Equality and Tradition

EQUALITY AND TRADITION

Questions of Value in Moral
and Political Theory

Samuel Scheffler

OXFORD
UNIVERSITY PRESS

OXFORD
UNIVERSITY PRESS

Oxford University Press, Inc., publishes works that further
Oxford University's objective of excellence
in research, scholarship, and education.

Oxford New York

Auckland   Cape Town   Dar es Salaam   Hong Kong   Karachi
Kuala Lumpur   Madrid   Melbourne   Mexico City   Nairobi
New Delhi   Shanghai   Taipei   Toronto

With offices in

Argentina   Austria   Brazil   Chile   Czech Republic   France   Greece
Guatemala   Hungary   Italy   Japan   Poland   Portugal   Singapore
South Korea   Switzerland   Thailand   Turkey   Ukraine   Vietnam

Published by Oxford University Press, Inc.
198 Madison Avenue, New York, New York 10016
www.oup.com

First issued as an Oxford University Press paperback, 2012

Oxford is a registered trademark of Oxford University Press

Library of Congress Cataloging-in-Publication Data

Scheffler, Samuel, 1951–
Equality and tradition : questions of value
in moral and political theory / Samuel Scheffler.
p. cm.
ISBN 978-0-19-539629-4 (hardcover); 978-0-19-989957-9 (paperback)
1. Values—Political aspects.   2. Equality.   3. Cosmopolitanism.
4. Toleration.   5. Liberalism.   I. Title.
JA79.S3167 2009
170—dc22   2009036139

Printed in the United States of America
on acid-free paper

For Deborah and Peter Goldberg

Contents

Equality and Tradition

Introduction

The twelve essays in this collection deal with questions of value in moral and political theory. The volume begins with an essay that takes up the very general question of what it is to value something and how valuing differs from other familiar attitudes. Several subsequent essays deal with the interpretation of particular values that play important roles in moral or political thought. Still other essays address tensions and conflicts that arise, both within and among individuals, in consequence of the diversity of human values. The volume closes with an essay about toleration, understood as a practice whose purpose is precisely to accommodate differences in people's evaluative convictions and commitments.

I have divided the essays into three groups under the very broad headings of Individuals, Institutions, and Society. These headings are, admittedly, a bit artificial, not just for the obvious reason that individuals and institutions themselves belong to society, but also because some of the essays are explicitly concerned with the relations between the values and norms that apply to individuals and those that apply at the level of society and its institutions. However, the headings are meant only to indicate the general emphases of the essays and not to suggest rigid or mutually exclusive categories. So, in particular, the essays in the first group deal primarily with questions about individual values and norms. Those in the second group explore the special moral significance that egalitarian liberalism assigns to basic social and political institutions. And the essays in the final group explore a number of important social values, such as the values of equality and tradition, as well as some of the urgent challenges facing contemporary societies, such as the challenges posed by immigration and by terrorism.

One general theme of the volume, which figures prominently in the essays included in the first section, is the importance of taking seriously those categories of value that seem most firmly entrenched in human life. The first essay ("Valuing") takes the phenomenon of valuing itself seriously, and argues against a variety of simple reductionist proposals, such as those that would reduce valuing to desiring, believing valuable, desiring to desire, or having a particular feeling. It develops a general account according to which valuing is instead to be seen as comprising a complex syndrome of interrelated dispositions and attitudes, including (at least) certain characteristic types of belief, dispositions to treat certain kinds of considerations as reasons for action, and susceptibility to a wide range of emotions.

The second essay, "Morality and Reasonable Partiality," draws on this general account of valuing to consider what, more specifically, is involved in valuing one's personal projects, interpersonal relationships, and membership in groups. Some philosophers believe that there is a tension and perhaps even an inconsistency between the kind of impartiality that morality requires and the kind of partiality that most of us routinely display in our behavior toward our intimates and associates and in our pursuit of the personal projects to which we are committed. This essay argues, however, that "reasons of partiality"—including "project-dependent," "relationship-dependent," and "membership-dependent" reasons—are concomitants of some of the most basic forms of human valuing, and that any credible morality will have to incorporate such reasons. This means not merely that it will permit or require partial behavior in some circumstances, but that it will treat reasons of partiality as bearing directly on the rightness or wrongness of actions. Most people do, in fact, treat reasons of partiality as morally relevant. The common-sense morality of our culture holds, for example, that we have "special obligations" to our intimates and associates that we do not have to other people. And it holds that, within limits, we may permissibly pursue our own projects and goals, even if we could do more good for humanity at large in some other way. In defending the moral significance of partiality, then, the second essay provides support for commonsense morality as against consequentialist outlooks, which take a more skeptical view both of special obligations and of the legitimacy of pursuing (what the consequentialist regards as) one's nonoptimal personal projects. The essay also tries to explain why relationship-dependent and membership-dependent reasons correspond to obligations while project-dependent reasons correspond only to permissions, and it considers the possibility, suggested by the writings of a number of philosophers, that morality as a whole may be interpreted on the model of reasons of partiality.

The third essay considers another striking feature of ordinary moral thought, which is the moral significance that it attaches to the distinction between doing and allowing. Although we ordinarily take ourselves to have a greater responsibility for what we do than for what we merely allow or fail to prevent, consequentialist philosophers have argued that this view is ultimately untenable, and that the distinction between doing and allowing lacks any fundamental moral significance. This essay maintains, however, that we have a deep commitment to drawing some such distinction in the context of our moral thought, and that people could not consistently hold themselves to norms of responsibility that did not assign them greater responsibility for what they did than for what they allowed. To this extent, the third essay is like the second one in defending a feature of commonsense moral thought against the challenge posed by consequentialism. These essays reflect my longstanding interest, dating back to my earliest work in philosophy, in trying to understand the bases for nonconsequentialist moral ideas.

It is noteworthy that the two elements of commonsense moral thought that I have mentioned—namely, reasons of partiality and the distinction between doing and allowing—have the effect of limiting the responsibility of individuals for the alleviation of suffering. Taken together, they imply that, so long as one has not caused the suffering of others oneself, and so long as one has no special personal or social relationship with the people who are suffering, it is permissible, within limits, to give the pursuit of one's own aims and aspirations priority over the provision of aid to those others. Yet these responsibility-limiting values, which are most at home in the context of small-scale personal relations and interactions, are in tension with other important values, such as the values of justice, fairness, and equality, to which many people are also deeply committed. If we are to accommodate all of our deeply held values, then some way must be found of addressing this tension. The fourth essay, "The Division of Moral Labor: Egalitarian Liberalism as Moral Pluralism," argues that egalitarian liberalism of the sort defended by John Rawls and others offers a distinctive response to this problem. This response, which contrasts naturally with those offered by utilitarianism on the one hand and libertarianism on the other, turns on the idea of a division of moral labor. According to this idea, the task of realizing the values of justice and equality belongs primarily to what Rawls calls "the basic structure" of society. The basic structure comprises a society's major social, political, and economic institutions, and it is to these institutions that the principles of justice are said in the first instance to apply. Individuals have a duty to support just institutions, but within the framework established by such institutions their actions may be guided by the values appropriate to small-scale interpersonal settings. In this way, both sets of values can be accommodated without either being reduced to or derived from the other.

This position implies that institutions are of great importance not only for political philosophy but also for moral philosophy, because they play a vital role in helping to resolve the tensions among the diverse moral values to which people are committed. Yet the Rawlsian emphasis on institutions and the associated idea of a division of moral labor have often been interpreted, not as facilitating the accommodation of diverse values, but rather as freeing individuals from the burdensome demands of justice and allowing them to engage in the unrestricted pursuit of their economic self-interest. The three essays in the second section defend the alternative interpretation I have sketched and consider some of its implications, including its implications for the way we think about the relations between moral and political philosophy, and between morality and politics. The fourth essay sets out the basic interpretation and discusses its motivation and significance. The fifth essay, "Is the Basic Structure Basic?," is a response to G. A. Cohen's influential critique of Rawls's institutional emphasis. The sixth essay, "Cosmopolitanism, Justice, and Institutions," considers the bearing of that emphasis on current debates about cosmopolitanism and global justice. If the values of justice and equality are taken to apply to the basic structure of society, then how should we think about the norms governing our relations to people in other societies? Some philosophers argue that, in this age of globalization, international institutions and organizations have become sufficiently important and consequential that they amount to a "global basic structure," so that the principles of justice should now be applied to the world as a whole rather than to the institutions of individual societies taken one by one. Other philosophers argue that, in the absence of a world state, there is not and cannot be a global basic structure, so that there remains a fundamental distinction between the principles of justice that apply domestically and the much weaker principles that apply globally. The sixth essay argues for an intermediate position. For all their importance, existing international institutions and arrangements cannot be said to constitute a basic structure in Rawls's sense. Nevertheless, these rapidly evolving institutions and arrangements may by now be sufficiently consequential that they require regulation by principles of justice that are more demanding than the traditional norms governing international relations. If we take seriously the institutional emphasis suggested by Rawls's philosophy, then one general lesson we should learn is that the emergence of new institutional forms may require the development of new moral norms. This means that, in order to decide what normative principles should be applied globally, we need to attend to the actual institutions and practices that emerge in our world. As those institutions and practices continue to develop, so too will our thinking about the normative standards that apply to them, and we may find that our existing repertoire of principles is insufficient to guide our reflections.

The aim of reconciling the values of personal life with a commitment to justice and equality is not, of course, unique to Rawls. It is, rather, a common feature of egalitarian liberal thinking. The view that has come to be called "luck egalitarianism," for example, attempts to demonstrate that an emphasis on individual choice and responsibility is not only compatible with egalitarian principles of distributive justice but is essential to the correct definition of such principles. In so doing, it seeks to defuse conservative criticism of the welfare state and to show that egalitarianism is not hostile to personal responsibility. Advocates of this position maintain that an egalitarian conception of justice, properly understood, seeks to neutralize the effects of brute luck on distribution, while allowing inequalities that derive from differences in the choices that people have freely made and for which they may reasonably be asked to bear responsibility. Although luck egalitarianism is often taken to have its origins in Rawls's own work, the seventh essay, "What Is Egalitarianism?," argues that his view is in fact very different, and that he should not be interpreted as an incipient luck egalitarian. In that essay and in the eighth essay, "Choice, Circumstance, and the Value of Equality," I criticize luck egalitarianism and argue that it misrepresents the nature of equality as a social value. I defend an alternative account of equality that I take to be much closer to Rawls's. According to this alternative account, equality is not, at the most fundamental level, a distributive ideal. It is, instead, an ideal of social and political relations, and what makes a conception of distributive justice an egalitarian conception is not that it seeks to neutralize the effects of luck on distribution but rather that it tries to identify the distributive principles that are appropriate to a society of equals.

Whereas the seventh and eighth essays consider how best to interpret the social values of justice and equality, the ninth and tenth essays deal with two significant challenges facing many contemporary societies. The ninth essay, "Is Terrorism Morally Distinctive?," discusses the challenge posed by terrorism, and attempts to explain why terrorism is often taken to be morally distinctive, even as compared with other forms of violence that may be equally objectionable. This essay argues that, in standard cases at least, terrorism involves a specific type of attack on social life. In these cases, violence or the threat of violence is used to generate fear, with the aim of degrading or destabilizing an existing social order. Some people are killed or injured (the primary victims), in order to create fear in a larger number of people (the secondary victims), with the aim of destabilizing or degrading the existing social order for everyone. What is peculiarly repellent about these cases is that the primary victims are killed or injured precisely in order to elicit fear, horror, and grief among the secondary victims, so that those reactions can in turn be exploited to promote the perpetrators' ultimate, destabilizing aims. This does not imply that terrorism is always worse than other forms of violence, but it does mean that it has a distinctive moral profile. Terrorism is distinctive in the way it exploits the power of fear in order to undermine the fragile values of social life.

Immigration presents societies with a number of different practical and theoretical challenges. "Immigration and the Significance of Culture," the tenth essay in this volume, argues that, in thinking about those challenges, an excessive reliance on the discourse of culture and identity has produced frequent distortions and oversimplifications. This essay maintains that, under circumstances of large-scale immigration, there is no possibility of preserving unaltered either the imported cultures of immigrant communities or the national cultures of host societies, and that neither side has any general right to such preservation. In a just society, immigrants and nonimmigrants alike should have the freedom to engage in the dynamic and interpretative process of extending their inherited cultures in the altered circumstances to which immigration gives rise, but it is a mistake to think that this requires the implementation of any special regime of "cultural rights." The constituents of political morality that are most relevant in thinking about the mutual responsibilities of immigrants and host societies alike are the principles of justice, which define a fair framework of social cooperation among equals; the basic liberties, including, especially, the liberties of speech, association, and conscience; and the important idea of informal mutual accommodation within the bounds of justice. Here again, as in the essays in Part II, the emphasis is on the importance of a just institutional framework within which people may lead their lives in ways that are responsive to the many other values that they recognize.

It is sometimes said, however, that there is just as much of a case within liberal theory for adopting regimes of rights that are tailored to accommodate cultural diversity as there is for adopting regimes to accommodate moral, religious, or philosophical diversity. This essay argues that it is a mistake to extrapolate from the case of moral, religious, and philosophical outlooks to the case of cultural affiliations. Liberalism has a special concern with the accommodation of *normative diversity*—that is, diversity with respect to people's normative and evaluative convictions—but cultural diversity is not a novel species of normative diversity over and above moral, religious, and philosophical diversity. That is because cultures are not perceived sources of normative authority in the same sense that moral, religious, and philosophical doctrines are. To classify something as a moral, religious, or philosophical value is to say something about the kind of authority its adherents take it to have. By contrast, to describe something as a cultural norm or value is not to characterize its perceived authority but rather to indicate its prevalence within a certain social group. To be sure, values and principles are important aspects of most cultures, but the reasons they generate are normally seen as deriving from those values and principles themselves, and not from the fact of their acceptance within the culture.

The case of tradition is different, or so I argue in the eleventh essay, "The Normativity of Tradition." By contrast with the case of culture, people do often act on reasons whose force they themselves ascribe to the authority of some tradition. In this sense, tradition is a normative notion, and the diversity of traditions is a species of normative diversity. But how is the normativity of tradition to be understood? Here we confront a skeptical dilemma. On the one hand, the mere fact that people have acted some way in the past does not seem like a good reason to act that way now. But, on the other hand, if to act on traditional reasons is to act for reasons that derive from the values that a tradition embodies or endorses, then the reference to the tradition seems otiose, for the force of the reasons seems to derive from the values rather than from the tradition. However, this essay identifies a variety of considerations that may speak in favor of adherence to a tradition, and argues that we should reject the form of skepticism embodied in the dilemma. Acting on traditional reasons is not a matter of doing something simply because people have done the same thing in the past, but neither is it a matter of acting on reasons that derive solely from certain abstract values that the tradition happens to endorse. The actual existence of a tradition gives its adherents reasons for action that they would not otherwise have had and that nonparticipants do not share. This conclusion is significant primarily for what it contributes to our understanding of human value and normativity, but it also holds an important lesson for liberal political theory. Because traditions are complex, multigenerational enterprises comprising elements of ritual, practice, historical memory, and collective aspiration no less than bodies of doctrine and individual conviction, one effect of recognizing the diversity of traditions as a species of normative diversity is to remind us that normative diversity is neither a purely individualistic nor a purely doxastic phenomenon. Although I do not believe that this supports the establishment of a novel regime of rights on the cultural-rights model, it is nevertheless relevant in thinking about the forms of mutual accommodation that a liberal society will want to encourage.

Liberal arrangements for the accommodation of normative diversity are the explicit focus of the final essay, "The Good of Toleration." Toleration is often seen as puzzling or paradoxical, in part because it seems to require us to concede normative authority to values that we reject. In other words, toleration requires us to treat other people's values, which we do not accept, as reasons for modifying our own conduct, which is rooted in values that we do accept. This is one reason why a compelling general justification for liberal toleration is often thought to be elusive. Rather than investigating the justification of toleration, however, this essay addresses a slightly different question, which is why so many people believe that toleration is an important value in its own right, despite its puzzling character. Questions about the good of toleration are, in one way, less ambitious than the question of its justification, since the features of toleration that recommend it to its supporters may not suffice to justify it to others. On the other hand, attempts to provide a general justification of toleration sometimes neglect the less ambitious question with which I am concerned. In seeking to identify reasons for toleration that everyone can accept, they sometimes neglect to consider why some people regard toleration as an especially good or valuable feature of a society. This essay argues that the answer lies in the very same feature of toleration that makes it look puzzling or paradoxical, namely, the fact that it requires us to concede authority to values that we do not accept. A regime of toleration amounts to a practice of mutual deference to one another's values, and it is not surprising that participation in such a practice is sometimes experienced as threatening or unwelcome. Yet, at the same time, the phenomenon of being linked to one's fellow citizens through a practice of mutual deference can also form the basis for relations of fraternity or solidarity, relations that are rooted, this essay argues, in the shared experience of subjection to the authority of norms.

The last essay ends on an optimistic note. The practice of liberal toleration emerged in the aftermath of the European Wars of Religion of
the sixteenth and seventeenth centuries, and comprised a set of practical
arrangements designed to break an apparently endless cycle of religious
violence and bloodshed. We may view it as a rare stroke of political good
fortune that, in their efforts to defuse violent sectarian conflict, liberal
societies devised arrangements and institutions that turn out also to
make available their own distinctive satisfactions and rewards. Of course,
intense conflicts of value are ineliminable and they certainly persist in
our world. There are conflicts within individuals and there are conflicts
among individuals and groups. The essays in this volume reflect two
general convictions. The first is that, if we are interested in understanding ourselves, then we need to explore the complexity of our diverse
evaluative commitments and to be wary of reductionist theorizing about
value and values. This is the spirit in which, for example, I have argued
against reducing valuing to desiring or believing, against consequentialist attempts to reduce normative ethics to a single master principle that
requires maximization of the good, against reducing the value of equality to a simple distributive formula, and against reducing the normative significance of participation in a tradition to the normativity of the
values that the tradition endorses. The second general conviction is that
liberal theory has a variety of resources, including but not limited to
those embodied in the practices of toleration, for accommodating the
diversity of human values. I have tried to identify some of the resources
of the Rawlsian branch of that theory, with its emphasis on the division
of moral labor, the moral role of social and political institutions, the
primacy of justice as a political virtue, and the necessity of providing a
fair framework of cooperation within which individuals can pursue their
diverse values and aims. It would be carrying optimism too far to suppose that liberal theory can provide us with a formula for eliminating
or defusing all the deadly conflicts of our own time. But, for all its flaws
and limitations, liberal theory still has much to offer as we think about
the possibilities for living together in a world where, despite rapid change
along many dimensions, deep conflicts of value endure and their capacity
to produce mischief and misery is undiminished.

Eight of the twelve essays included in this volume were originally
published elsewhere. The first two and final two essays have not been
previously published, although the first essay is also being published in
Reasons and Recognition: Essays on the Philosophy of T.M. Scanlon, edited
by R. Jay Wallace, Rahul Kumar, and Samuel Freeman, and the second
essay is also being published in *Partiality and Impartiality: Morality, Special Relationships, and the Wider World*, edited by Brian Feltham and

John Cottingham. Apart from updating a few references, I have made no changes in the previously published pieces. There is a bit of overlap among some of the essays, but since I wanted each essay to remain self-standing and capable of being read on its own, I have not attempted to eliminate this overlap.

PART I

Individuals

I

Valuing

Human beings are valuing creatures. One may value one's privacy, or one's relationship with one's brother, or a friend's sense of humor, or the opinion of a trusted advisor. But what is valuing? David Lewis says, "It is some sort of mental state, directed toward that which is valued. It might be a feeling, or a belief, or a desire."[1] He adds, parenthetically, that valuing might instead be "a combination of these; or something that is two or three of them at once; or some fourth thing."[2] But he proposes to set these more complicated possibilities aside, and to look for a simpler account. After quickly dismissing the idea that valuing is a feeling or a belief, Lewis defends a version of the view that it is a form of desiring.

The simplest version of this view, though not the one that Lewis himself endorses, is that to value something just is to desire it. This view has

1. See David Lewis, "Dispositional Theories of Value," as reprinted in Lewis, *Papers in Ethics and Social Philosophy* (Cambridge: Cambridge University Press, 2000): 68–94, p. 69.
2. *Ibid.*

been surprisingly influential, and it may seem plausible in some cases. For example, it may seem plausible that to value one's privacy just is to desire one's privacy. But does it seem plausible that to value one's friend's sense of humor is to desire one's friend's sense of humor? What does it even mean to say that one desires one's friend's sense of humor? On the most natural interpretation, it means that one would like to possess one's friend's sense of humor oneself. But this is clearly not what is meant by saying one values one's friend's sense of humor. If the suggestion that valuing is simply desiring is to have any plausibility, therefore, *desire* must be understood in a very special—and very broad—sense. Perhaps, for example, to desire something is to have a favorable attitude toward it. To value one's friend's sense of humor would then be to have a favorable attitude toward it. This may seem plausible. But is it plausible to equate desiring something with having a favorable attitude toward it? Offhand, it seems that I may have a favorable attitude toward something without desiring it. I have a favorable attitude toward Vaclav Havel, but I do not desire him, whatever that might mean, nor do I desire to see him, meet him, or talk to him.

Philosophers have offered other reasons for rejecting the reduction of valuing to desiring. Many have argued that valuing and desiring can come apart in cases of internal conflict or psychological disturbance. In some cases of this kind, it seems that a person may desire something without valuing it. As Harry Frankfurt has emphasized, for example, an addict may desire the drug to which he is addicted, yet despise that very desire and wish to be rid of it.[3] Similarly, a person may desire to engage in certain types of sexual activity yet disapprove of those activities and regard them as sinful or degrading. Or, as Gary Watson has suggested, a woman may have a momentary urge to drown her shrieking child in the bathtub, yet place no value at all on the drowning of her child.[4] There are also cases of emotional disturbance in which it seems that a person may value something without desiring it. For example, Michael Smith has argued, on the basis of an example of Michael Stocker's, that a person may value something, but as a result of depression or despair, feel no desire or motivation to pursue it.[5]

3. See Harry Frankfurt, "Freedom of the Will and the Concept of a Person," *Journal of Philosophy* 68 (1971): 5–20.
4. See Gary Watson, "Free Agency," as reprinted in Watson (ed.), *Free Will* (New York: Oxford University Press, 1982), pp. 96–110, at pp. 100–101.
5. Michael Smith, "Valuing: Desiring or Believing?" in D. Charles and K. Lennon (eds)., *Reduction, Explanation, and Realism* (Oxford: Oxford University Press, 1992),

This focus on cases of compulsion and conflict has led some philosophers to suppose that although valuing and desiring can indeed diverge, so that valuing cannot be reduced to desiring, such divergence is always a manifestation of deviance or irrationality. There are, however, quite mundane cases, involving no compulsion or inner conflict or emotional disturbance, in which valuing and desiring also come apart, in the sense that one of these concepts seems straightforwardly to apply but the other doesn't. In cases of trivial desires, for instance, the language of valuing seems overblown and out of place. I may want to thumb through a magazine in the doctor's office, or to eat some jellybeans, or to retie my loose shoelace, but it would be peculiar to describe these as things that I value. On the other hand, as we have already seen, I may value my friend's sense of humor, but it is not clear what it would even mean, in this context, to say that I desire my friend's sense of humor. Similarly, I may value the lessons I learned from my grandparents, but it is not clear what it would mean to say that I desire the lessons I learned from my grandparents.

Offhand, it seems that one significant difference between valuing and desiring is that the things we value are things that matter to us, or that we prize or cherish, or that have a certain importance for us. Not everything that we desire matters to us. And not everything that matters to us is a suitable object of desire. So although there are many things that we both value and desire, valuing cannot be reduced to simple desiring.

But if valuing cannot be reduced to simple desiring, then how is it to be understood? Gilbert Harman, after offering objections to a variety of proposals, says, "I conclude that valuing is a particular kind of desiring, but I am unable to say more about what kind."[6] Some philosophers, although not Harman, have suggested that the answer lies in the idea of a second-order desire, whose importance for our understanding of personhood has long been urged by Harry Frankfurt. This suggestion is in some ways surprising. Frankfurt himself does not attempt to explain valuing in this way. Although he places great emphasis on the related yet distinct notion of *caring*,[7] he uses the term *valuing* and its cognates only

---

pp. 323–359, at pp. 326–327. For Stocker's example, see Michael Stocker, "Desiring the Bad: An Essay in Moral Psychology," *Journal of Philosophy* 76 (1979), at p. 744.

6. Gilbert Harman, "Desired Desires," as reprinted in Harman, *Explaining Value and Other Essays in Moral Philosophy* (Oxford: Clarendon Press, 2000), pp. 117–136, at p. 135.

7. See, for example, Harry Frankfurt, "The Importance of What We Care About," as reprinted in *The Importance of What We Care About* (Cambridge: Cambridge University Press, 1988), pp. 80–94; "On Caring," in *Necessity, Volition, and Love* (Cambridge: Cambridge University Press, 1999), pp. 155–180; *The Reasons of Love* (Princeton, NJ: Princeton University Press, 2004).

sparingly, and it is not clear how, if at all, he sees his model as bearing on the understanding of valuing. Furthermore, one of the earliest and most influential objections to Frankfurt's position was Gary Watson's argument to the effect that the distinction between different orders of desire is an unsatisfactory substitute for the distinction between wanting and valuing.[8]

Nevertheless, others have sought to explain what valuing consists in by reference to Frankfurt's "hierarchical" model. David Lewis, for example, says that to value X is to desire to desire it.[9] This is meant to help with the case of the unhappy addict mentioned earlier. The addict craves his drug, but since he wishes he didn't, this view implies that he does not value it. Although what the addict values diverges from what he desires, it does not diverge from what he desires to desire. But does valuing always coincide with desiring to desire? In some cases, it seems, I can desire to desire something that I neither desire nor value. For example, I may want to want to become a regular operagoer—my opera-loving friends may have convinced me that I am missing out on a rich and rewarding dimension of aesthetic appreciation—but so long as I do not actually want to become a regular operagoer, it does not seem true that I value operagoing. It seems closer to the truth to say that I wish I valued operagoing. Perhaps, then, we need to modify Lewis's proposal. Perhaps to value X is (1) to desire it and (2) to desire to desire it. In the case just described, I do not value operagoing because I fail to satisfy the first condition. The unhappy addict, by contrast, does not value the drug he craves because he fails to satisfy the second condition. Yet there are, it seems, other cases in which I may value something without desiring to desire it at all. I may value the lessons that my grandparents taught me, but as earlier observed, it is not clear what would be meant by saying that I desire those lessons, and it is no clearer what would be meant by saying that I desire to desire them.

Perhaps it would become clearer if *desire* were taken to mean "have a pro-attitude toward." Then what it would be for me to value the lessons that my grandparents taught me would be for me to have a pro-attitude toward my having a pro-attitude toward those lessons. But while the idea of having a pro-attitude toward my having a pro-attitude toward the lessons may be easier to understand than the idea of desiring to desire the lessons, it does not seem to capture what is meant by saying that I value the lessons. Offhand, it seems that I might value the lessons my

8. See Watson, *op. cit.*, esp. pp. 107–109.
9. See Lewis, *op. cit.*

grandparents taught me without having any attitude at all toward my own attitude toward those lessons. At any rate, it may be clearer that I value the lessons than it is that I have a pro-attitude toward my having a pro-attitude toward the lessons. And even if I did have a pro-attitude toward my having a pro-attitude toward the lessons, this second-order attitude would be an attitude toward something about myself and my attitudes, whereas what I value are my grandparents' lessons and not some facts about myself. So how can my valuing of those lessons be equated with any attitude toward my own attitudes?

There are also cases in which one's second-order desires conflict with one's first-order desires, and yet it is the first-order desires, rather than the second-order desires, that are naturally taken to express what one values. In the movie *Casablanca*, Ilsa, played by Ingrid Bergman, says to Rick, played by Humphrey Bogart: "Richard, I tried to stay away. I thought I would never see you again, that you were out of my life…Now? I don't know. I know that I'll never have the strength to leave you again…I can't fight it anymore. I ran away from you once. I can't do it again…I wish I didn't love you so much."[10] Here, by contrast with the structurally parallel case of the unhappy addict, the viewer is presumably meant to understand that it is Ilsa's first-order attitude toward Rick, rather than her second-order desire not to love him so much, that indicates what she really values.[11]

Charles Taylor also relies on Frankfurt's notion of a second-order desire, but he uses the idea in a different way than Lewis does. He takes the general lesson of Frankfurt's discussion to be that "what is distinctively human is the power to *evaluate* our desires, to regard some as

10. *Casablanca* (Warner Brothers, 1942), screenplay by Julius J. Epstein, Philip G. Epstein, and Howard Koch (based on the play "Everybody Goes to Rick's" by Murray Burnett and Joan Allison), available online at http://www.imsdb.com/scripts/Casablanca .pdf, pp. 102–104 (last accessed on March 12, 2009).

11. It may seem that Rick himself draws a different conclusion, because, despite his love for Ilsa, and despite her declaration of love for him, he insists that she leave him behind and escape from Casablanca with her husband, Victor Laszlo: "Inside of us we both know you belong with Victor. You're part of his work, the thing that keeps him going. If that plane leaves the ground and you're not with him, you'll regret it…Maybe not today, maybe not tomorrow, but soon, and for the rest of your life" (*Ibid*, p. 121). Yet what makes him willing to help Ilsa and Laszlo escape together, which he had previously refused to do, is precisely his conviction that her declaration of love for him was sincere. Moreover, although it would have made for a worse movie, there would have been nothing jarring conceptually about having things end differently, with Rick simply accepting Ilsa's declaration of love and their living happily ever after.

desirable and others are [sic] undesirable."[12] And he appears to equate
second-order desires with evaluations of first-order desires. For example, he says that "a crucial feature of human agency is the capacity for
second-order desires or evaluation of desires."[13] Taylor is less concerned
to defend these claims than he is to argue for an additional distinction
between what he calls *strong* and *weak* evaluation of our desires. For our
purposes, however, the pertinent point is that, like Lewis, Taylor sees a
close connection between second-order desires and value. But whereas
Lewis's position is that to value X is to desire to desire X, Taylor's focus
is on the role of second-order desires in the evaluation not of X but of
the desire for X. There are a number of questions that might be raised
about Taylor's account. One question is whether what he means by *evaluation* is the same as what I mean by *valuing*, or, if not, how the two
notions differ. A second question, which Taylor anticipates,[14] is whether
his focus on the evaluation of our desires neglects the extent to which we
are concerned with the evaluation of the objects of those desires. A third
question is whether the close connection he draws between evaluation
and second-order desires is as faithful to Frankfurt's view as he takes it
to be. But for our purposes, the most important question concerns the
way that connection is to be understood. Do second-order desires in
and of themselves constitute evaluations of first-order desires, as Taylor
appears at times to suggest? Or does he think of second-order desires
as issuing from independent evaluations of the first-order desires that
are their objects? Either way, there are difficulties. On the one hand, as
Gary Watson argued in response to Frankfurt, it is unclear why a simple
second-order desire should count as an *evaluation* at all, any more than
a first-order desire does. A simple second-order desire is, after all, just
another desire, which happens to have a first-order desire as its object.
But if, on the other hand, second-order desires issue from independent
evaluations, then it seems that the concept of evaluation is presupposed
rather than illuminated by Taylor's appeal to second-order desires.

Perhaps, then, it is a mistake to construe valuing as a kind of desiring. Perhaps it is better thought of as a kind of believing. But what kind
of believing? The most obvious suggestion is that to value X is simply
to believe that X is valuable. This leaves open the question of what it
is to believe that something is valuable, and there is an obvious threat

12. Charles Taylor, "What Is Human Agency?" as reprinted in Taylor, *Human Agency
    and Language: Philosophical Papers 1* (Cambridge: Cambridge University Press,
    1985), pp. 15–44, at p. 16.
13. *Ibid.*, pp. 42–43.
14. *Ibid.*, p. 18n.

of circularity if we are tempted to think, as some philosophers do, that to believe that something is valuable is to believe that it is properly valued.[15] But the proposal that to value X is simply to believe that X is valuable is unsatisfactory in any case, for it is not only possible but commonplace to believe that something is valuable without valuing it oneself. There are, for example, many activities that I regard as valuable but which I myself do not value, including, say, folk dancing, bird-watching, and studying Bulgarian history. Indeed, I value only a tiny fraction of the activities that I take to be valuable. Of course, most of the valuable activities that I do not myself value are activities in which I also do not participate. So perhaps to value an activity is simply to regard as valuable an activity in which one participates. But this will not do. I can regard an activity in which I participate as valuable without valuing it myself. I may, for example, go to the opera from time to time, and I may regard operagoing as a valuable activity, and yet I may still not value it myself. Even though I participate in the activity and believe that it is a valuable activity, operagoing may leave me cold. Besides, this proposal only applies to activities. Yet there are many things besides activities that I regard as valuable, and many of these are also things that I myself do not value. There are, for example, many paintings, historical artifacts, and literary genres that I believe to be valuable but do not value myself. With respect to these things, the suggestion that to value them is to believe that they are valuable and to participate in them oneself would obviously make no sense.

It goes without saying, I hope, that I do not take these remarks to be merely autobiographical. I do not think that it is an idiosyncrasy of mine—or a sign that I am an especially crass or shallow person—that I fail to value so many of the things that I believe to be valuable. I think, instead, that the same is true of most people. The world contains many things that we regard as valuable; yet each of us values—indeed, I will offer reasons for thinking that each of us can value—only a small fraction of these valuable things. That is because valuing requires more of us than just belief. There is no limit in principle to the number of things whose value we can recognize or acknowledge. By contrast, there are severe limits to how much one can value within the confines of a single human life.

15. Elizabeth Anderson says in *Value in Ethics and Economics* (Cambridge, MA: Harvard University Press, 1993, p. 2) that "to judge that something is good is to judge that it is properly valued." Thomas Scanlon says in *What We Owe to Each Other* (Cambridge, MA: Harvard University Press, 1998, p. 89) that "the claim that friendship is valuable is best understood as the claim that it is properly valued."

The points I have been making have implications for the view of valuing defended by Michael Smith. Smith argues that "valuing is believing
valuable and believing valuable is believing that we have a normative
reason."[16] Or as he puts the point in another passage, "A has a normative reason to Φ iff A's Φing is valuable," and "A accepts that he has a
normative reason to Φ iff A values Φing."[17] In light of our discussion,
two related difficulties with these formulations are apparent. First, they
neglect the distinction between believing that something is valuable and
valuing it. Second, they overlook the fact that we can value many things
other than our own activities. As we have seen, for example, one may
value one's privacy, or one's friend's sense of humor, or the opinion of a
trusted advisor, or the lessons one learned from one's grandparents. None
of these is an action one performs or an activity in which one engages;
none of them is a type of Φing. So Smith's formulations wrongly equate
valuing and believing valuable, and they wrongly suppose that what people are capable of valuing is limited to their own activities. The scope of
what we value is in one way narrower and in one way broader than Smith
suggests. On the one hand, we do not value all the things that we regard
as valuable, but, on the other hand, we value many things in addition to
our own actions or activities.

But if valuing is neither a kind of desiring nor a kind of believing,
then what is it? The third of the three possibilities mentioned by David
Lewis was that valuing is a feeling. Lewis himself quickly rejects this possibility, on the ground that "the feelings we have when we value things
are too diverse."[18] This does seem like a reason to reject the simple view
that valuing consists in a single, distinctive type of feeling, but there
may be more plausible ways of analyzing valuing in terms of feelings
and emotions. One way to explore this possibility is by returning to the
thought that the things we value are things that matter to us, or that we
prize or cherish, or that have a certain importance for us. How are the
relevant notions of *mattering* and *importance* to be understood? Part of
the answer, at least, has to do with the role in our emotional lives of the
things that matter to us. If my relationship with my brother matters to
me, then I may feel pleased at the prospect of spending time with him,
saddened if we rarely have occasion to see one another, eager to help him
if he is in need, distressed if a serious conflict develops between us or if we
become estranged, and shocked and betrayed if he harms me or abuses

16. Smith, *op. cit.*, p. 344.
17. *Ibid.*, p. 329.
18. Lewis, *op. cit.*, p. 70.

my trust. Of course, these are only examples, and variations are possible depending on the details of our relationship. Perhaps my relationship with him matters to me, but in light of features of his character that are well known to me, I would not actually be shocked—only disappointed and resigned—if he abused my trust. Still, if the relationship does matter to me, then there will be a range of emotions that I am disposed to experience in various contexts, depending on how my brother fares and how our relationship fares. So if what it means to say that I value my relationship with my brother is that the relationship matters to me, then my valuing the relationship may consist, at least in part, in my being emotionally vulnerable in certain ways.[19]

We might, therefore, propose, not that valuing is a particular kind of feeling, but rather that valuing something makes one vulnerable to feelings and emotions of many different kinds concerning that thing. Following Niko Kolodny, we may say that to be "emotionally vulnerable to X" is to be vulnerable to a wide range of emotions regarding X depending on context and circumstance.[20] So the proposal might be that valuing X makes one emotionally vulnerable to X. Although this seems like a promising suggestion, care is required in developing it, and a number of significant qualifications are necessary if some version of the suggestion is ultimately to be defensible.

First, any plausible thesis connecting valuing with emotional vulnerability must acknowledge that the emotions to which valuing makes us vulnerable—call this our *value-dependent vulnerability*—will depend to some extent on the nature of the things that we value. For example, if I value our friendship, then I may feel a sense of betrayal if you fail to support me when I am in need. But if what I value is my privacy or some old family photographs, then I do not make myself vulnerable in the same way to feelings of betrayal. Neither my privacy nor the old

---

19. The connection between valuing and emotional vulnerability is emphasized by Elizabeth Anderson in Chapter One of *Value in Ethics and Economics*, and by Niko Kolodny in "Love as Valuing a Relationship," *Philosophical Review* 112 (2003), pp. 135–189. The notion of something being important to a person figures centrally in the writings of Harry Frankfurt cited in footnote 7. Frankfurt sees importance to a person as being closely connected with caring, but rather than analyzing these ideas in terms of emotional vulnerability, he interprets both of them as picking out essentially volitional phenomena. As will soon become clear, I distinguish between valuing and caring, and my account of valuing is not volitional in Frankfurt's sense. I regard the ideas of *mattering* and *importance to* as suggestive, but in the end I offer no analysis of them and nothing in my account of valuing turns on these notions.

20. Kolodny, *op. cit.*, pp. 150–152. Kolodny offers an account of valuing that has a good deal in common with the one I develop here.

photographs can betray me; only a person can do that. So the contours of one's emotional vulnerability depend on the nature of what one values.

Second, there are certain kinds of cases in which the degree of emotional vulnerability that one incurs by virtue of valuing something is likely to be highly attenuated. In general, one's value-dependent vulnerability is apt to be greatest when the things that one values are themselves things that can fare well or poorly, can be in good or bad condition, or can flourish or be damaged or destroyed. In short, one's emotional vulnerability is apt to be greatest when the things that one values are themselves vulnerable to changes in their condition. People, personal projects and relationships, and physical objects all fall in this category. But consider, by way of contrast, the lessons I learned from my grandparents. If we assume that these lessons are to be identified with the propositional content of what my grandparents taught me, then what I value, in valuing the lessons, is a set of propositions. Because those propositions cannot in any straightforward sense fare well or poorly, or flourish or be destroyed, I am not vulnerable, by virtue of valuing them, to the wide range of emotions that arise in response to variations in the fortunes or in the condition of the things that one values. This does not mean that I incur no value-dependent vulnerability at all by virtue of valuing the lessons that my grandparents taught me. Perhaps, for example, I am liable to feel sad or frustrated if I do not succeed in teaching those lessons to my own children and grandchildren. Perhaps I am liable to feel angry or indignant if other people mock or belittle the importance of those lessons. Still, the degree of emotional vulnerability one incurs in cases of this kind seems considerably reduced.

This suggests the third and most important qualification, namely, that valuing cannot be understood solely in terms of emotional vulnerability. There are other considerations that also support this conclusion. One of these has to do with the relation between *valuing* and *caring*. There is a great deal of overlap between these two notions. We can speak as easily, for example, of caring about one's relationship with one's brother as we can of valuing that relationship, and it is clear that caring, no less than valuing, renders one emotionally vulnerable. It is not surprising, then, that some writers treat the two concepts as interchangeable, as, for example, Elizabeth Anderson appears to do in the first chapter of *Value in Ethics and Economics.*[21] But, although caring and valuing are clearly related, there appear to be some significant differences between them. As noted earlier, Frankfurt treats caring as a central notion, but seldom uses

21. Anderson, *op. cit.*

the language of valuing. And after arguing, in an early paper,[22] that many patients with Alzheimer's Disease remain capable of valuing, Agnieszka Jaworska distinguishes, in her later work, between valuing and caring, and argues instead that some Alzheimer's patients are capable of caring even if they are not capable of valuing.[23] What might the differences between the two notions be?

English usage provides some clues. Although, as already noted, there are many cases in which it seems equally natural to speak either of valuing or of caring, there are other cases in which it seems more natural to use one of these terms rather than the other. To my ear, for example, it seems more natural to say that one values one's friend's sense of humor than that one cares about one's friend's sense of humor. Similarly, it seems more natural to say that one values a colleague's contributions to departmental discussions than that one cares about those contributions. On the other hand, it seems more natural to say that one cares about one's appearance or about how the Red Sox do against the Yankees than that one values those things. Indeed, to say that one values how the Red Sox do against the Yankees would be quite odd.

Although we should not assume that each nuance of English usage affords deep conceptual insight, some of the differences between the way *valuing* is used and the way *caring* is used do seem to me significant. Perhaps the most striking difference is that the objects of caring, unlike the objects of valuing, need not be things toward which one is favorably disposed. So, for example, it would be perfectly appropriate to describe someone as caring deeply about poverty and injustice. We have no difficulty in interpreting this description, and we do not take it to mean that the person is favorably disposed toward poverty and injustice. To describe the same person as *valuing* poverty and injustice, by contrast, would imply that the person was favorably disposed toward poverty and injustice. The second description, in other words, is naturally interpreted as meaning just the opposite of the first. This should make us wary of using *valuing* and *caring* interchangeably.

Perhaps, however, to value something is simply to care about *and* be favorably disposed toward it. But this will not do. What is meant by saying that I value my friend's sense of humor is not captured by saying that I care about and am favorably disposed toward her sense of humor.

22. Agnieszka Jaworska, "Respecting the Margins of Agency: Alzheimer's Patients and the Capacity to Value," *Philosophy & Public Affairs* 28 (1999): 105–138.

23. See, for example, Jaworska, "Caring and Internality," *Philosophy and Phenomenological Research* 74 (2007): 529–568, and "Caring and Full Moral Standing," *Ethics* 117(2007): 460–497.

As noted earlier, it is not even clear that it makes sense to speak of caring about one's friend's sense of humor. And if it does not, then adding that one is favorably disposed toward her sense of humor won't help.

In any case, to say that one is favorably disposed toward the things that one values is an underdescription. One may be favorably disposed toward something without valuing it. The pertinent point instead seems to be that valuing, unlike caring, involves a view of the object of one's attitude as being good or worthy or valuable. To view something as valuable goes beyond having a generically favorable disposition toward it. It is, one might say, a distinctive way of being favorably disposed toward it. And it is the fact that valuing involves this distinctive view of its objects that explains why there is such a difference between saying that someone cares about poverty and injustice and saying that the person values poverty and injustice. If this is correct, then even though, as we have seen, valuing cannot be reduced to or equated with believing valuable, nevertheless, valuing something does involve, in addition to emotional vulnerability, a view of the thing that one values as being good or worthy or valuable.[24]

These two dimensions of valuing are related to each other in at least two different ways. First, the emotions to which valuing makes us vulnerable normally present themselves to us as appropriate or merited, and this fact is closely connected to our belief that the things we value are good or valuable. The sadness I feel when a valued relationship ends is experienced as an appropriate response to what has happened, as is the annoyance I feel when the privacy I value is repeatedly disrupted, or the disappointment I feel when the colleague whose contributions to department meetings I value declines to offer an opinion on a matter of special importance. In each case, my experience of my reaction as merited or appropriate is closely connected to my view of the valued item as valuable. How is this "close connection" to be understood? On one interpretation, the fact that I view the item as valuable helps to explain why I think my reactions are merited: why sadness is an appropriate reaction to the end of

---

24. One class of (partial) exceptions should be noted. These are cases in which a person values something but describes it as having merely "sentimental" or "personal" value, or as being valuable only to him or herself. Because these very descriptions imply that in normal cases the value ascribed to valued items is not similarly qualified, I regard cases of "merely personal value" as being exceptions that prove the rule. (For a possible example of such a case, see Jerry Cohen's discussion of his eraser in Section 4 of his "Rescuing Conservatism: A Defence of Existing Value" [in *Reasons and Recognition: Essays on the Philosophy of T.M. Scanlon*].) It is also worth noting that even the ascription of "sentimental" or "personal" value to an item goes beyond having a generically favorable disposition toward it.

the relationship, why annoyance is an appropriate response to the violation of my privacy, and why disappointment is an appropriate response to my colleague's reticence. On another interpretation, my belief that the valued items are valuable just is, in part, a belief that these reactions, and other comparable reactions in other contexts, are merited or appropriate. To put it another way, it is a belief that there are good reasons for these reactions. On either interpretation, the fact that the items we value are seen as valuable has implications for the character and content of our emotional vulnerability.

Second, the fact that valuing involves emotional vulnerability helps to explain why there is a gap between believing valuable and valuing, that is, why believing that something is valuable does not automatically translate into valuing it. There are limits to our capacity for emotional vulnerability. Some of these limits are practical or psychological; they are limits of time or emotional resources. Some of them may instead be conceptual. To be emotionally vulnerable to X is for X to have a certain kind of importance in one's life, and there may be conceptual limits to the number of things that can be important to a person. If one has too many best friends, then one has no best friends, and if one has too many hobbies, then one has no hobbies. Similarly, perhaps, if too many things are important to us, then nothing is important to us. But whether the relevant limits are conceptual or "merely" practical and psychological, the fact is that most people have a capacity for the recognition of value that far outstrips their capacity for emotional vulnerability. That is one reason why we normally value only a small subset of the things that we regard as valuable.

We have identified two mutually related dimensions of valuing. To value X is normally both to believe that X is valuable and to be emotionally vulnerable to X. However, there is more to valuing than this. In particular, valuing also has deliberative significance: to value X involves seeing X as a source of reasons for action. By this I mean that one who values X is disposed to treat X-related considerations as constituting reasons for action in relevant contexts. For example, if I value my privacy, then I will be disposed in relevant contexts to treat considerations about the impact of proposed courses of action on my privacy as having deliberative relevance. Of course, the relevant contexts may not arise very often, and even when they do arise the privacy-related considerations may not be decisive. But if I never see those considerations as having deliberative relevance, then it is not true that I value my privacy. Similarly, if I value my relationship with my brother, then I will be disposed in suitable contexts to treat considerations about the impact of proposed courses of action on the state of our relationship as having deliberative relevance. If I had no disposition at all to do this, then it would not be correct to say that I valued the relationship. And so on for other cases. If I value my colleague's contributions to departmental meetings, then in suitable contexts I will treat considerations having to do with my ability to learn his opinion as relevant to my deliberations. In general, to value X is, *inter alia*, to be disposed in relevant contexts to treat X-related considerations as having deliberative relevance. Valuing, we may say, is deliberatively consequential.

It is clear from the examples I have mentioned that, just as the emotions to which valuing makes us vulnerable may vary depending on what it is that we value, so, too, the considerations that valuing disposes us to treat as reasons for action may vary depending on the nature of the things that we value. There is no precise formula that will cover every case. That is why I have spoken simply of a disposition to treat "X-related considerations" as reasons for action. This should not strike us as surprising. We should not expect the details either of our emotional engagement or of our practical orientation to be invariant across the wide range of things that we value. Instead, the emotions to which we are liable and the ways in which we have reason to act will, to some degree, vary depending on the nature of what we value. Consider, for example, that certain emotions, such as indignation, presuppose that the object of the emotion has the capacity to recognize and respond to reasons. Valuing one's relationship with another person involves a susceptibility to experiencing, toward that person, emotions that carry this presupposition. By contrast, valuing an inanimate object involves no comparable susceptibility. This illustrates the point that what it is to value something is conditioned by the nature of the object that is valued.

There is one obvious lesson that we should learn from this—a lesson which, despite its obviousness, has not been often enough noticed. The lesson is that any account of valuing *in general* will inevitably be both very abstract and, in important respects, incomplete. Beyond a certain point, we can make progress in understanding what valuing involves only by proceeding in a more piecemeal way, that is, by reflecting on the specific kinds of things that people value.[25] Nevertheless, my aim in this

---

25. In this spirit, I have elsewhere engaged in a number of such piecemeal inquiries. I have asked: What is involved in valuing a personal project? What is involved in valuing a personal relationship? What is involved in valuing one's membership in a group, community, or association? See "Relationships and Responsibilities," *Philosophy & Public Affairs* 26 (1997): 189–209, reprinted in *Boundaries and Allegiances* (Oxford: Oxford University Press, 2001), pp. 97–110; "Projects, Relationships, and Reasons," in R. Jay Wallace, Philip Pettit, Samuel Scheffler, and Michael Smith (eds.), *Reason and Value:*

essay is to see how far we can get in understanding valuing as a general phenomenon.

Our discussion to this point suggests that valuing involves a distinctive fusion of reason and emotion. It comprises a complex syndrome of interrelated dispositions and attitudes, including, at least, certain characteristic types of belief, dispositions to treat certain kinds of considerations as reasons for action, and susceptibility to a wide range of emotions. Somewhat more precisely, it seems that valuing any X involves at least the following elements:

1. A belief that X is good or valuable or worthy,
2. A susceptibility to experience a range of context-dependent emotions regarding X,
3. A disposition to experience these emotions as being merited or appropriate,
4. A disposition to treat certain kinds of X-related considerations as reasons for action in relevant deliberative contexts.

Three points should be noted by way of qualification and elaboration. First, I take this understanding of valuing to apply in the first instance to noninstrumental valuing. We can and often do value things instrumentally as well. Whether instrumental valuing can be understood as involving the same four elements, or whether some modification is required to cover the instrumental case, is a question I will not address here.[26]

Second, we have seen that the extent (and not merely the content) of one's emotional vulnerability can vary depending on the nature of what one values. It is likely to be greater when the things that one values are themselves vulnerable, and it is likely to be attenuated when they are not. But there are also other factors that can affect the extent of one's emotional vulnerability. Not everything that one values plays an equally central role in one's life. I may value both my relationship with my son and my colleague's contributions to department meetings, but they obviously do not play the same role in my life. Other things being equal, the degree of emotional vulnerability that one incurs in valuing a given thing will depend on the role that thing plays in one's life. These differences in role, in turn, are largely constituted by differences in the range

---

Themes from the Moral Philosophy of Joseph Raz (Oxford: Clarendon Press, 2004), pp. 247–269; and "Morality and Reasonable Partiality," Chapter 2 in this volume.

26. Nor shall I consider how the account might need to be modified to accommodate cases of "sentimental" or "personal" value like those discussed in footnote 24.

and character of the reasons for action with which different valued items are seen as providing us. I see my relationship with my son as providing me with compelling reasons for action in a very wide range of contexts, many of which are highly consequential. I also value my colleague's contributions to department meetings, but these provide me with reasons for action only in a very limited range of contexts. We speak of valuing things to different degrees, and of valuing some things more than others. To some extent, these ordinal and comparative judgments reflect judgments about how valuable different things are. But to a great extent they are best understood by reference to differences of role, reason, and emotional vulnerability.

Third, I said earlier that, according to one view, the belief that X is valuable just is, in part, the belief that one's context-dependent emotional reactions regarding X are merited. If one accepts this analysis, then it will seem a redundant feature of my account that it includes, as separate items, both the belief that X is good or valuable and the disposition to experience one's context-dependent emotions regarding X as being merited or appropriate. I will later provide reasons for doubt about this analysis of the belief that X is valuable, but for those who accept it, the redundancy in my account is easily remedied.

There is a potential difficulty with the kind of account I have been developing. One way of bringing out the difficulty is by comparing my account with Thomas Scanlon's, which is in some respects quite similar to mine, but which also differs from it in significant ways. Scanlon summarizes his account as follows:

> We value many different kinds of things, including at least the following: objects and their properties (such as beauty), persons, skills and talents, states of character, actions, accomplishments, activities and pursuits, relationships, and ideals. To value something is to take oneself to have reasons for holding certain positive attitudes toward it and for acting in certain ways in regard to it. Exactly what these reasons are, and what actions and attitudes they support, will be different in different cases. They generally include, as a common core, reasons for admiring the thing and for respecting it, although "respecting" can involve quite different things in different cases. Often, valuing something involves seeing reasons to preserve and protect it (as, for example, when I value a historic building); in other cases it involves reasons to be guided by the goals and standards that the value involves (as when I value loyalty); in some cases both may be involved (as when I value the U.S. Constitution).

> To claim that something is valu*able* (or that it is "of value") is to claim that others also have reason to value it, as you do.[27]

Scanlon's account is similar to the one I have been developing in its emphasis on the wide range of things that we value, in its assertion that valuing involves seeing oneself as having reasons for action of various kinds, and in its insistence on the diversity both of those reasons and of the actions they support. There are also some differences between the two accounts. For one thing, Scanlon does not identify emotional vulnerability as an aspect of valuing. His reference to taking oneself "to have reasons for holding certain positive attitudes" toward the things that one values covers some of this territory, but only some of it. As we have seen, the emotions to which valuing makes one vulnerable are not all positive in character; valuing a friendship makes one as vulnerable to feelings of grief at the friend's death as it does to feelings of delight in the friend's company. In addition, valuing involves a disposition actually to experience these attitudes, and not merely to see oneself as having reason for them. A second difference has to do with the way Scanlon draws the distinction between regarding something as valuable and valuing it oneself. His formulation (in the final sentence of the quoted passage) suggests that the only things that one can see as valuable are things that one values oneself.[28] In my view, this is a mistake. Valuing is not necessary for believing valuable, and believing valuable is not sufficient for valuing. I regard bird-watching and the study of Bulgarian history as valuable, but I do not value them myself. As I said earlier, it is partly the fact that valuing involves emotional vulnerability, while believing valuable does not, that explains why there is a gap between the two. So the second difference between Scanlon's account and mine is related to the first.

There is a third difference between the two accounts, and it is this difference that brings out a potential difficulty for the analysis of valuing that I have been developing. In my view, valuing something involves a belief that the valued item is good or valuable. In Scanlon's view it does not. As we have seen, Scanlon takes valuing to be a notion that is prior to the notion of believing valuable, and he analyzes claims about what is valuable with reference to this prior understanding of valuing. Indeed, Scanlon's primary motivation

<hr>

27. Scanlon, *op. cit.*, p. 95.
28. Actually, Scanlon's formulation is slightly ambiguous. The phrase *as you do* might mean either "as you value it" or "as you have reason to value it." In the text, for simplicity, I assume the first interpretation, and I criticize his formulation on that basis. But my arguments also apply, *mutatis mutandis*, to the version of his formulation that assumes the second interpretation.

for investigating the concept of valuing is because he sees it as a "helpful step-ping-stone" in the development of his buck-passing account of goodness and value.[29] The whole point of the buck-passing account is to deny that "being valuable" is itself a substantive, reason-generating property. Instead, "to call something valuable is to say that it has other properties that provide reasons for behaving in certain ways with regard to it."[30] So it suits Scanlon's wider purposes to explain valuing in terms of the perception of considerations as reasons and to explain believing valuable in terms of valuing.

I have already criticized Scanlon's statement that "To claim that some-thing is valuable is to claim that others also have reason to value it, as you do." As I have indicated, the suggestion that one must value something oneself in order to claim that it is valuable seems to me mistaken. A further worry is that Scanlon's statement, taken literally, appears to imply that there are two sets of reasons: the reasons that we take ourselves to have insofar as we value something, and the reasons that we have *for* valuing something. In addition to taking ourselves to have the first set of reasons, in other words, we also have a second set of reasons for taking ourselves to have the first set. But the content of this second set of reasons is not explained.[31]

---

29. Scanlon, *op. cit.*, p. 95. The buck-passing account is in turn meant to provide an alternative to the "teleological conception of value," which Scanlon takes to be asso-ciated with consequentialism but also to have wider appeal. In the course of his dis-cussion of the teleological conception, Scanlon criticizes my article "Agent-Centered Restrictions, Rationality, and the Virtues" (*Mind* 94 [1985]: 409–419; reprinted in S. Scheffler [ed.], *Consequentialism and Its Critics* [Oxford, 1988], pp. 243–260), but the extent to which our views differ is not clear to me. In the article that Scanlon discusses, I was attempting to diagnose the appeal of consequentialism and the cor-relative impression that there is something paradoxical about deontological prohibi-tions. My diagnosis was that consequentialism seems appealing because it embodies a form of rationality that I called "maximizing rationality." I maintained (1) that maximizing rationality is a familiar form of rationality, which plays a role outside consequentialist thought as well as within it, (2) that so long as one remains within the confines of maximizing rationality, deontological constraints do look puzzling, (3) that it might nevertheless be possible to reconcile the constraints with maximiz-ing rationality, (4) that it's in any case "not obvious that maximizing rationality con-stitutes the whole of rationality" (*Consequentialism and Its Critics*, 258), and (5) that an alternative defense of deontological constraints would involve showing that they "embody a limitation on the scope of that form of rationality, and give expression to a different form of rationality which we also recognize and which also has its place in our lives" (*Consequentialism and Its Critics*, 252). Despite the critical tone of Scan-lon's discussion, it's not clear to me which of these claims, if any, he actually rejects.
30. Scanlon, *op.cit.*, p. 96.
31. This is also a difficulty for the view I defended in "Relationships and Respon-sibilities."

These difficulties can, however, be deflected by formulating Scanlon's view in a slightly different way. He himself says in another place that the claim that "friendship is valuable is best understood as the claim that it is properly valued, that is to say, that the reasons recognized by someone who values friendship are in fact good reasons."[32] This alternative formulation avoids the second of the two problematic features I have mentioned. It does not imply that we have reasons for seeing ourselves as having the reasons involved in valuing. Nor does it imply that one must value something oneself in order to claim that it is valuable.[33] Yet this formulation retains the essentials of Scanlon's position. It preserves the buck-passing idea, as well as the idea that believing valuable should be defined in terms of valuing. To value something does not involve seeing it as valuable, on this account; instead, to claim that something is valuable is to claim that it is properly valued. Because it avoids the difficulties of the first formulation, I will treat this second formulation as the canonical statement of Scanlon's view of the relation between valuing and believing valuable.

Scanlon's view presents a challenge for the account of valuing that I have been developing. That account states that valuing X normally involves at least four elements, of which the first is a belief that X is good or valuable or worthy. But if the claim that something is valuable is in turn taken to mean that it is properly valued, then this element of my account looks to be circular. I noted earlier that the threat of circularity is a problem for views according to which valuing is simply equated with believing valuable. My own view, however, seems to suffer from a version of the same problem.

One response to this problem is to question the force of Scanlon's account of the relation between believing valuable and valuing. Although the second, "canonical" account of that relation does not imply that one must value something oneself in order to claim that it is valuable, it still takes the reasons of the people who do value a given thing as fixing the content of the claim that that thing is valuable. For example, if I say that bird-watching or studying Bulgarian history is valuable, my statement is to be understood as claiming that the reasons recognized by those who value these things are good reasons. But if claims to the effect that X is valuable are to be interpreted as claims about reasons, it is implausible to construe them solely as claims about the reasons recognized by people

---

32. Scanlon, *op.cit.*, p. 89.
33. Or, at any rate, it avoids this implication provided the claim that the reasons recognized by others are good reasons is not taken to commit one to treating them as reasons for oneself.

who value X. It is more plausible to suppose that they are, at least in part, claims about the reasons that even nonvaluers have. For example, if I say that bird-watching or studying Bulgarian history is valuable, despite the fact that I myself do not value those things, then my statement is most plausibly interpreted as being, at least in part, about the reasons that I—and other people generally—have with regard to those activities. We should not, for instance, cast aspersions on those who engage in the activities or disrupt what they are doing without good cause. Those who value bird-watching or the study of Bulgarian history have other reasons that the rest of us lack—such as reasons actually to engage in these activities. In general, those who value a given thing have distinctive reasons that are not shared by people who recognize the value of the thing but do not value it themselves.[34] If claims to the effect that something is valuable are to be construed as claims about reasons, then they are best understood as being, at least in part, claims about the reasons that even nonvaluers have.[35]

34. What is the source of these additional reasons? Since, by hypothesis, they are reasons that nonvaluers lack, it seems that their source cannot lie simply in the fact that the valued items are valuable. But this invites the following worry. If a person who values X has additional reasons that others lack, then perhaps the source of these additional reasons lies in the very fact that the person values X. But this would seem to imply that valuing is, so to speak, a reason for itself, which may seem circular or otherwise objectionable. Although I cannot address this worry adequately here, I believe that the additional reasons that valuers possess are to be accounted for, instead, by appealing to special features of the position that valuers occupy in relation to the valued item. For example, if I value my relationship with my son, the additional reasons that I have—but which others who recognize the value of that relationship lack—are to be explained by reference to the fact that I am a participant in the valuable relationship while they are not. Indeed, as I argue in the text that follows (at p. 37), there are some things (such as particular personal relationships) that only certain people can value, because only certain people can occupy the right position in relation to those things. Of course, what counts as being in the right position in relation to a given item will depend on the type of item it is. In the case of personal relationships, participation in the relationship may define the "right position," but for valuable objects or activities, other accounts may be required. For relevant discussion, see T. M. Scanlon, "Reasons: A Puzzling Duality?" in R. J. Wallace, P. Pettit, S. Scheffler, and M. Smith (eds.), *Reason and Value: Themes from the Moral Philosophy of Joseph Raz* (Oxford: Clarendon Press, 2004), pp. 231–246, and Niko Kolodny, "Aims as Reasons" (in *Reasons and Recognition: Essays on the Philosophy of T. M. Scanlon*).

35. It might be objected that people who value X will surely recognize, *inter alia*, those reasons that even nonvaluers have in regard to X. They will recognize, for example, reasons not to destroy or denigrate X. So if the claim that X is valuable is interpreted as a claim that the reasons recognized by those who value X are good reasons, then it *is* being interpreted, at least in part, as a claim about the reasons that even nonvaluers

These considerations may be taken to support a formulation of the buck-passing account that is not tied to the reasons of valuers in particular. And in fact, Scanlon formulates the buck-passing account itself in just this way. As we have seen, he says it asserts that "to call something valuable is to say that it has other properties that provide reasons for behaving in certain ways with regard to it."[36] Here there is no reference to the reasons of valuers specifically. Instead, the relevant reasons, and the persons for whom they are reasons, are left unspecified. This brings out a point that has so far been left implicit in my discussion, namely, that there are two distinct aspects of Scanlon's view that are, in principle, separable: the buck-passing account proper, and the claim that valuing has priority over believing valuable. The buck-passing account is the claim that to call something valuable is to say that it has other properties that provide reasons for behaving in certain ways with regard to it. The priority claim is the claim that valuing is a notion that is prior to believing valuable, and that believing valuable is to be explained in terms of valuing. The considerations we have been rehearsing provide reason to doubt the priority claim, but they do not count against the buck-passing account itself.

Suppose, however, that, while rejecting the priority claim, we do accept the buck-passing account. And suppose we also accept Scanlon's view that to value something is just "to take oneself to have reasons for holding certain positive attitudes toward it and acting in certain ways with regard to it." Then, because the buck-passing account, unsupplemented by the priority claim, interprets the statement that something is valuable without any reference to valuing or to the reasons of valuers in particular, and because, on Scanlon's account, valuing something involves no claim that the valued thing is valuable, the relation between valuing and believing valuable, on these assumptions, becomes elusive. On the one hand, it is no longer clear how the two phenomena differ from one another, inasmuch as both are said to consist solely in having certain very general

---

have. However, this interpretation fails to distinguish between the reasons that valuers alone have, such as reasons to engage in the activity (if X is an activity), and the reasons that nonvaluers also have, such as reasons not to denigrate or disrupt X. Even if it implies that reasons of both kinds are good reasons, in other words, it fails to distinguish between those good reasons that apply to valuers alone and those that apply to everyone. So even if, by virtue of its endorsement of the reasons recognized by valuers, it implies that any reasons that also apply to nonvaluers are good reasons, it makes no claim to the effect that certain reasons do in fact apply to nonvaluers. And that is the kind of implication that, in my view, a claim that X is valuable does carry.

36. Scanlon, *op.cit.*, p. 96.

beliefs about reasons. But if we assume, on the basis of the arguments given earlier, that they *do* differ from one another, then, because neither is defined with reference to the other, it is no longer clear that there is any relation between them at all. But this is implausible. Surely there is some connection between these cognate notions. One way of securing the connection it is to accept the priority claim and to define *believing valuable* in terms of valuing. But if we reject the priority claim, as I have argued we should, then we need to secure the connection in another way.

My proposal does this by asserting that to value something is in part to believe that it is valuable. This explains the difference noted earlier between valuing and caring and, as we have seen, it is compatible with the buck-passing account of value. On one interpretation, for example, the claim that X is valuable might here be understood, compatibly with the buck-passing account, as asserting that X has properties in virtue of which all people have reasons for behaving in certain (minimum) ways with regard to it. On a second, perhaps more plausible interpretation, it might be understood as the claim that X has properties in virtue of which (1) all people have reasons for behaving in certain (minimum) ways with regard to X, and (2) some people have reasons for additional actions with regard to X and for being emotionally vulnerable to it.[37] On either interpretation, to *value* X would involve believing that it is valuable in the specified sense, but it would also involve being emotionally vulnerable to it oneself and treating it as a source of additional reasons for action in one's own deliberations. Because—on either interpretation—my proposal is compatible with the buck-passing account, that account provides no objection to it. It is the priority claim, rather than the buck-passing account, that fuels the circularity objection to my proposal. However, I have argued that we should reject the priority claim. It overlooks the fact that to value something is in part to view it as good or worthy, and it treats the reasons of valuers as fixing the content of the claim that something is valuable. In so doing, it neglects the fact that valuable things give everyone, and not merely those who value them, certain minimal reasons for action, such as reasons not to destroy or denigrate those things.[38]

Let me conclude with two additional points about the distinction between valuing and believing valuable. First, I have said that nobody can

---

37. This interpretation is a variant of one suggested to me by Niko Kolodny.

38. If, despite my arguments, one continues to find the priority claim compelling, then one may simply eliminate the first element in my account of valuing, while retaining the other three. This would narrow the gap between Scanlon's account and mine, though the differences noted earlier concerning the role of the emotions would remain.

value all valuable things. However, I believe that something even stronger is true, namely, that there are some valuable things that can only be valued by certain people, even though everyone can recognize their value. Imagine, for example, that I have just heard a glowing account of the friendship between two people whom I have never met and with whom I have no connection. I might think, on the basis of this account, that their friendship sounds like a valuable one. It would be bizarre, however, for me to say that I value their friendship. Or, at any rate, it would be bizarre in the absence of some special explanation. Perhaps, for instance, it would make sense for me to say that I value their friendship as an example of a type of relationship that I took no longer to exist. Even in this case, however, I cannot value the friendship in the same way that the participants can; it cannot play the same role in my emotional life and practical deliberations. If it seemed to play such a role, we might have doubts about my mental well-being; we might fear that I had entered the psychological territory inhabited by groupies and stalkers. Yet even though I cannot value the friendship in the way that the participants can, I am just as capable as they are of recognizing its value. So not only is it the case that nobody can value all valuable things, but, in addition, some things whose value everyone can recognize can, nevertheless, only be valued by certain people. In this sense, at least some valuing is *positional* in a way that believing valuable is not. That is, there are some things of which it is true (1) that only those who occupy the right position in relation to the thing are capable of valuing it, or of valuing it in a certain way, and (2) that not everyone is capable of occupying the right position in relation to that thing. This provides an additional reason, beyond those already mentioned, why nobody can value all valuable things. Nobody can occupy all the relevant positions.

Second, in emphasizing the importance of the conceptual distinction between valuing and believing valuable, I have appealed at various points to ordinary usage. I believe that the conceptual distinction is firmly rooted in ordinary thought, and that this is clearly reflected in our linguistic practices. Nevertheless, ordinary usage is not so strictly regimented that our linguistic practices perfectly track the underlying conceptual distinction with which I am concerned. Despite what I have said, there are doubtless times when people use the verb *value* simply to mean something like "believe valuable." Someone may speak, for example, of valuing a colleague's contributions to department meetings when all she means is that she regards those contributions as valuable. This is especially likely to happen when, as in this example, the item that is the object of the attitudes in question is not one that gives much scope for emotional vulnerability and whose practical relevance is limited. In such cases, the differences between valuing in my sense and believing valuable are already attenuated, so it is perhaps not surprising that the boundaries between the two linguistic expressions should become blurrier. Still, the underlying conceptual distinction is clear, and as I hope to have demonstrated in this essay, it represents a stable and significant division in our attitudes.[39]

Appendix: Attaching Value

It is not uncommon to describe a person as "attaching value" to something, and, in context, this seems more or less equivalent to saying that he values it. For example, someone may be said greatly to value his relationship with his brother, or an old watch that his father gave him. But it may just as naturally be said that he "attaches great value" to the relationship or to the watch. We also speak—albeit, perhaps, in a somewhat narrower range of contexts—of people "assigning value" to one thing or another. These locutions may suggest that the phenomenon of valuing has—or is ordinarily understood as having—a voluntaristic dimension that my account neglects. The idea that, when we value something, we are "attaching" or "assigning" value to it may suggest that valuing consists in making a certain kind of decision—a decision to confer value on something that would otherwise lack it.

---

39. It might be suggested, however, that the difference between valuing and believing valuable is best thought of as a matter of a degree rather than as a sharp dichotomy. On the one hand, I have conceded that the level of emotional vulnerability involved in valuing may be attenuated in some cases, and on the other hand, it may be said that even believing something valuable brings with it some degree of emotional vulnerability. For example, I may be vulnerable to feelings of mild regret if I learn that something I regard as valuable (but do not value myself) has been destroyed.

It is important to distinguish between two different ways in which this suggestion might be developed. On one interpretation, being liable to experience certain (mild) emotions is part of what it is to believe that something is valuable. This seems to me implausible. On the other interpretation, which seems to me more plausible, the point is rather that a belief that X is valuable, when accompanied by a disposition to experience (say) mild X-related regret if X is destroyed, may not itself constitute an instance of valuing, but it may differ only in degree from a case of valuing in which the level of emotional vulnerability is attenuated. The two cases may still be distinguished from one another by reference to the degrees of emotional vulnerability involved and the kinds of reasons for action that the people in question recognize, but the difference may not be as stark as in some other pairs of cases. I am grateful to Kinch Hoekstra and Richard Fumerton for raising this issue.

I think that this is misleading, for at least two reasons. First, it is true that the expressions in question are often used in contexts of decision, but these are decisions about what to do and not decisions about what to value. For example, I may say, in explaining why I decided to pass up an evening at the theatre in order to spend time with an unhappy friend, that I attach greater value to the friendship than I do to going to the theatre. There is indeed a decision here, but it is a decision about how to spend the evening, not a decision about the items upon which I wish to confer value.

Second, our use of expressions like *attach value* and even *assign value*, in contexts where it would make equally good sense to speak simply of what we value, is partly a way of registering the fact that valuing something goes beyond merely recognizing that it is valuable, and that nobody can value every valuable thing. When we "attach" value to something, we are active not in the sense that we choose to make the thing valuable when previously it wasn't, for it may well be valuable already, and if it is not, then our valuing it does not make it so. Instead, we are active in the sense that we take up a certain orientation toward it; it becomes a focus of our emotions and a source of what we take to be our reasons. In this sense, it becomes important or valuable *to us*. But we need not decide to make this so, and usually we do not. Sometimes, to be sure, things become important to us—or we come to value them—as a consequence of decisions we have made, but that is not the same as our deciding to make them important to us or to value them. Often, the process of coming to value something happens quite gradually, without any conscious awareness on our part, and we simply find at some point that we do in fact value the thing: that we treat it as a source of reasons, and that we are emotionally vulnerable to it. Sometimes, far from deciding to value things, we find it difficult even to recognize or acknowledge that we value them. One familiar psychotherapeutic aim is to help people to attain greater reflectiveness about their emotions and motivations, and thereby to come to a better understanding of what they do and do not value, or of what actually matters to them. This reinforces the point that valuing or "attaching value" is not normally something that we decide to do. Instead, as I have argued, expressions like *attach value* register our implicit understanding of two points. First, valuing is a selective phenomenon, in the sense that nobody can value everything that is valuable, and that different people value different things. Second, in valuing something, we are taking up a practical and emotional orientation toward that thing, even though we do not normally decide to do this and may in some instances have a difficult time recognizing that we have done so.

Acknowledgments

This essay is also published in R. Jay Wallace, Rahul Kumar, and Samuel Freeman (eds.), *Reasons and Recognition: Essays on the Philosophy of T.M. Scanlon* (Oxford University Press). Printed here by agreement with the publisher. Earlier versions of the essay were presented to the Bay Area Forum for Law and Ethics (BAFFLE), to departmental colloquia at the University of Iowa and the CUNY Graduate Center, and to my Fall 2008 graduate seminar at NYU. I am grateful to all of these audiences for valuable discussion. I am also indebted to Macalester Bell, Josh Glasgow, Niko Kolodny, Stephen Neale, Derek Parfit, and Jay Wallace for helpful comments on previous drafts.

2

Morality and Reasonable Partiality

I. Introduction

What is the relation between morality and partiality? Can the kind of partiality that matters to us be accommodated within moral thought, or are morality and partiality rival sources of normative considerations? These are questions that moral philosophy has struggled with in recent decades.[1] They may not have much intuitive resonance, because the term *partiality* is not used much in everyday discourse. The June 2005 draft revision of the online OED offers two primary definitions of the word. The first definition is "[u]nfair or undue favouring of one party or side in a debate, dispute, etc.; bias, prejudice; an instance of this." The second definition is "[p]reference for or favourable disposition towards a particular person or thing; fondness; predilection; particular

---

1. See, for example, David Archard, "Moral Partiality," *Midwest Studies in Philosophy* 20 (1995): 129–141; Marcia Baron, "Impartiality and Friendship," *Ethics* 101(1991): 836–857; Lawrence Blum, *Friendship, Altruism, and Morality* (London: Routledge

affection; an instance of this."[2] To someone unfamiliar with debates in moral philosophy over the last quarter century, these definitions might seem to give us all the tools we need to answer the question of whether morality and partiality are compatible with one another. If, by *partiality*, we mean "bias" or "prejudice," then surely morality and partiality are not compatible, for bias and prejudice are antithetical to the kind of *im*partiality that is a fundamental feature of moral thought. But if, on the other hand, what we mean by *partiality* is a preference or fondness or affection for a particular person, then surely morality and partiality are compatible. Notwithstanding the importance that it assigns to impartiality in certain contexts, morality cannot possibly condemn our particular preferences and affections for one another.

Like many others who have written on these topics, I believe that this simple, commonsensical answer is basically correct. Yet the second half of the answer has been the subject of a surprising degree of controversy in recent moral philosophy. It has been challenged, from the one side, by defenders of morality—and especially by defenders of certain moral theories—who see our particular affections and preferences for one another as being in serious tension with the forms of impartiality and universality that are essential to morality. The most extreme versions of this challenge construe our particular affections and preferences as tantamount to forms of bias or prejudice; in effect, they see partiality in the second of the OED's senses as tantamount to partiality in the first sense. At the same time, the second half of the commonsensical answer has also been challenged by critics of morality, who believe that, in consequence of its commitments to impartiality and universality, morality cannot do justice to the role in our lives of particular attachments and affections.

and Kegan Paul, 1980); John Cottingham, "Ethics and Impartiality," *Philosophical Studies* 43 (1983): 83–99, and "Partiality, Favouritism, and Morality, *The Philosophical Quarterly* 36 (1986): 357–373; Owen Flanagan and Jonathan Adler, "Impartiality and Particularity," *Social Research* 50 (1983): 576–596; Marilyn Friedman, "The Impracticality of Impartiality," *Journal of Philosophy* 86 (1989): 645–656, and "The Practice of Partiality," *Ethics* 101 (1991): 818–835; Barbara Herman, "Integrity and Impartiality," *The Monist* 66 (1983): 233–250; Diane Jeske, "Friendship, Virtue, and Impartiality," *Philosophy and Phenomenological Research* LVII (1997): 51–72; Troy Jollimore, "Friendship Without Partiality?" *Ratio* 13 (2000): 69–82; John Kekes, "Morality and Impartiality," *American Philosophical Quarterly* 18 (1981): 295–303; Thomas Nagel, *Equality and Partiality* (New York: Oxford University Press, 1991); David Velleman, "Love as a Moral Emotion," *Ethics* 109 (1999): 338–374; Bernard Williams, "Persons, Character, and Morality," in *Moral Luck* (Cambridge: Cambridge University Press, 1981), pp. 1–19; and Susan Wolf, "Morality and Partiality," *Philosophical Perspectives* 6 (1992): 243–259.

2. http://dictionary.oed.com/cgi/entry/50172138 (last accessed June 15, 2006).

The fact that the relation between morality and partiality is seen as problematic testifies in part to the influence within modern moral philosophy of highly universalistic moral theories, especially consequentialist and Kantian theories, which have seemed to many of their supporters, and to at least as many of their critics, to make the relation between moral norms and particularistic loyalties and attachments appear problematic to one degree or another. More generally, and more speculatively, it is perhaps not surprising that, in a world where rapidly intensifying processes of global integration coexist uneasily and, at times, explosively with a range of identity-based social and political movements, there should be a perceived need, both within philosophy and outside it, to revisit the ancient issue of universalism and particularism in ethics.

As I said, the commonsense view of the relation between morality and partiality seems to me largely correct, but of course I have given only a crude statement of that view. And then there is the question of how to argue for it, since there are some who are not impressed by the authority of common sense, and still others who do not find the view commonsensical at all. In this essay, I cannot hope to discuss all the relevant issues. What I will try to do is to extend a line of argument I have developed elsewhere that bears on some of those issues. The general aim of this line of thought is to establish that what I will call *reasons of partiality* are inevitable concomitants of certain of the most basic forms of human valuing. This means that, for human beings as creatures with values, the normative force of certain forms of partiality is nearly unavoidable. If that is right, then for morality to reject partiality in a general or systematic way would be for it to set itself against our nature as valuing creatures. And that, I believe, would make morality an incoherent enterprise. My ultimate conclusion is that any coherent morality will make room for partiality, not merely in the sense that it will permit or require partial behavior in some circumstances, but also in the sense that it will treat reasons of partiality as having direct moral significance.

These are ambitious claims. I will not be able to give anything approaching a complete defense of them here. But I hope to take some steps toward such a defense. The structure of this essay will be as follows. In Section II, I will make some brief preliminary points about the nature and significance of the notion of valuing. In Section III, I will summarize arguments I have given elsewhere about the reason-giving status of personal projects and interpersonal relationships. Projects and relationships are among the most fundamental categories of human value, and to value a project or relationship is to see oneself as having reasons for action of a distinctive kind: *project-dependent reasons*, in the one case, and *relationship-dependent reasons* in the other. In a sense to be specified, these reasons amount to *reasons of partiality*.

In Section IV, I will extend this line of thought by introducing another category of reasons of partiality, which I will call *membership-dependent reasons*. In Section V, I will attempt to account for an asymmetry between the normative force of project-dependent reasons, on the one hand, and relationship-dependent and membership-dependent reasons, on the other hand. In Section VI, the longest section, I will consider the proposal, which is implicit in the work of a number of philosophers, that morality itself may be interpreted on the model of relationship-dependent reasons and membership-dependent reasons. This proposal suggests a radical extension of the line of argument developed in earlier sections of the essay, and it has the potential to cast debates about morality and partiality in a new light. It implies that the very impartiality that we rightly see as a defining feature of morality has its roots in the same structures of normativity that give rise to legitimate reasons of partiality. More generally, it supports a *relational* conception of morality— a conception that stands in contrast to the kind of impersonality associated with consequentialist conceptions. I will discuss several different versions of the proposal that moral reasons can be interpreted on the model of relationship-dependent reasons. I will articulate a number of questions and reservations about each of these versions, in the hope of identifying some of the issues that need to be addressed if some version of the proposal is ultimately to be vindicated. In Section VII, I will consider some general issues bearing on the prospects for a compelling relational view of morality. Finally, in Section VIII, I will explain how, in the absence of a fully satisfactory relational account, I see my discussion of project-dependent, relationship-dependent, and membership-dependent reasons as bearing on the issue of morality and partiality. As I have indicated, my claim will be, not merely that morality permits or requires partial behavior in some circumstances, but, in addition, that morality itself actually incorporates reasons of partiality. By this I mean that such reasons bear directly on the rightness or wrongness of actions.

II. Valuing

Much of the distinctiveness and appeal of utilitarianism derives from the fact that it gives priority to the good over the right, or to the evaluative over the normative. In the utilitarian view, moral norms that do not serve to advance the human good are to that extent pointless or arbitrary or worse; this is the meaning of the famous charge of "rule-worship."[3] To insist on

---

3. See J.J.C. Smart, "An Outline of a System of Utilitarian Ethics," in J.J.C. Smart and B. Williams (eds.), *Utilitarianism: For and Against* (Cambridge: Cambridge University Press, 1973), pp. 3–74, at p. 10.

obedience to a set of rules, however securely entrenched in custom and tradition they may be, is irrational and inhumane if it does not serve to secure for people the kinds of lives that they aspire to lead. Rules lack any legitimate purpose or normative significance, the utilitarian claims, if they do not serve to promote human well-being: if they fail to maximize value.

One response to utilitarianism is to point out that *value* is a verb as well as a noun. We can talk about value or values, but we can also talk about what *we value*. In asserting that right acts are those that maximize aggregate value, utilitarianism, in effect, privileges the noun over the verb. But the general idea that the evaluative has priority over the normative does not by itself dictate this choice. Since it is not obvious that the maximization of aggregate value coincides with what we do in fact value, it is reasonable to ask about the relation between these two notions. Is the maximization of aggregate value itself something that we do or should value? Is it at least compatible with what we value? Positive answers cannot be ruled out a priori, but to make such answers compelling would require sustained attention to questions about the nature of valuing, and these are questions that utilitarianism, with its emphasis on maximizing "the good," has tended to neglect. If utilitarianism says that the right thing to do is at all times to maximize aggregate value, and if doing this is incompatible with what people actually—and not unreasonably—value, then utilitarianism may itself be vulnerable to a version of the charge of rule worship. For, on these assumptions, the utilitarian norm of rightness is disconnected from basic human concerns, from what people themselves prize or cherish. And if that is so, then the utilitarian's allegiance to the norm may begin to look like a case of venerating the rule for its own sake, in isolation from any contribution it may make to the fulfillment of basic human purposes. It may begin to look, in other words, like an instance of the dreaded rule-worship.

Of course, one need not be a utilitarian for questions about the nature of valuing to be significant. Indeed, my position will be that questions about the nature of valuing lead us away from utilitarianism and other forms of consequentialism. To that extent, I am in agreement with the position defended by Thomas Scanlon in Chapter Two of *What We Owe to Each Other*.[4] But Scanlon is also interested in the nature of valuing because he regards at as a "helpful stepping-stone"[5] in the development of his "buck-passing account" of goodness and value. By contrast, I will not be presenting any account of goodness—or of "value as a noun"—and,

---

4. Cambridge, Mass.: Harvard University Press, 1998.
5. *What We Owe to Each Other,* p. 95.

as far as I can see, my arguments are neutral with respect to the truth or falsity of the buck-passing account.

I take valuing in general to comprise a complex syndrome of dispositions and attitudes. These include dispositions to treat certain characteristic types of consideration as reasons for action. They also include certain characteristic types of belief and susceptibility to a wide range of emotions. For the purposes of the arguments I will be developing in this essay, the connection between valuing and the perception of reasons for action is particularly important. However, the role of the emotions is also important and is not to be overlooked. To value something is in part to be susceptible to a wide range of emotions, depending on the circumstances and on the nature of the thing that is valued. We learn what people value by attending not merely to what they *say* they value but also to the emotions they experience in different circumstances. Someone who values a personal project, for example, may feel anxious about whether the project will be successful, frustrated if it encounters obstacles, depressed at not having enough time to devote to it, ambivalent if forced to choose between it and other valued pursuits, defensive if other people criticize it or regard it as unworthy, exhilarated if the project goes better than expected, and crushed or empty if it fails.[6] We expect someone who values a project to be vulnerable to emotions of these types. A person may sincerely profess to value something, but if he does not, in the relevant contexts, experience any of the emotions characteristically associated with valuing something of that kind, then we may come to doubt that he really does value it, and upon reflection he may himself come to doubt it as well.

What is involved in valuing a particular thing will depend to some extent on the type of thing that it is. For example, certain emotions presuppose that the object of the emotion has the capacity to recognize and respond to reasons. Valuing one's relationship with another person involves a susceptibility to experiencing emotions toward that person that carry this presupposition. By contrast, valuing an inanimate object— a work of art, say, or a beautiful rock formation—does not. This illustrates the point that what it is to value something is conditioned by the nature of the object that is valued. It follows that any account of valuing

---

6. This sentence is taken, with slight alterations, from my essay "Projects, Relationships, and Reasons," in R. Jay Wallace, Philip Pettit, Samuel Scheffler, and Michael Smith (eds.), *Reason and Value: Themes from the Moral Philosophy of Joseph Raz* (Oxford: Clarendon Press, 2004), pp. 247–269, at pp. 253–254. Elizabeth Anderson makes a very similar point in her *Value in Ethics and Economics* (Cambridge, Mass.: Harvard University Press, 1993), p. 11.

in general must remain highly abstract and limited. To make further progress in understanding what is involved in valuing, we need to proceed in a more piecemeal way by reflecting on the specific kinds of things that people value. That will be how I proceed in this essay. I will ask: What is involved in valuing a personal project? What is involved in valuing a personal relationship? What is involved in valuing one's membership in a group, community, or association?

III. Relationships and Projects

In a series of earlier essays, I have argued that to value one's relationship with another person noninstrumentally is, in part, to see that person's needs, interests, and desires as providing one, in contexts that may vary depending on the nature of the relationship, with reasons for action, reasons that one would not have had in the absence of the relationship.[7] Of course, the needs and interests of strangers also give one reasons for action. The fact that I lack a relationship with you does not mean that I never have reason to take your interests into account or to act in your behalf. But if I do have a relationship with you, and if I attach noninstrumental value to that relationship, then I will be disposed to see your needs, interests, and desires as providing me, in contexts of various kinds, with reasons that I would not otherwise have had, and with which the needs, interests, and desires of other people do not provide me. This means that I will see myself both as having reasons to do things in your behalf that I have no comparable reason to do for others, and as having reason to give your interests priority over theirs in at least some cases of conflict. This is part of what valuing one's relationships involves. If there are no contexts whatsoever in which I would see your needs and interests as giving me reasons of this kind, then it makes no sense to say that I value my relationship with you, even if I profess to do so. Of course, not all of your needs, interests, and desires give me these *relationship-dependent reasons*, and even those that do may at times be silenced or outweighed or overridden by other considerations. Still, if I value my relationship with you noninstrumentally, then I will treat that relationship as a source of

7. The relevant essays are: "Relationships and Responsibilities," *Philosophy & Public Affairs* 26 (1997): 189–209, reprinted in *Boundaries and Allegiances* (Oxford: Oxford University Press, 2001), pp. 97–110; "Conceptions of Cosmopolitanism," *Utilitas* 11 (1999): 255–276, reprinted in *Boundaries and Allegiances*, pp. 111–30; and "Projects, Relationships, and Reasons." My discussion in this section draws on these earlier essays.

reasons that I would not otherwise have. To value one's relationships is to treat them as reason-giving.

This does not mean that to value a personal relationship is to regard the person with whom one has the relationship as more valuable than other people, or to regard the relationship itself as more valuable than other people's relationships. On the contrary, valuing one's relationships is fully compatible with a recognition of the equal worth of persons and with a recognition that other people have relationships that are just as valuable as one's own. Yet, at the same time, there is more to valuing one's relationships than simply believing that they are instances of valuable types of relationship. To value one's relationships is not to regard them as more valuable than other people's relationships, but neither is it merely to believe that they are valuable relationships that happen to be one's own. To value one's relationships is also to see them as a distinctive source of reasons. It is, in other words, for the needs, desires, and interests of the people with whom one has valued relationships to present themselves as having deliberative significance, in ways that the needs and interests of other people do not.

There are clear parallels between what is involved in valuing a personal relationship and what is involved in valuing a personal project. Valuing a personal project, like valuing a personal relationship, involves seeing it as reason-giving. In other words, to value a project of one's own is, among other things, to see it as giving one reasons for action in a way that other people's projects do not, and in a way that other comparably valuable activities in which one might engage do not. Again, this does not mean that one sees one's projects as being more valuable than anybody else's projects or than any other activity in which one might engage. Nor does it mean that one's *project-dependent* reasons always take priority over other reasons. Still, if I value my projects noninstrumentally, then I will see them as a distinctive source of reasons for action, and there will be contexts in which I see myself as having reasons to pursue those projects, even though doing so means passing up opportunities to engage in other equally valuable activities or to assist other people with their equally valuable projects. This is simply what valuing one's personal projects noninstrumentally involves. If I do not see myself as having any more reason to attend to my own projects and goals than I do to engage in other activities or to attend to the projects and goals of other people, then it no longer makes sense to think of them as my projects and goals at all, still less to think that I value them noninstrumentally.

There are few things to which people attach greater value than their personal projects and interpersonal relationships. I take this claim to be uncontroversial. Our projects and relationships are among the primary things that we value. They give purpose and shape to our lives.

Of course, particular projects and relationships are open to criticism of various kinds. A project may be pointless, misguided, shallow, corrupt, or evil. A relationship may be unhealthy or exploitative or oppressive. The fact that someone values a particular project or relationship does not mean that it is worth valuing. Yet any suggestion that people should in general cease to value their personal projects and relationships would be difficult to take seriously. From what vantage point might such a claim be put forward? And on what authority might one presume to tell people that they should abandon these basic categories of human value? There are religious ideals that hold that one should strive to detach oneself from worldly concerns and to transcend the self altogether. Whatever the attractions of these ideals, they do not provide grounds for criticizing the particular categories of value we are discussing. They aspire to something more radical: a rejection of all valuing, indeed a rejection of the self as normally understood. I won't engage with these ideals here, because debates about morality and partiality normally take it for granted that we are dealing with human beings as creatures with values who have distinct identities as persons. So long as we proceed on that assumption, I see little basis for any credible argument to the effect that people should cease to value their projects and relationships.

If the arguments I have been sketching are correct, this means that partiality is a deeply entrenched feature of human valuing. To value one's projects and relationships is to see them as sources of reasons for action in a way that other people's projects and relationships are not. Personal projects and relationships by their nature define forms of reasonable partiality, partiality not merely in our preferences or affections but in the reasons that flow from some of our most basic values. To be sure, I have so far argued only that valuing one's projects and relationships involves *seeing them as* sources of reasons. I have not argued that these reasons of partiality really exist. Yet if there is no general ground for insisting that we are mistaken in valuing our projects and relationships, then neither is there any ground for denying the validity of project-dependent and relationship-dependent reasons as a class. By virtue of what we value, we see ourselves as having reasons of these types. We may on occasion value things that shouldn't be valued, and so we may on occasion see ourselves as having reasons that we do not have. But to say that we are fallible is not to say that we are systematically misguided. Absent any reason for repudiating our valuation of projects and relationships as a class, there is no basis for denying that we have project-dependent and relationship-dependent reasons at all. Contrapositively, skepticism about such reasons is tantamount to the rejection of fundamental categories of human valuation.

IV. Membership-Dependent Reasons

In addition to valuing their personal projects and interpersonal relationships, people value their membership in groups and associations of various kinds. They value group membership even when the groups in question are large enough that there is no prospect of knowing individually, let alone having a personal relationship with, each of the other members. It is possible, of course, to value one's membership in a group in a purely instrumental way, as a means of achieving one's long-term goals or obtaining the discrete benefits that group membership makes available. For example, an ambitious white-collar worker may apply for membership in an exclusive club in the hope that it will enhance his career. Or, again, one may value one's membership in the American Association of Retired People solely because AARP members receive a discount on the purchase of prescription drugs. Here it is perfectly imaginable that one might receive such a discount without belonging to the AARP, and if one could, then, by hypothesis, one would see no loss in surrendering one's membership and obtaining the discount in other ways.

Often, however, people value their membership in groups noninstrumentally. They find membership rewarding in its own right. Even in such cases, there may seem to be a sense in which they can be said to value membership for the sake of the benefits it provides. Perhaps, for example, one values one's membership in a particular community because of the bonds of trust and solidarity that members share. However, this is merely a way of characterizing the respects in which membership in the group is a good. It is not a specification of a good that is independent of membership and to which membership is a means. In other words, the benefits mentioned are not separable even in principle from one's membership; one could not, even in principle, receive them without belonging to this community. One might, of course, come to develop bonds of trust in some other community, but the bonds that unite members of *this* community have a distinctive character and are not fungible. If one ceased to be a member of the community, one would experience a sense of loss even if one were assured that one would be welcomed into some other community. Since one cannot make sense of the idea that one might obtain the benefits of belonging to this particular community without actually belonging to this particular community, it would be wrong to say that one values one's membership only as a means of obtaining those benefits. In valuing the benefits one is valuing one's membership.

It is not surprising that people should value group membership. Human beings are social creatures, and we express our social natures through participation in a rich variety of formal and informal groups, associations, and organizations. This is one of the basic ways in which we find fulfillment. So it is not at all surprising that we should value our membership in groups. This form of valuation is firmly rooted in our nature as social creatures. What is involved in valuing noninstrumentally one's membership in a group or association? As with projects and relationships, valuing one's membership in a group or association is in part a matter of seeing it as reason-giving, as a source of what I will call *membership-dependent reasons*. In general, membership-dependent reasons are reasons for doing one's share, as defined by the norms and ideals of the group itself, to help sustain it and contribute to its purposes. Most groups and associations have formal or informal ways of communicating what is expected of individual members. To value one's membership in a group or association is, in part, to see these expectations as presenting one with reasons for action in a way that the expectations of other worthy groups do not. One need not believe that the group to which one belongs is the most valuable group of its kind, still less that it is the most valuable group of any kind, in order for its expectations to be perceived as presenting one with reasons for action in a way that other groups' expectations do not. Nor need one believe that fulfilling the group's expectations will have better overall results, in the consequentialist sense, than engaging in other valuable activities would. The capacity of my membership in a group to provide me with reasons for action is not dependent on a conviction that the group is worthier than other groups or that fulfilling its expectations is the most valuable thing I could do. Of course, my membership-dependent reasons may in various contexts be overridden or outweighed or silenced by reasons of other kinds. And if an otherwise worthy group articulates expectations in a given case that strike me as foolhardy or unjust, then I may not see myself as having any reason to fulfill those expectations. But if I never see myself as having any more reason to respond to the group's expectations than I do to engage in other valuable activities, then it no longer makes sense to suppose that I value my membership in the group noninstrumentally.

If these arguments are correct, then, like personal projects and relationships, group membership defines a form of reasonable partiality, partiality in the reasons that flow from deeply entrenched categories of human valuation. If there is no ground for insisting that we are mistaken in valuing group membership in general, then neither is there any ground for denying the validity of membership-dependent reasons as a class. By virtue of what we value, we see ourselves as having reasons of these types. To be sure, some groups are evil or corrupt, and if we value our membership in such a group we may see ourselves as having reasons that we do not really have. As with projects and relationships, however, to say that we are fallible is not to say that we are systematically misguided. Absent any reason for repudiating our valuation of group membership in general, there is no basis for denying that we have membership-dependent reasons at all. Contrapositively, skepticism about such reasons is tantamount to rejecting a fundamental category of human valuation.

V. The Asymmetry between Projects and Relationships

Despite the strong parallels between project-dependent reasons and relationship-dependent reasons, there is, as I've noted elsewhere,[8] an important asymmetry between them. Oversimplifying slightly, we may characterize the asymmetry as follows. We normally suppose that many of our relationship-dependent reasons are reasons on which we are required or obligated to act. It is not merely that we have reasons to attend to the needs of, say, our children or elderly parents, but that we have obligations to do so. By contrast, even when we have strong project-dependent reasons, we do not normally suppose that we are obligated or required to act on them. I may have strong reasons to complete my novel, but if I fail to do so I will not have violated any obligation or deontic requirement. And this remains the case even though these reasons may strike me with the force of practical necessity; prospectively I may say that I *have to* finish my novel or that I simply *must* do so. This means that there are really two puzzles to be addressed. One puzzle is how to account for the asymmetry between project-dependent and relationship-dependent reasons. But in order to address that puzzle, we need to characterize more clearly the content of the asymmetry. If reasons of both kinds may strike us with the force of practical necessity—as reasons on which we must act—then how can it also be true that we are required or obligated to act on reasons of one kind but not the other?

The key to solving both puzzles lies in the observation that many relationship-dependent reasons are reasons that one lacks the authority to disregard, not merely in the sense that the reasons may be compelling or rationally decisive, but in the sense that there are specific people who are entitled to complain if one neglects those reasons. If I fail to act on compelling relationship-dependent reasons to attend to my son's needs, then, other things being equal, I have wronged him and he has a legitimate complaint against me. But if I fail to act on compelling

---

8. In "Projects, Relationships, and Reasons."

project-dependent reasons to finish my novel, I have wronged no one and no one is in a privileged position to complain.[9] This gives content to the claim that, despite the fact that both relationship-dependent reasons and project-dependent reasons may strike us with the force of practical necessity, we are required or obligated to act on the former but not the latter.

But why is someone entitled to complain in the one case but not the other? Why is it the case that, if I neglect compelling relationship-dependent reasons to attend to my son's needs, then I will have wronged him, whereas, if I neglect compelling project-dependent reasons to finish my novel, then I will not have wronged anyone? It would, of course, be circular to reply that, in the first case, I lack the authority to disregard the reasons in question, whereas in the second case I retain that authority. Nor will it do to say that, in the first case, my failure will affect my son adversely, while in the second case my failure will have adverse effects on nobody but myself. One's failure to act on one's project-dependent reasons may well have adverse effects on other people. My failure to complete my novel may disappoint admirers of my fiction. My failure to complete the design for a new product may deprive others of its benefits. My failure to open the small business I had dreamed about may deprive the local economy of a badly needed boost. My failure to complete my medical studies may mean that someone does not receive medical care that is as good as the care I would have provided.

A more promising answer would proceed along the following lines.[10] To value our relationships is to see them as sources of reasons. Insofar as we are correct to value our relationships—insofar as our relationships are valu*able*—they are indeed sources of reasons. So if we ask why the needs, interests, and desires of people with whom we have valuable relationships give us reasons for action, the answer lies in the fact that we have those relationships with them. A valuable relationship transforms the needs and desires of the participants into reasons for each to act in behalf of the

9. Compare the view that Milan Kundera attributes to Stravinsky: "[W]hat an author creates doesn't belong to his papa, his mama, his nation, or to mankind; it belongs to no one but himself; he can publish it when he wants and if he wants; he can change it, revise it, lengthen it, shorten it, throw it in the toilet and flush it down without the slightest obligation to explain himself to anybody at all" (M. Kundera, "What Is a Novelist?" *The New Yorker* [October 9, 2006], pp. 40–45, at p. 44).

10. The discussion in this paragraph derives from but also revises and supersedes my earlier discussion of this issue in "Projects, Relationships, and Reasons," pp. 266–268. In making these revisions, I largely follow the account given by R. Jay Wallace, in "The Deontic Structure of Morality," unpublished draft, December 3, 2005.

other in suitable contexts. At the same time, it gives each of them reasons to form certain normative expectations of the other, and to complain if these expectations are not met.[11] In particular, it gives each of them reason to expect that the other will act in his or her behalf in suitable contexts. These two sets of reasons—reasons for action on the one hand and reasons to form normative expectations on the other—are two sides of the same coin. They are constitutively linked and jointly generated by the relationship between the participants. Insofar as we have a valuable relationship, I have reasons to respond to your needs, desires, and interests, and insofar as those reasons are compelling or decisive, you have complementary reasons to expect that I will do so. And vice versa. This is neither a coincidence nor a mystery. It is simply the normative upshot of valuable human relationships. The fact that two human beings have a valuable bond or tie is a source of interlocking reasons and expectations for each of them. That is the kind of normative significance that valuable relationships have for their participants. I might have compelling pragmatic or prudential reasons to respond to your needs or desires without your being entitled to form an expectation that I will do so or to hold me to account if I do not. But if the source of my reason to respond to your needs and desires lies in the value of our relationship, and if that reason is compelling, then my reason for action is complemented by your entitlement to expect that I will respond. The very same consideration that gives me reason to act in your behalf gives you reason to complain if I do not. In this sense, I lack the authority unilaterally to disregard my reason to act in your behalf; I cannot waive your entitlement to complain.

This argument needs refinement and qualification, but something along these lines seems to me basically correct. And even without having the refinements and qualifications in hand, it is clear that no comparable argument applies to the case of project-dependent reasons. Insofar as they arise outside the context of interpersonal relations, my project-dependent reasons are not accompanied by complementary entitlements on the part of other people to form expectations of me. Interpersonal relationships are collaborative enterprises by definition, and the normative considerations they generate for each party are constitutively linked to the normative considerations they generate for the other. In giving me a decisive reason to act in your behalf, they give you a claim that I should do so. By contrast, nobody but me need be a party to my project,

---

11. The idea of holding agents to a set of normative expectations is central to the account of responsibility developed by R. Jay Wallace in *Responsibility and the Moral Sentiments* (Cambridge, Mass.: Harvard University Press, 1996). Here I focus on the distinctive expectations of the participants in interpersonal relationships.

and so my project can give me reasons to act without giving anyone the normative standing to complain if I fail to do so. In this sense, my purely project-dependent reasons might be described as *normatively individualistic*. I have unilateral authority to disregard such reasons, however strong they may be, and this gives content to the idea that, even though I might be foolish or unreasonable not to act on them, nevertheless I am not required or obligated to do so. In practice, of course, project-dependent reasons often overlap with relationship-dependent reasons, both because the participants in personal relationships sometimes develop joint projects and because personal projects sometimes involve relationships with other people. In cases of either of these types, it may be impossible to distinguish one's project-dependent reasons from one's relationship-dependent reasons, and when this happens it is the normative character of the relationship-dependent reasons that is dominant. That is, one's reasons lose the normative characteristics of purely project-dependent reasons, and one may be required or obligated to act on them. Still, purely project-dependent reasons do exist, and they differ in their deontic character from relationship-dependent reasons.

The normative characteristics of membership-dependent reasons do not correspond precisely to those of either relationship-dependent or project-dependent reasons. On the one hand, membership in a group implicates one directly in relations of co-membership with others, and membership-dependent reasons lack the normatively individualistic character of purely project-dependent reasons. One may be required or obligated to act on them. On the other hand, the relations that are constitutive of group membership may be highly attenuated. One need not have a face-to-face relationship or even a personal acquaintance with each of the other members of a group to which one belongs, and in larger groups one may know personally only a very small proportion of them. This means that the normative significance of membership-dependent reasons has a more diffuse character than is typical of relationship-dependent reasons. Although one's failure to act on one's membership-dependent reasons does give others grounds for complaint, it may not always be clear who exactly has the standing to complain. Perhaps all the members of the group do, or perhaps only those group members who are most affected by one's failure to act, if they can be identified, or perhaps only the officials or designated representatives of the group, if it has any. It may be even less clear who can reasonably be said to have been wronged by one's failure to act. Is it the entire membership of the group, or is it the group itself—considered as something over and above its membership—or some subset of group members? Or does it not make sense to speak of wronging in such cases? One reason for doubt is that, in large groups, at least, the failure of any one individual to satisfy the group's expectations may have no perceptible effect on the other members, who may not even be aware of the failure. So it may seem overblown to use the language of wronging.

In any event, the answers to questions about who is wronged and who has standing to complain when an individual fails to act on his membership-dependent reasons may vary depending on the nature, size, and organizational structure of the group of which he is a member. What does seem clear is that the relatively simple pattern of reciprocal normativity that characterizes two-person relationships may not apply straightforwardly in these cases.

VI. A Relational View of Morality?

I have argued that our project-dependent, relationship-dependent, and membership-dependent reasons all define important forms of reasonable partiality. This list may not be exhaustive. At the very least, though, the three types of reason I have identified cover much of the territory of reasonable partiality. So it is noteworthy that various philosophers have seen personal relationships as crucial to understanding the normative force of morality itself. On the face of it, many moral reasons are relationship-independent. That is, they are reasons to treat other people in certain ways regardless of whether we have any personal relationship with them. Yet a number of philosophers have suggested, in effect, that these reasons are best understood as constituting a species of relationship-dependent or membership-dependent reason, and the idea that morality has an essentially relational structure has been presented as an alternative to the consequentialist emphasis on the impersonal aggregation of value. In an early essay,[12] for example, Thomas Nagel characterized the difference between utilitarianism and absolutist deontology in the following terms: "Absolutism is associated with a view of oneself as a small being interacting with others in a large world. The justifications it requires are primarily interpersonal. Utilitarianism is associated with a view of oneself as a benevolent bureaucrat distributing such benefits as one can control to countless other beings, with whom one may have various relations or none. The justifications it requires are primarily administrative."[13] Nagel suggests in the same essay that the key to understanding the basis of deontological restrictions may lie in "the possibility that to treat someone

12. "War and Massacre," reprinted in Samuel Scheffler (ed.), *Consequentialism and Its Critics* (Oxford University Press, 1988), pp. 51–73.
13. *Ibid.*, p. 67.

else horribly puts you in a special relation to him which may have to be defended in terms of other features of your relation to him."[14]

More recently, Jay Wallace has argued that the "deontic structure" of morality—the fact that moral reasons present themselves to us in deliberation as requirements or obligations—can be understood by reference to the same kind of reciprocal normativity that characterizes personal relationships, such as friendship, and the reasons arising from them.[15] Just as we lack the authority unilaterally to disregard our relationship-dependent reasons because they arise from valuable relationships that also ground corresponding expectations and complaints on the part of the people with whom we have those relationships, so, too, there are "valuable relationships [that lie] at the heart of morality," and these relationships, in providing us with reasons for action, also generate legitimate expectations and grounds for privileged complaint on the part of other people. Like relationship-dependent reasons, Wallace argues, moral reasons have the character of requirements because they arise within structures of relational or reciprocal or "bipolar" normativity.[16]

These ideas suggest a radical extension of the line of argument that I have been developing. My aim has been to argue that project-dependent, relationship-dependent, and membership-dependent reasons all represent forms of reasonable partiality, which morality should be thought of as incorporating. But the remarks of Nagel and Wallace may be taken to suggest, more radically, that moral reasons are always relationship-dependent. This suggestion has the potential to transform debates about morality and partiality. Whereas the presupposition of those debates is that there is at least a prima facie tension between morality and partiality, the suggestion here is that even those moral reasons that appear superficially to be relationship-independent nevertheless have their source in

14. *Ibid.*, p. 66.
15. Wallace, "The Deontic Structure of Morality." I am here oversimplifying Wallace's position. He also cites two other factors that may contribute to our understanding of moral reasons as having the status of requirements. These factors are the inescapability of such reasons—the fact that they apply to all people—and their weightiness or importance. However, the central argument of his paper is that the deontic structure of morality cannot be fully explained by these other factors alone. There is, he says, a "distinct source of deontic structure" (p. 2), and he appeals to the notion of reciprocal or relational normativity to account for this additional dimension of the normativity of morality. I will ignore this complication in the remainder of my discussion, since I don't believe that it affects the points I want to make.
16. The notion of bipolar normativity derives from Michael Thompson, "What is it to Wrong Somebody? A Puzzle about Justice," in *Reason and Value: Themes from the Moral Philosophy of Joseph Raz*, pp. 333–384.

relations among people, so that moral reasons and reasons of partiality arise ultimately in just the same way.

I find the idea of interpreting morality in fundamentally relational terms attractive, yet I believe that a satisfactory relational interpretation continues to elude us. Several versions of a relational interpretation have been suggested in recent philosophical work. These versions differ from one another in significant ways, but in each case there are puzzles or obscurities that bar the way to unqualified acceptance. In the remainder of this section, I will discuss three of these versions, and in each case I will try to identify some of the issues that need to be addressed if a compelling position is to emerge.

One way of modeling moral reasons on relationship-dependent reasons is suggested by Nagel's frankly speculative proposal that "to treat someone else horribly puts you in a special relation to him which may have to be defended in terms of other features of your relation to him."[17] However, Nagel offers this as a suggestion about how deontological restrictions in particular might be justified or explained. He does not purport to be offering a relational account of morality as a whole. And since the "special relation" he invokes is supposed to be called into being by mistreatment—by the violation of a deontological restriction—it is not clear how readily this proposal could be generalized to explain moral reasons as a class. The suggestion that "to treat someone horribly puts you in a special relation to him" implies that the relation arises from the fact of mistreatment. It is the mistreatment that "establishes"[18] the relation. But this means that, if a person respects deontological restrictions, then there is no relation of the relevant kind between him and those who would otherwise have been his victims. Since it is unclear how the deontological reason the agent respects could have its source in a relation that doesn't exist, this raises a question about whether Nagel's appeal to the relation between agent and victim can fully explain how such reasons arise. It is even less clear how that appeal might be extended to provide a relational account of moral reasons in general.

There is a deeper point here. I have argued that personal relationships can be sources of reasons for action because they are among the most basic objects of human valuation, and because valuing is always connected to the perception of reasons. But the relevant notion of a *relationship* requires clarification. As Niko Kolodny has observed, there is a thin, logical sense in which, whenever two people satisfy some two-place

17. Nagel, "War and Massacre," p. 66. The next several paragraphs expand on points I made in footnote 25 of "Projects, Relationships, and Reaons," pp. 267–268.
18. Nagel, "War and Massacre," p. 67n.

predicate, they can be said to stand in an interpersonal relation.[19] But the valuable reason-giving relationships that I have been discussing are relationships in a more robust sense. They are ongoing bonds between individuals who have a shared history that usually includes patterns of engagement and forms of mutual familiarity, attachment, and regard developed over time.[20] In such cases, we can usually say, not merely that the participants *stand in some relation to* one another, but that they *have a relationship with* one another. My argument has been that relationships of this kind are among the most basic and deeply entrenched categories of human valuation and the most important sources of human fulfillment and that, as such, they have the capacity to give us reasons for action if anything does. In this sense, I have attempted to explain the source of relationship-dependent reasons.

The pertinent question to ask about relational views of morality is whether they can provide a comparable explanation of the source of moral reasons, by showing how those reasons arise from valuable human relationships of some kind. The "special relation" between agent and victim that Nagel speaks of is not, however, a valuable relationship. Indeed, it is not a human relationship in the sense just described at all. Rather than being a temporally extended pattern of mutual engagement, the relation between agent and victim supervenes on a discrete interaction between two individuals who may have no independent relationship of any kind.[21] In speaking of a special relation between those two individuals, Nagel means to be emphasizing that what is wrong about the violation of a deontological restriction has to do with features of the interaction *between them*. It does not have to do with the wider effects or overall consequences of such a violation. In *The View from Nowhere*, he suggests that the wrong-making feature is the fact that the agent's actions are guided by or aim at the victim's harm or injury or evil.[22] But to say this is clearly not to ground moral reasons in an ongoing human

19. Niko Kolodny, "Love as Valuing a Relationship," *Philosophical Review* 112 (2003): 135–189, at p. 147.
20. See Kolodny, "Love as Valuing a Relationship," p. 148. Kolodny particularly emphasizes the importance of a shared history.
21. Thus I find misleading Christine Korsgaard's comment that "the relationship of agents and victims, like that of love or friendship, is a *personal* relationship" ("The Reasons We Can Share," *Social Philosophy and Policy* 10 [1993]: 24–51, at p. 48). Niko Kolodny makes similar points in his "Partiality and the Contours of the Moral" (unpublished).
22. Nagel writes that a deontological restriction "expresses the direct appeal to the point of view of the agent from the point of view of the person on whom he is acting. It operates through that relation. The victim feels outrage when he is deliberately

relationship, let alone a valuable one. So it does not by itself take us very far down the road toward a satisfactory relational view of morality.

Perhaps the most straightforward way of trying to develop such a view is to argue that, in addition to their other personal relationships and social affiliations, all people share the bond of their common humanity. In Locke's words, all of "*mankind are one community*, make up one society, distinct from all other creatures."[23] Or, in Christine Korsgaard's more Kantian formulation, each person is not only "a member of many smaller and more local communities," but also "a member of the party of humanity, a Citizen of the Kingdom of Ends."[24] This argument proposes that, just as it is possible to value noninstrumentally one's relationships with particular individuals and one's membership in various social groups and associations, so, too, it is possible to value one's membership in the wider human community. And just as valuing one's relationships or one's membership in groups and associations involves seeing those bonds as reason-giving, so, too, valuing one's membership in the wider human community involves seeing it as reason-giving. Moral reasons, this proposal concludes, are simply membership-dependent reasons that arise from the value of belonging to the human community.

One initial worry about this proposal, which I will mention only to set aside, is that it may provide a relatively weak motivational foundation for morality. Most people do have projects and relationships that they value, and few of them doubt that those projects and relationships give them reasons for action. But skepticism about morality is more widespread, and moral skeptics may be happy to deny that they value something called "membership in the human community." So if moral reasons do arise from the value of this kind of membership, this may do little to persuade the skeptic. Of course, a central aspiration of Kantian moral philosophy is to establish that one must value one's own humanity as a condition of valuing one's other relationships and affiliations, or indeed of valuing anything at all. I will not engage with this dimension of the Kantian project here, since I want to concentrate on the prior question of whether a viable relational interpretation of morality is available in the first place.

---

harmed even for the greater good of others, not simply because of the quantity of the harm but because of the assault on his value of having my actions guided by his evil. What I do is immediately directed against his good: it doesn't just in fact harm him" (*The View from Nowhere* [New York: Oxford University Press, 1986], at p. 184).

23. John Locke, *Second Treatise of Government* (1690), Section 128 (emphasis in the original).

24. Christine Korsgaard, *The Sources of Normativity* (Cambridge University Press, 1996), p. 127.

More immediately pressing puzzles emerge if we ask the following question. If valuing one's membership in the human community involves seeing it as reason-giving, what is the content of those reasons? If they are construed on the model of relationship-dependent reasons, then perhaps they are reasons to respond to the needs and interests of human beings, reasons that one does not have to respond to the needs and interests of nonhumans. I have two reservations about this proposal. First, as Locke's emphasis on our being "distinct from all other creatures" suggests, it treats the distinction between human and nonhuman creatures as the linchpin of morality, as if the primary moral imperative were to give the interests of human beings priority over those of the beasts or of aliens from outer space. Second, it says nothing about the kind of response to the needs and interests of human beings that is called for, and, in particular, it says nothing to rule out the utilitarian idea that one should respond to those needs and interests by maximizing their aggregate satisfaction. To that extent, it does nothing by itself to flesh out the idea of a relational conception of morality as an alternative to impersonal, aggregative forms of consequentialism.

If the reasons involved in valuing one's membership in the human community are instead construed on the model of other membership-dependent reasons, then perhaps they are reasons to do one's fair share, as defined by the norms and ideals of the human community itself, to help sustain the community and contribute to its purposes. The problem, of course, is that in asking about the content of our moral reasons, the norms of the human community are precisely what we are trying to characterize. There is, by hypothesis, no independent characterization of those norms to which noncircular appeal can be made, so, on this interpretation, the proposal is vacuous.

Underlying many of these worries is a more basic doubt about the plausibility of grounding moral reasons in the value of membership in the human community. One way of articulating this doubt is to suggest that this proposal takes too literally what is in fact a metaphorical way of formulating a very different view. The alternative view is that moral reasons are grounded in the value of humanity, or of persons. This view can be expressed metaphorically by speaking of the value of membership in the human community, but the metaphor should not be taken literally. A literal reading makes morality seem too much like a matter of group loyalty—of loyalty to one's fellow humans—and in so doing it puts the accent in the wrong place.[25] It is not really the value of *membership* that

---

25. I take this to be an objection to the view of morality defended by Andrew Oldenquist in "Loyalties," *Journal of Philosophy* 79 (1982): 173–193. But see Bernard Williams,

gives rise to moral reasons, according to the alternative view, but rather the value of humanity—of persons—and talk of membership in the human community is simply a picturesque way of reminding us that all persons have moral standing. This contrasts with cases of genuinely relationship-dependent and membership-dependent reasons.[26] In such cases, one's reasons do not arise simply from the value of the person with whom one has the relationship or shares the group affiliation. Instead, it is one's participation in the valuable group or relationship that is the source of one's reasons, and nonparticipants do not have the same reasons, even though they may recognize the value of the persons involved. If this is correct, and if the doubts articulated here are well-founded, then what looks like a relational conception of morality may turn out in the end not to be one after all.

A third way of grounding moral reasons in valuable human relationships is suggested by Thomas Scanlon in *What We Owe to Each Other*. Scanlon's contractualism "holds that an act is wrong if its performance under the circumstances would be disallowed by any set of principles for the general regulation of behavior that no one could reasonably reject as a basis for informed, unforced general agreement."[27] Scanlon takes it to be an advantage of this view that it provides a compelling explanation of the reason-giving force of moral judgments. The core idea is that the distinctive reason that we have to avoid doing what is wrong is a reason to want our behavior to be justifiable to others on grounds they could not reasonably reject. Scanlon writes: "When I reflect on the reason that the wrongness of an action seems to supply not to do it, the best description of this reason I can come up with has to do with the relation to others that such acts would put me in: the sense that others could reasonably object to what I do."[28] This suggests that moral reasons are rooted in considerations about our relations to other people.

Scanlon elaborates on this suggestion in the course of explaining how the contractualist account of moral motivation makes available a convincing reply to "Pritchard's dilemma." This dilemma asserts that any account of moral motivation will be either trivial (if it says that we have reason to avoid

---

"The Human Prejudice," in *Philosophy as a Humanistic Discipline* (Princeton, N.J.: Princeton University Press, 2006), Chapter 16.

26. This is related to the contrast drawn by Niko Kolodny, in "Partiality and the Contours of the Moral," between the "person-based" conception of morality and the "owed-to" conception. Significantly, Kolodny argues that a commitment to the person-based conception is what motivates the view that morality excludes partiality.

27. Scanlon, *What We Owe to Each Other*, p. 153.

28. *Ibid.*, p. 155.

doing what's wrong just because it's wrong) or unacceptably "external" (if, for example, it says that avoiding wrongdoing will conduce to our own interests). Scanlon develops his reply by first considering the case of friendship. In this case, a similar dilemma might seem to arise, for we can ask why we should be loyal to our friends, and any answer we give may appear either trivial (if it says that loyalty is what friendship requires) or unacceptably external (if it appeals to the benefits of having friends). The solution to the friendship dilemma, Scanlon believes, is to characterize friendship in such a way as to make clear why it is a relationship that is "desirable and admirable in itself."[29] If we do this, we will see that there is really no dilemma. Rather than being competing answers to a single question, the two horns of the supposed dilemma capture "two essential aspects of friendship."[30] On the one hand, part of what friendship involves is seeing loyalty to one's friends as a sufficient reason for performing what may sometimes be burdensome actions. On the other hand, being a friend also involves an appreciation of the way in which the friendship enriches one's life and contributes to one's good.

Analogous points hold, Scanlon maintains, in the case of morality. Here his solution to Pritchard's dilemma is to represent our reasons to avoid wrongdoing as rooted in a certain ideal of interpersonal relations that is intimately connected with morality, but that has enough independence from it to provide a nontrivial account of those reasons. He writes:

> There are obvious similarities between the case of friendship as I have described it and that of the morality of right and wrong, and my strategy in responding to the problem of moral motivation is analogous to the response I have just sketched to Pritchard's dilemma in the case of friendship. The contractualist ideal of acting in accord with principles that others (similarly motivated) could not reasonably reject is meant to characterize the relation with others the value and appeal of which underlies our reasons to do what morality requires. This relation, much less personal than friendship, might be called a relation of mutual recognition. Standing in this relation to others is appealing in itself—worth seeking for its own sake. A moral person will refrain from lying to others, cheating, harming, or exploiting them, "because these things are wrong." But for such a person these requirements are not just formal imperatives; they are aspects of the positive value of a way of living with others.[31]

29. *Ibid.*, p. 161.
30. *Ibid.*, p. 162.
31. *Ibid.*

Scanlon's position, then, is that a relation of mutual recognition, which is in some ways analogous to friendship but is less personal, underlies our reasons to conform with moral requirements. If this is correct, then it seems that moral reasons may be thought of as relationship-dependent reasons arising from the valuable relation of mutual recognition. Furthermore, as Wallace suggests, the deontic character of moral reasons may then be understood on the model of other relationship-dependent reasons, such as those arising from friendship. The suggestion, in other words, is that, in the moral case as in the case of friendship, our relationship-dependent reasons belong to structures of reciprocal normativity, which means the same considerations that generate reasons for an agent to conform to moral requirements also generate reasons for others to complain if he does not. In the moral case, the people who may complain are those to whom the action could not have been justified on grounds they would have been unreasonable to reject. As Wallace puts the point: "What makes an action of mine morally wrong is the fact that it cannot be justified to someone affected by it on terms that person would be unreasonable to reject. In a situation in which I do something morally wrong, the person adversely affected will have been wronged by me, and have privileged basis for moral complaint, resentment, and so on, precisely insofar as I have acted with indifference to the value of relating to them on a basis of mutual recognition and regard. The very principles that specify what I have moral reason to do, on this relational conception, equally serve to specify normative expectations and entitlements on the part of others. Those principles are thus implicated in a bipolar normative nexus very like the one that defines the reciprocal reasons and expectations constitutive of a relationship of friendship."[32] This explains why, in the moral case as in the case of friendship, one's relationship-dependent reasons have the character of requirements; as elements belonging to a "bipolar normative nexus," they are reasons that one lacks the authority unilaterally to disregard.

Attractive as this picture is, the force of the analogy between friendship and the relation of mutual recognition seems to me uncertain. Scanlon

32. Wallace, "The Deontic Structure of Morality," p. 35. As Frances Kamm has emphasized in discussion, one obvious question is whether a view of this kind can account for imperfect duties, which are not owed to any particular individual. Another obvious question is whether it can account for the norms governing our treatment of nonhuman animals. However, Scanlon says clearly that his view is meant only to account for the portion of morality that concerns "what we owe to each other," and that questions about the treatment of nonhuman animals may fall outside the scope of that part of morality. See Scanlon, *What We Owe to Each Other*, pp. 177–188.

identifies one source of doubt when he says that the relation of mutual recognition may seem "implausibly ideal." He adds, "The motivational basis of friendship makes sense because friends play a real and important role in one's life. But morality, as I am describing it, requires us to be moved by (indeed to give priority to) the thought of our relation to a large number of people, most of whom we will never have any contact with at all. This may seem bizarre."

Scanlon's reply to this objection is that "if the alternative is to say that people count for nothing if I will never come in contact with them, then surely this is bizarre as well."[33] This reply seems curiously unresponsive to the objection as stated, because the relevant alternative to Scanlon's position is not that people count for nothing if one will never come into contact with them, but rather that the reason why they count for something does not derive from the value of the relation of mutual recognition.[34] More significantly, Scanlon's characterization of the objection to his view seems to run together two different worries. The first worry is that, whereas one's friendships play a "real" role in one's life, the relation of mutual recognition is "ideal." The second worry is that, whereas friends are people one actually knows, the relation of mutual recognition is supposed to be capable of holding among people who do not know and will never meet one another. Scanlon's response focuses on the second of these worries, but if we are attempting to evaluate the analogy between friendship and mutual recognition, both worries need to be addressed.

The way I would formulate the second concern is as follows. In what sense may two people be said to stand in a relation of mutual recognition if they have never met or interacted, will never meet or interact, and do not even know of each other's existence? Clearly, Scanlon does not mean to be using the term *relation* merely in the thin, logical sense identified earlier. But in what more substantive sense do people in the circumstances described stand in a relation of mutual recognition? Perhaps the idea is that, even though they do not know of each other's existence, each wants his behavior to be justifiable to everyone, and so, by implication, each wants his behavior to be justifiable to the other. Now if this is what is meant by saying that the two people stand in a relation of mutual recognition, the pertinent notion of *relation* would seem to be very different from the one that is operative in the case of

---

33. Scanlon, *What We Owe to Each Other*, p. 168.
34. Scanlon goes on to consider a version of this objection, but the version he considers denies the relevance, not of the relation of mutual recognition *per se*, but rather of the idea of justifiability to others. This deflects attention away from the questions about the relation of mutual recognition that I am discussing.

valuable personal relationships like friendship. As we have seen, the latter are ongoing relationships between individuals who have a shared history that usually includes patterns of engagement and forms of mutual familiarity, attachment, and regard developed over time. Even if we can find a use of the term *relation* or *relationship* that goes beyond the thin, logical sense and applies in the case of mutual recognition, it is not clear that there is enough substantively in common between that case and the case of friendship to support an analogy between the reason-giving characteristics of each.

The other worry is this. In the case of friendship, what gives rise to reasons is an actual relationship. In general, relationship-dependent reasons, as I have characterized them, are simply reasons that one has by virtue of participation in a valuable relationship, and this model applies straightforwardly to the case of friendship as Scanlon discusses it. In the moral case, however, Scanlon does not say that we do, in fact, stand in relations of mutual recognition with others. Nor, *a fortiori*, does he say that we have moral reasons in virtue of our participation in actual relations of mutual recognition with others (a claim that might have the awkward implication that moral norms do not apply to our treatment of those with whom we lack such relations). What he tends to say instead is that what underlies moral reasons is the "appeal" or "ideal" of standing in relations of mutual recognition. If I understand him correctly, the idea is that we value a certain way of living with others, which we may or may not have achieved in practice, and insofar as we respond to moral reasons, we seek to realize that way of living together. Now, this may be a plausible account of how moral reasons arise. However, the role it assigns to the relation of mutual recognition in generating such reasons is not analogous to the role that a person's friendships play in generating relationship-dependent reasons. In the friendship case, it is the value of an actual relationship in which one is a participant that generates the reasons. In the moral case, as here understood, what seems to generate the reasons is not any actual relationship at all, but rather a certain ideal of how human beings should relate to one another. If this is correct, then moral reasons are not relationship-dependent reasons in the sense that I have specified. And despite what Scanlon suggests, morality does not give one reasons in the same way that one's friendships do.

This is not an objection to Scanlon's contractualism or even to the account he gives of moral motivation, except insofar as that account relies on an analogy between the way friendships generate reasons and the way relations of mutual recognition generate reasons. But it does mean that, as it stands at least, Scanlon's contractualism does not provide us with a way of construing moral reasons as a species of relationship-dependent reason. Nor, contrary to what Wallace suggests, does it yet enable us to see how a relational conception of morality might be grounded. To be sure, contractualism as Scanlon presents it, with its emphasis on the justifiability of one's actions to others who are affected by them, coheres smoothly with an interpretation of the deontic character of morality that links it to structures of reciprocal or bipolar normativity, in which reasons for action are constitutively connected to grounds for privileged complaint. But in the case of valued personal relationships like friendship, the value of the relationships provides an explanation of how these structures of reciprocal normativity arise. The appeal to relations of mutual recognition does not play a comparably explanatory role, for the relations in question are not actual, ongoing human relationships at all. One thing that may serve to obscure this disanalogy is the fact that a structure of reciprocal normativity can itself be taken to define or constitute a relationship of a certain kind between two people. If I have reason to act in your behalf and you have reason to complain if I do not, then those facts themselves might be said to define a *normative relationship* between us. Clearly, however, structures of reciprocal normativity cannot be grounded in the very normative relationships that they are said to define, for there is no content to these relationships other than the facts of reciprocal normativity themselves.[35] In the case of friendship, the normative relationship supervenes on an ongoing historical relationship between the participants, and it is the value of that ongoing relationship that is explanatory. But nothing comparable is true in the case of the relation of mutual recognition. So, as it stands, at least, the appeal to that relation does not explain how structures of reciprocal normativity arise.

To sum up: The function of the relation of mutual recognition in the contractualist arguments I have been discussing is ideal and prospective; rather than being an ongoing relationship that gives rise to moral reasons, it is a relation that is supposed to be realized or made possible by acting on such reasons. If the appeal to this relation is to explain how reciprocal moral reasons arise, we need a clearer understanding of how ideal, prospective relations can generate reasons. The character of the relation of mutual recognition also requires further elucidation. It must be a relation that can plausibly be said to obtain between people regardless of whether they ever meet or know of each other's existence, and regardless of whether the actions of either ever affect the other. And it must be sufficiently independent of the structures of reciprocal

---

35. This is a point that has been emphasized by Kerstin Haase in her unpublished writing on this topic.

normativity themselves that it is capable of providing a noncircular grounding for them.

VII. Relational Views, Deontic Character, and the Consequentialist Challenge

It is beyond the scope of this essay to consider whether a successful account of moral reasons along these lines can be provided. Perhaps there is a way of interpreting the appeal to relations of mutual recognition that would make clear its capacity to generate structures of reciprocal normativity. Still, I take the lesson of the discussion in the previous section to be that, even if such an interpretation is forthcoming, it is unlikely to represent moral reasons in general as relationship-dependent reasons in my sense. And this, after all, is not surprising. Relationship-dependent reasons are reasons of partiality arising from the value of particular, historical relationships between specific individuals. Even if moral norms can be represented as relational in important respects, morality aspires to the regulation of behavior among strangers as well as intimates, and it seems implausible that moral reasons of all kinds should have their source in particular, historical relationships.[36]

However, the idea that morality is relational in the sense that its deontic character is to be understood with reference to structures of reciprocal normativity has much to recommend it. In other words, we can distinguish between a *relational view* of morality—the view that the deontic structure of morality is best understood with reference to notions of reciprocal normativity—and the thesis that moral reasons are in general *relationship-dependent*. Even if we do not accept the relationship-dependency thesis, a relational view of morality remains attractive. For one thing, the fact that the deontic character of relationship-dependent reasons is best understood in terms of reciprocal normativity speaks in favor of a relational view of morality, even if morality itself is not in general relationship-dependent. Of course, my own view is that, despite not

---

36. In *Moral Dimensions: Permissibility, Meaning, Blame* (Cambridge, Mass.: Harvard University Press, 2008), Scanlon develops an analogy between friendship and what he calls "the moral relationship." What he says about this analogy differs in some significant respects from his discussion of the analogy between friendship and the relation of mutual recognition in *What We Owe to Each Other*. I do not have space here to give Scanlon's new discussion the careful consideration it deserves. Suffice it to say that it does not allay my doubts about the plausibility of construing moral reasons as relationship-dependent (or membership-dependent) reasons in my sense.

being generally relationship-dependent, morality does incorporate many relationship-dependent reasons, and this already implies that the deontic character of at least some moral reasons must be understood in terms of reciprocal normativity. But even if one rejects this view, the fact remains that relationship-dependent reasons frequently present themselves to us in deliberation and reflection as requirements or obligations, and that their deontic character is best understood in terms of reciprocal structures of reasons and complaints. If that is right, then there is at least prima facie reason to think that the deontic character of other reasons that present themselves as requirements or obligations should be understood in the same way.

This consideration is reinforced by the fact that consequentialism, the most influential and best developed alternative to a relational view, has a hard time accounting for the deontic character of morality at all. Although many consequentialists argue that promoting optimal outcomes is what we have *most reason* to do, this is not yet to explain the peculiar deontic character of morality—the fact that we see moral norms as defining a set of *requirements* or *obligations*. This is a point that Jay Wallace has made very effectively.[37] To my knowledge, consequentialists have done little to explain how morality could have this kind of deontic character, although some of them have, in effect, tried to explain the phenomenon away, by construing questions about what it is to have an obligation as questions about the utility of blaming the agent. But this is a significantly revisionist move. It amounts to denying that morality has a distinctively deontic character at all, and substituting a set of very different considerations about the utility of blame. If we are resistant to this kind of revisionism, and believe that the deontic character of morality is something to be explained rather than explained away, then a relational conception of morality will seem much more promising than a consequentialist conception.

On the other hand, even if one has doubts about consequentialist revisionism in general, there is something to be said on behalf of revisionism about the deontic character of morality in particular, especially if deontic character is understood in terms of structures of reciprocal normativity. Beginning with the great utilitarian writers of the eighteenth and nineteenth centuries, one of the strengths of the consequentialist tradition—and one of its most striking features—has been its insistence on the need to think about moral questions in a systematic and holistic way, focusing not merely on individual actions in isolation but also on

---

37. In "The Deontic Structure of Morality."

the way in which our actions are structured by social institutions and are related to wider patterns of human conduct. In the utilitarian view, the traditional moral norms that serve to regulate the conduct of individual agents in their dealings with one another may not, despite their commonsense credentials, be adequate to the circumstances of the modern world. Although it is understandable that people should once have thought about questions of right and wrong primarily in the context of the relationships among single individuals or the members of relatively small groups, the fates of people in the modern world are tied together in complex ways through their shared participation in vast social, political, and economic structures. Individual actions must, therefore, be assessed, and the norms governing them must be rationalized, from a broader perspective, which takes into account the entire web of causal connections in which both the actions and the norms are embedded.

Among philosophers, utilitarianism has been severely criticized for its many counterintuitive implications and for its insensitivity to the complex structures of value that inform our practical deliberations and interpersonal relations. But economists and social policy makers have continued to find utilitarianism's broad institutional perspective congenial, and among them its influence has never waned. In *A Theory of Justice*, John Rawls wrote:

> We sometimes forget that the great utilitarians, Hume and Adam
> Smith, Bentham and Mill, were social theorists and economists
> of the first rank; and the moral doctrine they worked out was
> framed to meet the needs of their wider interests and to fit into
> a comprehensive scheme. Those who criticized them often did
> so on a much narrower front. They pointed out the obscurities
> of the principle of utility and noted the apparent inconsisten-
> cies between many of its implications and our moral sentiments.
> But they failed, I believe, to construct a workable and systematic
> moral conception to oppose it. The outcome is that we often
> seem forced to choose between utilitarianism and intuitionism.[38]

Much has changed since Rawls wrote these words, not least because of the great impact of his own work. But the influence of utilitarianism endures among social and economic policy makers and theorists, and for many of the same reasons. Viewed in this light, the failure of

---

38. John Rawls, *A Theory of Justice* (Cambridge, Mass.: Harvard University Press, 1971),
    pp. vii–viii.

consequentialism to explain the deontic character of morality may be cast by its defenders, not as an embarrassing omission, but rather as a deliberate challenge to more conventional forms of moral thought, a challenge that might be spelled out as follows.

The idea of *deontic character*, understood with reference to structures of reciprocal normativity, is indeed at home in a morality of interpersonal relations. But a morality of interpersonal relations is no longer an adequate morality for our world. In trying to decide how people should act, we cannot think about their actions and the implications of those actions solely or primarily in the context of their personal relationships with their friends, family, and associates. The most important moral questions to ask about individual actions often pertain instead to the social and institutional forms that structure the options available to individuals, and the wider social and global impact of patterns of activity to which each of a very large number of individuals makes only a tiny contribution. This is evident, for example, if we think about global warming and other environmental problems, or if we think about the relation between consumer behavior in affluent countries and labor practices in developing countries. In this context, it is a mistake to think that what is crucial for moral thought is to preserve the deontic character of morality—where this means identifying, for each act of wrongdoing, particular people who have been wronged and have privileged ground for complaint. To do this is to mistake the phenomenology of traditional morality for a fundamental feature of moral thought, and to deprive ourselves of the tools we need to address the moral problems we actually face. Some of those problems are difficult precisely because, although they have clearly been caused by the actions of human beings, no specific individuals have privileged grounds for complaint about the behavior of any other specific individuals. So as long as we insist that structures of reciprocal normativity are essential to morality, our moral thought will lack the concepts it needs to address these problems. The task we face is not to preserve the notions of obligatoriness and privileged complaint, but rather to persuade people that they have reason to avoid certain kinds of actions even when no particular individuals have special grounds for complaint about those actions.

To describe this consequentialist challenge is not, of course, to endorse it, still less to concede that consequentialism itself represents an adequate moral outlook—in contemporary conditions or any others. I have argued in various places that, for a number of different reasons, among which its failure adequately to accommodate reasonable partiality is one of the most important, consequentialism does not provide a viable alternative to the traditional morality it criticizes. Still, the consequentialist challenge reinforces the importance of addressing the lacuna we have identified in the relational view of morality. The question is how, on the relational view, to explain the source of moral reasons in a way that preserves the view's emphasis on reciprocal normativity, while at the same time demonstrating its applicability outside the context of relatively small-scale interpersonal relationships. This means providing a sensible treatment of the structural, institutional, and aggregative phenomena that the consequentialist challenge highlights, and accounting in a plausible way for the norms that govern our treatment of distant strangers. Whatever the failings of the consequentialist position, the structural and institutional phenomena to which it calls attention are of undeniable importance, and their perceived salience is likely to grow in coming years. These phenomena are not themselves artifacts of consequentialism, and no moral outlook can ultimately be acceptable unless it addresses them in a satisfactory way. Nor can a moral outlook be acceptable if it fails to account for the norms governing our treatment of distant strangers. So it is essential to establish that a relational view of morality can be convincingly applied outside the context of actual interpersonal relationships. As I have argued, although appeals to the relation between agent and victim, to membership in the human community, and to relations of mutual recognition are all suggestive, none establishes a convincing parallel with personal relationships like friendship, and none, without further development, provides a clear explanation of the source of moral reasons in general. I continue to believe that the capacity of a relational view to provide a nonskeptical interpretation of the deontic character of morality is a great advantage. But the worry persists that this may be an illusion, deriving from an understandable but mistaken tendency to apply essentially interpersonal concepts outside the domain in which they have a genuine application.

VIII. *Morality and Partiality*

Setting relational views to one side, the question of morality and partiality remains. Even if morality is not generally relational, I believe that it incorporates project-dependent, relationship-dependent, and membership-dependent reasons, and in so doing accommodates reasonable partiality. When I say that it incorporates these reasons, what I mean is that reasons of these types bear directly on the rightness or wrongness of actions, in much the same way that the fact that one has promised to act in a certain way bears directly on the rightness or wrongness of acting in that way. In my view, moral norms aim to regulate the conduct of people who are understood from the outset as valuing creatures, creatures with projects, relationships, and group affiliations. Like other forms of regulation, morality simultaneously constrains and legitimates. On the one hand, not only does it limit what may be done in the service of our projects, relationships, and group affiliations, it shapes our understanding of what counts as a worthy project or relationship or association in the first place. It tells us not merely that there are limits to what may be done in the name of a personal project or relationship, but also that a project that is evil or corrupt, or a relationship that is destructive or abusive, lacks the value that makes it a source of reasons to begin with. Yet morality also assumes that, within these limits and constraints, it is appropriate and often obligatory that people should act on the reasons that arise from their projects, relationships, and group affiliations. It tells us that we may legitimately pursue our projects, that we are obligated to address the needs and interests of our intimates, and that we should do our fair share in the joint enterprises in which we participate.

None of this is argument, of course, and it is in fact quite difficult to argue in a non–question-begging way for this or any other view of the relation between morality and partiality. That is because the issue turns ultimately on some of the most basic and abstract questions about the nature and function of morality, and it is difficult to produce arguments about morality and partiality that do not already presuppose some answers to those questions. My strategy in this essay has been indirect. By examining project-dependent, relationship-dependent, and membership-dependent reasons, I have sought to emphasize that partiality is a dimension of practical rationality, and so to undercut the tendency to associate morality with detached reason and partiality with nonrational feeling or affection. I have also tried to highlight two features of these reasons that, to my mind, make it implausible to situate them outside the ambit of morality. The first is the fact that they are concomitants of basic categories of human valuation; in other words, the recognition of such reasons is part of what is involved in valuing some our deepest commitments. The second is that reasons of partiality exhibit precisely the deontic characteristics that we associate with moral norms; we see ourselves, for example, as having obligations to our families, friends, and associates, as being entitled or permitted to develop and pursue personal projects, and so on. Indeed, obligations to family, friends, and associates are often viewed as paradigmatic moral requirements. Taken together, these considerations seem to me to make a strong, albeit indirect, case for incorporating reasons of partiality within morality. At the very least, they shift the burden of proof to those who would exclude such reasons from morality's ambit. Those who wish to do this cannot deny that we are valuing creatures at all. Nor can they deny that morality appeals to our nature as valuing creatures, since morality is itself a realm of value, and the capacity of moral norms and ideals to motivate and engage us depends on the fact that we are valuers. So the position must be that although humans are valuing creatures, and although morality appeals to our nature as valuing creatures, morality nevertheless gives no direct weight to some of the most basic reasons we have by virtue of what we value; instead, whatever morality asks of us, it asks of us on the basis of reasons that have some other source, and whose roots in what we actually value remain to be explained. And this despite the fact that the excluded reasons are often taken as paradigmatic moral considerations and exhibit precisely the deontic characteristics associated with moral norms. What exactly might the motivation for this exclusivist position be?

The point can be sharpened. Morality aspires to regulate our conduct toward all people, strangers and intimates alike. The exclusivist position is that, at the most fundamental level, the moral reasons that apply to intimates are no different from those that apply to strangers. But once we accept that reasons of partiality are genuine reasons that flow from some of our most basic values and do in fact apply to our treatment of our intimates, the insistence that these reasons have no direct moral relevance risks making morality itself seem irrelevant. If morality were to give no weight to these reasons, then instead of looking authoritative, moral judgments might appear simply to be based on an incomplete accounting of the pertinent considerations. And if that were so, then it would be unclear why people should acknowledge the authority of those judgments or even take them into account. Ultimately, then, the basic reason for thinking that morality incorporates reasons of partiality is that no credible system for the regulation of human behavior can possibly exclude them.

Acknowledgments

This essay is also published in Brian Feltham and John Cottingham (eds.), *Partiality and Impartiality: Morality, Special Relationships, and the Wider World* (Oxford University Press). Printed here by agreement with the publisher. An earlier version of the essay was presented as the Mala Kamm Memorial Lecture at NYU. Versions were also presented to audiences at Reading, MIT, Cornell, Oslo, Iowa, and

MORALITY AND REASONABLE PARTIALITY

the Ethics Center at the University of Zurich. I am grateful to all of these audiences for helpful discussion. Special thanks to Nick Sturgeon, who served as commentator on the paper at Cornell, and to Niko Kolodny and Jay Wallace, who provided helpful comments on the earliest draft.

3

Doing and Allowing

Many philosophers have said, though some consequentialists have denied, that people have a greater responsibility, in general, for what they do than for what they merely allow or fail to prevent. There is little doubt that some idea of this sort has an important role to play in ordinary moral thought. I say "some idea of this sort" because there is considerable disagreement about how best to characterize the distinction on which the idea rests. Many philosophers have tried to make the idea more precise and have put forward alternative

Originally published in *Ethics* 114 (January 2004): 215–239. © 2004 by The University of Chicago. All rights reserved. An early version of this article was presented as a keynote address at the Oxford Graduate Philosophy Conference in November 2000. Subsequent versions were presented to a meeting of the Bay Area Forum for Law and Ethics (BAFFLE) and to departmental colloquia at New York University and Bowdoin College. Many members of these audiences made helpful comments, but I am conscious of specific debts to Eric Beerbohm, Michael Bratman, Bill Brewer, Cheshire Calhoun, Meir Dan-Cohen, Brad Hooker, Frances Kamm, Thomas Nagel, Derek Parfit, and Larry formulations that revolve around different but overlapping distinctions. Among the candidate distinctions that have been discussed are the distinctions between doing and allowing, between doing and failing to prevent, between doing and letting happen, between doing and not doing, between action and inaction, between acts and omissions, between positive agency and negative agency, between what one does to another person directly and what merely happens to that person as a result of what one does, and so on. I will not attempt in this article to adjudicate among these different candidate distinctions. What I will instead try to show is that, despite the absence of any consensus about which of the candidates is to be preferred, our practice of treating one another as responsible agents requires us to make some distinction of this kind.

I

I will begin by asking what it is that proponents of the various candidate distinctions are all trying to characterize. In each case, we may say that the aim is to specify what, for purposes of moral assessment, are to count as primary manifestations of individual agency and what are to count as secondary manifestations. In saying this, I do not mean to be adding yet another candidate distinction to the list. Instead, I am trying to give an intuitive characterization of a generic contrast, with the thought that all the distinctions I have listed may be conceived of as candidate specifications of that generic contrast. They all purport to distinguish between cases in which our agency is implicated in a primary way and cases in which it is implicated only secondarily, if at all.

For many philosophers, the point of trying to draw such a distinction with precision is to provide a formulation that will at once capture, clarify, and supply a principled basis for extending our commonsense judgments about the content of people's responsibilities, or, as I shall sometimes say, about the allocation of *normative responsibility*. The idea,

Simon. I am also indebted to Seana Shiffrin and Jay Wallace for valuable discussion, and I am grateful for the many comments that I received from two anonymous reviewers and the editors of *Ethics*. Finally, I must record my indebtedness to Bernard Williams, news of whose death arrived as I was preparing the final version of this article for publication. Bernard gave me very helpful written and oral comments on an early version of the article. It was my great good fortune to have had him as a friend and colleague for many years. The importance of his work and his influence on moral philosophy are too obvious to require comment.

in other words, is that we normally make a distinction of some kind
between primary and secondary manifestations of our agency and that
we operate with an intuitive picture according to which, in general, the
norms of individual responsibility attach much greater weight to the primary than to the secondary manifestations. According to this picture,
for example, we normally have a greater responsibility to avoid harming people ourselves than we do to prevent them from being harmed
in other ways. This means that we must go to greater trouble in order
to avoid harming them than we must in order to prevent them from
being harmed. It also means that we are expected not to harm one person
even in order to prevent harms of equal severity from befalling a greater
number of people. Harming someone, according to the intuitive picture,
is normally a primary manifestation of one's agency, whereas failing to
prevent someone from being harmed is normally only a secondary manifestation. This is true even if the "other way" in which the person will be
harmed is by someone else's harming him. If Zelda fails to prevent Zane
from being harmed by Zack, that is still only a secondary manifestation
of Zelda's agency.

Attempts to provide a more precise formulation of the contrast
between primary and secondary manifestations of agency are often motivated by a desire to vindicate some version of this intuitive picture of
normative responsibility. More specifically, the aim is to formulate the
distinction in a way that enables it to satisfy two sets of desiderata. On
the one hand, the distinction should be clear, consistent, and capable
of being formulated without relying on moral concepts. On the other
hand, it should strike us upon reflection as morally relevant. It should
largely correspond to, and thus help to illuminate, an important class of
commonsense judgments about the content of people's responsibilities.
There will undoubtedly be some of those judgments that it fails to capture, but in such cases it should point to a convincing reason for rejecting
the discordant judgments, and it should also provide a plausible way of
guiding and extending our judgment in cases in which we are intuitively
uncertain. In short, the goal is to vindicate an important class of commonsense judgments about the allocation of normative responsibility by
showing how those judgments are, on the whole, responsive to a clear
and significant action-theoretic distinction.

Once the goal has been described in this way, there are a variety of
doubts that may be raised about its attainability. Perhaps the distinctions
we draw in moral contexts between primary and secondary manifestations of our agency reflect prior moral judgments and cannot be characterized using only nonmoral, action-theoretic concepts. Alternatively,
even if our judgments can, with a certain number of modifications and

adjustments, be construed as responsive to some action-theoretic distinction, some may wonder how much justificatory weight such a distinction can bear. Why should an action-theoretic distinction have the authority to determine how normative responsibility should be allocated? Why should any nonnormative distinction have such ethical significance?

Even those who believe that the goal is attainable, or at any rate worth pursuing, are almost certain to agree that none of the proposed distinctions is likely to be wholly satisfactory without considerable refinement and qualification. And the project of trying to formulate appropriate refinements and qualifications has proven fiendishly complex. Furthermore, some who are sympathetic to the basic project would nevertheless argue that no single distinction, however qualified and refined, will ever be adequate by itself, for there is more than one such distinction that plays an important role in our moral thought.[1]

I shall not directly address the various doubts just mentioned, although some of what I say will have an indirect bearing on some of them. As I have already suggested, however, my own aim is neither to provide a precise formulation of the distinction between primary and secondary manifestations of agency nor to defend the moral relevance of any particular candidate formulation. Instead, the question that I wish to explore concerns the source and the depth of our commitment to drawing *some* sort of distinction, in the moral judgments that we make, between what I have been calling primary and secondary manifestations

1. The literature on the issues summarized in the preceding two paragraphs is enormous, but an adequate bibliography would surely include the following works among others: Jonathan Bennett, "Whatever the Consequences," *Analysis* 26 (1966): 83–102, and "Morality and Consequences," in *The Tanner Lectures on Human Values*, vol. 2, Sterling M. McMurrin (ed.) (Salt Lake City: University of Utah Press, 1981), pp. 45–116; Philippa Foot, "The Problem of Abortion and the Doctrine of Double Effect," in *Virtues and Vices* (Berkeley: University of California Press, 1978), pp. 19–32; Frances Kamm, *Morality, Mortality*, vol. 2 (Oxford: Oxford University Press, 1996); Shelly Kagan, *The Limits of Morality* (Oxford: Oxford University Press, 1989); Warren Quinn, "Actions, Intentions, and Consequences: The Doctrine of Doing and Allowing," *Philosophical Review* 98 (1989): 287–312, and "Actions, Intentions, and Consequences: The Doctrine of Double Effect," *Philosophy & Public Affairs* 18 (1989): 334–351; Judith Thomson, "Killing, Letting Die, and the Trolley Problem," pp. 78–93, and "The Trolley Problem," pp. 94–116, both in *Rights, Restitution, and Risk* (Cambridge, Mass.: Harvard University Press, 1986). Two useful anthologies, each of which includes many significant writings on these issues (including some of those mentioned above), are Bonnie Steinbock (ed.), *Killing and Letting Die* (Englewood Cliffs, N.J.: Prentice-Hall, 1980); and John Martin Fischer and Mark Ravizza (eds.), *Ethics: Problems and Principles* (Fort Worth, Tex.: Harcourt, Brace, Jovanovich, 1992).

of our agency. I will remain agnostic on the question of how exactly we do or should draw this distinction. Indeed, I shall not assume that most people have any very precise criterion for drawing it, still less that they all have precisely the same criterion. Thus, although I shall usually speak of the distinction as a distinction between doing and allowing or between doing and failing to prevent, these formulations are to be understood merely as placeholders and not as attempts to provide a precise or authoritative version of the distinction. I believe that we have a deep commitment to drawing some distinction, in the context of our moral thought, between primary and secondary manifestations of our agency—even if we would be hard-pressed to formulate the distinction clearly and consistently—and that we are also committed to seeing ourselves as more responsible in general for the primary than for the secondary manifestations. That we have these commitments does not seem to me to be in serious doubt, notwithstanding any lack of clarity or precision there may be in the way we distinguish between the two types of manifestation. My interest is in exploring the question of why exactly we have these commitments.

When I say that "we" have these commitments, I do not mean to imply either that absolutely everyone does in fact accept moral principles that rely on a distinction between primary and secondary manifestations of agency or that every rational agent must do so. For I do not mean to deny that there are people who reject norms of responsibility altogether, nor do I wish to argue here against the moral skeptic who challenges the rationality of a commitment to such norms. What I do plan to argue is that those of us who are not moral skeptics, but who instead see ourselves as subject to norms of responsibility, must employ some distinction between primary and secondary manifestations of agency. Thus, my arguments will be directed not at moral skeptics who reject responsibility but at consequentialist reformers who advocate its radical expansion. I will argue that people cannot consistently hold themselves to norms of responsibility that do not draw some distinction between primary and secondary manifestations of agency, and assign individuals somewhat greater responsibility for the primary than for the secondary manifestations.

Given that this is the aim I want to pursue, I will begin by asking the following question. Suppose we have a group of people who are not moral skeptics, but who instead regard themselves and one another as subject to norms of individual responsibility. What additional conditions must these people satisfy in order for it to be true of them that, if they are to remain consistent, the norms to which they view themselves as subject must make use of a distinction between doing and allowing (or some comparable distinction between primary and secondary manifestations of individual agency)? The answer to this question that I wish to explore is *none*. That is, I want to argue that, provided people view themselves as subject to norms of individual responsibility in the first place, they cannot accept any system of normative responsibility that does not, to some extent at least, assign them greater responsibility for what they do than for what they allow.[2]

This suggestion may be thought of as a weaker version of a famous Kantian claim. In the second section of the *Foundations of the Metaphysics of Morals*, Kant argues that it is possible to derive the formula of the only possible Categorical Imperative from the very idea of such an imperative.[3] The proposal that I want to consider is more modest. It does not claim that there is a single, fundamental norm of individual responsibility that can be used to identify all of our more specific responsibilities, let alone that the content of that norm can be entirely derived from the mere idea of such a norm. But it does claim that, by considering what is involved in viewing oneself as subject to norms of individual responsibility, one can derive a certain constraint on the content of such norms.

My defense of this conclusion will be developed in stages. In Section II, I will argue that to see oneself as subject to norms of responsibility is already to draw a normatively relevant distinction between primary and secondary manifestations of one's agency, and I will defend this claim against an important challenge. In Section III, I will explain in general terms what I take the argument of the preceding section to imply about the content of the norms of responsibility. In Section IV, I will confront a crucial objection which denies that the argument of

2. There might, in principle, be a form of consequentialism that treated certain kinds of "doings" as having special disvalue and directed agents to minimize total overall occurrences of such doings. This form of consequentialism would not assign individuals greater responsibility for what they themselves did than for what they allowed; instead, one's responsibility for preventing others from performing objectionable doings would be just as great as one's responsibility for not performing such doings oneself. For the purposes of my argument in this article, a consequentialist view of this kind would not count as one that distinguished between doing and allowing. A system of normative responsibility employs a distinction between doing and allowing, in the sense that I intend, only if it does assign individuals greater responsibility for what they themselves do than for what they allow.

3. Immanuel Kant, *Foundations of the Metaphysics of Morals*, trans. L. W. Beck (Indianapolis: Library of the Liberal Arts, 1959), pp. 38–39 (corresponding to 4:420–21 in the Prussian Academy edition).

Section II has any bearing at all on the content of such norms. According to this objection, the argument at most establishes that a formal distinction between primary and secondary manifestations of agency is implicit in the idea of holding oneself to norms of responsibility; it does not establish that such a distinction is required at the first-order substantive level, as part of the content of the norms to which people hold themselves. In responding to this objection, I will present the core of my case for thinking that such norms must indeed incorporate a distinction between primary and secondary manifestations of agency. Finally, in Section V, I will set my overall argument in a broader context.

II

To begin with, I need to explain what I mean when I talk about viewing oneself as subject to norms of responsibility. Here I will be relying heavily on the ideas of Jay Wallace, who argues that to treat any person—whether oneself or someone else—as a responsible agent is to hold that person to a set of normative standards or expectations.[4] To hold a person to a set of standards or expectations is, in turn, to see the person as having reasons to live up to those standards, and as an appropriate object of reactive attitudes if he or she fails to do so. Typical examples of such attitudes are resentment and indignation, in the case of breaches of expectations committed by others, and guilt, in the case of breaches one has committed oneself. However, what is important for present purposes is not the status of these examples in particular but, rather, the fact that there are *some* special, expectation-sensitive attitudes that are seen as constituting merited or appropriate responses to people who have violated the normative standards to which we hold them. I will follow Wallace in reserving Strawson's term "reactive attitudes" for this special class of attitudes.[5] One need not actually have a reactive response every time one perceives an expectation as having been breached, but if, on a given occasion, one does not do so, and if one genuinely has expectations of the agent who (without any justification or excuse) committed the breach,

---

4. See R. Jay Walace, *Responsibility and the Moral Sentiments* (Cambridge, Mass.: Harvard University Press, 1996), chaps. 1–3.
5. Ibid., chap. 2. See also P. F. Strawson, "Freedom and Resentment," in *Free Will*, Gary Watson (ed.) (Oxford: Oxford University Press, 1982), pp. 59–80.

then one will at least believe that such a response would be justified or appropriate.[6] This is one of the things that distinguishes the expectations we have of one another as responsible agents from forms of grading or appraisal in which one merely notes, perhaps with disappointment or surprise but perhaps in a spirit of clinical detachment, that the object of one's assessment has fallen short of some standard of merit or excellence. It is possible, in a similar spirit, merely to note that an agent has not acted as he or she had reason to act, without experiencing any reactive attitude toward the agent or having any view about the appropriateness of such attitudes. But this will be an indication that one did not have expectations of the agent in the relevant sense: that one was not holding the agent to a standard of conduct. Instead, one was—so to speak—merely grading or appraising his or her conduct.

Thus, to view oneself as subject to norms of individual responsibility, in the sense I have in mind, is not merely to accept the fact that one is eligible for a certain form of grading or appraisal. It is, instead, to hold oneself to a standard: to see oneself as having reasons to conform to the standard, and as an appropriate target of reactive responses, by oneself and others, when one fails to do so.

If one does, in this sense, view oneself as subject to norms of individual responsibility, then, of course, one already perceives a normatively relevant distinction between one's own conduct and that of other people, since it is one's own conduct, not theirs, that one sees oneself as having reason to bring into conformity with the relevant standards or norms. More generally, to view oneself as subject to norms of individual responsibility is to draw a normatively relevant distinction between one's own conduct and all other causal processes. It is, in other words, to see oneself as responsible for regulating the exercise of one's own agency, as opposed to the exercise of anyone else's agency or any other causal processes, by reference to those norms. It is also true, I want now to argue, that to see oneself as subject to norms of individual responsibility is already to draw a normatively relevant distinction of some kind between primary and secondary manifestations of one's agency.

What I have in mind is this. To see oneself as subject to norms of responsibility is to see oneself as having reason to bring one's conduct into conformity with those norms. But bringing one's conduct into

---

6. The last several sentences have been taken, with only minor modifications, from my article "Distributive Justice and Economic Desert," in *Desert and Justice*, Serena Olsaretti (ed.) (Oxford: Clarendon, 2003), pp. 69–91, at pp. 70–71.

conformity with norms of individual responsibility is itself something that one does, and not something that one merely allows to happen. It requires marshaling the full resources of one's agency, including one's capacities for deliberation, choice, and action. There is no ongoing process with which one need only avoid interfering in order to bring one's conduct into conformity with norms of responsibility. Instead, if one sees oneself as subject to a standard of responsibility and holds oneself to that standard, then one sees oneself as responsible for exercising a kind of overall regulative control of one's conduct, and the exercise of such control is itself a full-fledged expression of one's agency. According to some philosophical traditions, of course, it is much more than that; it is the purest or truest or freest expression of one's agency. For the purposes of this argument, however, we need not claim so much. It is enough to point out that, from the perspective of the individual agent, the internalized demand that one live up to a standard of responsibility always presents itself as a demand that one do something, namely, that one regulate the exercise of one's agency in conformity with the relevant norms. This means that to view oneself as subject to such norms is already to attach a special importance to, and to see oneself as having a special responsibility for, what one does. The distinction between primary and secondary manifestations of agency is a presupposition of viewing oneself as subject to norms of responsibility in the first place.

This argument invites an immediate challenge. The argument seems to assume that responsible agents recognize reasons of two different kinds. In specific contexts of decision and action, they acknowledge the force of the particular normative reasons that apply to those contexts. In addition, they recognize general reasons "to bring their actions into conformity with the norms of responsibility." It is to the recognition of these general reasons that the argument appeals in seeking to establish that responsible agents are committed to a distinction between primary and secondary manifestations of agency. But, the challenge runs, responsible agents need not acknowledge reasons of the second kind at all. Holding oneself to a standard of responsibility need not amount to anything over and above being stably disposed to respond, on a case-by-case basis, to the specific normative reasons that arise in particular contexts. One need not recognize any additional, general reasons to conform with the norms of responsibility, if that is supposed to mean that, in addition to acting in conformity with the balance of specific reasons on a case-by-case basis, one sees oneself as having reason to perform some further "action" of "bringing one's [other] actions into conformity with the norms of responsibility." In short, this challenge asserts, the argument multiplies reasons and actions needlessly. Responsible agents need only recognize the specific reasons for action that apply to them. They do not need, in addition, to recognize general reasons to act in accordance with those specific reasons.

There are two points to be made in response to this challenge. First, the argument as I have stated it does indeed suppose that guiding one's life in accordance with standards of normative responsibility is itself a manifestation of agency, which involves something over and above a disposition to recognize reasons of responsibility on a case-by-case basis. I do not think that this is an implausible way of understanding what it means to hold oneself to standards of responsibility, at least for minimally reflective agents. Minimally reflective agents will have had occasion to notice that it can sometimes be difficult or costly to respond to the reasons of responsibility that arise in particular situations. They will have noticed that there can be circumstances in which the prospect of ignoring or neglecting such reasons has its attractions and that many people do in fact ignore them more or less frequently. By this route if by no other, minimally reflective agents will have been led to consider the force and authority of specific reasons of responsibility. And if, in the end, they affirm the authority of such reasons—if they affirm that, for them, such reasons are indeed *reasons*—then they are doing something more than manifesting a stable disposition to respond to those reasons on a case-by-case basis. They are resolving to regulate their agency in conformity with those reasons. Thus, for minimally reflective agents at least, it does not seem implausible to suppose that holding oneself to a standard of normative responsibility involves something over and above the possession of a stable disposition to respond to reasons of certain kinds on a case-by-case basis.

The second point is this. Suppose that what I have just said is wrong and that one can hold oneself to a standard of normative responsibility without having made any higher-order resolution to conform to normative reasons on a case-by-case basis. All that is necessary is that one should, as a matter of fact, be stably disposed to respond to such reasons. Even if this is so, I believe that, in the end, the claims I have made also apply to the recognition of specific, first-order normative reasons. To see oneself as having a specific normative reason, in other words, is already to distinguish between primary and secondary manifestations of one's agency. That is because the fundamental point I am making is really a point about normativity. To see oneself as subject to a practical require-ment—however specific to a given case that requirement may be—is in the first instance to see oneself as a *subject*: as an agent who is constrained by the force of rational considerations to exercise his agency in some ways rather than others. To put it another way, the very fact that one acknowledges a practical reason presupposes that one sees oneself as a subject, a locus of agency, who is charged with the task of exercising that agency in accordance with reasons of some kind. In short, responding to a practical reason—trying to be guided by that reason—is always a primary manifestation of one's agency. It is always, we may say, something that one does. Thus, even if holding oneself to norms of responsibility involves nothing over and above a disposition to respond to specific normative reasons on a case-by-case basis, it is still a primary manifestation of one's agency.

III

If the considerations just presented are correct, then the challenge to my argument fails. The distinction between primary and secondary manifestations of one's agency is, as I have said, a presupposition of viewing oneself as subject to norms of responsibility in the first place. It follows, I believe, that the norms to which one views oneself as subject must themselves incorporate such a distinction; they must, to some extent at least, assign us greater responsibility for the primary than for the secondary manifestations of our agency.[7]

---

7. I have presented this as an anticonsequentialist conclusion, but one may wonder how far it actually counts against consequentialism. At the level of fundamental principle, consequentialism denies that one has a greater responsibility for the primary than for the secondary manifestations of one's agency. So my argument, if correct, implies that people cannot consistently see themselves as being "subject to" (fundamental) consequentialist principles. However, I have said that to see oneself as being, in the relevant sense, subject to certain norms is to see oneself as having reason to live up to those norms and as an appropriate target of reactive attitudes when one fails to do so. Yet many consequentialists reject the reactive attitudes as misguided and unjustified, and there are well-known consequentialist arguments to the effect that people should not treat consequentialist principles as guides to personal decision making; they should not, in that sense, see themselves as having reason to live up to those principles. Thus, a consequentialist might, it seems, accept the conclusion that individuals cannot consistently see themselves as subject to consequentialist principles, while denying that this conclusion is damaging to consequentialism. Although I do not find this kind of position plausible, my arguments do not by themselves show that it is untenable. What my arguments do aim to establish is that consequentialist principles cannot feature in our actual practices of treating one another as responsible agents. For the participants in those practices regard themselves and one another as subject to norms of responsibility in just the sense that I have specified. Thus, if my arguments are correct,

Before attempting to defend this assertion, let me explain what I mean when I say that the norms must assign us greater responsibility for the primary than for the secondary manifestations. It goes without saying that the norms will also attach some weight, at least in contexts of certain kinds, to the secondary manifestations. To do otherwise would be simply to ignore the fact that the exercise of human agency is firmly embedded within the larger causal order, from which there is no way of detaching it. In fact, I believe that one of the functions of norms that rely on the distinction between doing and allowing is to regulate the effectively ineliminable tension between the special importance we attach to our own actions, and our recognition that those actions are nevertheless subsumed within the larger causal web. In other words, attaching special significance to what one does is a condition of viewing oneself as subject to norms of responsibility in the first place. Yet the exercise of one's agency is itself part of the larger causal order and, as our freedom of action increases, so, too, do the opportunities deriving from our causal position—the opportunities to intervene in causal processes that we did not initiate, and that may be quite alien to our purposes. Principles of individual responsibility modulate their reliance on distinctions like the distinction between doing and allowing so as to balance the normative force of these two different factors. In normal circumstances, they assign us greater responsibility for what we do than for what we allow or fail to prevent. Yet they also attach some weight to what might be termed the responsibilities of causal position. That is, they treat us as responsible, in some circumstances, for the way we respond to relevant causal opportunities that present themselves to us. If one is in a position to prevent some disastrous chain of events from unfolding and does not do so, then the fact that one did not initiate the chain or make a direct causal contribution to it cannot be relied upon to provide one with an automatic justification or excuse. The norms of individual responsibility attach some weight to what we fail to prevent.

Given that one of the functions of such norms is to strike a balance between the two very different types of consideration I have described, I do not believe that there is any way of specifying the distinction between doing and allowing that could render the norms immune from controversy. No candidate specification of the distinction, however

---

the norms to which responsible agents hold one another cannot be consequentialist norms. Readers must decide for themselves how damaging they think this conclusion is for consequentialism.

precisely drawn, and however firmly rooted in the theory of action or causation, could either produce consensus about how the balance should optimally be struck or allay the ambivalence people often feel in hard cases.

Consider, for example, the kinds of cases in which the distinction comes under the greatest pressure. These are cases in which the only way of preventing a great harm from befalling some group of innocent people is by harming an innocent person oneself. Suppose I find myself in a situation of this kind. Even if we stipulate that my choice is between doing harm and failing to prevent harm, that by itself will not produce consensus about which choice I should make, because it was not uncertainty on that point that made the choice look difficult to begin with. And even if we stipulate that it would be wrong of me to inflict the harm, the fact remains that, if I defer to this judgment, I will have passed up the only available opportunity to prevent great suffering. Thus, even if this is a situation in which I must give normative priority to my own agency—to the consideration that inflicting a harm would be *my doing*—the fact remains that, in not harming, I will also be passing up a certain causal opportunity—an opportunity to avert suffering. And there is no way of drawing the line between doing and allowing that can make ambivalence an inappropriate response to this fact. That is because such ambivalence is, at least in part, responsive to the tension between two views of myself: between the view of myself as an agent, with a special responsibility for the primary manifestations of my own agency, and the view of myself and my actions as belonging to the causal order of nature. So long as we see ourselves as moral agents at all, there is no way of eliminating this tension, and thus no way of eliminating its capacity to generate ambivalence in hard cases.

The fact that we should not expect too much of the distinction between doing and allowing, however, does not mean that we can make do without it. It is certainly possible to argue that commonsense norms of individual responsibility attach too much weight to the distinction and assign us too little responsibility for the alleviation of suffering that we did not cause. But if we are persuaded by such arguments and seek to live up to a more expansive or inclusive set of norms, then, on any plausible way of drawing the distinction between doing and allowing, that itself will have to be something that we do. The influence of the more inclusive norms will have to run through our deliberations, decisions, and intentions to our actions. If, under the influence of such norms, I am resolved to take more responsibility for the alleviation of suffering in distant lands, and not to content myself with the thought that I did not cause it, then of course what follows is that I will have to change how I live—to change

what I do. My determination to live up to the inclusive norms will have
to be reflected in my decisions and my actions. Indeed, there is a way
in which I will have to attach much more normative importance to my
own actions than I previously did. I will have to hold each action to a
higher standard and to be much less willing to treat certain of my acts as
too trivial, too innocuous, or too purely self-regarding to require much
in the way of normative scrutiny or justification. Thus, the idea that we
should accept a maximally expansive conception of individual responsibility that attaches no normative significance to the distinction between
what we do and what we allow has a paradoxical flavor. If we succeed in
convincing ourselves that the idea is correct, then there is a clear sense
in which we will see our own agency, and what we ourselves do, as more
rather than less significant.

IV

There is an obvious objection to the line of thought I have been developing. The objection is that this line of thought confuses two different
ways in which one's own actions might be said to be of special normative
significance. At one level, it is a truism that any plausible conception of
individual normative responsibility must treat the individual's actions as
important. After all, a standard of normative responsibility itself takes the
form of a criterion (or set of criteria) for right and wrong action, and its
aspiration is to tell people something about how they should lead their
lives. Clearly, then, if one views oneself as subject to norms of responsibility, there is a way in which one must treat one's own actions and one's
own agency as having a special kind of normative importance. However,
it does not follow from this that the norms to which one views oneself as
subject must, as part of their content, attach significance to the distinction between what one does and what one allows. It would be perfectly
coherent, for example, to hold oneself to a standard that treated the harms
one fails to prevent as no less significant, in determining the rightness or
wrongness of one's actions, than the harms one inflicts oneself. There is no
inconsistency in assessing people's conduct by reference to a standard that
directs them to make optimal use of the causal opportunities available to
them and attaches no weight to the distinction between those unfavorable outcomes that they directly bring about and those that they fail to
prevent. Formally, of course, the claim that one ought always to make
optimal use of the causal opportunities available to one is itself a criterion
of right action, a conception of what one should do. However, a conception of normative responsibility can acknowledge the formal role of the

distinction between what one does and what one allows without treating it as having substantive importance.

The same objection can be put another way. I have argued that responding to practical reasons—trying to be guided by them—is always a primary manifestation of one's agency. I have also claimed that the standards of responsibility to which one holds oneself must, as part of their content, attach significance to the distinction between what one does and what one allows—between primary and secondary manifestations of one's agency. But, it may be said, the first of these claims undermines the second. The first claim entails that holding oneself to norms of responsibility is a primary manifestation of one's agency, no matter what the content of those norms is. If that is correct, then the fact that holding oneself to norms is a primary manifestation of one's agency places no constraints at all on the content of the norms. Holding oneself to a norm of causal optimality is just as much a primary manifestation of one's agency as is holding oneself to a norm that distinguishes between doing and allowing. So even if holding oneself to norms is a primary manifestation of one's agency, that fact has no implications whatsoever for the content of the norms.

In order to respond to this objection, let us begin by thinking more carefully about the position of a man who views himself as subject to norms of individual responsibility but takes the content of the norms to be insensitive to the distinction between what one does and what one allows. I have suggested, in effect, that there is an instability in this man's position, for he is committed to thinking both that the distinction between primary and secondary manifestations of his agency is normatively significant and that the distinction is not significant. Insofar as he is determined to comply with the norms of responsibility, he treats the distinction as significant, for securing compliance with the norms is itself a primary manifestation of his agency. But insofar as he treats the outcomes he directly brings about and those that he fails to prevent as having equal weight in determining the rightness or wrongness of his actions, he denies that the distinction is significant. The objection we are considering asserts that there is no instability in this man's position, because his two apparently inconsistent beliefs operate on different levels or in different contexts.

I doubt, however, whether the two beliefs can be compartmentalized in a way that avoids instability. To see why not, let us begin by considering some of the implications of the fact that he treats the distinction between what he does and what he allows as irrelevant to the rightness or wrongness of his actions. One of the implications is that if, in order to make optimal use of the causal opportunities available to him, he would have to harm an innocent person, he does not see that fact in itself as providing any special reason for him to refrain from pursuing what is, by hypothesis, the optimal course of action. To be sure, the fact that an innocent person will be harmed is itself a pro tanto reason against the action, but we are supposing that, on balance, the action nevertheless represents his optimal response to the available causal opportunities, perhaps because a still greater number of people will be harmed if he acts in any other way. If so, then he does not see the fact that he will have to inflict the harm himself as providing any independent reason for him to refrain.

But if this is how he assesses the situation, then we must ask what he thinks about the reactions that his prospective victim, and the victim's friends and associates, are likely to have to his decision. After all, even if he does not see the fact that he will have to inflict the harm himself as providing a reason for him to refrain, the victim and the people who care about her are likely to see things differently. At the very least, they are likely to make him the target of reactive responses like resentment and indignation. He will have harmed an innocent person, and the victim and those who care about her are likely to regard this as a breach of normative expectations for which the agent is appropriately held accountable.

The question that I want now to ask is what he is likely to make of their response. By hypothesis, the fact that he would be harming the woman makes no normative difference to him, provided that by doing so he would be making optimal use of his causal opportunities. We may therefore assume that, prospectively, he does not view the likelihood that the victim and her associates will hold him accountable for harming her as providing him with a normative reason—that is, a reason recognized by the norms of individual responsibility that he accepts—to refrain from doing so. He may anticipate that it will be unpleasant for him to be the target of the woman's resentment and indignation, but we may assume that the prospect of such unpleasantness does not alter his judgment that harming her represents his optimal response to the causal opportunities that are open to him. Since he holds himself to norms of responsibility that require him always to make the optimal use of such opportunities, he must treat the reaction of the woman and her associates as having no normative weight.

In order for him to discount their reaction in this way, of course, he must assume that the reaction is misguided: that they are holding him to an inappropriate standard of individual responsibility. By hypothesis, he views himself as subject to norms of responsibility, and if he thought that the standard to which they were holding him was an appropriate one, then he would not discount their reaction. Instead, he would hold himself to the same standard. In that case, he presumably would not harm the woman at all, but if he did, he would then view himself as an appropriate target of reactive responses on the part of other people, and he would also be disposed to experience self-reactive attitudes like guilt and remorse. Thus, in order for him to discount the reaction of the woman and her associates, he must assume that they are wrong to hold him to a standard of individual responsibility that requires him not to harm her.

Of course, he does not think that they are wrong to hold him to any standard of individual responsibility at all. Nor does he think that they are wrong to treat him as being, in principle, an eligible target of reactive attitudes like indignation and resentment. After all, he holds himself to a standard of individual normative responsibility, and this means, in part, that he thinks he is an appropriate target of reactive responses, by himself and others, when he fails to meet that standard. So he would not think that the woman and her associates were in error if they held him to the same standard to which he holds himself, and responded with attitudes like resentment and indignation when he failed to live up to that standard. Since the standard to which he holds himself is one that requires him at all times to make optimal use of the causal opportunities available to him, that is the standard to which he thinks that they may appropriately hold him as well. Thus, although he thinks that the innocent woman and her associates are wrong to react with resentment and indignation when he harms her, he would think it appropriate of them to experience such attitudes toward him if he failed to make optimal use of his causal opportunities. For example, it would be appropriate of them to experience such attitudes if he failed to harm the woman, since, by hypothesis, he would then be making less than optimal use of the opportunities available to him.

Now the idea that it would be wrong for the innocent woman and her associates to resent the man for harming her in order to make optimal use of his causal opportunities, but appropriate for them to resent or be indignant with him for not harming her, seems psychologically and humanly absurd.[8] It does not seem to correspond to any reasonable or

---

8. It may be protested that, as a conceptual matter, only a person who (believes that he or she) has been harmed or injured can feel resentment, so that it could not possibly be an implication of the view under consideration that the women and her friends may appropriately resent the man for not harming her. Whether or not this point is correct (I have doubts), it is clear that a parallel point does not apply to indignation. In order

realistic pattern of human reaction.[9] But this is just one symptom of a deeper instability in the position of someone who views himself as subject to norms of responsibility but takes the content of those norms to be insensitive to the distinction between doing and allowing. To see this, let us make one further assumption, namely, that our man does not consider himself to be exceptional in being subject to norms of responsibility that require individuals to respond optimally to their causal opportunities. Instead, he takes the same norms to apply to other people as well. Thus, he expects others to conform their behavior to those norms, and he believes that they should expect the same of him and of one another. Furthermore, he believes that, in general, people are appropriately subject to reactive attitudes like resentment and indignation when they fail

---

to feel indignant about a breach of expectations, one does not need to believe that one has personally been injured by that breach or suffered as a result of it. (Indeed, Strawson describes indignation as "the vicarious analogue of resentment" or, again, as "resentment on behalf of another, where one's own interest and dignity are not involved" [p. 71].) Thus, whatever may be true of resentment, there is no conceptual impediment to supposing that, according to the view under consideration, the woman and her friends may appropriately be indignant about the man's failure to harm her. Hence my use in the text of the phrase "resent or be indignant."

9. Is this really true? We can perhaps imagine that the innocent victim of a justified act (e.g., the bombing of an aggressor's munitions factory) might have her resentment diminished by the recognition that the act was indeed justified, especially if the harm to her was an unintended side effect of that act. But this is a far cry from experiencing resentment or indignation about *not* being harmed whenever harming would be causally optimal. A case that comes a bit closer might be the case of a soldier in an elite military unit who is genuinely indignant about not being chosen for a mission in which he would almost certainly be killed. As this example suggests, however, the most compelling instances of people who may be indignant about not being asked to make some sacrifice for the sake of a group all seem to presuppose a background of special solidaristic ties and identifications among the members of the group. What is more difficult to imagine is that people should, in general, be indignant when other agents do not harm them as a way of making optimal use of their causal opportunities. It is difficult to conceive of this as a stable and routine feature of human moral psychology. It is also noteworthy that, in the example of the soldier, one of the things that unites the group for which the sacrifice is to be made is shared experience of facing extreme danger together. Indeed, this is one of the things that makes the example credible, a fact that has important implications when considering a subject in which recent moral philosophy has not displayed much interest, namely, the moral psychology of danger. It presents a challenge to the Hobbesian assumptions that tend, almost by default, to dominate the philosophical discussion of that subject. However, it would be a mistake to construct a general moral psychology on the basis of this important but special case.

to make optimal use of the causal opportunities that are available to them, but that otherwise such attitudes are out of place.

The central difficulty with this is that it requires him to take, and to suppose that others should take, a purely instrumental view of his own actions and of theirs, but such an attitude is incompatible with viewing himself and them as being subject to norms of responsibility in the first place. The norms that the man accepts require him to take an instrumental attitude because they assert that each action is to be assessed solely in terms of its optimality relative to the other causal opportunities available to the agent. Each action, then, is to be assessed in terms of its causal instrumentality. The fact that a given action might help to realize some value (other than causal or instrumental optimality) about which the agent cares, to instantiate a principle or ideal that matters to him, or to contribute to the flourishing of one of his projects or relationships is of no direct significance. The only question is whether, in these circumstances, the agent's optimal causal contribution would be made by realizing that value, instantiating that ideal, or attending to that project or relationship. Many philosophers have argued that taking such an attitude toward one's own actions is incompatible with genuine allegiance to a principle or value, or with genuine attachment to a project or relationship.[10] I will return to this point, with which I agree, but the argument I want now to make is different. I want to argue that such an attitude is incompatible with viewing oneself as subject to norms of responsibility.

There are two different ways of bringing out this incompatibility. First, let us assume, for the sake of argument, that the standards of normative responsibility do require that we abide solely by the norm of instrumental optimality. And let us also assume for the moment that holding oneself to a standard of normative responsibility involves a higher-order resolution to conform to that standard, and not merely a stable disposition to respond to specific reasons on a case-by-case basis. We have already seen that holding oneself to a standard of responsibility is itself a primary manifestation of one's agency, even if the standard consists solely in the norm of instrumental optimality. To this we can now add that the perceived imperative to hold oneself to that very norm cannot derive from the instrumental optimality of so doing, for at least two reasons. First, there is no guarantee that one's efforts to conform to the norm will in fact be instrumentally optimal; in some circumstances, making

---

10. The locus classicus is Bernard Williams, "A Critique of Utilitarianism," in *Utilitarianism For and Against,* by J. J. C. Smart and Bernard Williams (Cambridge: Cambridge University Press, 1973), pp. 77–150.

such efforts may be counterproductive, and the resolution to conform with the norm of causal optimality may itself be causally nonoptimal. In addition, the perceived imperative to hold oneself to the norm of instrumental optimality cannot derive from the instrumental optimality of so doing because, if it did, one would need already to have accepted the norm in order to see oneself as having reason to accept it, which means that the proposed derivation is circular. The perceived imperative to hold oneself to the instrumental norm must instead be based on a perception of that very norm as being, in itself, rationally compelling, whether or not trying to abide by it is instrumentally optimal. But this means that the perceived imperative depends on a view of the instrumental norm as having independent, rational force. And if this is correct, then not only is holding oneself to the norm of instrumental optimality a primary manifestation of one's agency, but, in addition, it is a manifestation of one's agency that is justified by considerations other than instrumental optimality.[11]

Thus, even if we assume, for the sake of argument, that the norms of responsibility are themselves norms of instrumental optimality, the perceived imperative to abide by those very norms must be based on a conviction that there are noninstrumental reasons for doing so. This means that one can only view oneself as subject to norms of responsibility if one already accepts a distinction between what one does and what one allows and views at least some of the things that one does as justified by considerations that are independent of their instrumental optimality. Nor is this conclusion altered if we give up the assumption that holding oneself to a standard of responsibility involves a higher-order resolution to conform to the standard, and if we suppose instead that it involves nothing more than a stable disposition to respond to specific reasons on a case-by-case basis. Even if this is so, the perceived force of those reasons cannot derive from the instrumental optimality of trying to adhere to

11. Suppose an instrumentalist were to say instead that, although the first-order norms of responsibility may have a noninstrumental character, and although holding oneself to those norms may be a primary manifestation of one's agency, one's reasons for doing so are themselves reasons of instrumental optimality. For example, the instrumentalist may say that the real reason for holding ourselves to the first-order norms is because this form of inner vigilance is the only causal mechanism we have available for ensuring an optimal level of compliance with the norms. However, if our reasons for holding ourselves to the noninstrumental norms are themselves reasons of instrumental optimality, then we still need some reason for abiding by the norm of instrumental optimality, and, as argued in the text above, that reason cannot also be a reason of instrumental optimality.

them; and if they have their force independently of the instrumental optimality of trying to adhere to them, then trying to adhere to them is itself a manifestation of one's agency that is justified by noninstrumental considerations.

The second way of bringing out the incompatibility is this. We are supposing that the man holds himself and others to the norm of causal optimality, which means that he views breaches of that norm as meriting some reactive response. But the relevant notion of merit is itself independent of considerations of causal optimality. To say that breaches of the norms of responsibility merit a reactive response is to say that the occurrence of a breach provides a justification for such a response. The response may or may not be instrumentally optimal. Perhaps the optimal thing to do would be to train oneself to avoid having such responses, so far as possible. But since, by hypothesis, breaches of the normative standard are seen as meriting reactive responses, those responses need not be instrumentally optimal in order to be warranted. To hold oneself and others to a normative standard is to commit oneself to a notion of merit that is not subject to a norm of causal optimality.

It may be suggested that the consistency of the man's attitudes could be preserved if he were to adopt a revised notion of merit that was in fact subject to a norm of causal optimality. In this spirit, for example, he would see people's conduct as "meriting" a reactive response when and only when such a response would be causally optimal. But, setting aside the cluster of issues that nest around the word *adopt*, the central point is that the revised notion of *merit* is not really a notion of merit at all, and the resulting attitudes are not reactive attitudes. Reactive attitudes are experienced as merited responses to breaches of expectations, which means that they are experienced as responses that are justified or made appropriate by those breaches. If we imagine that our man experiences certain attitudes as causally optimal responses to particular bits of behavior, then we are no longer ascribing to him reactive attitudes. A blast of hostile affect delivered in the hope of achieving some instrumental advantage is not the same thing as resentment or indignation. It is not a reactive attitude at all, because it is not a reaction to a perceived failure by the agent who is the target of the attitude to respond to available reasons. Yet, by hypothesis, to hold people to standards of normative responsibility is precisely to see them as appropriate targets of reactive attitudes when they are insensitive to those standards. It is to expect of them that they will be responsive to a certain class of reasons and to view breaches of these expectations as providing a justification for a reactive response. Thus, if our man really does deploy items from his own affective repertoire solely on the basis of his calculations of their instrumental efficacy, then he is not treating the targets of those deployments as agents who are subject to, and expected to live up to, norms of individual responsibility. He is not in that sense treating them as responsible agents.[12]

Thus, to summarize, I have argued that there is a deep instability in the position of someone who views himself as subject to norms of responsibility but takes the content of those norms to be completely insensitive to the distinction between doing and allowing. In order to regulate one's life by reference to a normative standard that requires one always to make optimal use of the causal opportunities one has available, one must take a purely instrumental attitude toward one's own actions. But in order to view oneself as subject to norms of individual responsibility at all, one must think of one's actions very differently. At the most fundamental level, one must see oneself as having noninstrumental reasons to hold oneself to the normative standard. In addition, one must view oneself as subject to reactive responses that are governed by a noninstrumental conception of merit or desert. Furthermore, what is true of one's view of oneself is also true of one's view of others. In order to see other people as subject to norms of individual responsibility, one must see them as having noninstrumental reasons to conform to the relevant norms and as subject to reactive responses that cannot be understood in purely instrumental terms.

It may be protested that the conclusions that can be drawn from these arguments are quite limited. If the arguments are correct, they show that holding oneself to a standard of normative responsibility constitutes an exercise of agency that is not itself subject to a norm of instrumental optimality, and that our practices of responsibility involve reactive responses that are also not subject to such a norm. However, it may be said, this does not show that the norm of instrumental optimality does not suffice to govern all other areas of human conduct. With the two exceptions just mentioned, the standards of normative responsibility may still require agents always to act in such a way as to make optimal use of their causal opportunities.

This suggestion seems to me untenable, however, for at least two closely related reasons. First, whether or not holding oneself to a standard

---

12. Of course, as I said in n. 7, some consequentialists view the reactive attitudes as misguided and unjustified. These consequentialists might argue that, insofar as our practice of treating one another as responsible agents depends on such attitudes, the practice should be rejected or revised. As I have indicated, I find this kind of position implausible but do not argue against it here. My aim is only to show that a distinction between doing and allowing is required by our actual practices of responsibility.

of normative responsibility involves a higher-order resolution to conform to that standard, it certainly requires more than just a single, discrete exercise of one's agency. In holding oneself to such a standard, and in viewing oneself as subject to reactive responses when one violates that standard, one manifests an ongoing practical orientation. That orientation includes a set of standing dispositions to think about one's actions in certain ways. For example, it includes a standing disposition to treat the fact that an act would violate the standard as constituting a noninstrumental reason not to perform it. It also includes a standing disposition to treat any violations of the standard that one may nevertheless commit as making certain reactive responses noninstrumentally appropriate. These dispositions systematically constrain all of one's deliberations and decisions, even on occasions when no considerations of the relevant kinds happen to arise. For example, even if none of the acts among which one is choosing on a given occasion does in fact violate the norms of responsibility, it remains true that one would be disposed to reject any act that one did take to violate the norms and to regard a reactive response as appropriate if one nevertheless performed such an act. Thus, the significance of the fact that one has noninstrumental reasons for holding oneself to a standard of normative responsibility is not confined to a single type of act or area of human conduct. Instead, that fact shapes the exercise of one's agency more generally. The distinctive practical orientation of someone who holds himself to a normative standard is characterized by a pervasive sensitivity to noninstrumental reasons.[13]

Second, I have been arguing that our practice of treating one another as responsible agents rests on a conception of what it means to be an agent that excludes a purely instrumental view of our actions. One important feature of this noninstrumental conception of our agency is that it is a conception of ourselves as temporally extended beings—beings whose responsiveness to noninstrumental reasons is a standing feature of their participation in a stable social world. The practical orientation described in the previous paragraph would be impossible without this feature. Once one has the noninstrumental conception of one's agency, moreover, this is the conception that one has. One does not simply turn it on and off depending on the context, for if one did turn it on and off then one's actual conception of oneself would not be the noninstrumental conception. Indeed, the very idea that one might "turn on and off" a

---

13. Similar points are developed at greater length in my *Human Morality* (New York: Oxford University Press, 1992).

view of oneself as a temporally extended creature with a standing disposition to respond to noninstrumental reasons is incoherent, for there is no coherent way of conceiving of either the self that would be doing the turning on and off or its reasons for doing this. Thus, the suggestion that, within their area of application, the norms themselves may require that we adopt a purely instrumental stance toward one another's conduct makes neither psychological nor conceptual sense. If we are to hold ourselves and others to norms of individual responsibility at all, then the norms in question will, within their area of application, have to provide a standard of assessment that is not purely instrumental.

Now the only alternative to an instrumental standard is one that treats the agent's actions as having independent normative significance—as having a kind of significance, in other words, that does not derive from their instrumental efficacy. And any such standard requires us to treat the distinction between doing and allowing as normatively relevant, for it tells us that there is a distinctive kind of normative significance that attaches to what we do—to the primary manifestations of our agency. To be sure, such a standard need not draw the distinction between doing and allowing in just the same way that commonsense morality does. Indeed, I have already questioned whether there is a single "commonsensical" way of drawing it. Nevertheless, a noninstrumental standard of responsibility must employ, and attach normative significance to, some version of the distinction.

V

The points that I have been making can be put in a slightly different way and set in a somewhat broader context. A large part of the achievement of interpersonal understanding consists in learning about the characters, values, and commitments of other people. These are among the most important dimensions of individuals' distinctiveness, of their "individuality." And the way that we come to understand the characters, values, and commitments of other people is, to a very great extent, by coming to appreciate the kinds of considerations that they treat as reasons for action. It is through the kinds of reasons they recognize that individuals reveal the regulative structure of their characters. It is through those patterns of reasons, in other words, that they make manifest the values that they treat as basic, the concerns that matter most to them, the commitments they regard as fundamental, and the ideals and principles to which they strive to be faithful. In an important sense, it is through the recognition of reasons that people express themselves.

What makes this kind of self-expression possible for human beings—indeed, what makes it possible for them to have selves to express in the first place—is the fact that they respond to such a rich and varied range of reasons. They are moved by their attachment to particular people, their loyalty to causes, their pursuit of goals, their respect for principles, and their delight in forms of activity. They are also moved by their fears, hatreds, and antipathies, of course, and this too reveals aspects of their characters—this too tells us something about their values and commitments. The important point, for our purposes, is that the constitution and expression of distinct human selves could not take the form that it does if human beings did not treat such a wide and diverse range of considerations as providing them with reasons for action.[14]

A norm requiring individuals always to make optimal use of the causal opportunities available to them would, if internalized, make it impossible for human beings to respond in a direct and consistent way to the many other kinds of reasons that they recognize, and whose recognition gives definition and expression to a person's character and values. For someone to regard his actions solely as instruments for the promotion of optimal states of the world would, to adapt a remark that Rawls makes in a slightly different context, represent "the dissolution of the person as leading a life expressive of character and of devotion to specific final ends and...values."[15] If a life of character is to be sustainable, the norms to which people hold one another must distinguish between what individuals do and what they allow—between primary and secondary manifestations of their agency. Without some conception of what are to count as the primary manifestations of our agency, the kind of responsiveness to diverse practical reasons that defines us as distinct persons is not possible.[16]

14. The relation between self-constitution and the diversity of reasons is an important theme in the writings of Joseph Raz. See, e.g., *The Morality of Freedom* (Oxford: Clarendon, 1986), chap. 14.
15. John Rawls, "Social Unity and Primary Goods," in *Utilitarianism and Beyond*, ed. Amartya Sen and Bernard Williams (Cambridge: Cambridge University Press, 1982), pp. 159–85, at p. 181.
16. I leave open the question of whether there are forms of consequentialism that can accommodate the points made in this paragraph. Certainly, as suggested in n. 7, there have been many defenders of consequentialism who have been prepared to deny that people should treat consequentialist principles as guides to personal decision making, and who would accordingly be happy to agree that people should not regard their actions solely as instruments for the promotion of optimal states of the world. Once again, I do not find these forms of consequentialism plausible, but their assessment lies beyond the scope of this article. Nor shall I discuss views like those of Amartya

It is important not to overstate the conclusions of this line of thought. I have been arguing that there are certain conditions that candidate norms of responsibility must meet if they are to be capable of being accepted and internalized by people who view themselves and one another as subject to such norms. In particular, candidate norms must make a distinction between doing and allowing—or some other distinction between primary and secondary manifestations of individual agency—and they must, to some extent at least, assign individuals greater responsibility for the former than for the latter. As we have seen, however, it does not follow from this, nor is it true, that acceptable norms of individual responsibility cannot attach any weight whatsoever to what is merely allowed. Any plausible set of norms will need to attach some weight to the responsibilities of causal position, since to do otherwise would be to ignore the way in which the exercise of human agency is embedded within the larger causal order. Nor is it a requirement of selfhood or self-expression that individuals must ignore their causal position: that they must attach no significance to the causal opportunities they forgo or to the outcomes they fail to prevent. Although, as I have argued, it is a requirement of self-constitution and self-expression that individuals be capable of responding to diverse sources of practical reasons, the existence of indefinitely many causal opportunities is one of the conditions that defines the background against which that capacity is normally exercised. One of the challenges of being an agent—of making one's way in the world—is to reconcile oneself to the omnipresence of such opportunities. The difficulty of this challenge is indicated by the imaginative power of questions about what might have been, and by the rich array of emotions—from regret, bitterness, and self-reproach to profound gratitude and relief—that we are prone to experience in response to missed opportunities and failures to act.

One familiar Kantian theme is the opposition between theoretical and practical perspectives on human action. From a theoretical standpoint, human beings are part of the natural order, and their actions are subject

---

Sen, who insists on the relevance, within a framework of "consequential evaluation," of the distinction between doing and allowing, but whose commitment to "evaluator relativity," or "situated evaluation," distinguishes his position from consequentialism as I understand it. For Sen's view see his "Rights and Agency," *Philosophy & Public Affairs* 11 (1982): 3–39, "Evaluator Relativity and Consequential Evaluation," *Philosophy & Public Affairs* 12 (1983): 113–132, "Positional Objectivity," *Philosophy & Public Affairs* 22 (1993): 126–45, and "Consequential Evaluation and Practical Reason," *Journal of Philosophy* 97 (2000): 477–502.

to causal laws. From a practical standpoint, we have no alternative but to conceive of ourselves as agents whose choices are guided by reasons. The argument that I have been developing suggests something slightly different. Insofar as we regard ourselves as subject to norms of responsibility, we must indeed see a normatively relevant distinction between our own actions and other causal processes. We must see ourselves as responsible for regulating the exercise of our agency by reference to reasons deriving from the applicable norms. At the same time, however, part of the pathos of human agency lies in the fact that, notwithstanding our commitment to viewing ourselves as responsible choosers whose deliberations are guided by reasons, our sense of ourselves as agents is also conditioned by an awareness of our subsumption within the larger causal web, and by the resulting recognition that missed opportunities, of many different kinds, are an ineliminable feature of human life. No amount of rational self-regulation or self-control can guarantee that we will never feel regret about a missed opportunity or a lost chance. Even the fact that we passed up some opportunity for good reasons does not guarantee that it will never make sense to regret having done so.[17]

As I have said, part of the function of norms that distinguish between doing and allowing is to strike a balance between considerations of two very different kinds: between the inevitable priority and distinctiveness of action, on the one hand, and its unavoidable subsumption within a larger causal web, on the other. For this reason if for no other, it is unlikely that there is any way of delineating the boundary between doing and allowing that can shield that distinction from normative controversy. But, as I have argued in this article, neither is there any way of eliminating the distinction in favor of a radically expansive conception of normative responsibility that treats doing and allowing symmetrically. Some distinction between what one does and what one allows is an ineliminable feature of any conception of normative responsibility to which responsible agents can consistently hold one another, even though the contours of the distinction are likely to remain both imprecise and contested, and

---

17. Another position with which mine has something in common, but from which it also differs, is Thomas Nagel's view that there is a division within each individual between two opposing standpoints—standpoints that Nagel has variously characterized over the years as the internal and the external, the subjective and the objective, and the personal and the impersonal. See, e.g., *The Possibility of Altruism* (Oxford: Clarendon, 1970), *Mortal Questions* (Cambridge: Cambridge University Press, 1979), *The View from Nowhere* (New York: Oxford University Press, 1986), and *Equality and Partiality* (New York: Oxford University Press, 1991).

even though it is likely to be of limited assistance in resolving the hardest cases. Of course, it remains perfectly possible to argue that the conventional moral wisdom in our culture assigns individuals too little responsibility for assisting those who are suffering or in need. The claim that there are limits to how expansive a conception of responsibility individuals can accept need not amount to an endorsement of the moral status quo. Still, in considering how individuals might reasonably be asked to conceive of their responsibilities for the alleviation of suffering, it is important to keep the limits in mind. Complete symmetry between doing harm and failing to prevent harm is not to be expected.

PART II

Institutions

4

The Division of Moral Labor:

Egalitarian Liberalism as Moral Pluralism

By any reasonable standard of assessment, it is clear that human beings lead lives of wildly varying quality. People who live in different societies or belong to different social classes often differ greatly in their life expectancy, material resources, political rights and personal freedoms, and levels of nutrition and health, as well as in their access to education and medical care and their vulnerability to violence and assault. At the extremes, at least, these differences are normally accompanied by great differences in the range of options people have available to them, in their prospects of achieving their aims, and in their sense of satisfaction with their own lives. Whereas many people in many countries enjoy a high level of prosperity and material comfort, and have a reasonable chance of achieving a significant measure of personal fulfillment over the course of their lives,

Originally published in the *Proceedings of the Aristotelian Society*, Supplementary Volume 79 (2005): 229–253. Reprinted by courtesy of the Editor of the Aristotelian Society. © The Aristotelian Society 2005.

there are many others who can look forward to little more than a miserable life and an early death. Although great progress has been made in combating the worst forms of poverty in recent decades, there continue to be people who live in conditions of extreme deprivation and malnutrition; people whose lack of medical care leaves them defenseless against infection and disease; people who have never received a formal education, have no political influence or representation, and do not enjoy the protection of the rule of law; and people whose utter powerlessness leaves them vulnerable to degrading and humiliating social and political arrangements or even, at worst, to policies of deliberate savagery and brutality.

All of this is well known. Among people who have the good fortune to live in circumstances characterized by material prosperity and political freedom, few are unaware of the continued existence of widespread suffering resulting from poverty, famine, disease, political oppression, and organized violence. Searing images of human suffering appear on television and in other media with sufficient regularity that it is difficult to remain completely ignorant of the extremes of human misery.

Although the very familiarity of these images tends to diminish their capacity to produce shock, and may even induce a certain degree of callousness at times, many people never cease to find such images deeply disturbing and unsettling. Nevertheless, few people are moved by their awareness of human suffering to alter their lives in fundamental ways. To be sure, there are some people who—motivated perhaps by principle, or by religious or ideological conviction, or by an unusual degree of personal empathy—choose to devote their lives to the alleviation of human misery. However, the number of people whose response to the facts of human suffering extends beyond an occasional contribution of time or money, on a fairly modest scale, to a "charitable" or "humanitarian" organization, is relatively small. And although there are many morally sensitive people who are subject to intermittent feelings of unease about the discrepancy between their own comfortable circumstances and the plight of those who are worst off, few are plagued by profound and persistent feelings of guilt or shame about their failure to do more to alleviate human misery.

One thing that undoubtedly helps to explain why individuals do not do more in response to the suffering of others is that often they are not certain what kind of response would be useful or effective. When people are made aware of widespread suffering resulting from famine, war, extreme poverty, or political oppression, they are frequently daunted by the scale of the problems, frustrated by the absence of any consensus either about the causes of those problems or about the best ways of solving them, and inhibited by their own geographic or social distance from the victims. The perceived absence of clear, effective, and readily available mechanisms for assisting those in need often leaves people in doubt as to what, other than writing a check, they might usefully do to help. Even when deciding where to send a check, people may doubt their capacity to judge the relative effectiveness of the different organizations to which they might contribute.

Of course, the main reason why people don't do more to help alleviate human misery may seem simpler than this: most people, after all, have problems of their own. Living an ordinary life, even in reasonably comfortable circumstances, is usually difficult and often exhausting. Most people struggle just to keep up. They have their hands full trying to cope with the daily challenges of life, and it is not easy for the plight of the needy to get a grip on the structure of their motivations. Yet this cannot by itself be a complete explanation. Most people are capable of shouldering a variety of responsibilities and of observing numerous constraints on their activities when there are well-established norms requiring them to do so. Part of the explanation for people's failure to do more to aid those who are in need is that the predominant values and norms of our culture do not in fact require them to do so.

To the contrary, many familiar moral ideas have the effect of limiting individual responsibility for the alleviation of suffering. Let me mention four such ideas by way of illustration. First, there is the idea that we have a greater responsibility for what we ourselves do than for what we merely fail to prevent. Although there are times when one ought to help alleviate suffering one did not cause, one's primary responsibility, in general, is to avoid harming others oneself. The second idea is that one has greater responsibilities toward some people than toward others: greater responsibilities toward one's family and friends, for example, than toward strangers and people with whom one lacks any significant social bond. The third idea is that one is normally entitled to try to lead a decent and fulfilling life oneself, even if that means forgoing opportunities to assist others who are in need. One is not expected to wait until all the more urgent needs of others have been met before pursuing one's own aims and aspirations.

The final idea is that, for purposes of moral assessment, responsiveness to a value does not in general require optimization or maximization of the value. Even the most favorable sorts of moral assessment do not normally depend on one's having done as much as possible to attain some morally admirable end. Consider, for example, a physician who, out of a desire to help people, passes up the opportunity to join a lucrative urban practice and chooses instead to work as a family doctor in a poor, medically under-served rural community. The doctor is hardly to be faulted if it turns out that there was some other career path available that would have enabled her to help people even more. (Perhaps she could have joined *Médecins Sans Frontières* and provided medical care for people whose needs were more urgent.) Not only will she have done nothing wrong, by our lights, in making the choice she made, but we are apt to regard her as particularly admirable or virtuous for having made that choice. It is not necessary, in order to see her as virtuous, still less in order to see her choice as morally defensible or justified, that we regard her as having done the most helpful thing she could possibly have done, or as having realized her values in the best possible way. The standard of maximization or optimization is not one that we apply in these contexts.

I have formulated these four ideas only very roughly, and each can be interpreted in importantly different ways. In addition, it is clear that each admits of various exceptions and qualifications. Yet the influence of these ideas on people's habits of thought and feeling is no less strong for that. Taken together, they imply that, so long as one has not caused the suffering or misery of others oneself, and so long as one has no special personal or social relationship with the victims, it is legitimate, at least within certain broad limits, to pass up opportunities to assist those who are suffering in order to pursue one's own aims and aspirations, especially if achieving one's aims will contribute in some way to the realization of some significant human value. In this way, these ideas serve to limit indi-vidual responsibility for the alleviation of suffering. They imply that, in respect of human misery, the world of individual responsibility is much smaller than the world as a whole.

More generally, the ideas I have mentioned, like many other familiar values and norms, encourage us to focus attention on the ways in which we interact with the people we know and the people we meet, especially those people with whom we have significant social or communal or insti-tutional ties. The kind of moral reflection they promote is reflection about our treatment of the other people we encounter and about the quality of our personal relations. They encourage us to be, as it were, good citizens of our moral neighborhood: to be mindful of how we conduct ourselves toward those people who, because of their physical or social or emotional proximity, or because of the directness or immediacy of our causal interac-tions with them, are taken to fall within the proper sphere of our moral concern. These "limiting" values and norms, as we may call them, are most at home in the context of small-scale personal relations and interac-tions. That context provides the setting in which they normally have their clearest application, and which people who have internalized them are encouraged to treat as morally salient. One symptom of their influence is the fact that even morally sensitive people are likely to feel guiltier about having broken a promise or slighted a friend or neglected a family member than about not having done more to alleviate global suffering.

Nevertheless, many people do feel intermittently uneasy about their own failure to do more to help alleviate extreme human misery. They may be subject to occasional episodes of self-doubt about their justification for living as they do, and they may be prone to defensiveness if challenged. This suggests, what should in any case be clear, that many people who have internalized the limiting norms also have other values with which those norms are perceived as being in tension. For example, many people acknowledge ideas of justice, fairness, equality, human rights, and the equal worth of persons, which have, and are understood to have, implications that transcend the arena of small-scale interpersonal relations, and which reflect an expansive understanding of the proper scope of moral concern. Values of this second kind play a particularly central role in political morality, and many people are troubled—or are capable of being troubled—by institutional arrangements and practices that they take to be incompatible with these values. They may be disturbed, for example, about political or economic arrangements that they regard as unfair or exploitative. They may be troubled by large variations in levels of income, wealth, or life-expectancy; or by widespread suffering resulting from avoidable famine, disease, or poverty; or by instances of political oppression or tyranny; or by systems of caste or hierarchy or other forms of systematic discrimination and marginalization. Notwithstanding their internalization of the limiting norms, then, many people also affirm other values and principles—ideas of justice and equality, perhaps, or conceptions of the value of human life—about which they feel strongly, and whose compatibility or incompatibility with the limiting norms is a matter of at least sporadic concern to them.

There are a number of possible responses to the perceived tension between these two sets of values. In this paper, I want to discuss the response offered by egalitarian liberals, such as Rawls, Nagel, and Dworkin, and to highlight what I take to be its distinctiveness. In order to help motivate this response, I will begin by giving brief and highly stylized summaries of two different approaches with which the egalitarian response may be contrasted.

The first of these approaches is the one taken by libertarianism. The libertarian gives priority to the values and principles that regulate small-scale interactions among individuals, and treats the larger-scale values of social justice and equality as valid only insofar as they can be construed as applications of values and norms that are at home in the context of one-on-one personal interactions. For example, the human rights that it is appropriate to recognize at the social or institutional level are limited to those rights that already constrain the way individuals treat one another in their personal interactions; there is no human right to be provided by institutions with additional "social welfare" benefits. Although some people may voluntarily choose to live in accordance with a more demanding set of personal or social ideals, it is not mandatory that they do so and such ideals should not be imposed upon them. For the libertarian, one might say, micro-level norms define the content and limits of macro-level norms.[1]

By contrast, something like the reverse is true for utilitarians and other consequentialists. The consequentialist response to the perceived tension is, roughly, to give priority to considerations of aggregate well-being, and to make room for the traditional norms of personal life only insofar as their use can be justified at a putatively more fundamental level where a thoroughly impartial concern for all individuals prevails. For the consequentialist, individuals' reliance on the limiting norms may be legitimate up to a point, insofar as such reliance may itself promote conditions that are optimal from a less restricted moral perspective. But consequentialists deny that the limiting norms have any independent moral standing or justification. Moreover, the general tendency of consequentialist thought is to suggest that the limits on individual responsibility that we have internalized may not ultimately be defensible. Insofar as it is feasible to do so, we should embrace a more inclusive understanding of our responsibilities. We should see ourselves as more responsible for the plight of strangers, more responsible for things that happen far away, more responsible for preventing and not merely avoiding the infliction of harm, more responsible for the foreseeable but unintended consequences of our actions. By circumscribing the boundaries of our responsibilities, limiting norms serve to insulate us, as moral agents, from much of what happens in the world at large. The general tendency of consequentialist thought is to suggest that we should expand our moral horizons, and stop seeing ourselves as quite so well insulated.

Obviously, these are only the barest sketches of the libertarian and consequentialist positions, each of which admits of considerable development, refinement, and internal variation. But since my aim in this paper is to discuss a different response to the perceived tension between the values of personal life and the values of political morality, I will simply assert that, in my view, it is a mistake to treat either set of values as having merely derivative significance, as both the libertarian and the

1. See Robert Nozick, *Anarchy, State and Utopia* (New York: Basic Books 1974), 204–213.

consequentialist do. Although I cannot argue the point here, I believe that to do this is to understate the importance and mutual independence of these values. On the one hand, the "limiting norms" are deeply rooted in the structure of human agency and human interpersonal relationships.[2] On the other hand, our normative reflection about the larger social world in which we live cannot plausibly be represented as drawing solely on the values and norms that inform small-scale interpersonal relations. No response that fails to treat each set of values as having autonomous standing—as having moral importance in its own right—can do justice to the place of these values in our normative thought.

One way of interpreting egalitarian liberalism is as attempting to provide a response that does do justice to both sets of values. Rather than seeking to derive one set of values from the other, the egalitarian liberal proposes what amounts to a division of moral labor. The task of realizing the values of justice and equality will be assigned primarily to what Rawls calls "the basic structure of society." The basic structure, which comprises a society's major social, political, and economic institutions, will be regulated by a distinctive set of normative principles. Individuals will be assigned a duty to support just institutions, but within the framework established by those institutions, they will be able to lead their lives in such a way as to honor the values appropriate to small-scale interpersonal relationships. Both sets of values will be accommodated without either being reduced to or derived from the other.[3]

2. Elsewhere I have argued for this claim as it applies to each of the first three limiting norms mentioned above. On the idea that we have a greater responsibility for what we do than for what we allow, see 'Doing and Allowing', Chapter 3 in this volume. On our special responsibilities toward those with whom we have close personal ties, see "Relationships and Responsibilities," *Philosophy & Public Affairs* 26, n. 3 (Summer 1997), 189–209 (reprinted in *Boundaries and Allegiances* [Oxford: Oxford University Press 2001], 97–110). On the legitimacy of pursuing one's own aims even if that means forgoing opportunities to do good, see "Projects, Relationships, and Reasons," in R. J. Wallace, P. Pettit, S. Scheffler, and M. Smith (eds.), *Reason and Value: Themes from the Moral Philosophy of Joseph Raz* (Oxford: Oxford University Press 2004), 247–269, and *The Rejection of Consequentialism* (Oxford: Clarendon Press, rev. ed. 1994). Special responsibilities and the legitimacy of pursuing one's own aims are also discussed in "Morality and Reasonable Partiality," Chapter 2 in this volume.

3. As is clear from the text, this division of moral labor is framed in the first instance as applying within a single society. One of the most important and contested questions about egalitarian liberalism, which I cannot discuss here, is how it is properly to be applied to the world as a whole. Ultimately, both the content and the plausibility of the division-of-labor idea as a response to the tension within our values will depend in part on how this issue is resolved. For some preliminary discussion, see "Cosmopolitanism, Justice & Institutions," Chapter 6 in this volume.

In one way, this interpretation of the aims of egalitarian liberalism is hardly novel. Both Rawls and Nagel explicitly employ the division-of-labor metaphor. And in his most developed explanation of his reasons for treating the basic structure as the primary subject of justice, Rawls contrasts his own view with precisely the two positions I have mentioned: libertarianism and consequentialism (utilitarianism).[4] Indeed, to a very great extent, egalitarian liberalism has developed in explicit dialogue with, and in explicit opposition to, these two contrasting views. Each of them is seen as privileging one set of values at the expense of another equally important set.

Nevertheless, the division-of-labor metaphor has been understood in different ways, both by egalitarian liberals themselves and by their critics. The result, I think, is that different strands within egalitarian liberalism have not been adequately distinguished from one another, and that some of the appeal of the position has been obscured. In this paper, my aim is to disentangle some of the different ways in which the division-of-labor metaphor has been understood, with an eye to clarifying both the appeal of the egalitarian-liberal project and the challenges that it faces.

The obvious place to begin is with Rawls,[5] and the first thing to notice is that he actually draws two different distinctions between the rules and principles that apply to the basic structure of society and those that apply elsewhere. The first distinction follows more or less directly from his claim that the basic structure is the primary subject of justice. In making this claim, Rawls means in part to be asserting that the principles that apply to the basic structure may not be appropriate for regulating groups and associations of other kinds, nor for regulating the conduct of individuals. As he says: "The principles of justice for institutions must not be confused with the principles which apply to individuals and their actions in particular circumstances. These two kinds of principles apply to different subjects and must be discussed separately."[6] In Rawls's view, there are many different normative principles and ideals that apply to individuals and their conduct. "Justice as fairness" does not purport either to codify those principles and ideals or to preempt them. His conception of justice

4. John Rawls, *Political Liberalism* (New York: Columbia University Press 1993), Chapter 7 (especially sections 2 and 3). Cited hereafter as PL, with page references given parenthetically in the text.

5. My summary of Rawls's views in the next several pages draws on my more extensive discussion in "Is the Basic Structure Basic?", Chapter 5 in this volume.

6. John Rawls, *A Theory of Justice* (Cambridge, MA: Harvard University Press 1971), pp. 54–55, and rev. ed. (Harvard University Press 1999), p. 47. Cited hereafter as TJ, with page references to the original and revised editions given parenthetically in the text.

is intended for a particular kind of subject, and for that subject only. Whereas utilitarianism is usually thought of as a "completely general theory" that "applies equally to all social forms and to the actions of individuals" (PL 260), the "first principles of justice as fairness are plainly not suitable for a general theory" (PL 261). In effect, then, Rawls endorses a form of pluralism about moral values and principles. Social institutions should be regulated by his principles of justice, but other groups and individual agents should in general be guided by other principles and may legitimately aim to realize other values and ideals. Although Rawls does not use the division-of-labor metaphor in drawing this distinction, it seems like a natural way of expressing his view.

Rawls draws his second distinction in the course of explaining his reasons for treating the basic structure as primary. He gives three main reasons for this emphasis. First, the basic structure has profound and far-reaching effects. The social position into which one is born helps to determine one's expectations in life, and any inequalities resulting from differences in people's initial social positions are likely to be particularly deep and pervasive. So it is of the utmost importance that the basic structure of society, and the social positions that it establishes, should satisfy the demands of justice. Second, the basic structure helps to shape people's characters, desires, aims, and aspirations. It is not merely a device for satisfying existing wants, but also a way of creating new wants in the future. Since the basic structure inevitably has this function, and since the question of how people and their aspirations are to be shaped is a moral question, it is again essential that the basic structure should be regulated by norms of justice. Finally, Rawls says that agreements and transactions among individuals will be just or fair only if certain background conditions are satisfied, and that there are no feasible rules of individual conduct that can secure background justice or prevent its erosion over time. Given the scale of a modern economy, the establishment and preservation of background justice requires far too much information and is far too complex a task to be accomplished by any set of rules that might plausibly guide individual conduct. Instead, it is the function of the basic structure to secure and preserve background justice. "The role of the institutions that belong to the basic structure is to secure just background conditions against which the actions of individuals and associations take place. Unless this structure is appropriately regulated and adjusted, an initially just social process will eventually cease to be just, however free and fair particular transactions may look when viewed by themselves" (PL 266).

It is in connection with this last reason that Rawls draws his second distinction between the norms that pertain to the basic structure and norms of other kinds, and it is here that he explicitly employs the division-of-labor metaphor. What he says is that, in order to secure the background conditions necessary to ensure the fairness of individual transactions, we look for an "institutional division of labor" between "two kinds of social rules, and the different institutional forms in which these rules are realized" (PL 268). The basic structure includes one set of "operations"—Rawls cites income and inheritance taxation as examples—that "continually adjust and compensate for the inevitable tendencies away from background fairness." It also "enforces through the legal system another set of rules that govern the transactions and agreements between individuals and associations," and which "satisfy the requirements of simplicity and practicality" (PL 268). In other words, he writes: "What we look for, in effect, is an institutional division of labor between the basic structure and the rules applying directly to individuals and associations and to be followed by them in particular transactions. If this division of labor can be established, individuals and associations are then left free to advance their ends more effectively within the framework of the basic structure, secure in the knowledge that elsewhere in the social system the necessary corrections to preserve background justice are being made" (PL 268–269).

It is clear that Rawls's two distinctions represent two very different contrasts. The first contrast, which I will refer to as "the division of moral labor," is between the principles of justice that apply to the basic structure and those values and norms that apply elsewhere. Whereas the basic structure of society should be designed in such a way as to satisfy the principles of distributive justice, both individual conduct and other groups and associations should in general be guided by other principles and should strive to realize other virtues and ideals. The point of this distinction is to acknowledge the diversity of values and principles, and to emphasize the limited scope of Rawls's conception of justice. The second contrast, which Rawls speaks of as the "institutional division of labor," is between two sets of rules: the rules constituting those social forms that are part of the basic structure and are necessary to ensure background justice, and the rules that directly regulate economic transactions and agreements among individuals. This contrast has nothing to do with value pluralism. It is motivated instead by the challenge of preserving background justice, given that this cannot feasibly be accomplished through norms of individual conduct alone.

Rawls's emphasis on the basic structure has been vigorously criticized by a number of philosophers, including most notably G. A. Cohen and Liam Murphy. One important line of criticism has focused on the implications for individual motivation of treating institutions as the primary

subject of distributive justice. Cohen thinks that, by restricting the principles of justice to the institutional structure of society, Rawls reveals
a willingness to tolerate "unlimited self-seekingness in the economic
choices" that individuals make within that structure.[7] On this interpretation of Rawls, individuals must abide by the rules established by the basic
structure, but they are free to act on purely self-interested motives whenever they are deciding among options that the rules do not prohibit. In
response, Cohen argues that this kind of self-interested economic behavior would inevitably compromise the justice of society in Rawls's own
terms. In Cohen's view, the establishment of a society that is just by
Rawlsian standards would require the prevalence of an "*ethos* of justice
that informs individual choices"[8] and leads individuals to restrain their
self-interested economic behavior. Cohen's claim, in other words, is that
the norms of justice must guide individual conduct as well as regulating
institutional design, if a just society is to be achieved.

Liam Murphy, meanwhile, thinks that the point of Rawls's institutional division of labor is "to take the business of securing justice off
people's plates in their day-to-day lives" so that "they can devote most of
their concerns to their own affairs."[9] The point is "to minimize the costs
people must sustain to secure justice" (IDJ 259). Ultimately, Murphy
believes, Rawls's aim is to develop a conception of justice that is "less
intrusive, and in that sense less demanding" (IDJ 288) of individuals.
The institutional division of labor, according to Murphy, is offered by
Rawls as a device for doing this. As such, Murphy says, it is taken by
Rawls as counting in favor of what Murphy calls "dualism," which in his
parlance is the view that different normative principles apply to the basic
structure and to individual action, and which thus corresponds to what
I have called the division of moral labor.

Murphy agrees that it is desirable to reduce the burdens for individuals of securing justice, so far as this is possible, and he finds the idea of
an institutional division of labor plausible, at least up to a point. But he
denies that this idea provides any support for dualism. Indeed, he argues
that the implications of the dualistic view for questions of individual
duty are perverse. Rawls says that individuals have a duty to support

7. G. A. Cohen, "Where the Action Is: On the Site of Distributive Justice," *Philosophy & Public Affairs* 26, n. 1 (Winter 1997), 3–30, at p. 16.

8. *Ibid.*, p. 10.

9. Liam Murphy, "Institutions and the Demands of Justice," *Philosophy & Public Affairs* 27, n. 4 (Fall 1998), 251–291, at p. 258. Cited hereafter as IDJ, with page references given parenthetically.

just institutions when they exist and to assist in the establishment of such institutions when they do not already exist. Yet Murphy argues that, because Rawls interprets the principles of justice themselves as purely institutional norms, he does not ascribe to individuals any duty directly to address the concerns that underlie and motivate an interest in justice. Instead, individuals' "concern with inequality or the amount of suffering abroad is necessarily *mediated* through institutional structures" (IDJ 280). Murphy finds this implausible. "If people have a duty to promote just institutions, why do they lack a duty to promote whatever it is that just institutions are *for*?" (IDJ 280). Often, he concedes, the best way for people to promote the ends that underlie our interest in justice will be precisely by promoting just institutions. However, the Rawlsian position would appear to require a person "to promote just institutions even if she is sure that the *aim* of the just institutions she is promoting would be better served if she herself pursued that aim directly" (IDJ 281). And it is this that Murphy finds implausible.

In their different ways, both Cohen and Murphy insist that a concern with justice must directly inform the motives of individual agents. Unless the aim of achieving justice has its place in the motivational repertoire of individuals, a just society will, in Cohen's view, be unattainable, and the duty to promote just institutions will, in Murphy's view, seem perverse. Both Cohen and Murphy object to the sharp discontinuity they see in Rawls's account between the values that regulate institutional design and those that regulate individual conduct. Combining their objections, we might say: treating justice as a purely institutional value is both incompatible with the attainment of a just society and incongruous with any reasonable account of the bases for our concern with the justice of our institutions.

Thomas Nagel is more sympathetic than either Cohen or Murphy to the idea of a division of moral labor (or what he calls a "moral division of labor"), but he agrees that the motive of securing justice must somehow inform the choices of individuals if the division of labor is to be both stable and successful in achieving its aims. He believes that, in order for a successful division of labor to be achievable, its motivational basis must derive from the "division in each individual between two standpoints, the personal and the impersonal."[10] His idea is that, although the division of labor assigns the task of securing justice mostly to social institutions, that task is congenial to the impersonal standpoint and hence to

---

10. Thomas Nagel, *Equality and Partiality* (New York: Oxford University Press 1991), p. 3. Cited hereafter as EP, with page references given parenthetically.

one aspect of the self. In consequence, it is possible that individuals can be motivated to support just institutions in such a way as to stabilize the division of labor. As Nagel puts the point, "the aim is to external-ize through social institutions the most impartial requirements of the impersonal standpoint, but our support of those institutions depends on the fact that they answer to the demands of a very important part of ourselves" (EP 53).

Nevertheless, Nagel is not altogether confident that it will be possible in the end to achieve a successful division of labor of the kind that egali-tarian liberals seek. He fears that the tension within egalitarian liberalism "between its public impersonal egalitarianism and its encouragement of the private pursuit of personal aims may be too sharp to permit coher-ent reflection in the integrated but internally differentiated personality of the individuals who are supposed to embrace them both" (EP 59). Echoing a point made forcefully by Cohen, he says that, within a Rawl-sian scheme that provides talented people with inequality-generating economic incentives when this is necessary to maximize the position of the worst-off group, "the egalitarian sense of fairness must make us regard as unfortunate those very inequalities which as economic actors we are bent on getting the benefit of" (EP 116). This requires a "parti-tion of motives" which enables us simultaneously to regard some of the inequalities tolerated by the system as "unfair and morally suspect" (EP 117) and to believe that "one is entitled to try to get as much out of the system as one can" (EP 117). This partition of motives, he believes, is "not strictly intelligible" (EP 117). As he puts it, "the combination of egalitarian public values and inegalitarian personal aims to which we are forced by motivational logic simply lacks the character of an integrated moral outlook" (EP 117).

The various criticisms and doubts expressed by Cohen, Murphy, and Nagel present a significant set of challenges to egalitarian liberalism. At the same time, some of those criticisms and doubts seem to me to involve misinterpretations of Rawls, and some of them rest on what I take to be an unattractive interpretation of the idea of a division of moral labor. I want now to clarify these points in order to bring into sharper focus both the problems and the attractions of egalitarian liberalism.

To begin with, it is important not to exaggerate the extent to which Rawls insulates individual conduct and motives from considerations of justice. As we have seen, and as Cohen, Murphy, and Nagel all recognize, Rawls says that individuals have duties to support and to comply with just institutions, and that they must have a "strong and normally effec-tive...sense of justice" that leads them to do this (TJ 454/398 rev.). In addition, one of Rawls's reasons for treating the basic structure as the primary subject of justice has to do with the way in which social institutions inevitably shape individuals' wants and aspirations. Because of these effects, the choice of institutions must be made on moral grounds, and institutions "must be not only just but framed so as to encourage the virtue of justice in those who take part in them" (TJ 261/231 rev.). In other words, the institutions that make up the basic structure must be designed "to foster the virtue of justice and to discourage desires and aspirations incompatible with it" (TJ 261/231 rev.). Thus, although the basic structure is the primary subject of justice, and although the principles of justice are not framed as direct or general guidelines for individual conduct, those principles do have implications both for individuals' duties and for questions of individual motivation.

Contrary to what Murphy maintains, moreover, the point of the institutional division of labor, according to Rawls, is not to make the task of achieving social justice less burdensome or demanding for individuals. Nor, a fortiori, is the ability of the institutional division of labor to accomplish this aim supposed to count as an argument in favor of dualism (the division of moral labor). Rather, the point of the institutional division of labor is to secure the background conditions necessary to ensure that voluntary transactions among individuals are fair. And the importance of securing background justice is, again, one of the reasons Rawls gives for treating the basic structure as the primary subject of justice. As we have seen, he believes that background justice must be secured by institutions because it cannot be secured through individual action alone. In other words, Rawls's concern is not that it would be excessively intrusive or costly or burdensome for individuals to achieve background justice, but rather that it is simply beyond their capacity to do so. As evidence for his interpretation, Murphy cites Rawls's statement that "[i]f this division of labor can be established, individuals and associations are then left free to advance their ends more effectively within the framework of the basic structure, secure in the knowledge that elsewhere in the social system the necessary corrections to preserve background justice are being made" (PL 269). But the context of this remark makes it clear that the implied contrast is not with a situation in which, because there is no division of labor, individuals are compelled, at great cost, to preserve background justice themselves. The contrast is rather with a situation in which, because there is no division of labor, background justice is unachievable, and individuals must live with the knowledge that this is so.[11]

11. My discussion of this point is indebted to an unpublished presentation given by Jake Bassett in a graduate seminar I taught at Berkeley in 2000.

Although neither Cohen nor Nagel ascribes to Rawls the aim of making justice less costly for individuals, they both agree that the effect of the division-of-labor idea is to provide individual agents with a wide-ranging justification for self-interested economic behavior. This interpretation inverts the explicit motivation for Rawls's institutional division of labor, which, as we have seen, is to put constraints on individual economic transactions in order to preserve background justice. And it effaces the distinctive form of moral pluralism that is reflected in the idea of a division of moral labor. After all, Rawlsian pluralism does not imply that individuals should be guided solely by economic self-interest, but rather that they should be responsive to the full range of values and norms that apply to individuals and their conduct.

It is worth noting in this connection that, in Nagel's own development of the idea of a "moral division of labor," he does not mark the difference between the two contrasts I have located in Rawls's work. That is, he does not distinguish between what I have called "the division of moral labor" and what I have called "the institutional division of labor." Since Nagel does not purport to be describing Rawls's view, this is not, of course, an interpretative failing. But it does mean that, in his own development of the division-of-labor idea, he tends to elide the difference between the two contrasts. In consequence, a general problem concerning the implications of moral pluralism tends to be assimilated to a specific problem about the role of the market in an egalitarian society. The general problem is how different kinds of moral values and norms can be jointly realized in practice. The specific problem is how to reconcile an egalitarian tax structure with a market framework that provides incentives to those with scarce talents and assumes that individuals will be motivated primarily to advance their economic self-interest. Thus, on the one hand, Nagel gives a general characterization of the idea of a division of labor that is cast in the language of value pluralism: "Ideally the moral division of labor would assign the bulk of agent-neutral values to be realized by background institutions, leaving us relatively free to pursue agent-relative values in our personal lives' (EP 85–6). On the other hand, however, his discussion of the prospects for a division of labor is concerned primarily with the difficulty of "combining political egalitarianism with personal acquisitiveness" (EP 121).

The tendency to assimilate these two problems is facilitated by the close connection Nagel draws between his moral division of labor and the distinction between the personal and impersonal standpoints. His reliance on that distinction, which is purportedly internal to each individual, is intended to provide a way of securing the motivational conditions for a successful division of labor. By associating institutional norms with the impersonal standpoint, which is itself construed as a feature or aspect of each individual's outlook, Nagel means to give justice a motivational base within the self. Yet, at the same time, his position seems to imply that all noninstitutional norms should be associated with "the personal point view," and this makes it easier to overlook the variety and heterogeneity of noninstitutional values and norms. For example, it makes it easier to overlook the point, on which Rawls for one insists, that the distinction between the principles that regulate the basic structure and those that apply to individual conduct is not exhaustive; there may be independent values and principles that apply to groups and associations of other kinds. In Nagel's rendering, all noninstitutional values, having been associated with the personal point of view, tend to be grouped together as "personal concerns," for which economic self-interest may then seem like a plausible proxy.

Even if the distinction between the principles that regulate the basic structure and those that apply to individual action were exhaustive, any attempt to ground it in the distinction between the personal and impersonal standpoints would be incongruous with the psychologically unified character of our reactive responses to individual and institutional misconduct. I may resent my own mistreatment, or be indignant at the mistreatment of someone else, by either an individual agent or an institution. At the level of psychology, there is no discontinuity in these responses, as one might expect there to be if the distinction between individual and institutional norms were associated with divergent aspects of the self or with sharply opposed sources of motivation. Instead, our reactive responses routinely and unreflectively stray back and forth across the conceptual line that distinguishes individual from institutional misconduct, with no sense that this very continuity of response results from a heroic feat of psychological integration. Thus, there is no reason to suppose that our moral assessments of individual agents and our moral assessments of institutions are associated with fundamentally different ways of looking at the world, or that the values that we apply to individuals derive from the personal side of ourselves whereas the values we apply to institutions derive from the impersonal side. Indeed, if the distinction between individual and institutional norms is associated with the distinction between the personal and impersonal standpoints, the psychologically unified character of our reactive responses seems difficult to explain.

This is symptomatic of a more general problem with Nagel's approach, to which I am otherwise sympathetic. We have seen that, by associating institutional norms with the impersonal standpoint, which he takes to be one of two divergent perspectives within each individual, Nagel aims to give egalitarian justice a motivational base within the self. The difficulty with this strategy, however, is that it relocates within the structure of the self the sharp discontinuity between institutional norms and personal motives that was taken by Cohen and Murphy to constitute the basic problem for the division-of-labor idea. Once this discontinuity is taken to have its roots in the opposition between two diametrically opposed aspects of the self, it becomes more rather than less difficult to see how it might be overcome. As Nagel observes, "motivational logic" then makes it seem as if the concerns associated with the two different standpoints are doomed to pull in different directions, and it is this that leaves him pessimistic about the prospects for a successful division of labor. I have been arguing, however, that there is no discontinuity at the level of moral psychology that corresponds to the distinction between institutional and noninstitutional values, and so it is a mistake to associate the division of moral labor with a distinction between two aspects of the self.

The upshot of these reflections is that, although the idea of a division of labor has featured prominently in a number of discussions of egalitarian liberalism, these discussions have offered differing interpretations of the idea and its motivations, and they have tended to obscure its appeal. "The division of moral labor," as I understand it, is not intended to make justice less burdensome or costly for individuals; it does not provide a justification for "unlimited self-seekingness in the economic choices" of individuals; and it is not a device for reconciling divergent aspects of the self. Instead, it represents a distinctive form of pluralism about value, and it suggests a way of reconciling diverse values that would otherwise come into conflict with one another. The idea is that social institutions inevitably play a special role in determining people's economic expectations, shaping their characters, and structuring the background against which they enter into agreements with one another. In view of these features, social institutions are subject to special normative principles, and the achievement of social justice will depend primarily on the extent to which the basic structure of society conforms to those principles. One particularly important task for the basic structure will be to put in place an "institutional division of labor," comprising a set of institutional mechanisms and a set of legal regulations governing individual transactions, whose joint effect will be to establish background justice and ensure that it is not undermined by the cumulative effects of voluntary exchanges over time. Despite the primary role of the basic structure, justice is not exclusively an institutional value. Individuals too have duties of justice, and just institutions will shape people's motives so as to discourage individual conduct that is incompatible with justice. But, on the one hand, the primary subject of justice remains the basic structure of society and, on the other hand, there are many other values and norms that should appropriately regulate individual conduct within the basic structure.

The main appeal of the division of labor so understood lies in its affirmation of pluralism and in the strategy it suggests for accommodating that pluralism. Its attractions can be exhibited most readily by contrasting it again with consequentialism and libertarianism. Egalitarian liberalism insists on the autonomy of the values and norms governing human interpersonal relations, and it refuses to treat them, in the consequentialist manner, as having only derivative significance. Those values are part of a conceptual and normative repertoire that we are given by virtue of our participation in forms of human interaction and aspiration that are so basic that we cannot really envision what human social life would be like without them. They do not need to be justified by reference to some putatively more fundamental level of value. To this extent, egalitarian liberalism acknowledges the force of the libertarian position. Yet, at the same time, it denies that our normative repertoire is exhausted by the values that govern our personal lives and small-scale interpersonal relations. The profoundly formative institutions of complex, modern societies have capabilities, natures, and social roles that differ radically from those of individual human agents, and different principles apply to them. The familiar commonsense principles of individual conduct are not an adequate guide to institutional design. To this extent, egalitarian liberalism acknowledges the force of the consequentialist position. Moreover, as I have argued elsewhere,[12] egalitarian liberalism also agrees with consequentialism that, in matters of distributive justice, the assessment of overall social arrangements takes conceptual and normative priority over the assessment of individual shares. For both views, in other words, the justice of a single individual's share always depends on the justice, as judged by an independent standard, of the overall social distribution that obtains. In this sense, both views endorse *holistic* accounts of distributive justice. This contrasts with the libertarian approach, which treats the justice of overall distributions as dependent on and derivative from a prior accounting of what each individual is due.[13]

In addition to affirming a form of pluralism that distinguishes egalitarian liberalism from both libertarianism and consequentialism, the idea of

---

12. "Rawls and Utilitarianism," in S. Freeman (ed.), *The Cambridge Companion to Rawls* (Cambridge: Cambridge University Press 2003), 426–459, reprinted in *Boundaries and Allegiances*, 149–172. See also the Introduction to *Boundaries and Allegiances*.
13. I have discussed holism about distributive justice in the following writings, in addition to those cited in note 12 above: "Justice and Desert in Liberal Theory," *California Law Review* 88, n. 3 (May 2000), 965–990, reprinted in *Boundaries and Allegiances*, 173–196; "Distributive Justice and Economic Desert," in S. Olsaretti, (ed.), *Desert and Justice* (Oxford: Clarendon Press 2003), 69–91; "Replies to Ashford, Miller, and Rosen," *Philosophical Books* 44, n. 2 (April 2003), 125–134.

a division of moral labor embodies a strategy for resolving the tensions to which pluralism gives rise. If social institutions are designed in conformity with the principles of justice, then, it suggests, individual conduct within those institutions may legitimately be responsive to the various norms and ideals that govern our personal lives and interpersonal relationships. Since some of these norms and ideals may be quite stringent, it does not follow that the division of moral labor liberates individuals from moral demands, still less that it enables them to engage in the unlimited pursuit of self-interest, economic or otherwise. The division of labor is appealing because it offers a strategy, not for the reconciliation of egalitarian justice and personal acquisitiveness, but rather for the joint accommodation of diverse values.

Yet if recent discussions have tended to obscure the appeal of the division-of-labor idea, they have also tended to mischaracterize its real difficulties. The central question is not whether equality can be reconciled with personal acquisitiveness but whether the proposed strategy for accommodating pluralism can succeed. As I have said, it is an advantage of egalitarian liberalism that, unlike either libertarianism or consequentialism, it affirms the autonomy and mutual independence of two sets of values whose place in our normative thought is secure. But this means that, unlike either of those other views, egalitarian liberalism needs to show that both sets of values can coherently be incorporated within a single normative scheme and jointly accommodated within a single social world. It is not enough, by way of demonstrating this, simply to say that institutions have the primary responsibility for achieving social justice and that individuals and groups may legitimately be responsive to values of other kinds. It needs to be shown that these different sets of values can be jointly realized without undermining one another. For example, can the limitations on bequest that may be necessary to achieve and preserve a just distribution of resources be imposed without undermining the ability of parents to discharge their obligations to their children? Are the limitations on voluntary transactions that may be necessary to preserve background justice compatible with individual autonomy and with individuals' legitimate interest in developing their own projects and plans? What is to guarantee that it will not be necessary to choose, in these and many other cases, between the achievement of social justice and a respect for other, noninstitutional values and norms?

The same point can be put another way. The idea of a division of moral labor represents an attempt to accommodate the multifaceted character of our own values: to make room for the irreducibly heterogeneous character of the evaluative concerns that move us. The aim is to accommodate these different values by allowing them regulative authority over different aspects of our lives and social arrangements. A successful allocation of this kind must be capable of being stably embedded within human social practices and (as Nagel emphasizes) within the motivational repertoires of individual human agents, and it must leave us feeling that we have succeeded in doing justice to the diversity of our own values. This means that such an allocation must be a social and not purely a theoretical achievement, and there is no a priori guarantee that a successful allocation will be available. This is a fundamental problem for egalitarian liberalism, and its character is only obscured if one treats the division-of-labor idea as a way of justifying the pursuit of individual self-interest rather than as an expression of value pluralism.

The temptation to do this, however, does not result from a simple misunderstanding. It arises because there are two strands in egalitarian liberalism that have not always been sufficiently distinguished. The first strand, which I have been emphasizing, is the pluralistic strand. This is the dimension of egalitarian liberalism that opposes the libertarian and consequentialist conceptions of the normative realm. The second strand is what might be called the economic strand. This is the dimension of egalitarian liberalism that seeks to reconcile an egalitarian conception of justice with some form of market economy. The first strand corresponds roughly to what I have been calling the division of moral labor, while the second corresponds roughly to the division of institutional labor. The tendency of recent discussions has been to assimilate the first strand to the second, thus obscuring the differences between them. But it is the first strand that is normatively fundamental, for if it is desirable to reconcile egalitarian justice with a market economy that is only because such a reconciliation would make possible the joint accommodation of diverse values. So the assimilation of the first strand to the second also obscures the ultimate appeal of egalitarian liberalism, as well as the real difficulties that it faces.

This is not to dismiss or deny the importance of the various challenges that have been posed to the economic strand. Many people are understandably sceptical about the extent to which market mechanisms can coherently be included within the framework of an egalitarian conception of justice. Cohen in particular has developed this kind of scepticism with great force, and liberal egalitarians cannot afford to ignore his arguments.[14] Defenders of Rawls's position, for example, must respond

14. See, in addition to the article by Cohen cited above, the following of his writings: "Incentives, Inequality, and Community," in Grethe B. Peterson, (ed.), *The Tanner Lectures on Human Values* 13 (Salt Lake City: University of Utah Press 1992), 263–329; "The Pareto Argument for Inequality," *Social Philosophy and Policy* 12, n. 1 (Winter 1995), 160–185; *If You're an Egalitarian, How Come You're So Rich?* (Cambridge, MA: Harvard University Press 2000).

to Cohen's claim that the achievement of Rawlsian justice would be compromised by the economic incentives allowable under the terms of the "lax interpretation" of the difference principle and by the kind of self-interested economic behavior that would be legitimate within the rules established by the basic structure. I have discussed Cohen's arguments at length elsewhere[15] and cannot give them serious consideration here, but let me conclude by indicating in a very general and I'm afraid rather cryptic way what I take to be the bearing on his critique of the arguments I have been developing in this essay.

Suppose we distinguish among three different questions: (1) To what extent would individuals in a society with a just basic structure be motivated by economic self-interest? (2) To what extent should individuals in such a society be motivated by economic self-interest? (3) To what extent would a just society accede to the demands of talented people that they be provided with economic incentives to work more productively? Keeping in mind the idea of a division of moral labor, it seems to me natural for egalitarian liberals to respond along the following lines. First, the institutions of a just society would support the development of aspirations and traits of character that would limit the extent of personal acquisitiveness among citizens.[16] Second, individual conduct should be guided by the full range of applicable norms and values, and should not consist solely or primarily in the pursuit of economic self-interest. Third, a just society would accede to demands for economic incentives only if those demands could be justified by reference to the norms and values that apply to individual conduct: by reference, for example, to individuals' obligations to assist members of their own families, or to their legitimate interest in developing their own projects and plans. Of course, these replies all require elaboration and defense, but I hope that the general moral is clear. The egalitarian-liberal idea of a division of moral labor represents an acknowledgment of, and a strategy for accommodating, the diversity of our values. It is not an apology for economic self-interest or a device for justifying personal acquisitiveness. What the division of moral labor tells us about economic self-interest is that its legitimate social role will depend on the place of self-interest among the full range of our values. The larger challenge for the division-of-labor idea, and for egalitarian liberalism more generally, derives from the same pluralism that is the primary source of its appeal. Egalitarian liberalism is an optimistic view,

---

15. In "Is the Basic Structure Basic?" *op. cit.*
16. For helpful discussion of this point, see Joshua Cohen, "Taking People as They Are?" *Philosophy & Public Affairs* 30, n. 4 (Fall 2001), 363–386.

because, unlike forms of pluralism that treat painful conflicts among our values as ineliminable, it supposes that we can design our social world in such a way as to accommodate the most important of those values and to reconcile the conflicting tendencies to which they give rise. There may be more reasons to hope than there are to believe that this sort of optimism is warranted and that the project of joint accommodation can succeed. But the tradition of egalitarian liberalism has enough to recommend it, and it has proved sufficiently resourceful to date, that it would be premature to declare the project a failure.

5

Is the Basic Structure Basic?

Rawls says in *A Theory of Justice* that, for him, "the primary subject of justice is the basic structure of society, or more exactly, the way in which the major social institutions distribute fundamental rights and duties and determine the division of advantages from social cooperation" (1971 [1999]: 7[6]).[1] In the course of his sustained and wide-ranging critique of Rawls's political philosophy, G. A. Cohen subjects this aspect of Rawls's view to withering critical scrutiny. In this chapter,

Originally published in *The Egalitarian Conscience: Essays in Honour of G. A. Cohen*, Christine Sypnowich (ed.) (Oxford University Press, 2006), 102–129. Reprinted by permission of the Oxford University Press. I am grateful to Jerry Cohen, Samuel Freeman, Niko Kolodny, and Michael Titelbaum for valuable written comments on an earlier version of this chapter. I have also benefited from discussions with Meir Dan-Cohen, Kerstin Haase, Thomas Nagel, and Eric Rakowski.
1. Cited hereafter with page references to both editions (1971 [1999]).

I want to assess the force of Cohen's objections. I will begin by considering what Rawls means when he says that the basic structure is the primary subject of justice, and by examining the motivations for his view. I will then summarize Cohen's arguments and ask whether those arguments succeed in undermining Rawls's position. My ultimate aim is not to interpret or defend Rawls, but rather to consider the merits of focusing on the basic structure as the primary subject of justice.

As I have noted, Rawls takes the "basic structure" to comprise a society's "major social institutions." These institutions are understood to include "the political constitution and the principal economic and social arrangements" (ibid.). Rawls emphasizes that his inquiry is a limited one and that the justice of the basic structure is only "a special case of the problem of justice" (ibid. 7[7]). The principles of justice that apply to the basic structure may not be the appropriate principles of justice for regulating private groups or associations, the customs and conventions of everyday life, the law of nations, or voluntary cooperative agreements in general. Thus, for example, his defense of "justice as fairness" should not be taken to imply that churches and scholarly organizations must seek to implement the difference principle or that the conventions of etiquette must incorporate the principle of fair equality of opportunity.

Nor should we assume that the principles of justice that are appropriate for the basic structure can also serve to regulate individual conduct in general. "The principles of justice for institutions must not be confused with the principles which apply to individuals and their actions in particular circumstances. These two kinds of principles apply to different subjects and must be discussed separately" (ibid. 54–5[47]). The principles of individual conduct must address the full range of moral requirements and permissions that apply to us as individuals. They must clarify the nature of our obligations and natural duties, and they must address a wide variety of topics including supererogation, mutual aid, and personal virtues such as beneficence, courage, and mercy (ibid., sect. 18). In contrast to utilitarianism, as it is usually interpreted, Rawls does not suppose that his theory is a completely general moral outlook that "applies equally to all social forms and to the actions of individuals" (Rawls 1993: 260). Indeed, he says that "[t]he first principles of justice as fairness are plainly not suitable for a general theory" (ibid. 261). He is, in this sense, a pluralist about moral principles, and his claim that the basic structure is the primary subject of justice is in part an expression of methodological modesty. Rawls presents his principles as having limited scope; they are framed so as to apply to major social institutions and do not constitute principles for the general regulation of groups, associations, and individuals.

To be sure, he believes that certain principles for individuals "are an essential part of any theory of justice" (1971[1999]: 108[93]), because they specify how individuals are to conduct themselves in relation to just institutions. He includes as part of his theory two such principles: the principle of fairness, which accounts for all of our voluntarily incurred obligations, and the principle governing the natural duty of justice. "This duty," Rawls says, "requires us to support and to comply with just institutions that exist and apply to us," and "to further just arrangements not yet established, at least when this can be done without too much cost to ourselves" (ibid. 115[99]). He also emphasizes that, in order for a society to be "well ordered," its major institutions "must be not only just but framed so as to encourage the virtue of justice in those who take part in them" (ibid. 261[231]). Citizens must have a "strong and normally effective" (ibid. 454[398]) sense of justice. They must be motivated to "accept the just institutions that apply to" them, to do their "part in maintaining these arrangements," and to "work for (or at least not to oppose) the setting up of just institutions, and for the reform of existing ones when justice requires it" (ibid. 474[415]). Despite the fact that the principles of justice for the basic structure are framed so as to apply to institutions and do not constitute principles for the general regulation of individual conduct, then, Rawls takes them to have an important bearing both on individuals' responsibilities and on their motives. At the same time, this formulation itself reveals another aspect of the claim that the basic structure is the primary subject of justice: the principles for the basic structure are primary in the sense that the principles for individuals depend on them. We cannot know how considerations of distributive justice should affect individual conduct until the principles for the basic structure are in hand. Appealing to "the social nature of the virtue of justice," Rawls asserts "that a person's obligations and duties presuppose a moral conception of institutions and therefore that the content of just institutions must be defined before the requirements for individuals can be set out" (ibid. 110[95]).

In *A Theory of Justice* and in subsequent writings, Rawls gives a number of different reasons, beyond those that are implicit in what has already been said, for treating the basic structure as primary. His various discussions of this topic differ in emphasis, organization, and detail, but I want to highlight three considerations he mentions that seem to me particularly significant. In summarizing these considerations, I will quote extensively from Rawls's texts, because I think that his views have been frequently misunderstood and I want to convey some of the substance and flavor of his own formulations. First, he says that the "basic structure is the primary subject of justice because its effects are so profound and present from the start" (ibid. 7[7]). People born into different social positions have different expectations in life, and their more or less favorable prospects cannot possibly be justified by an appeal to their prior merit or desert. Because one's initial social position has such a profound effect on one's chances in life, and because any inequalities resulting from differences in people's starting places are "especially deep" and "pervasive," it is essential that a society's major institutions, and the social positions they determine, should be regulated by norms of justice (ibid.).

Second, the basic structure "shapes the wants and aspirations that its citizens come to have. It determines in part the sort of persons they want to be as well as the sort of persons they are. Thus an economic system is not only an institutional device for satisfying wants and needs but a way of creating and fashioning wants in the future" (ibid. 259[229]). Because of this, the choice of social institutions "involves some view of human good and of the design of institutions to realize it" (ibid. 259–260[229]). This is a choice that must "be made on moral and political as well as on economic grounds" (ibid. 260[229]). After all, people's wants and interests "are not fixed or given" (Rawls 1993: 269). The desires and aspirations that individuals happen to have at any given moment enjoy no default moral authority. Antecedently, there is no more reason to endorse the status quo with respect to the distribution of desires and interests than there is to endorse the existing distribution of property. A "theory of justice must take into account how the aims and aspirations of people are formed" (ibid.), and it cannot remain "at the mercy, so to speak, of existing wants and desires" (Rawls 1971[1999]: 261[231]). It must instead consider how "the basic structure shapes the way the social system produces and reproduces over time a certain form of culture shared by persons with certain conceptions of their good" (Rawls 1993: 269). Just institutions must be designed so as "to foster the virtue of justice and discourage desires and aspirations incompatible with it" (Rawls 1971[1999]: 261[231]).

Third, we cannot tell whether agreements and transactions among individuals are just simply by looking to the local contexts of those agreements and transactions. Instead, "certain background conditions are necessary if transactions between individuals are to be fair" (Rawls 1993: 269). Moreover, even if fair background conditions exist at a particular time, that does not suffice to ensure the fairness of all subsequent transactions among individuals. "Even though the initial state may have been just, and subsequent social conditions may also have been just for some time, the accumulated results of many separate and seemingly fair agreements entered into by individuals and associations are likely over an extended period to undermine the background conditions required for

IS THE BASIC STRUCTURE BASIC?

free and fair agreements" (Rawls 2001: 53). In order for agreements and transactions among individuals to be just, it is necessary both to secure and to preserve just background conditions. This task cannot be accomplished by individuals, for "there are no feasible and practicable rules that it is sensible to impose on individuals that can prevent the erosion of background justice" (Rawls 1993: 267). The rules applying to individual transactions and agreements are "practical and public directives" (ibid. 268). As such, they "cannot be too complex, or require too much information to be correctly applied" (ibid. 267). They cannot "exceed the capacity of individuals to grasp and follow them with sufficient ease," nor can they "burden citizens with requirements of knowledge and foresight that they cannot normally meet" (ibid. 268). Rawls argues that there simply are no feasible rules of individual conduct that are capable of preserving background justice and that do not violate these conditions. He writes:

> Individuals and associations cannot comprehend the ramifications of their particular actions viewed collectively, nor can they be expected to foresee future circumstances that shape and transform present tendencies. All of this is evident enough if we consider the cumulative effects of the purchase and sale of landed property and its transmission by bequest over generations. It is obviously not sensible to impose on parents (as heads of families) the duty to adjust their own bequests to what they estimate the effects of the totality of actual bequests will be on the next generation, much less beyond. (ibid.)

Rawls believes that the task of ensuring background justice can only be performed by the institutions that make up the basic structure:

> The role of the institutions that belong to the basic structure is to secure just background conditions against which the actions of individuals and associations take place. Unless this structure is appropriately regulated and adjusted, an initially just social process will eventually cease to be just, however free and fair particular transactions may look when viewed by themselves. (ibid. 266)

He concludes that we should seek "an institutional division of labor between the basic structure and the rules applying directly to individuals and associations and to be followed by them in particular transactions" (ibid. 268–269). The basic structure includes "those operations that continually adjust and compensate for the inevitable

tendencies away from background fairness, for example, such operations as income and inheritance taxation designed to even out the own-
ership of property" (ibid. 268). The rules applying to individuals and
associations include such things as "rules relating to fraud and duress,"
which "satisfy the requirements of simplicity and practicality" (ibid.).
Rawls says that if "this division of labor can be established, individuals
and associations are then left free to advance their ends more effectively
within the framework of the basic structure, secure in the knowledge
that elsewhere in the social system the necessary corrections to preserve
background justice are being made" (ibid. 269).

Before turning to a consideration of Cohen's criticisms of Rawls, let
me make three observations about Rawls's account. First, Rawls actually
draws two different contrasts between the norms that govern the basic
structure and norms of other kinds. As we have seen, he draws a general
distinction between the principles of justice that apply to the basic structure and the principles that apply to individual conduct and to groups
and associations. The point of this contrast is to allow for the plurality of
values and principles and to clarify the limited scope of Rawls's project.
His two principles of justice are not proposed as a codification of the
entire content of morality, nor are they meant to preempt or supersede
the many other norms that also apply to individuals and associations. In
addition, however, Rawls also speaks more narrowly of an "institutional
division of labor" between "two kinds of social rules, and the different
institutional forms in which these rules are realized" (ibid. 268). The idea
is that the basic structure includes one set of operations (such as income
and inheritance taxation) that is designed to preserve background justice
over time, and that it "also enforces through the legal system another set
of rules that govern the transactions and agreements between individuals and associations" (ibid.). This other set of rules includes the law of
contract, and its function is to provide individuals with a set of clear and
practical guidelines that they can use to guide their economic transactions within a background framework whose fairness will be monitored
and preserved by the first set of institutional mechanisms and arrangements. The point here is not about pluralism or methodological modesty, but rather that, given the feasibility constraints that apply to the
rules regulating individual conduct, the institutional forms required to
ensure background justice will have to go beyond and help fix the content of those rules. At the risk of causing confusion rather than dispelling
it, I will refer to the first contrast as "the division of moral labor" between
the principles of justice that apply to the basic structure of society and
the values and principles that apply to other areas of life; and to the
second contrast, following Rawls, as the "institutional division of labor"

between those social forms that are required to ensure background justice and those that directly regulate individual economic transactions.

The second observation is that neither of these contrasts implies that the principles of justice for the basic structure have no bearing on individuals' duties and responsibilities. Nor do they imply that individuals' motives and attitudes can properly remain unaffected by those principles. As we have already seen, Rawls insists, to the contrary, that individuals have a natural duty to support just arrangements, and that a just and stable society will be impossible unless the members of society have a strong and normally effective sense of justice. Moreover, he says that just institutions must have the aim of encouraging the virtue of justice among citizens and "discouraging desires that conflict with the principles of justice" (Rawls 1971[1999]: 261 [230–231]). These claims are entirely consistent with the pluralism about value to which the division of moral labor is responsive. They are also consistent with Rawls's notion of an institutional division of labor, since his idea is merely that rules of individual conduct are insufficient to preserve background justice, not that individual conduct can properly remain uninformed by considerations of justice.

Finally, in drawing the two contrasts I have mentioned, Rawls's aim is not to explain how individuals can be freed from the burdensome responsibility of securing social justice. Nor is he attempting to demonstrate that a just set of social institutions would make it possible for individuals as economic actors to behave as unrestrained self-interested maximizers. The division of moral labor, as we have seen, responds to a form of pluralism about moral values and principles. The idea is not that there are no moral principles that regulate individual conduct, so that the field is clear for the unrestricted pursuit of self-interest, but rather that the principles for the basic structure do not supersede the complex and varied principles and values that apply to individuals. The institutional division of labor, meanwhile, responds to a problem about how background justice can be secured and preserved. The idea here is not to relieve individuals of a burdensome but feasible task, but rather that the task in question is one that individuals are incapable of discharging. Admittedly, Rawls courts misunderstanding of this point when he says: "If this division of labor can be established, individuals and associations are then left free to advance their ends more effectively within the framework of the basic structure, secure in the knowledge that elsewhere in the social system the necessary corrections to preserve background justice are being made" (1993: 269). This can easily be taken to mean that the division of labor is intended to leave individuals "free to advance their ends" rather than requiring them to preserve background justice. In this spirit,

Murphy interprets Rawls as wanting "to take the business of securing justice off people's plate" so that they can "devote most of their concerns to their own affairs," thus leading "freer and better lives" (1999: 258).[2] However, Rawls's point is very different, and it is clear enough in context. If the division of labor were not established, individuals would have no basis for confidence in the justice of their economic arrangements, even if each individual transaction were conducted in conformity with the fairest set of rules that it was feasible for individuals to abide by. The implication of Rawls's argument is not that, in the absence of a just basic structure, individuals would have to pick up the slack, which would be

---

2. Murphy gives what I regard as a misleading account of the relation between the institutional division of labor and the division of moral labor. He thinks that the former is motivated by a desire to limit the burdens on individuals and that, as such, it is meant to provide an *argument* for what he calls "dualism," which corresponds (roughly) to the division of moral labor. I have argued, by contrast, that the division of moral labor is a response to a general pluralism about value, whereas the institutional division of labor is responsive to an independent concern about the need to ensure background justice.

Murphy equates Rawls's account of the institutional division of labor with the idea of a "moral division of labor" described by Nagel (1991: ch. 6 in particular). Although Murphy's characterization seems fair enough as a description of Nagel's view, Rawls's view is very different. There is nothing in Rawls that corresponds to Nagel's distinction between the personal and impersonal standpoints within each individual, still less is the institutional division of labor proposed as a way of integrating those two standpoints. Julius (2003) also equates (one strand of) Rawls's position with Nagel's. He describes what he calls the "separation view," according to which the "separation of institutional and personal spaces of decision affords a division of labor whose function is to *externalize* the burdens of attention to justice" (ibid. 326–327), so that it is possible, compatibly with equality, for people "to pursue good lives for themselves, with every person attaching special importance to her own success" (ibid. 326). Although Julius says that "[t]he key to this outlook is Rawls's image of a *moral division of labor*" (ibid.), both the italicized phrase itself and the view to which it refers are drawn from Nagel rather than Rawls.

More generally, I believe that it is anachronistic to interpret Rawls, as both Murphy and Julius do in the passages I have cited (see also Murphy 1999: 288–291), as preoccupied with questions about the burdensomeness of justice or the demandingness of morality. Such questions began to attract widespread philosophical scrutiny with the publication of Williams's essay, "A Critique of Utilitarianism" (1973). But although, as I (Scheffler 1982: ch. 1) have argued, there are connections between Williams's and Rawls's criticisms of utilitarianism, questions about the relative demandingness of different moral norms did not loom large in *A Theory of Justice*, which was published two years before Williams's essay. I believe it is a mistake to read those preoccupations back into Rawls's text and treat them as supplying the motivation for his emphasis on the basic structure.

very burdensome for them, but rather that they would have no choice but to concede the injustice of their economic arrangements, at least until they were able to establish just institutions.[3]

Before turning to Cohen, let me address one question raised by the observations that I have made. I have emphasized that, despite Rawls's insistence that the basic structure is the primary subject of justice, he also thinks that just institutions must shape individuals' characters and regulate their conduct. A just social system must encourage the development within citizens of the virtue of justice, and it must discourage the formation of desires that conflict with the principles of justice. In

---

3. I am indebted here to an unpublished presentation given by Jake Bassett in a graduate seminar I taught in 2000. Murphy criticizes the suggestion Rawls (1993: 268) makes, when illustrating the idea of an institutional division of labor, that devices like income and inheritance taxation belong to the basic structure whereas the law of contract belongs to the rules that apply to individuals. Murphy argues that the institution of taxation is not intrinsically "less intrusive on people" (1999: 260) than the law of contract, so that the distinction Rawls draws "does not correspond to any principled doctrinal or structural division in legal systems" (ibid. 261). As I have argued, however, the point of the institutional division of labor is not to ensure that justice is achieved in a way that individuals do not find intrusive. Nor is it essential for Rawls that this division of labor should correspond to a deep or principled distinction in the law. His point is that the basic structure will need to include some institutional mechanisms that serve to adjust and compensate for deviations from background justice. Suitably designed institutions will be capable of gathering the extensive information and performing the complex calculations on which background justice depends, but which individuals could not reasonably be expected to have available to them for use in personal decision-making. There is no reason why the specific institutional mechanisms that are used to ensure background justice must be fixed or invariant, or why the distinction between those mechanisms and the rules applying to individual transactions must correspond to a deep, doctrinal division. The distinction between tax and contract is illustrative, not definitional or essential. All that is necessary is that the basic structure should include some mechanisms that go beyond the rules for individuals and that are designed to ensure background justice. Murphy protests that the rules applying to individuals cannot plausibly be thought to lie "entirely outside the purview of justice" (ibid.). But, as Murphy indirectly acknowledges, Rawls is clear about the fact that the rules applying to individual transactions are themselves rules that the basic structure "enforces through the legal system" (Rawls 1993: 268), so that they are not outside the purview of justice. Nor, as I will argue, does this undermine Rawls's claim that his principles of justice are framed so as to apply to institutions rather than individuals. On the one hand, the fact that just institutions will establish and enforce legal rules that apply to individuals does not imply that the principles of justice themselves apply directly to individual conduct; on the other hand, the fact that the principles will indirectly affect individuals, through the operation of just institutions, is not something that Rawls has any wish to deny.

addition, the basic structure must enforce through the legal system a set of rules that governs individual economic transactions. How, then, can Rawls continue to say that his principles of justice apply to the basic structure rather than to individual actions? This question will seem troubling, I believe, only if we suppose that Rawls's distinction between the principles that apply to institutions and those that apply to individuals is intended to place individuals beyond the reach of justice and to insulate them from its influence. However, Rawls's point is merely that his principles of justice are not framed as direct or general guidelines for individual conduct. On the one hand, the principles are framed in such a way as to guide institutions in securing the background justice and fairness of the social system, a task that individual agents cannot feasibly accomplish by themselves. On the other hand, the principles do not purport to codify or supersede the many other values and norms that appropriately apply to individual conduct. So individuals should not, in general, treat them as guides to personal decision making. But that is not to say that the principles of justice should have no impact on individuals' motives or that the basic structure cannot in turn enforce rules that apply to individuals. On the contrary, one of the most important tasks of the basic structure is to influence people's wants and aspirations, and another of its tasks is to regulate individual conduct in such a way as to preserve background justice. Yet we cannot know how considerations of justice should affect individuals until the principles for the basic structure are in hand.

As we will see, these points bear directly on the objections raised by Cohen. Cohen's critique of Rawls's focus on the basic structure begins with the observation that Rawls's difference principle is ambiguous as between a "strict" reading and a "lax" reading. The difference principle says "that inequalities are just if and only if they are necessary to make the worst-off people in society better off than they would otherwise be" (Cohen 1997: 5). The ambiguity to which Cohen calls attention concerns the interpretation that is given to the idea of a "necessary inequality." Suppose that, in order to maximize the position of the worst-off group, talented people are offered economic incentives to induce them to work more productively. Assuming that the talented would be unwilling to do this work unless they were given these incentives, are we to suppose that the difference principle treats the resulting inequalities as necessary in order to maximize the position of the worst-off people, and hence as just? According to the strict reading, the answer is no. Inequalities are necessary, in the relevant sense, only when, without them, the better paid would be *unable* to work as productively as they could have with extra income. In the case just described, the talented are not unable to work as productively without extra income, they are merely unwilling to do so. According to the lax reading, however, the answer is yes. Given that the talented will not in fact work as productively unless they are given extra income, the inequalities that result from giving them that income are indeed necessary in order to maximize the position of those who have least.

Cohen believes that there are strands in Rawls's work that support each of these incompatible interpretations, but he thinks that Rawls is sufficiently committed to the justice of economic incentives that the lax reading must be taken to represent his official position. Yet Cohen argues that the lax difference principle is not a principle of justice at all, as opposed to a principle of expediency, and that it is in any case incompatible with Rawls's own aspiration to provide a conception of justice for a well-ordered society in which all citizens have a strong and normally effective sense of justice that leads them willingly and wholeheartedly to support the conception of justice that regulates their social institutions. The talented members of a well-ordered Rawlsian society could not claim with a straight face that it was necessary to pay them extra to induce them to work more productively, since the only thing that could make this necessary would be a decision on their part not to work productively for less money, and that is not a decision they could defend compatibly with a wholehearted commitment to the difference principle itself.

Cohen concludes from this that, assuming the difference principle is meant to regulate "the affairs of a society whose members themselves accept that principle" (ibid. 6), it must be given a strict, rather than a lax, reading. Moreover, he thinks that the principle so construed justifies "hardly any serious inequality" (ibid.), for it is almost never true that the talented could not work just as productively without extra remuneration as they do with such remuneration. He also thinks it follows from his argument that "the justice of a society is not exclusively a function of its legislative structure, of its legally imperative rules, but also of the choices people make within those rules" (ibid. 9). These choices must be "appropriately informed by the difference principle" (ibid.). Or, as he says elsewhere, a "government cannot by itself implement" (1992: 315) the strict difference principle. In order for "the strict difference principle to prevail, there needs to be an ethos informed by the principle in society at large" (ibid.).

Cohen (1997) imagines that Rawlsians would reply to his argument by insisting that the difference principle is meant to apply only to the basic structure, and not to choices made by individuals within that structure. Although individuals must uphold the distributive principles governing the basic structure, this means only that they must willingly abide by the economic rules established by the structure. The principles need not, in addition, inform the choices that people make within the basic structure, from among those options not prohibited by the rules. Within the basic structure, the principles simply do not apply, and so they do not exclude purely self-interested economic decisions by individuals. Indeed, the principles are compatible with "unlimited self-seekingness in the economic choices of well-placed people" (ibid. 16).

Cohen labels this the "basic structure objection" (BSO) to his argument, and he offers two rejoinders. First, he says that the objection is inconsistent with a variety of comments Rawls makes about the role of principles of justice within the lives of citizens in a well-ordered society. Second, he asserts that there is another ambiguity in Rawls's position, an ambiguity in the concept of the basic structure itself. Sometimes Rawls seems to imply that the basic structure comprises only legally coercive social institutions, while at other times he says that institutions like the family, which, according to Cohen, depend less on law than on "convention, usage, and expectation" (ibid. 19), are also included within it. Cohen argues that if noncoercive practices and institutions are included, the BSO fails, because the behavior of individuals is constitutive of such practices and institutions. This implies that individual conduct cannot be excluded from the ambit of the principles of justice that apply to noncoercive structures. But if, on the other hand, Rawls limits the basic structure to legally coercive institutions, he contradicts his own rationale for treating the basic structure as the primary subject of justice, which has to do with the profound and far-reaching effects of that structure. Noncoercive practices and institutions have effects that are just as profound as the effects produced by coercive institutions, Cohen argues, so Rawls has no non-arbitrary grounds for excluding them. Cohen concludes that there is no way of disambiguating the concept of the basic structure that can vindicate the BSO. Furthermore, he says, the "fatal ambiguity" of that concept constitutes "a major fault line in the Rawlsian architectonic [which] not only wrecks the basic structure objection but also produces a dilemma for Rawls's view of the basic structure from which I can imagine no way out" (ibid. 18).

Cohen's masterful arguments expose two highly significant areas of unclarity in Rawls's theory. It is indeed unclear whether the difference principle should be given a strict or a lax interpretation, or perhaps some other interpretation altogether. It is also unclear how exactly Rawls understands the basic structure. These are issues of great importance for the interpretation of Rawls's theory and, in both cases, there are conflicting tendencies in his writing. Nevertheless, I do not believe that Cohen's arguments suffice to undermine Rawls's view of the basic structure as the primary subject of justice, nor do I believe that they undermine the two distinctions I have labelled 'the division of moral labor' and 'the institutional division of labor.'

Let me say, to begin with, that I very much doubt whether the BSO, as Cohen formulates it, is an objection that Rawls himself would have offered in response to Cohen's arguments against the legitimacy of incentive inequalities. This may seem a surprising thing to say, given Rawls's undoubted insistence on the primacy of the basic structure. However, the BSO, as Cohen develops it, goes beyond the claim that Rawls's principles of justice apply primarily to the basic structure. It includes, in addition, the idea that a just society is compatible with "unlimited self-seekingness in the economic choices of well-placed people" (ibid. 16). I doubt that Rawls would have taken this position. This is partly because, as we have seen and as Cohen himself emphasizes, there are many passages in Rawls's writing that are inconsistent with it. For example, it is very difficult to square the BSO, as Cohen formulates it, with Rawls's emphasis on the importance of the sense of justice and with the elaborate moral psychology that he develops in Part III of *Theory*. But there is also a deeper point lying behind the textual counter-evidence. When Cohen rejects the claim that the basic structure is the primary subject of justice, he does so because he associates it with a failure to condemn "the self-interested motivation of market maximizers" (Cohen 1997: 16). The alternative view with which he contrasts it, and which he himself recommends, is that individual behavior must be "appropriately informed by" (ibid. 9) the principles that regulate the basic structure. But when Rawls himself proposes the basic structure as subject, he does not say that individuals should be motivated purely by economic self-interest, nor does he contrast his position with the view that the principles of social justice should "appropriately inform" individual conduct. Instead, he contrasts it, in the case of the division of moral labor, with the view—exemplified by utilitarianism—that a single master principle or theory suffices to regulate both social institutions and individual conduct. He also contrasts it, in the case of the institutional division of labor, with the view that there are feasible principles of individual conduct that do not themselves presuppose principles for the basic structure and that are capable of preserving background justice. Neither of these contrasts implies any endorsement of "unlimited self-seekingness," or any hostility to the idea that individual conduct should be "appropriately informed" by the principles for the basic structure. Rawls does not claim that individual motivation should be entirely unaffected by the principles of social justice, nor do I believe he thinks any such thing. Indeed, as we have seen, one of his explicit reasons for giving primacy to the basic structure has to do with the role of social institutions in "creating and fashioning" (Rawls 1971[1999]:259[229]) citizens' wants and aspirations. Just institutions cannot treat existing desires as "fixed or given" (Rawls 1993: 269); they must instead "shape" those desires in accordance with "some view of human good" (Rawls 1971[1999]:259[229]) and they must have the aim "of discouraging desires that conflict with the principles of justice" or are "incompatible" with "the virtue of justice" (ibid. 261[230–231]).

Of course, as Cohen makes clear, Rawls never squarely confronts the question of how exactly individual economic choices should be informed by the principles of justice, and that is a significant omission. Yet, it is one thing to recognize the significance of the omission, and quite another to conclude that Rawls endorses unlimited self-seekingness or that he wishes to insulate individual motivation from any influence by the principles of justice. Neither of these things seems to me to be true. For this reason, I doubt whether Rawls would have offered the BSO, as Cohen has formulated it, in reply to Cohen's argument against incentive inequalities.

In view of these doubts, and in view of the fact that Cohen himself thinks that the BSO fails, it is worth asking whether there are other replies to the incentives argument that might be available to Rawls, and whether those replies would undermine Rawls's view that the basic structure is the primary subject of justice. To avoid misunderstanding, let me clarify the dialectical position as I understand it and the theoretical option that I wish to investigate. Cohen's original incentives argument confronts Rawls with the need to disambiguate the difference principle in light of the divergent interpretations provided by the lax and strict readings of that principle. Cohen imagines Rawls offering the BSO as a reply to the incentives argument, but Cohen argues that the ambiguity of the concept of the basic structure not only "wrecks the basic structure objection" but also poses an insuperable difficulty for the claim that the basic structure is the primary subject of justice. Cohen thus implies that Rawls would have to give up that claim even if he did not offer the BSO in reply to the incentives argument. It is the truth of this last contention that I wish to explore.

Suppose, then, that Rawls declined to offer the BSO in reply to Cohen. What other response to the incentives argument might be available to him? Recall, to begin with, that in Cohen's view, the correct interpretation of the difference principle, given Rawls's characterization of his enterprise, is the strict version, which, according to Cohen, licenses little or no inequality. As we have seen, however, Cohen believes that, while there is support for both interpretations of the principle in Rawls's texts, Rawls's commitment to incentives is sufficiently fundamental that he must be assumed to endorse the lax version. Now let me observe, parenthetically, that I am not convinced that Rawls's endorsement of incentives is as clear and unqualified as Cohen takes it to be, nor do I fully understand the basis on which Cohen, when confronted with what he sees as a conflict between passages in Rawls that support a lax reading and those that support a strict reading, decides that Rawls's actual position should be identified with the pro-lax passages. A similar point—or perhaps it is exactly the same point—applies to Cohen's handling of the conflict he perceives between passages in Rawls that support the BSO and those that are inconsistent with it.

However, I will not pursue this issue. Instead, I want to call attention to a feature of Cohen's presentation that seems to me even more puzzling. Suppose that Rawls—influenced by Cohen's arguments, perhaps—were to endorse the strict difference principle as the correct principle of justice to regulate the basic structure of society, which we may here take, counterfactually, to include only the coercive structure of its economic institutions. It follows that, in a well ordered Rawlsian society, just economic institutions would permit only those inequalities that were necessary, independently of people's choices, to maximize the position of the worst-off group. The choice-dependent incentive inequalities that the lax principle allows would not be provided to the talented in such a society and, if Cohen is correct, this means that there would be little or no inequality in that society. And this would be the result of the configuration of the coercive basic structure alone. Why, then, does Cohen conclude that "the government cannot by itself implement" the strict difference principle, or that in order for that principle "to prevail, there needs to be an ethos informed by the principle in society at large" (Cohen 1992: 315)? The answer, it seems to me, is obscure. It may well be true that, if the coercive structure were regulated by the *lax* principle, then economic equality would be achieved only if talented citizens had an egalitarian ethos, in consequence of which they did not demand special incentives to work productively. But it does not follow that, if the coercive structure were regulated by the *strict* principle, the achievement of equality would depend on such an ethos. Nor, so far as I can see, does Cohen ever argue for this conclusion. Indeed, he never seriously considers what it would mean for the coercive structure to be regulated by the strict principle. Instead, what he says is the following:

> . . . if we begin with an uninterpreted statement of the [difference] principle, where it is ambiguous across strict and lax interpretations, *and* we suppose that all of the people in the society it governs comply wholeheartedly with it, by which I mean that they are concerned to ensure that their own conduct is just in the

sense defined by the principle, then what they comply with is the principle in its strict interpretation.

   In such a society, the difference principle affects the motivation of citizens in economic life. It controls their expectations about remuneration, that is, what they will regard as acceptable pay for the posts they are invited to fill. It is generally thought that the difference principle would be used by government to modify the effect of choices which are not themselves influenced by the principle, but, so I claim, in a society of wholehearted commitment to the principle, there cannot be so stark a contrast between public and private choice. Instead, citizens want their own economic behavior to satisfy the principle, and they help to sustain a moral climate in which others want the same. . . . [M]uch of what Rawls says commits him to such an understanding of the difference principle, even though his approval of incentives embodies a rejection of that understanding, since approving of incentives means accepting the difference principle in its lax form, and in that form it can be satisfied in a society where it has no direct influence on economic motivation. (ibid. 312)

Now, leaving aside any worries one might have about what exactly is involved in wholehearted compliance with an ambiguous principle, we may grant the point made in the first paragraph: that if everyone were motivated by an ethos of justice to comply wholeheartedly with the uninterpreted difference principle, they would not demand incentive inequalities, and in that sense what they would comply with is the strict version. We may also grant that, in a society in which an ethos of justice prevailed, people would want their own behavior to satisfy the difference principle, and in that sense there would not be a stark contrast between public and private choice. Still, it does not follow from either of these points singly, or from both of them taken together, that a government could not implement the strict difference principle by itself. In fact, it is not at all obvious why a government could not implement that principle, by simply prohibiting incentive payments, or taxing them at 100 percent (absent compelling evidence that the recipients *could* not work as productively in the absence of such payments).[4] Of course, if the society in which the

4. Cohen mentions the possibility of eliminating all inequality through "income taxation which redistributes to fully egalitarian effect" (1997: 9), but he does not consider how this bears on the question of whether a government by itself could implement the strict difference principle.

government did this were well ordered, citizens would *also* have a sense of justice leading them wholeheartedly to comply with the strict principle. If, on the other hand, citizens lacked such motivation, then some of the talented might refuse to work as productively as they could.[5] But it does not follow from the first of these points that a government could not implement the strict principle by itself. And, notwithstanding the second point, equality would prevail in the society in question, even if some of the talented refused to work as productively as they could. Cohen is, therefore, mistaken when he says that, in the absence of an ethos of justice, "inequalities will obtain that are not necessary to enhance the condition of the worst off" (1997: 10). Nor does he establish that the strict principle requires all citizens to be as productive as they could possibly be.[6]

5. Indeed, as suggested in the final sentence of this paragraph of text and argued in note 6, even citizens in a well-ordered society who were wholeheartedly motivated to comply with the strict principle might decline to work as productively as they could.

6. It may be suggested that, in order to sustain his conclusion that the government alone could not implement the strict principle, Cohen needs only to show that the principle requires all people to be as productive as they would have been had the incentives allowable under the lax principle been in place. The strict principle so understood would still need an ethos of justice in order to be implemented fully, albeit a (morally if not epistemically) less demanding one than the ethos described earlier in the text. Pogge (2000: 149–152) suggests something like this as an interpretation of Cohen, citing Cohen's discussion (1995: 171–175). (See also Julius 2003: 349–355.) Although I remain agnostic on this interpretive question, let us suppose for the sake of argument that this is indeed what Cohen believes. What exactly is supposed to support the conclusion that implementation of the strict principle requires such an ethos? As far as I can see, the only argument Cohen gives is that, absent the ethos, inequalities will prevail that are not necessary to enhance the position of the worst off and that cannot, therefore, be produced compatibly with a wholehearted commitment to the difference principle. As we have seen, however, this simply is not true of a society whose coercive structure is regulated by the strict principle. Nor is it clear why the content of the productive ethos that is required by the strict principle should be determined by the choices that people would make under a regime regulated by the (discredited) lax principle. Why shouldn't people living under a strict regime instead regard those counterfactual choices as being symptomatic of the distorting effects of incentive payments, and decide that they were unwilling to sacrifice other goals and values to achieve greater productivity, even though greater productivity would increase the size of each person's (equal) share of primary goods? More generally, the difference principle says that *inequalities* must maximize the position of the worst-off group. It does not specify any particular level of equality as the one that justice requires in circumstances where there are no justified inequalities. To be sure, the parties in the original position are said to be motivated in choosing principles of justice by a desire to secure the largest possible shares of primary goods for themselves. Yet the

It is important to be clear about what I take these considerations to show. The main conclusion I am trying to establish is that there is nothing in Cohen's challenge to the legitimacy of incentive inequalities per se that undermines Rawls's claim that the basic structure is the primary subject of justice. Cohen imagines Rawls responding to his challenge by offering the "basic structure objection," and in reply Cohen argues that that objection cannot survive the attempt to disambiguate the concept of the basic structure. But if, instead of offering the BSO in response to Cohen's original challenge, Rawls were to affirm the strict version as the correct interpretation of the difference principle, nothing in Cohen's argument about the implications of the strict principle establishes that Rawls's emphasis on the basic structure would then be unsustainable. Cohen thinks otherwise because he never actually considers the implications of having the (coercive) basic structure regulated by the strict principle. He only considers the implications of people having a whole-hearted commitment to the difference principle in circumstances where the coercive structure is regulated by either (1) the lax principle; or (2) the uninterpreted, ambiguous principle.

There are two possible misunderstandings that I particularly want to forestall. First, I am not denying that, in a society that was just and well-ordered by Rawls's lights, and whose coercive economic institutions were regulated by the strict principle, people would have a strong sense of justice, in consequence of which they would be strongly and whole-heartedly motivated to comply with the strict principle. In this sense, they would have an ethos of justice. What I am denying is that this fact undermines Rawls's claim that the basic structure is the primary subject of justice. I deny this for two reasons: (1) an ethos of justice would not actually be *necessary* to produce an economic distribution satisfying the strict principle—such a distribution *could* be achieved by the coercive structure alone; and (2) Rawls's claim that the basic structure is

difference principle as Rawls formulates it does not require that equal shares be maximized, and he emphasizes that citizens in real life may well lack the maximizing motivation that he ascribes to the parties. Indeed, he asks: "[W]hy wouldn't it turn out that a society that follows the principles of justice allows, and even encourages, associations in which individuals abjure the desire for wealth beyond some amount appropriate for their common purposes?" (1999: 273). In any case, it would fundamentally transform the thrust of Cohen's critique if he were to argue that an egalitarian ethos is needed not to avoid unjust inequalities but rather to ensure that equal shares are as high as they could possibly be.

primary was never meant to exclude an ethos of justice—even if he is not clear about the precise content and contours of such an ethos—nor is it incompatible with the idea that the difference principle should influence people's motivations.

Second, I am not claiming that Rawls would or should endorse the strict difference principle. There are other possible replies Rawls might make to the incentives argument. For example, Joshua Cohen has suggested that rather than "introducing qualifications or limiting conditions in the statement of the principles [of justice] themselves" (2002: 372), Rawls's "alternative strategy is to argue in effect that the objectionable incentive inequalities will not arise and therefore do not command separate treatment in an account of justice" (ibid.). Such inequalities will not arise, according to this interpretation, because the difference principle as stated—understood nonstrictly—requires institutions to maximize the position of the worst-off group, and one thing that institutions may need to do in order to achieve this aim is precisely to generate a social ethos that limits the incentive demands that people make. This reply, too, preserves Rawls's view that the basic structure is the primary subject of justice while denying that justice condones unlimited self-seekingness in the economic choices of individual agents.[7] Moreover, as I will soon explain, G. A. Cohen himself provides reasons for doubting whether the strict principle is acceptable, and his doubts point to still another possible reply to the incentives argument. Since my aim is not to evaluate the incentives argument per se, but rather to assess its implications for Rawls's claim about the primacy of the basic structure, I can afford to remain agnostic about what Rawls's best reply to that argument is. The point of my discussion has simply been this: since one of the options with which the incentives argument presents Rawls is to endorse the strict principle, and since doing this would not require him to abandon

---

7. One aspect of Joshua Cohen's position strikes me as less clear than it might be. On the one hand, he says that what he calls the "ultralax" difference principle, which countenances all incentives that are necessary in an intention-relative sense, "is not at all plausible as a requirement of justice" (Cohen 2002: 371), and that Rawlsian justice does not condone it. Yet he also says that "there is nothing in the formulation of the principles of justice as fairness that directly condemns the inequalities" (ibid. 372) that the ultralax principle permits. As I have noted in the text, he thinks that Rawls hopes to exclude such inequalities without modifying the principles of justice themselves. But this seems to imply that the difference principle, as Rawls formulates it, just *is* the ultralax principle. This sits uneasily with the judgment that the ultralax principle is not at all plausible as a requirement of justice, even if we suppose that "the objectionable inequalities will not arise" in a Rawlsian society.

the claim that the basic structure is the primary subject of justice, it follows that the incentives argument does not by itself undermine that claim.

Thus, to repeat, there is nothing in Cohen's challenge to the legitimacy of incentive inequalities per se that undermines Rawls's claim that the basic structure is the primary subject of justice.[8] Nor is it apparent that Rawls needs to rely on the BSO in order to respond to Cohen's challenge. So even if, as Cohen argues, the ambiguity of the concept of the basic structure is fatal to that objection, this may not by itself pose a difficulty for Rawls. Still, it may seem that, whether or not Rawls relies on the BSO, any ambiguity in the concept of the basic structure cannot help but jeopardize his claim that the basic structure is the primary subject of justice. Cohen goes even further when he says that, in addition to undermining the BSO, the ambiguity of the concept "produces a dilemma for Rawls's view of the basic structure from which I can imagine no way out" (1997: 18). Clearly, then, it is important to consider the implications for Rawls's project of the ambiguity that Cohen alleges. Before doing that, however, let me digress briefly to explain why I said in the previous paragraph that Cohen himself provides reasons for doubting the acceptability of the strict difference principle.

As we have seen, Cohen's confidence that Rawls should reject the lax interpretation of the principle derives from his conviction that people who were genuinely committed to the difference principle would have no justification for demanding special incentives to work productively. Yet it is a curiosity of Cohen's "Incentives" paper (1992) that he himself suggests the basis for such a justification. For he agrees with the view, which, as it happens, he attributes to me, that *"every person has a right to pursue self-interest to some reasonable extent"* (ibid. 302, emphasis in original; see also Cohen 2000: 206, n. 24). He denies, rightly in my view, that such a prerogative could "justify the range of inequality, the extremes of wealth and poverty that actually obtain" (1992: 303) in western societies. But he seems to allow that a prerogative of the sort he endorses might justify some more modest degree of inequality. Within limits, in other words, one might justify one's demand for incentives by invoking one's prerogative to advance one's own interest. When Cohen considers the implications of this point for the interpretation of the difference principle, what he says is that the legitimacy of a prerogative

---

8. Thus, I disagree with the argument developed by Murphy (1999), at 267–269.

justification for modest incentives does not vindicate the lax difference principle, since the lax principle might justify incentive payments that were either more or less generous than what a reasonable prerogative would allow. Granting this point, however, the natural next question is whether the endorsement of prerogatives suggests still another interpretation of the difference principle, one that does not coincide with either the lax version or the strict version. Cohen comes closest to addressing this question when he says, in a footnote, that the strict version is the only alternative to the lax version: "there is no third way of playing the difference principle game." He then adds, "A further alternative would be the strict difference principle constrained by an agent-centered prerogative. But the added constraint *modifies*—it does not interpret—the difference principle" (ibid. 315 n.).

I find this reply unpersuasive. As we have seen, the strict and lax readings of the difference principle are distinguished by their differing interpretations of the word *necessary*, as it occurs in that principle. The lax reading allows that inequalities can be justified by what Cohen calls "intention-relative" necessities, whereas the strict reading countenances only "intention-independent necessities" (ibid. 311). But why should the notions of intention-relativity and intention-independence exhaust the field of possible interpretations of *necessary*? Why couldn't a supporter of the difference principle who was impressed by Cohen's endorsement of an agent-centered prerogative say that inequality-generating incentives should be deemed necessary, in the relevant sense, if and only if either (1) the talented are unable to work as productively without them; or (2) the insistence of the talented on such incentives falls within the scope of their "right to pursue self-interest to some reasonable extent"? On this reading, the difference principle countenances both intention-independent necessities and those intention-relative necessities that are morally justifiable. Whether this reading is best described as a "modification" or an "interpretation" of the difference principle, the fact remains that it is another possible version of that principle: more tolerant of incentives than the strict reading, but less tolerant of them than the lax reading. We might call it *the moderate* reading. I do not claim that Rawls himself had this reading in mind. But I do think that the availability of the moderate reading casts doubt on the idea that, in light of Cohen's arguments, Rawls should have accepted the strict reading. Indeed, if one agrees both with Cohen's criticism of the lax principle and with his endorsement of an agent-centered prerogative, then it would seem to be the moderate reading, rather than the strict reading, that one has most reason to recommend. Given that Cohen himself satisfies the conditions set out in the antecedent of the previous sentence, I do not understand why he fails to take this reading seriously.[9]

Let me now return to the alleged ambiguity of the concept of the basic structure and its implications for Rawls's argument. As we have seen, Cohen claims both that this ambiguity "wrecks" the BSO and that it poses an insuperable difficulty for Rawls's view of the subject matter of justice. It is the second of these claims that we are now considering. Cohen argues that Rawls faces a dilemma. If the basic structure is limited to coercive institutions, then the focus on that structure is arbitrary, given that Rawls's stated reason for this focus has to do with the profound effects of the basic structure, and noncoercive institutions have effects that are just as profound as coercive institutions. If, on the other hand, the basic structure includes noncoercive practices and institutions, then it becomes untenable to exclude individual conduct from the ambit of justice, for individual behavior is constitutive of noncoercive institutional structure.

Before attempting directly to assess the force of this argument, let me mention three respects in which Cohen's presentation of the argument is either incomplete or unclear. First, when formulating the first horn of his dilemma, Cohen acknowledges only one of Rawls's stated reasons for treating the basic structure as the primary subject of justice: namely, the profound effects of that structure on people's life prospects. "[W]hat *other* rationale," he asks, "could there be for calling it the *primary* subject of justice?" (1997: 21). This rhetorical question overlooks the two other reasons Rawls cites: (1) the fact that the basic structure shapes people's wants and aspirations, which should not be treated as fixed or given; and (2) the fact that a just basic structure is necessary to ensure the background justice of economic transactions, since no feasible rules of individual conduct are adequate for that task. Since Cohen neglects these considerations, his claim that a focus on coercive structure would

---

9. David Estlund has also emphasized the significance of Cohen's endorsement of agent-centered prerogatives, pointing out that such prerogatives must be understood to legitimate more than just the pursuit of self-interest narrowly understood. Estlund argues that "inequality producing incentives will still be required by many conscientious citizens exercising certain prerogatives that Cohen must allow" (1998: 101).

   Andrew Williams (1998: sect. 6) suggests that an agent-centered prerogative cannot be incorporated into a theory of justice for the basic structure because it violates the "publicity condition" on which Rawls insists. However, this cannot be Cohen's view because he rejects the publicity condition that Rawls and Williams favor (see Cohen 2000: 212–213, n. 36).

be arbitrary is, at best, premature. To defend it fully, he would need to establish that all three of Rawls's reasons apply to noncoercive structure as well.[10]

Second, Cohen's allegation that Rawls's concept of the basic structure is ambiguous relies on the distinction Cohen draws between coercive and noncoercive institutions. In the case of coercive institutional structure, Cohen says, we can distinguish between the structure itself and individual actions that occur within it. In contrast, no such distinction can be drawn in the case of noncoercive structure, for "behavior is *constitutive of noncoercive structure*" (ibid. 20). But the coercive/noncoercive distinction is itself not altogether clear, for implicit in Cohen's argument (and in the account I have so far given of it) are two different ways of drawing the distinction.[11] On one interpretation, it is a distinction between two kinds of institution: an institution is to be classified as coercive if its structure is legally coercive, and it is to be classified as noncoercive if its structure depends "far less on law than on convention, usage, and expectation" (ibid. 19). Cohen says that the family is "a signal example" of a noncoercive institution in this sense. On the second interpretation, the distinction is not between two kinds of institution but rather between two kinds of "structure," and one and the same institution may comprise both coercive and noncoercive structure. This second formulation creates no presumption, as the first one does, that each institution will be classifiable either as coercive or as noncoercive. Cohen suggests both interpretations when he says, in characterizing the supposed ambiguity of Rawls's account of the basic structure: "Sometimes it appears that coercive (in the legal sense) institutions exhaust it, or, better, that *institutions belong to it only insofar as they are (legally) coercive*" (ibid. 18; emphasis added).

The difference between the two interpretations is relevant for the following reason. On the first interpretation, it is debatable whether Cohen is correct in saying that the family counts as a noncoercive institution. After all, there is a large body of family law, and all societies engage

---

10. This point also bears on the effectiveness of Cohen's argument against the basic structure objection.

11. Cohen himself concedes that it may not be a sharp one, because coercive structures may also not be fully separable from individual behavior. In other words, the characterization he gives of noncoercive structure may apply equally to putatively coercive structure. Cohen says that he can contemplate this idea with equanimity because, if true, it only reinforces his claim that justice cannot plausibly be thought to apply exclusively to structures and not to individual actions. However, the unclarity to which I call attention in the text is independent of this point.

in the legal regulation of marriage, adoption, divorce, child custody, child support, alimony, parental responsibility, and the like. There is, for example, nothing noncoercive about the practice of restricting marriage to a pair of adults consisting of one man and one woman. To be sure, the structure of the family may also be taken to include uncoerced patterns of individual conduct and "socially constructed expectations" (ibid. 20), but the same is true of putatively coercive institutions, so the grounds for classifying the family as noncoercive remain unclear on this interpretation. Perhaps, then, Cohen's argument is best understood as relying on the second interpretation. On this interpretation, the distinction between coercive and noncoercive structure is not a distinction between two different kinds of institution: those that are coercive and those that are not. Instead, the idea is that many institutions, of which both the family and the market economy are important examples, have frameworks that are partly coercive but are also partly constituted by non-mandatory conventions and practices. Cohen may be interpreted as arguing that, inasmuch as some of these nonmandatory practices seem to fall clearly within the purview of justice, Rawls cannot without arbitrariness exclude them from the basic structure or limit that structure solely to the coercive elements of an institution's framework.

This may indeed be the more plausible interpretation of Cohen's argument, and it certainly presents a challenge to a purely coercive understanding of the basic structure. At the same time, however, it also implies that such an understanding *need not exclude the family* from the basic structure. In other words, if Rawls wants to say that institutions belong to the basic structure "only insofar as they are (legally) coercive," then he can say that of the family as well as any other institution, for much of family structure *is* legally coercive. Although Cohen does not explicitly deny this point, he does not explicitly acknowledge it either.[12] As I will

---

12. Furthermore, the following passage, in which Cohen describes what he sees as Rawls's noncoercive specification of the basic structure, encourages us to overlook the point:

> Rawls often says that the basic structure consists of the *major* social institutions, and he does not put a particular accent on coercion when he announces *that* specification of the basic structure. In this second reading of what it is, institutions belong to the basic structure whose structuring can depend far less on law than on convention, usage, and expectation: a signal example is the family, which Rawls sometimes includes in the basic structure and sometimes does not. But once the line is crossed, from coercive ordering to the non-coercive ordering of society by rules and conventions of accepted practice, then the ambit of justice can no longer exclude chosen behavior, since the usages which constitute informal structure (think, again, of the family) are bound up with the customary actions of people. (1997: 19–20)

explain below, I think it is a point of some importance. For now, suffice it to say that, although Cohen may still argue that it is arbitrary to include only coercive structure within the basic structure, his argument cannot legitimately derive any support from the thought that a purely coercive specification flatly excludes the family from the basic structure, for that simply is not true.

Finally, the members of any human society will inevitably have developed many informal practices and shared expectations, and it will be possible to discern patterns of many kinds in the choices they make. These practices and patterns will differ considerably in their social visibility, internal uniformity, invariance across different societies, and robustness in the face of various forms of change, and the individual choices they subsume will differ in their degrees of self-consciousness, perceived dependence on social values and norms, and amenability to modification through incentives and pressures of various kinds. In pressing his *ad hominem* case for the inclusion of "informal structure" within the scope of Rawls's principles of justice, Cohen does not distinguish among the many important respects in which informal practices and patterns may differ from one another. Some of Cohen's critics have pointed out that the two examples of informal structure that he considers—namely, patterns of individual choice within the market economy and the family—differ from each other in ways that may well affect the relative strength of the arguments for including each of them respectively within the ambit of Rawlsian principles (see Murphy 1999: 269; Williams 1998: 242–243). Whether or not this is so, there is clearly a great deal more that needs to be said about the varieties of informal structure and about the character of the norms that are appropriate to patterns and practices of various kinds.

Having mentioned these respects in which Cohen's argument seems to me in need of further development, I will now set them aside. I will assume for the sake of argument that, as Cohen says, Rawls's concept of

---

In effect, this passage equivocates between the two interpretations of the coercive/ noncoercive distinction. It begins by classifying the family as a noncoercive institution because it depends "less on law than on convention, usage, and expectation," and concludes that the noncoercive elements of family structure must be included within the basic structure if the institution of the family is included at all. This overlooks the fact that the family might be included within the basic structure only "insofar as it is legally coercive." It is not true that the coercive elements of family structure can be included only if the noncoercive elements are included as well.

the basic structure is ambiguous as between an interpretation that limits it to coercive structure and one that includes noncoercive structure as well. The question I want to consider now is whether this ambiguity undermines Rawls's claim that the basic structure is the primary subject of justice. The ambiguity will have this undermining effect if—but only if—Rawls's claim fails however the concept is disambiguated. Of course, it would in any case be desirable to resolve any ambiguity the concept may display. But unless there is no way of disambiguating it that is compatible with Rawls's claim about the primacy of the basic structure, the ambiguity of the concept will not undermine that claim.

So suppose, to begin with, that Rawls were to insist on a purely coercive specification of the basic structure. As we have seen, Cohen thinks that this would be arbitrarily narrow, because it is not only the coercive structure that has profound effects on people's life prospects. However, although I am not sure that Rawls would or should construe the basic structure in purely coercive terms, there is one obvious reason for doing so that does not seem arbitrary, namely, that the coercive structure is *coercive*. Coercion always requires justification, and this requirement is particularly urgent with respect to the coercive political power of the state. In Rawls's view, a society is to be conceived of as a fair system of cooperation among free and equal people. Any such system will require the coercive enforcement of the fundamental terms of cooperation. But given the status of individuals as free and equal, the establishment of coercive institutions poses a special justificatory problem. The role of principles of justice, as Rawls understands it, is to specify fair terms of cooperation, terms that free and equal persons themselves could endorse. On this view, the justice of coercive institutions, if it can be secured, provides a solution to the justificatory problem posed by the coercive character of those institutions. The importance of achieving such a solution cannot be underestimated, for the use of the coercive power of the state to impose unjust social arrangements is a great evil, greatly to be feared. However unjust or otherwise unacceptable a social arrangement may be, the coercive enforcement of such arrangements is even worse.

Ironically, one reason why this is so emerges from Cohen's arguments *against* a purely coercive specification of the basic structure. In the case of noncoercive practices, Cohen writes, "people do have choices: it is, indeed, *only* their choices that reproduce [noncoercive] social practices; and some, moreover, choose *against* the grain of nurture, habit, and self-interest" (1997: 25). Thus, if a noncoercive practice is unjust, there is room for an "incremental process" in which a small number of "moral pioneers" initiate a virtuous cycle; they revise their own unjust behavior, and this affects the expectations of others, who in turn change their behavior, which leads to still more widespread changes in expectation, and so on. Eventually the unjust practice simply disappears through the uncoerced, everyday choices of individuals (ibid. 26). But in the case of coercive structure, no such process is available because, Cohen says, "*coercive* structure arises independently of people's quotidian choices" (ibid. 20). This reveals one respect in which the effects of coercive structure are, *pace* Cohen, more "profound" than those of noncoercive structure: they are more insulated against the possibility of change through ordinary individual choices. For this reason among others, it does not seem entirely arbitrary to suggest that the basic structure is limited to "the *broad coercive outline* of society" (ibid. 19).

It is worth noting, moreover, that a purely coercive specification of the basic structure need not be nearly as tolerant as Cohen suggests of sexist patterns within the family. First, as we have seen, much of family structure is legally coercive. It would, therefore, be included within the basic structure under a purely coercive specification and directly regulated by the principles of justice. Second, as we have also seen, one of the functions of just social institutions is to shape individuals' characters in such a way as to discourage desires and motivations that are incompatible with justice. Assuming that the principles of justice that apply to the coercive structure of the family are egalitarian in their content, it follows that just coercive institutions will also seek to discourage wants and aspirations that are inconsistent with gender equality. Nor does it seem implausible that they should have this effect. Cohen says that "sexist family structure is consistent with sex-neutral family law" (ibid. 22). As a logical matter, perhaps. But the extent to which the two can in fact coexist is an empirical issue, which Cohen does not investigate. Moreover, the relevant question for our purposes concerns the extent to which sexist family structure can coexist with genuinely egalitarian family law (which may or may not be sex-neutral). If family law were thoroughly egalitarian, and if norms of gender equality pervaded other areas of the law that have served to enforce gender differences, it is far from obvious to me that the egregious sexist patterns that Cohen cites could indeed survive and flourish. Just as Cohen underestimates the degree of economic equality that could be achieved if the coercive basic structure were regulated by the strict, rather than the lax, difference principle, so too he may underestimate the degree of gender equality that could be achieved if the coercive structure were regulated by genuinely egalitarian norms.

Despite Cohen's arguments, then, I am not persuaded that a purely coercive specification would be arbitrarily narrow or, a fortiori, that the arbitrariness of such a specification would undermine Rawls's claim that the basic structure is the primary subject of justice. But let us suppose, for the sake of argument, that Cohen is right about this. Let us suppose that, in order to avoid arbitrariness, the basic structure must be interpreted expansively to include not only coercive institutions but also some noncoercive institutions and practices.[13] Assuming that this is correct, does it undermine Rawls's claim about the subject matter of justice? Note that it does not follow from this assumption that there is no distinction to be drawn between the expanded basic structure and individual choices made within that structure. Even if the noncoercive institutions that are part of the expanded structure are constituted by individual choices, the structure also comprises coercive institutions that are not so constituted.[14] Furthermore, there are, presumably, many individual actions that are not constitutive of any of the noncoercive institutions that are candidates for inclusion in the basic structure. So even if the basic structure, properly understood, includes some noncoercive institutions, it does not comprise all or only individual conduct, and it is still possible to distinguish between the basic structure and choices made within that structure. Moreover, there may still be good reasons for treating the (expanded) basic structure as the primary subject of justice. For it may still be true that:

1. the basic structure so understood has profound effects on people and their prospects;
2. the background justice of individuals' economic transactions can be preserved only if the basic structure is regulated by a special set of principles;
3. the influence of the basic structure on human wants and aspirations is acceptable only if the structure satisfies those principles;
4. the principles do not constitute appropriate guides to every type of individual decision;
5. there are other values and norms that should properly influence individual conduct in certain areas; and
6. the correct principles of justice for individuals depend on the correct principles of justice for the basic structure.

In short, the inclusion of noncoercive institutions within the basic structure would perhaps be fatal to the idea, which I take Rawls in any

---

13. Here, for ease of exposition, I treat the coercive/noncoercive distinction as a distinction between two types of institution, rather than between two types of structural element within a single institution. Nothing substantive turns on this.
14. This will be true, at any rate, so long as we set aside, as Cohen himself does for most of his discussion, the concession mentioned in n. 11.

case to reject, that the principles of justice should have no influence on individual motivation or conduct; however, it would not undermine the Rawlsian claim that, given the distinctive functions of the basic structure, the principles for regulating that structure (including those individual choices and actions that may be constitutive of parts of it) are of primary importance from the standpoint of justice.

I have been examining Cohen's charge that the ambiguity of the concept of the basic structure undermines Rawls's claim about the subject matter of justice. I have argued that, insofar as the distinction between coercive and noncoercive institutions is clear, there are at least some considerations that count in favor of a purely coercive specification of the basic structure, so the claim that such a specification would be arbitrarily narrow has not been established. If that claim proves to be compelling, however, then noncoercive practices and institutions can be included within the basic structure, where appropriate, without jeopardizing the view that the basic structure is the primary subject of justice.

Let me conclude with a brief summary of the overall argument of this chapter. Cohen's challenge to the legitimacy of economic incentives exposes an indeterminacy in the difference principle, an indeterminacy whose resolution is crucial if the content and implications of that principle are to be clear. Yet there are a number of different ways in which Rawls might respond to the incentives challenge. I doubt whether he would respond by offering what Cohen calls the "basic structure objection," and the other responses available to him are all compatible with his claim that the basic structure is the primary subject of justice. Thus, the incentives challenge does not by itself suffice to undermine that claim. It is true that Rawls does not demarcate precisely the contours of the basic structure, but this fact also does not undermine his claim that the basic structure is the primary subject of justice. Although it is clearly desirable to clarify the scope of the basic structure, there is no reason to think that this cannot be done consistently with Rawls's claim about the subject matter of justice.

As I indicated at the outset, my ultimate aim in this chapter has not been to interpret or defend Rawls, but rather to consider the merits of an emphasis on the basic structure. Although I have not established that the basic structure is the primary subject of justice, I have tried to show that Cohen's arguments do not defeat this view. Indeed, once one appreciates Rawls's reasons for emphasizing the basic structure, and once one recognizes that such an emphasis does not require one to endorse the lax difference principle or to condone "unlimited self-seekingness in the economic choices of well-placed people," it is not clear to me what residual reason Cohen himself has for resisting this emphasis. I do not believe that he would reject the pluralism about value to which "the division of moral labor" is responsive. His endorsement of an agent-centered prerogative seems to involve a tacit acknowledgment of the plurality of values, and elsewhere he (2003: 244–245) has directly embraced a form of pluralism.[15] Similarly, I would be surprised if he were to dispute the importance of securing background justice, which is what motivates Rawls's call for an "institutional division of labor." Nor do I imagine that Cohen would disagree with Rawls about the role of the basic structure in shaping people's wants and aspirations. At the very least, we can say this: once the claim that the basic structure is the primary subject of justice is decoupled from the idea that justice condones unlimited self-seeking behavior, the considerations that count in its favor need to be evaluated in their own right. As far as I can see, the arguments of Cohen that I have discussed in this chapter do little to diminish the force of those considerations.

References

Cohen, G. A. (1992). "Incentives, Inequality, and Community," in G. B. Peterson (ed.), *The Tanner Lectures on Human Values*, vol. 13. Salt Lake City, UT: University of Utah Press.

———(1995). "The Pareto Argument for Inequality," *Social Philosophy and Policy* 12.

———(1997). "Where the Action Is: On the Site of Distributive Justice," *Philosophy & Public Affairs* 26.

———(2000). *If You're an Egalitarian, How Come You're So Rich?* Cambridge, MA: Harvard University Press.

———(2003). "Facts and Principles," *Philosophy & Public Affairs* 31.

Cohen, J. (2002). "Taking People As They Are?," *Philosophy & Public Affairs* 30.

Estlund, D. (1998). "Liberty, Equality, and Fraternity in Cohen's Critique of Rawls," *Journal of Political Philosophy* 6.

Julius, A. J. (2003). "Basic Structure and the Value of Equality," *Philosophy & Public Affairs* 31.

15. "Justice is not the *only* value that calls for (appropriately balanced) implementation: other principles, sometimes competing with justice, must also be variously pursued and honored" (Cohen 2003: 244–245).

   Julius (2003: 344–345) says that "monists" can accept an agent-centered prerogative. But this is because monism, as he understands it, is compatible with the existence of multiple values; it insists only that individuals have some reason to promote distributive justice. But this is as much as to say that "monism" in his sense is compatible with the pluralism about value to which the division of moral labor is responsive.

Murphy, L. (1999). "Institutions and the Demands of Justice," *Philosophy & Public Affairs* 27.

Nagel, T. (1991). *Equality and Partiality*. New York: Oxford University Press.

Pogge, T. (2000). "On the Site of Distributive Justice: Reflections on Cohen and Murphy," *Philosophy & Public Affairs* 29.

Rawls, J. (1971). *A Theory of Justice* (rev. edn. 1999). Cambridge, MA: Harvard University Press.

———(1993). *Political Liberalism*. New York: Columbia University Press.

———(1999). *Collected Papers*, S. Freeman (ed.). Cambridge, MA: Harvard University Press.

———(2001). *Justice As Fairness: A Restatement*, E. Kelly (ed.). Cambridge, MA: Harvard University Press.

Scheffler, S. (1982). *The Rejection of Consequentialism* (rev. edn. 1994). Oxford: Clarendon Press.

Williams, A. (1998). "Incentives, Inequality, and Publicity," *Philosophy & Public Affairs* 27.

Williams, B. (1973). "A Critique of Utilitarianism," in J. J. C. Smart and B. Williams (eds.), *Utilitarianism For and Against*. Cambridge: Cambridge University Press.

6

Cosmopolitanism, Justice, and Institutions

Cosmopolitanism is not—or not yet—the name of a determinate political philosophy. Although many contemporary theorists have put forward views that they describe as cosmopolitan, there is little agreement among them about the central elements of a cosmopolitan position. Almost nobody advocates the development of the kind of global state that would give the idea of "world citizenship" literal application. Instead, disparate views have been advanced under the heading of cosmopolitanism, and these views share little more than an organizing conviction that any adequate political outlook for our time must in some way comprehend the world as a whole.

To some people cosmopolitanism is primarily a view about sovereignty. To others it is primarily a view about culture and identity. To many philosophers, however, it is primarily a view about justice, and

Originally published in *Daedalus* 137 (Summer, 2008): 68–77. © 2008 by the American Academy of Arts and Sciences.

in recent years there has been an increasing flow of books and articles devoted to the subject of "global justice."

In part, the focus on justice reflects the continuing influence of John Rawls, who insisted that "[j]ustice is the first virtue of social institutions, as truth is of systems of thought."[1] In so doing, Rawls elevated the concept of justice above other important political ideas such as liberty, law, equality, power, rights, obligation, security, democracy, and the state, and gave it a privileged place on the agenda of contemporary political philosophy. It is testimony to Rawls's influence that justice—especially "distributive," or economic, justice—has remained a central preoccupation of political philosophers ever since.

Yet there is disagreement about the bearing of Rawls's own work on cosmopolitanism considered as a view about justice.

In the cosmopolitan literature, Rawls figures both as hero and as villain. As hero—for saying that a just society cannot permit the distribution of income and wealth to be influenced by morally arbitrary factors such as people's native abilities or the social circumstances into which they are born. Cosmopolitans see this as paving the way for a recognition that national boundaries are equally arbitrary from the standpoint of justice. As a matter of justice, the accident of where one is born should have no effect on one's economic prospects.

As villain—because Rawls himself refused to draw this conclusion. In *A Theory of Justice*, he argued that the "primary subject of justice" is the "basic structure" of an individual society. The basic structure comprises a society's major social, political, and economic institutions. Rawls's principles of distributive justice are universal in the sense that they apply to the basic structure of each society taken one at a time, but not in the sense that they apply to the global distribution of income and wealth as a whole. So, according to Rawls's "difference principle," the laws and institutions of the United States should be designed in such a way as to maximize the position of the worst-off Americans, and the laws and institutions of Bangladesh should be designed in such a way as to maximize the position of the worst-off Bangladeshis. But justice does not require that the worst-off Bangladeshis should be as well-off as the worst-off Americans. Indeed, it does not require that the best-off Bangladeshis should be as well-off as the worst-off Americans. According to Rawls, the principles of distributive justice impose no constraints at all on the distribution of income and wealth between the United States and Bangladesh or among citizens of the two countries.

1. John Rawls, *A Theory of Justice* (Cambridge, Mass.: Harvard University Press, 1971), 3.

A Theory of Justice was published at a time when *globalization* was not yet a word in our everyday lexicon and few people described themselves as cosmopolitans. Virtually all political philosophers at the time assumed that the individual society was the default unit of analysis. So if he had written nothing further on the subject, Rawls's failure to question this assumption might have been taken to reveal nothing more damning than a lack of prescience or a failure of imagination. Yet when, late in his career, Rawls explicitly addressed issues of global justice in light of the extensive literature that had by then emerged on the subject, he refused the invitation of sympathetic cosmopolitan critics to apply his theory of distributive justice globally. Instead, he argued that relations among societies are governed by the "law of peoples."[2] The law of peoples sets out principles of justice to govern international relations, but they are not principles of *distributive* justice. In other words, they do not concern themselves with the distribution of income and wealth per se, but instead presuppose the existence of separate societies within which distributive principles do apply. In taking this position, Rawls cemented his ambiguous status—part hero, part villain—within the cosmopolitan literature.

I believe that this mixed assessment gets things backwards. On the one hand, Rawls is not the hero that cosmopolitans take him to be, because he never did say that morally arbitrary factors should not be allowed to influence the distribution of income and wealth. Any distribution, including distributions that conform to Rawls's own difference principle, will inevitably be influenced by such factors. What Rawls said was that a just distribution must not be *improperly* influenced by morally arbitrary factors. But to decide what counts as an improper influence we need a substantive theory that we have compelling independent reasons to accept. Rawls took himself to have provided such a theory for the special but crucial case of the basic structure of an individual society. Cosmopolitans would have to do something comparable for the global case. The mere observation that national boundaries are morally arbitrary—hardly controversial if what it means is just that nobody deserves to be born in one country rather than another—does not take us very far.

On the other hand, Rawls's emphasis on the basic structure as the primary subject of justice does not qualify him as the villain of the piece either, for its real effect is to clarify the form that a compelling argument for cosmopolitanism would have to take. If anything, it is this feature of Rawls's view, rather than his claim about the moral arbitrariness of

---

2. See John Rawls, *The Law of Peoples* (Cambridge, Mass.: Harvard University Press, 1999).

natural talents and social class, that paves the way for the development of a credible cosmopolitan position.

There is one well-known argument for cosmopolitanism that does take its inspiration from Rawls's claims about the primacy of the basic structure. Rawls is correct, according to this argument, to stress the importance of regulating the basic structure by norms of justice, but what he fails to recognize is that there is now a global basic structure—a worldwide network of economic and political institutions. It is to this structure, rather than to the institutions of a single society, that the principles of justice properly apply.

Samuel Freeman, a prominent defender of Rawls, has responded forcefully to this line of argument.[3] He emphasizes that, for Rawls, distributive justice is not concerned with the allocation of goods in the abstract. Nor, contrary to what some philosophers appear to believe, are we to decide on the principles of distributive justice by comparing the intrinsic attractiveness of different allocative patterns. Instead, distributive justice is a response to social and political cooperation and the possibilities and problems that cooperation brings with it. As such, it is an essentially social and political value, and it governs the basic social institutions that make possible the production, exchange, distribution, and consumption of goods. The institutions in question include the legal systems of property and contract, and they are political products, the results of political decisions and political action. The principles of distributive justice provide standards for designing and assessing such institutions. The role of these principles is to specify fair terms of cooperation for people who are conceived of as engaged in a complex cooperative project governed by a strong notion of reciprocity.

Since, in Rawls's view, a world government is neither feasible nor desirable, and since the basic institutions to which distributive justice applies must be constructed politically, there is no global basic structure and no reasonable expectation that one will emerge in the future. There are, to be sure, global institutions and arrangements of various kinds, but they do not add up to a global basic structure that is remotely analogous to the domestic case. Instead, these institutions are largely the product of international agreements among independent states, and they presuppose the existing legal and institutional structures of those states. In the absence of a global state with a world government, there is nothing that would count as a global basic structure in Rawls's sense.

---

3. In Samuel Freeman, *Justice and the Social Contract* (New York: Oxford University Press, 2007), part III.

This response is effective against the simple cosmopolitan strategy of generalizing Rawls's claims about the basic structure to the case of the so-called "global basic structure." Yet even if this simple generalizing strategy fails, Rawls's focus on the basic structure holds a more encouraging lesson for cosmopolitans.

To see why, it will help to review some of the motivation for that focus. One place to start is with utilitarianism—the theory that Rawls treats as the primary rival to his own—and in particular with utilitarian revisionism. Utilitarians hold that the correct normative standard to apply both to individual actions and to institutional policies and arrangements is the standard of maximizing average or aggregate utility or welfare. Utilitarianism is famous—or notorious—for its willingness to deviate from traditional or "commonsense" moral principles whenever a deviation will promote maximum utility overall. The simplest form of utilitarianism holds, for example, that killing innocent people is normally wrong because it normally fails to maximize the general welfare. But if, in extraordinary circumstances, killing some innocent person *would* maximize the general welfare, perhaps because it would prevent the deaths of more innocents overall, then it is the right thing to do.

Utilitarian revisionism is motivated by two mutually reinforcing convictions. The first is that there is a strong connection between morality, properly understood, and well-being. If adherence to a given set of values and norms does not serve to enhance human well-being, then it is irrational and inhumane to insist on those norms, however firmly entrenched in tradition and common sense they may be. The dead hand of tradition should not blind us to the fact that the only possible point of morality is to make our lives better, nor should it lead us to acquiesce in values and norms that fail to contribute to that aim.

The second conviction is that it is essential to think about moral questions in a systematic and holistic way, focusing not merely on individual actions in isolation but also on the way in which our actions are structured by social institutions and are related to wider patterns of human conduct. The fates of people in the modern world are tied together in complex ways through their shared participation in vast social, political, and economic structures. In these circumstances, we cannot continue to rely uncritically on the heterogeneous assortment of commonsense values and principles that people are used to applying in their daily lives. Instead, individual actions must be assessed, and the norms governing them must be rationalized, from a broader perspective. In formulating social policy, we must consider how and when the competing interests of different people should be balanced and aggregated, and we must decide what principles should guide the design of the massive social and political institutions that structure individuals' lives.

Among philosophers, utilitarianism has long been criticized for its many counterintuitive implications and its willingness to reject or revise values and principles in which most people have great confidence. Yet economists and social policymakers have continued to be attracted by its broad institutional perspective, its simple maximizing structure, and its foundational reliance on an inclusive notion of well-being. Despite its revisionism, utilitarianism has seemed to them to provide a rational, humane, and systematic basis on which to address the large-scale questions of institutional policy and design that are so important in the modern world. Rawls himself regarded it as extremely significant that the great classical utilitarians were also leading economists and social reformers with a primary interest in institutions. Indeed, an institutional emphasis of some kind seems to be required if we are to develop norms and principles capable of regulating the structural and aggregative phenomena to which the utilitarian is rightly sensitive. If the influence of utilitarianism is to be challenged, an alternative must be found that shares some of its virtues.

Now, Rawls cannot accept utilitarian revisionism, which he sees as a threat to the basic values of freedom and equality that are the foundation of a democratic society. And he believes that utilitarianism's reliance on well-being as a fundamental notion is deeply misguided. Yet he shares the institutional focus and systematic aims of utilitarianism. In the Preface to *A Theory of Justice* he says that his aim is to give a systematic account of justice that will be superior to the utilitarian account. This account is meant to apply specifically to the basic institutional structure of society. The claim that the basic structure is the primary subject of justice gives social institutions priority over individual actions, from the standpoint of justice, and it reveals important affinities with the utilitarian view. In so doing, it confirms Rawls's intention to offer a serious alternative to utilitarianism at the level of institutional design for a democratic society.

Although Rawls's position is in general much less revisionist than utilitarianism, there is one respect in which it is actually more revisionist, for Rawls believes that social institutions require special normative principles that do not apply directly to individual agents. This represents a departure from the dominant historical tradition within moral and political philosophy. Not even utilitarianism, with its avowedly institutional emphasis, maintains that the norms governing institutions differ fundamentally from those governing individual conduct. On the contrary, a striking feature of the utilitarian view is its insistence that, ultimately, there is but a single fundamental principle that regulates both individuals and institutions.

Rawls's claim about the primacy of the basic structure, expressed in his characteristically colorless prose and initially presented as part of an informal introductory exposition of the main outline of his theory, did not become a major focus of attention during the outpouring of critical discussion that greeted the publication of *A Theory of Justice*. Although it attracted the interest of a few commentators, it was generally overshadowed by other more striking and more obviously consequential features of his theory. Nor did Rawls do much at first to highlight the significance of his emphasis on the basic structure. In fact, he tends in *Theory* to understate the novelty of this emphasis, insisting, for example, that his view of justice is entirely compatible with Aristotle's.

However, critics have maintained, rightly in my view, that Rawls's focus on the basic structure marks a sharp departure from traditional philosophies of justice. Indeed, as Samuel Fleischacker has argued,[4] although the term *distributive justice* is an ancient one, the actual idea of distributive justice that Rawls employs, and which receives its fullest and best developed account in his work, appears to be a relatively modern one. But whereas his critics believe that this is a serious failing of his view, it seems to me to be one of its most important features.

Rawls's insistence on the primacy of the basic structure amounts to an attempt to redirect liberal theory away from a focus on individual acts, agents, and transactions, and toward a focus on the fairness of basic social institutions. More precisely, his aim is to reorient liberal theory in two ways: first, by making justice its primary virtue, and then by interpreting justice to apply in the first instance to social institutions rather than to individual actions. A concern with the justice of fundamental social arrangements, Rawls insists, must take priority over, and is a precondition for, any legitimate concern with the justice of individual actions and transactions. This focus on the basic structure represents, among other things, an attempt to incorporate into liberal theory what Rawls sees as the legitimate insights not only of utilitarianism but also of the socialist tradition. In their different ways, each of these traditions has emphasized the extraordinary and transformative significance of modern social and economic institutions. Rawls's focus on the basic structure represents an attempt to incorporate these insights securely within liberal, democratic thought.

Now we live in a time when, in the United States of America, there has been a massive retreat from the kinds of social welfare policies that Rawls's theory recommends, and the idea that our economic institutions must satisfy a test of fundamental fairness has fallen into disfavor. This means that the reorientation of liberal thought that Rawls sought to

---

4. Samuel Fleischacker, *A Short History of Distributive Justice* (Cambridge, Mass.: Harvard University Press, 2004).

achieve in theory has, for the time being at least, been stymied in practice. But its theoretical importance remains undiminished.

Rawls provides a number of explicit reasons for his focus on the basic structure. First, he says in *A Theory of Justice* that the basic structure is the primary subject of justice because its effects in shaping people's life prospects are so profound. Individuals born into different social positions have different expectations in life, some of them more favorable than others. These inequalities of expectation are obviously not grounded in considerations of merit or desert, and because they affect people at birth they are especially "deep" and "pervasive." We cannot simply eliminate them all, for "any modern society…must rely on some inequalities to be well designed and effectively organized."[5] But their depth and pervasiveness make it essential that such inequalities should be regulated by principles of justice.

A second reason Rawls mentions has to do with the way the basic structure shapes people's desires and their characters. Citing "economists as different as Marshall and Marx,"[6] he says that a social system inevitably shapes people's desires and aspirations, and helps to determine the kinds of persons they are and want to be. The choice among different systems, therefore, implicates different views of the human good and different moral assumptions. Yet these issues are not always confronted openly. Rawls's emphasis on the basic structure is meant to counteract our tendency "to acquiesce without thinking in the moral and political conception implicit in the status quo, or [to] leave things to be settled by how contending social and economic forces happen to work themselves out."[7]

Taken together, these two considerations highlight the formative role of social institutions in shaping people's desires, characters, and differing expectations in life. In view of the massively consequential social role of the basic structure, bringing it under the control of a regulative conception of justice is a matter of the first importance. Any failure to do so will mean that matters of great moral urgency are left to be settled by default or by the play of "contending social and economic forces."[8]

In "The Basic Structure as Subject," first published in 1977, Rawls provides an additional reason.[9] He argues that agreements among

---

5. John Rawls, *Justice as Fairness: A Restatement* (Cambridge, Mass.: Harvard University Press, 2001), 55.
6. Rawls, *A Theory of Justice*, 259.
7. Ibid., 260.
8. Ibid.
9. John Rawls, "The Basic Structure as Subject," *American Philosophical Quarterly 14* (April 1977). A revised and expanded version was published the following year, and is included as Lecture VII of *Political Liberalism* (New York: Columbia University Press, 1993).

individuals should be treated as morally authoritative only if they are made freely and under fair conditions, and that only the basic structure can secure the background conditions necessary to ensure that agreements are free and fair. Even if such conditions happen to obtain at a given moment, the cumulative effect of many separate and seemingly fair individual transactions may be to alter the distribution of resources and opportunities in ways that erode background justice. With the best of intentions, individuals cannot sustain background justice over time, for the task is too complex and requires too much information. There are no feasible rules of individual conduct full compliance with which would suffice to prevent the erosion of background justice. Instead, it is the role of the basic structure to secure and preserve just background conditions. As Rawls puts the point,

> When our social world is pervaded by duplicity and deceit we are tempted to think that law and government are necessary only because of the propensity of individuals to act unfairly. But, to the contrary, the tendency is rather for background justice to be eroded even when individuals act fairly: the overall result of separate and independent transactions is away from and not toward background justice. We might say: in this case the invisible hand guides things in the wrong direction and favors an oligopolistic configuration of accumulations that succeeds in maintaining unjustified inequalities and restrictions on fair opportunity. Therefore, we require special institutions to preserve background justice, and a special conception of justice to define how these institutions are to be set up.[10]

This reason differs from the two previously mentioned. In appealing to the profound effects of the basic structure and its role in shaping individuals' wants and aspirations, Rawls had emphasized some of the potentially problematic ways in which the basic structure can affect individuals' lives and the attendant need to bring it under normative control. But in calling attention to its role in achieving background justice, he makes a complementary point. There are profound moral problems that only the basic structure can solve. In view of the tendency of individual transactions to erode background justice, and the unavailability of feasible rules of personal conduct to counteract this tendency, individuals by themselves cannot

10. Ibid., 267.

achieve a just society. Only a properly designed basic structure can secure the background conditions that are a precondition of such a society.

In this same essay, Rawls retracts his earlier claim that his focus on the basic structure is in accord with traditional thinking about justice. Conceding that this claim was misleading, he instead highlights the distinctiveness of his approach by contrasting it with utilitarianism on the one hand and libertarianism on the other. Neither of these two otherwise opposed positions sees a need for special principles to regulate the basic structure. Utilitarians recognize the moral importance of social institutions, but they believe that the same principles that regulate institutions can also be applied to individual conduct, even if this means departing from the traditional norms of personal morality. This is in keeping with the revisionism noted earlier.

Libertarians, meanwhile, see no difference between a political society and any other form of association, and regard basic social and political institutions as having no special moral status or importance at all. Instead, the same principles that govern the justice of individual transactions can be used to assess the justice of social arrangements. By contrast, Rawls insists that the institutional framework of a complex, modern society constitutes a distinctive kind of moral subject, with a social role and a set of capacities that differ from those of individual agents. As such, it requires regulation by a distinctive set of principles.

One striking implication of Rawls's position is that, as the social world develops, new social and political forms may emerge, and some of these forms may come to play such a distinctive and consequential role in human life—creating new problems, compounding old ones, and being indispensable to the solution of new and old alike—that they constitute, in effect, new types of moral subject, requiring regulation by *sui generis* normative principles. If this is correct, then morality depends on politics in the sense that, in order to know what normative principles should be applied to institutions, we need to attend to the actual institutions that have emerged in our world, to the problems they have created and the problems they can solve, and to the social roles that they play. In short: new social forms may require new moral norms.

Of course, this slogan is too simple, for these new moral norms may in turn require the modification of the new social forms or even their replacement by still newer forms. But the direction of influence runs two ways: moral norms may require changes in existing institutions and practices, but changes in existing institutions and practices may also create new forms of agency and give rise to a need for new moral norms. We should understand complaints about the novelty of Rawls's emphasis on the basic structure in this light. Critics may well be right to say that the very idea that there are special principles of "social justice" that do not apply directly to individual agents is a distinctively modern one, which finds no echo in the thought of the ancients or their successors up to the modern age. But as a modern idea it presumably emerged in response to a modern predicament and, as far as I can see, it is none the worse for that.

The bearing of these considerations on the case for cosmopolitanism should be clear. Even if there is no "global basic structure" to which principles of distributive justice should be applied, there is another way of generalizing Rawls's argument, and one that is potentially more encouraging to cosmopolitan ideas. This alternative strategy involves arguing that the processes of globalization have given rise to new human practices and institutional arrangements, which, whether or not they add up to a global basic structure, nevertheless require regulation by distinctive principles of justice.

Rawls's arguments for the primacy of the basic structure suggest that, for this alternative generalization strategy to succeed, three things would have to be established. The first is that at least some of the new global practices and arrangements have come to exert a profound and morally consequential role in human affairs. The second is that it would be either unfeasible or undesirable simply to undo the relevant practices and arrangements. And the third is that there are urgent moral problems— akin to the problem of background justice—that could not be solved either by individual agents or by the basic structures of individual societies even if both complied fully with the respective norms that apply to them, but which could be solved if the relevant global practices and organizations were regulated by *sui generis* principles of justice. Call the first of these conditions the *consequential role condition,* the second the *irreversibility condition*, and the third the *moral indispensability condition*.

It is not as easy as it may seem to tell whether these three conditions have been satisfied. One implication of Rawls's argument in *The Law of Peoples*, for example, is that the shocking facts of global poverty and inequality do not by themselves establish that the moral indispensability condition has been met. The relevant question, from a Rawlsian perspective, concerns the extent to which these appalling problems would persist even if all of the world's states were domestically just and complied fully with the law of peoples. The answer to this question is not obvious.

Nevertheless, the global economic, legal, and regulatory terrain is complex, rapidly changing, and difficult to survey. It is hard to take the measure of these developments, and easy to mistake transient features of current arrangements for permanent ones. But it seems clear that accelerating global integration is giving rise to new social forms and practices, to new patterns of interaction and interdependence, and to new modes of governance involving a heterogeneous assortment of rule-making bodies charged with fixing the terms of global economic activity. It would be rash to assume that the principles of justice with which we are already familiar, whether they apply to individuals or to the institutions of an individual society or to relations among "peoples," in Rawls's sense, will suffice to regulate all of these new social forms.

Nor should we assume that none of the new norms that may be required will be norms of distributive justice in particular. There is a tendency to frame discussions of global distributive justice as debates about how much people in affluent countries owe to those in poorer countries. This invites attention to questions about the moral significance of membership in a political society, the relative strength of our duties to conationals and to others, and the limits of required self-sacrifice. Important as these questions are, however, there is a more direct way in which economic globalization can raise issues of distributive justice—namely, by facilitating modes of interaction that have significant distributive effects that cut across national borders and elude political control by the institutions of individual societies. Consider, for example, the claim that increased access by Western capital to labor markets in developing countries has depressed the wages of Western workers while improving the prospects of poor workers in the Third World. If true, this claim seems to implicate issues of distributive justice that may be difficult to address solely at the level of the individual society.

Furthermore, the absence of a global basic structure does not mean that problems of background justice cannot arise on the global level. After all, it is not the existence of the basic structure that gives rise to the need for background justice. Cosmopolitans may argue that, if injustice is to be avoided, it is as important to impose background constraints on the processes of economic globalization as it is to impose them on a domestic market economy. One effect of globalization, in other words, may be to shift the locus of the problem of background justice by making it difficult for any single society to ensure just background conditions for transactions involving its citizens. Under these conditions, cosmopolitans may argue, using Rawls's words in a different context, that we "require special institutions to preserve background justice, and a special conception of justice to define how these institutions are to be set up."

One lesson of Rawls's theory for philosophers is that we should be wary of trying to address problems of distributive justice by debating rival allocative formulae in a political and institutional vacuum. This is a lesson that some cosmopolitan theorists have at times perhaps neglected.

But another lesson is that it is not the job of philosophers to announce a priori limits on the social and political forms that may emerge in our world, or to foreclose the possibility that at least some of those forms will require new regulative norms. This is a lesson that some *anti*cosmopolitan theorists have at times perhaps neglected.

It is worth remembering that Rawls devised his own theory of distributive justice, with its novel insistence on the primacy of the basic structure and on maximizing the position of the worst-off social group, only after the institutions of the welfare-state had already become familiar and well-established. If cosmopolitanism is the view that, similarly, the continued emergence and development of new global practices, bodies, and organizations may require the development of new and previously unanticipated kinds of regulative moral norms, then there is nothing in Rawls's theory to rule that out. Indeed, there is no better illustration of the view that changes in our social world may require changes in our repertoire of moral principles than Rawls's own arguments for the basic structure as the primary subject of justice.

PART III

Society

7

What Is Egalitarianism?

One of the most significant theories of distributive justice to have emerged since the publication of *A Theory of Justice* is the form of distributive egalitarianism that Elizabeth Anderson has dubbed "luck egalitarianism."[1] This theory has

Originally published in *Philosophy & Public Affairs* 31, no. 1. Copyright © 2003 by Princeton University Press. Used by permission of John Wiley & Sons, Inc. An earlier version of this article was presented as the 2002 Sir Malcolm Knox Memorial Lecture at the University of St. Andrews. Versions were also presented to the Philosophy Department at the University of Pennsylvania; to the Colloquium in Legal and Social Philosophy at University College London; and as a Keynote Address to the 2002 Berkeley-Stanford Graduate Student Philosophy Conference. I am grateful for the helpful comments, questions, and suggestions that I received from many people, including David Archard, Elizabeth Ashford, Sarah Broadie, Samuel Freeman, Christopher Kutz, Véronique Munoz-Dardé, Michael Otsuka, Stephen Perry, Eric Rakowski, Thomas Ricketts, Debra Satz, John Skorupski, Gopal Sreenivasan, Jay Wallace, Andrew Williams, and Jonathan Wolff. I am particularly indebted to G. A. Cohen for detailed written comments; to Ronald Dworkin for extensive discussion; and to three readers for *Philosophy & Public Affairs*, who made many extremely valuable suggestions for improvement. I thank Sarah Goldberg for research assistance.
1. Elizabeth Anderson, "What Is the Point of Equality?" *Ethics* 109 (1999): 287–337.

different variants, but the central idea is common to all of these variants. The core idea is that inequalities in the advantages that people enjoy are acceptable if they derive from the choices that people have voluntarily made, but that inequalities deriving from unchosen features of people's circumstances are unjust. Unchosen circumstances are taken to include social factors like the class and wealth of the family into which one is born. They are also deemed to include natural factors like one's native abilities and intelligence.

Luck egalitarianism overlaps with but also diverges from the prevailing political morality in most liberal societies, both with respect to the unacceptability of inequalities deriving from people's circumstances and with respect to the acceptability of inequalities deriving from their choices. Consider first the unacceptability of inequalities deriving from people's circumstances. The prevailing political morality holds that intentional discrimination based on largely unchosen factors such as race, religion, sex, and ethnicity is unjust, and that distributive inequalities resulting from such discrimination are unjust as well. It also holds that people of equal talent from different social classes should have equal access to the social positions for which their talents qualify them, and that it is unjust if inequalities result from a society's failure to provide this kind of equal opportunity. Thus, the prevailing morality agrees with luck egalitarianism in rejecting certain kinds of inequalities deriving from unchosen features of people's circumstances. However, in rejecting all inequalities of advantage resulting from differing circumstances, luck egalitarianism goes far beyond the prevailing political morality, which, against a background of nondiscrimination and equal opportunity, is prepared to tolerate significant distributive inequalities deriving from differences of talent and ability. By contrast, luck egalitarianism denies that a person's natural talent, creativity, intelligence, innovative skill, or entrepreneurial ability can be the basis for legitimate inequalities.

Consider next the acceptability of inequalities deriving from people's choices. If some people make more money than others because they choose to work longer hours, then the prevailing morality certainly agrees with luck egalitarianism that that is not in itself objectionable. Unlike luck egalitarianism, however, the prevailing political morality does not go so far as to say that any extra income deriving from people's choices should, in principle, be exempt from redistributive taxation. In determining one's tax burden, the prevailing morality makes no attempt to identify, let alone to shield from taxation, the portion of one's income that is traceable specifically to one's choices as opposed to one's natural abilities.

The upshot is that although there are substantial areas of overlap between luck egalitarianism and the prevailing political morality, luck egalitarianism is in one way much more willing than the prevailing morality to engage in redistributive taxation, but also in one way much less willing. In this sense at least, luck egalitarianism is both more and less egalitarian than the prevailing political morality.[2]

Unlike Rawls's theory, which became the focus of intense critical scrutiny as soon as *A Theory of Justice* appeared in print, luck egalitarianism has been relatively slow to attract critical attention, despite the impressive level of influence it has attained and the lively debates that have taken place among proponents of its different variants. This state of affairs has begun to change, however, and in this article I wish to make a modest contribution to the project of critical examination that Anderson and others have initiated.[3] I am indebted to Anderson's discussion in many ways, some of which I will acknowledge more specifically as I proceed. But my primary emphases will be different from hers, and I hope that my main points are sufficiently independent as to be of interest in their own right.

Luck egalitarianism is often presented as an extension and generalization of some Rawlsian arguments whose substantive implications Rawls himself failed fully to appreciate. Thus, luck egalitarianism is often said by its advocates to be truer than Rawls's own conception of justice to some of his fundamental insights. In part because of its putative Rawlsian pedigree, perhaps, luck egalitarianism's supporters have done less than one might expect to provide an independent defense of the position at the fundamental level. In this article, however, I argue

2. I do not mean to imply that these two factors cancel each out so that there is no net difference in the redistributive implications of the two positions. Luck egalitarians differ among themselves about the how much redistribution is justified, in part because they disagree about the extent to which actual inequalities are the result of differences in people's circumstances as opposed to differences in their choices. The "prevailing political morality" also encompasses a range of positions on the extent of legitimate redistribution, for although, as I have said, adherents of the prevailing morality have no principled objection to taxing income that derives from people's choices, they disagree among themselves about how much taxation is justified and why. In general, however, most luck egalitarians think that the economic regimes of contemporary liberal societies should be significantly more redistributive than those regimes have usually been in practice, and more redistributive than the prevailing political morality would allow. As I note in Section II, it is therefore striking that the rise of luck egalitarianism occurred during a period in which liberal societies were in fact becoming much less redistributive.

3. See, in addition to the paper of Anderson's cited above, Jonathan Wolff, "Fairness, Respect, and the Egalitarian Ethos," *Philosophy & Public Affairs* 27 (1998): 97–122; Seana Valentine Shiffrin, "Paternalism, Unconscionability Doctrine, and Accommodation," *Philosophy & Public Affairs* 29 (2000): 205–250; Timothy Hinton, "Must Egalitarians Choose Between Fairness and Respect?" *Philosophy & Public Affairs* 30 (2001): 72–87. Debra Satz has also pursued related themes in her as yet unpublished work.

that luck egalitarianism can draw little support from Rawls. In addition, I present reasons for doubting whether it is either a plausible position in its own right or a compelling interpretation of egalitarianism.

My article is organized as follows. In Section I, I will summarize a familiar version of the recent history of political philosophy—a version that locates the origins of luck egalitarianism in Rawls's thought but insists that he himself fails to develop the view in a consistent or thoroughgoing way. Although I will make clear my disagreement with the interpretation of Rawls as an incipient luck egalitarian, I will postpone a complete account of the bases for my disagreement until Section III. In the intervening section (Section II), I will present some reasons for doubting the plausibility of the luck-egalitarian position. In the course of my discussion, I will argue that any form of distributive egalitarianism, if it is to be persuasive, must be rooted in a more general conception of equality as a moral value or normative ideal. With that argument as background, I will return in Section III to Rawls. I will attempt to show that his work, properly understood, provides no support for luck egalitarianism; his position is better understood as helping to illustrate how a plausible form of distributive egalitarianism can be anchored in a conception of equality as a social and political ideal. Finally, in Section IV, I will consider some attempts to demonstrate that luck-egalitarian principles can also be anchored in a broader conception of equality.

I

As I have noted, it is often said that luck egalitarianism has its origins in Rawls's work, but that Rawls himself fails to develop the view in a consistent or thoroughgoing way. According to this interpretation, Dworkin subsequently builds on the basic Rawlsian insight to provide the first systematic formulation of a luck-egalitarian position, a formulation that is more faithful to Rawls's original insight than is Rawls's own conception of justice. Alternative versions of luck egalitarianism are then developed in response to Dworkin and Rawls. Will Kymlicka offers a clear description of this putative progression of ideas. Kymlicka says that "[o]ne of Rawls's central intuitions...concerns the distinction between choices and circumstances,"[4] and that Rawls is "motivated"[5] by the desire to produce a theory

4. Will Kymlicka, *Contemporary Political Philosophy* (Oxford: Clarendon Press, 1990), p. 70.
5. Ibid., p. 76.

that is "ambition sensitive" but "endowment insensitive"—a theory that makes people's fortunes depend on their choices but not on their natural endowments or other unchosen circumstances. However, Kymlicka adds, "Rawls seems not to have realized the full implications of his own argument,"[6] for "while Rawls appeals to th[e] choices-circumstances distinction, his difference principle violates it."[7] By contrast, he continues, "Dworkin accepts the 'ambition sensitive' and 'endowment insensitive' goal that motivated Rawls's difference principle. But he thinks a different distributive scheme can do a better job living up to that ideal."[8]

There are two primary aspects of Rawls's work that are usually cited as evidence for his (imperfectly developed) luck egalitarianism. The first is his informal moral argument for the superiority of his two principles of justice of the laissez-faire "system of natural liberty." That rival scheme allows for the operation of a free market economy constrained only by a background of equal liberty and formal equality of opportunity. Rawls observes that the system of natural liberty permits the distribution of resources to be "strongly influenced"[9] by people's natural attributes and the social positions into which they are born. But these factors, he argues, are "arbitrary from a moral point of view."[10] Because they are so arbitrary, we should not allow the distribution of resources "to be improperly influenced by" them.[11] Instead, we should strive "to mitigate the influence of social contingencies and natural fortune on distributive shares."[12] Rawls goes on to say that this line of thought does not, "strictly speaking,"[13] count as an argument for his conception of justice, since he is undertaking to develop a kind of social contract theory and, as he understands it, this means that the "official" arguments for his conception must be arguments that establish that it would be rational for the parties in the original position to choose it. Nevertheless, the "unofficial" moral argument that I have sketched is often cited as the initiating formulation of the luck-egalitarian idea that inequalities deriving from unchosen circumstances are unjust.

The second aspect of Rawls's view that has been understood as luck egalitarian in its tendency is the appeal to responsibility that he makes

6. Ibid., p. 72.
7. Ibid., p. 76.
8. Ibid.
9. John Rawls, *A Theory of Justice* (Cambridge: Harvard University Press, 1971), p. 72.
10. Ibid.
11. Ibid.
12. Ibid., p. 73.
13. Ibid., p. 75.

in the course of defending primary social goods as the appropriate basis for interpersonal comparisons. Some critics argue that primary goods are not a reasonable basis for such comparisons because a theory that relies on them takes no account of variations in the costs of satisfying different people's preferences. Two people with identical bundles of primary goods may have very different levels of utility or welfare because one of the people has simple tastes that can be inexpensively satisfied while the other has preferences that are very costly to satisfy. Since primary goods take no account of these variations, a theory that uses them as the basis for interpersonal comparisons will treat the two people as enjoying the same level of well-being and will make no provision for the greater difficulty that the second person has in satisfying his preferences. In response, Rawls argues that we have "a capacity to assume responsibility for our ends,"[14] and that "citizens can regulate and revise their ends and preferences in the light of their expectations of primary goods."[15] In a just society, therefore, "those with less expensive tastes have presumably adjusted their likes and dislikes over the course of their lives to the income and wealth they could reasonably expect; and it is regarded as unfair that they now should have less in order to spare others from the consequences of their lack of foresight or self-discipline."[16] This response has been cited as an early expression of the luck-egalitarian position that people must bear the cost of their own choices and that economic inequalities are, therefore, legitimate provided they arise from differences in the choices that people make.[17]

Despite what he sees as the luck-egalitarian strands in Rawls's thought, Kymlicka argues that Rawls's own theory of justice is incompatible with luck egalitarianism in at least two significant respects. First, the difference principle does not make any special provision for those who have special medical needs, even when those needs result from unchosen natural conditions, since the principle takes only primary *social* goods, such as money, into account when assessing individuals' well-being. Thus, the principle treats two individuals with identical bundles of primary social goods as being equally well-off, even if one of the individuals is in normal health while the other suffers from a congenital medical condition that is very costly to treat. Second, the difference principle seeks to maximize the position of the worst-off social class, as measured by an index of

14. Rawls, "Social Unity and Primary Goods," in *John Rawls: Collected Papers*, Samuel Freeman (ed.) (Cambridge: Harvard University Press, 1999), pp. 359–397, at p. 369.
15. Ibid., p. 370.
16. Ibid., pp. 369–370.
17. See, for example, Kymlicka, p. 75.

primary goods, even if the reason that some members of that class have small shares of those goods is that they freely choose to work shorter hours because of a preference for greater leisure over greater income. In this way, the difference principle interferes with the processes by which differences in people's choices may generate economic inequalities, and it requires some people to bear the costs of the free choices made by others.

The fact that these features of the difference principle are incompatible with a luck-egalitarian position has led some interpreters to conclude that Rawls's view is inconsistent and that he fails to appreciate fully the implications of his own luck-egalitarian arguments and premises. I think that this interpretation is misleading, and that it is a mistake to construe Rawls as appealing to a general distinction between circumstances and choices, which his difference principle then fails to respect. I do not see any evidence that Rawls relies on such a distinction or that he ever expresses the aim of producing a theory that is "endowment insensitive" but "ambition sensitive." In my view, the best explanation of the fact that Rawls's theory of justice does not respect the distinction between choices and circumstances is that Rawls is not attempting to respect it. He simply does not regard the distinction as having the kind of fundamental importance that it has for luck egalitarians.

To be sure, Rawls does make the arguments against the system of natural liberty and in favor of a reliance on primary goods as the basis for interpersonal comparisons, which have been seen as congenial to a luck-egalitarian position. But Rawls deploys those arguments in the service of a view that is substantively quite different from luck egalitarianism. Nor does Rawls's view have the same theoretical motivations as the ones articulated by luck egalitarians. Richard Arneson, for example, when introducing his preferred version of a luck-egalitarian position,[18] says that it "is addressed to egalitarians"[19] and that it seeks to answer the following question: "Insofar as we care for equality as a distributive ideal,

---

18. Richard J. Arneson, "Equality and Equal Opportunity for Welfare," *Philosophical Studies* 56 (1989): 77–93. More recently, Arneson has abandoned the version of luck egalitarianism defended in this article, in favor of a view that he calls "responsibility-catering prioritarianism." See, for example, Richard J. Arneson, "Equality of Opportunity for Welfare Defended and Recanted," *Journal of Political Philosophy* 7 (1999): 488–497; and "Luck Egalitarianism and Prioritarianism," *Ethics* 110 (2000): 339–349. In the second of these two articles Arneson describes responsibility-catering prioritarianism both as an "(outlier) member of the luck egalitarian family" (p. 340) and as "a close cousin of luck egalitarianism" (p. 341).

19. Arneson, "Equality and Equal Opportunity for Welfare," p. 77.

what is it exactly that we prize?"[20] His reply is that "the idea of equal opportunity for welfare is the best interpretation of the ideal of distributive equality."[21] In posing this question and developing his reply, Arneson takes himself to be entering into a discussion initiated by Rawls and Dworkin. Their writings, he says, "have debated the merits of equality of welfare and equality of resources taken as interpretations of the egalitarian ideal."[22] I will postpone until Section IV the question of how best to characterize Dworkin's enterprise, but I believe it is a mistake to present Rawls as aiming to persuade an audience of fellow distributive egalitarians that equality of resources is a better interpretation of the egalitarian ideal than equality of welfare. As I shall try to show, Rawls's theory has different aims and ambitions, and relies on different moral premises. Thus, it is hardly surprising, and certainly no sign of inconsistency, that his theory should end up having a different content as well.

Of course, someone might insist that whatever Rawls himself may think, a luck-egalitarian position does in fact follow from his arguments against natural liberty and in favor of primary goods, once the full implications of those arguments are properly understood. To the extent that he fails to recognize this consequence, his theory is so much the worse for that. I do not find this convincing. In Section III, I will outline briefly the kind of alternative view that Rawls's arguments seem to me intended to support. Although there are certainly areas of overlap between Rawls's position and luck egalitarianism, and although there are certainly strands of argument in his work that luck egalitarians are bound to regard as congenial, my own view is that, on the whole, Rawls's arguments support his own position rather than luck egalitarianism. In certain fundamental respects, moreover, Rawls's position seems to me more attractive than luck egalitarianism. For the moment, however, I want to set Rawls's view to one side and explain some of the reasons for my reservations about the luck-egalitarian position.

II

As I have already suggested, many discussions of luck egalitarianism are addressed primarily to other egalitarians. They simply assume that an ideal of distributive equality has an important role to play in our

20. Ibid.
21. Ibid.
22. Ibid.

thinking about distributive justice, and they ask how that ideal is best to be understood. Arneson makes the point explicitly. His arguments, he writes, are "addressed to egalitarians, not their opponents."[23] As with Arneson's own essay, most of the luck-egalitarian literature is devoted to considering two closely related questions. The first question is what exactly egalitarians wish to equalize.[24] This question is often formulated as a question about the correct "metric" of equality. The candidates for equalization that have been debated include welfare, resources, opportunity for welfare, and access to advantage, among others. The second question is which forms of disadvantage should receive compensation in the name of equality. Here there has been discussion of physical handicaps, medical needs, limited talents, unfavorable social positions, unsuccessful gambles, expensive tastes, expensive religious commitments, undesirable aspects of temperament, and so on.

Although the debates about how best to respond to these questions have been intense, it is by no means clear how much the different versions of luck egalitarianism differ in their practical, political implications. Arneson, speaking of the choice between some version of "equality of resources" and his own preferred principle of "equal opportunity for welfare," concedes that "the practical implications of these conflicting principles may be hard to discern, and may not diverge much in practise."[25] But if the practical import of the intra-egalitarian debates is not always clear, there is no doubt that there are great differences, of considerable political significance, between luck egalitarians as a group and nonegalitarians. Yet luck egalitarians have spent relatively little time defending the moral core of the luck-egalitarian position against skeptics and proponents of other views. An analogy would be a debate among defenders of rival versions of utilitarianism in which the practical stakes were unclear and little attempt was made to persuade others that maximizing some version of utility was the right approach to take in the first place.

Of course, there is certainly a place for internal discussions, among the proponents of any broad philosophical position, about how that

23. Ibid.
24. Indeed, in some luck-egalitarian writings, this is not only the first question but also the first sentence. John Roemer, for example, begins his essay "Equality of Talent" by asking: "If one is an egalitarian, what should one want to equalize?" And Roemer's essay "A Pragmatic Theory of Responsibility for the Egalitarian Planner" begins: "What should an egalitarian seek to equalize?" Both essays are included in Roemer's *Egalitarian Perspectives* (New York: Cambridge University Press, 1994), pp. 119–147 and 179–196, respectively.
25. Arneson, "Equality and Equal Opportunity for Welfare," p. 87.

position is best to be interpreted. Utilitarians do in fact engage in such discussions, as do proponents of every other philosophical position that is appealing enough to attract a wide and diverse group of supporters. Important as these internal discussions are, however, they do not obviate the need to motivate, explain, and defend the core of a philosophical position to those who are not yet persuaded. In the specific case of luck egalitarianism, moreover, this task is especially important in light of the stark contrast between the theory's political implications and the political context in which it was developed. The rise of luck egalitarianism as an important position within political philosophy, which took place during roughly the last two decades of the twentieth century, coincided with a marked increase in inequalities of income and wealth in the United States and other liberal societies.[26] Those decades were characterized by a strong trend, intensified by the collapse of the Soviet Union, toward increased privatization and reliance on the market, and a steady erosion in political support for distributive egalitarianism of any kind. Thus there was a sharp disparity between the luck egalitarianism that was becoming increasingly influential in philosophical discussions of distributive justice, and the actual distributive practices of the societies in which those discussions took place—and this despite the fact that one of the aims of luck-egalitarian theorists is to demonstrate that egalitarians need not, in general, be hostile to markets, and must indeed rely upon them in important ways. Of course, the existence of a disparity between luck-egalitarian theory and actual political practice does not by itself tell against the luck-egalitarian position. Justice is a normative notion, and so no proposed principle of justice can be falsified simply by pointing out that actual practice does not, in fact, conform to it. Yet the starkness of the contrast between luck-egalitarian theory and contemporary political practice makes it especially important to address fundamental questions about the moral defensibility of the core luck-egalitarian idea. What needs to be considered is whether luck egalitarians have latched on to an idea of equality that has real appeal as a social and political value.

The importance of addressing this issue can be brought out in another way. A moment ago I suggested a parallel between debates among luck egalitarians and intra-utilitarian debates. The relation between luck egalitarianism and utilitarianism is an interesting and, I think, an instructive

26. For some of the relevant U.S. data, see U.S. Census Bureau, *Income Inequality (1967–1998)*, at www.census.gov/hhes/income/incineq/p60204/. For data on other liberal democracies, see Timothy M. Smeeding, "Changing Income Inequality in OECD Countries: Updated Results from the Luxembourg Income Study," *Luxembourg Income Study Working Paper No. 252* (March 2000).

one, which merits closer scrutiny. For those who interpret Rawls as an early adherent of luck egalitarianism, his defense of primary goods as the basis for interpersonal comparisons has been taken to place him squarely on the side of those who advocate equality of resources, and in opposition to those who advocate some version of equality of welfare. Yet Rawls' defense of primary goods is of course part of an argument against utilitarianism, not equality of welfare. His target, in other words, is the position that we should maximize welfare, not that we should equalize it. Now for utilitarians, the notion of utility or welfare—whether it is interpreted hedonistically or is instead construed as consisting in the satisfaction of preferences—plays a double role. First, it supplies the content of the utilitarian theory of what is genuinely valuable or good, both for an individual and *sans phrase*. Second, it is treated as the appropriate measure to use in assessing personal well-being. These two roles are related, inasmuch as it is the utilitarian theory of the good that underwrites the reliance on utility as the measure of individual well-being. And both of these features of utilitarianism are distinct from its third crucial claim, which is that the right or just thing to do is to maximize overall utility.

Rawls is sensitive both to the distinctions and to the relations among these three features of the utilitarian position. He rejects the utilitarian theory of the individual good, which he regards as indefensibly monistic, in favor of the pluralistic view that the good for an individual consists in the successful development and execution of a rational plan of life. And the switch from a monistic to a pluralistic account of the good helps in turn to motivate his rejection of utility in favor of primary goods as the measure of personal well-being, as well as his rejection of maximizing conceptions of justice in favor of the idea that what justice requires is the establishment of a fair framework of cooperation within which people can pursue their diverse plans of life.

When the position that one ought to maximize aggregate welfare is replaced by the position that one ought to equalize welfare levels, certain objections to the maximizing view are transformed. For example, utilitarianism is often said to be embarrassed by the possibility of "utility monsters"—that is, by the possibility of people who are unusually efficient at converting resources into utility. The objection is that if there were such people, utilitarianism would dictate that resources should be channeled disproportionately to them, without regard for the distributive implications of such a policy. When utilitarianism is replaced by a welfarist version of luck egalitarianism, the problem of utility monsters is replaced by the problem of expensive tastes. Here the objection is that if one aims to equalize welfare, then the distribution of resources in society is held hostage to those whose tastes and preferences are unusually costly to satisfy—that is, to people who are unusually inefficient at converting resources into utility. Welfarist egalitarianism is said to imply that resources should be channeled disproportionately to these people, without regard for the way in which doing so may depress the levels of well-being that others can achieve.

In view of the relation between these two objections, it would be instructive to compare the respective conclusions that critics have drawn from them. It would also be useful to explore other connections between utilitarianism and luck egalitarianism. But although a number of luck-egalitarian writers have in fact compared the two positions, their comparisons usually begin from the premise that utilitarianism is most plausible when construed as a theory of equality, rather than as a teleological view that is concerned with maximizing the good.[27] Since, as these writers invariably go on to point out, utilitarianism is actually quite implausible when construed as a theory of equality, their discussions rarely amount to more than a rehearsal of the advantages of luck egalitarianism. But the interpretation of utilitarianism as a theory of equality is itself implausible in my view,[28] and so a less narrowly structured investigation of the relations between utilitarian and luck-egalitarian principles would be welcome.

27. Dworkin makes this claim in *Sovereign Virtue* (Cambridge: Harvard University Press, 2000), pp. 62–64. It is developed at length by Kymlicka (*Contemporary Political Philosophy*, chaps. 2 and 3, and *Liberalism, Community, and Culture* [Oxford: Clarendon Press, 1989], chap. 3), who absorbs it into (what might be called) his "egalicentric" narrative of the history of political philosophy. Kymlicka argues that Rawls's theory of justice is motivated by inadequacies in the utilitarian conception of equality, and that Dworkin's theory of justice is then motivated by inadequacies in Rawls's conception of equality. ("Dworkin's theory was a response to problems in Rawls's conception of equality, just as Rawls's theory was a response to problems in the utilitarian conception of equality" [*Contemporary Political Philosophy*, p. 85].) Eric Rakowski seems also to endorse the claim in his *Equal Justice* (Oxford: Clarendon Press, 1991), pp. 23–25. Amartya Sen, who does not himself put forward a luck-egalitarian theory but whose emphasis on the question "equality of what" has exerted a powerful influence on the development of luck egalitarianism, speaks of the "'hidden' egalitarianism in utilitarian philosophy" (*Inequality Reexamined* [Cambridge: Harvard University Press, 1992], p. 13). By this he means that utilitarianism attaches equal importance to the utilities of all people, and that this "egalitarian foundation is…quite central to the entire utilitarian exercise" (p. 14). Sen is surely correct to say that the fact that utilitarians attach equal importance to the interests of all people is a very significant feature of their view. However, it is a further step to the conclusion that utilitarianism is best thought of simply as a theory of equality. Not every theory that favors equality in some respect is best interpreted as being motivated, ultimately, by a conception of what equality requires.

28. For reasons that are well explained in Samuel Freeman, "Utilitarianism, Deontology, and the Priority of Right," *Philosophy & Public Affairs* 23 (1994): 313–349.

Discussions of luck egalitarianism have also done a less thorough job, in general, of addressing the most fundamental questions about the justification of that position, than utilitarians and their critics have done in addressing the analogous questions about the justification of utilitarianism. For example, luck-egalitarian debates between welfarists and resourcists do not always distinguish clearly between the question of whether welfarism is an adequate theory of the good, and the question of whether it is the individual good itself, or instead the means of achieving it, that egalitarians should be seeking to equalize. And the idea that justice requires the equal distribution of *something* is often simply taken for granted as the starting point of discussion.

In my view, the luck-egalitarian position is open to doubt on a number of grounds. Perhaps the most obvious difficulty is that the degree of weight that the luck egalitarian places on the distinction between choices and circumstances seems, on its face, to be both philosophically dubious and morally implausible. Philosophically, the question is whether the distinction is deep enough to bear the kind of weight that luck egalitarians place on it. Some luck-egalitarian writings seem implicitly to suggest that whatever is assigned to the category of unchosen circumstance is a contingent feature of the causal order, which is not under the individual's control and does not implicate his or her personhood, whereas voluntary choices are fully under the control of individuals and constitute pure expressions of their agency. But this contrast is, of course, untenable. In any sense of identity that actually matters to people, unchosen personal traits and the social circumstances into which one is born are importantly, albeit not exclusively, constitutive of one's distinctive identity.[29] And, in any ordinary sense of *voluntary,* people's voluntary choices are routinely influenced by unchosen features of their personalities, temperaments, and the social contexts in which they find themselves. In his defense of a version of luck egalitarianism,[30] G. A. Cohen concedes that reliance on the distinction between choices and circumstances may leave luck egalitarians "up to our necks in the free will problem," but he says— perhaps with some irony?—that "that is just tough luck."[31] Cohen points out that one of the achievements of luck egalitarianism is to demonstrate that egalitarians can incorporate "the most powerful idea in the arsenal of the anti-egalitarian right: the idea of choice and responsibility."[32] Yet, in

---

29. This is a theme of several of the essays included in my *Boundaries and Allegiances* (New York: Oxford University Press, 2001).
30. G. A. Cohen, "On the Currency of Egalitarian Justice," *Ethics* 99 (1989): 906–944.
31. Ibid., p. 934.
32. Ibid., p. 933.

so doing, luck egalitarianism invites the objection that, like the political philosophies of the anti-egalitarian right, it tacitly derives much of its appeal from an implausible understanding of the metaphysical status of the category of choice.

This objection would be easier to dismiss if the luck-egalitarian account of the significance of choice were morally compelling. But in fact that account seems on its face to be morally implausible. It is morally implausible, for example, that justice requires individuals to be fully compensated for disadvantages that derive from unchosen features of their circumstances but not to be compensated at all for disadvantages that result from their voluntary choices. As Anderson has argued, it is morally implausible that choice should have that kind of significance or make that degree of difference. On the one hand, there are many unchosen personal attributes that may be disadvantageous but for which we do not, in fact, demand compensation from others. On the other hand, the fact that a person's urgent medical needs can be traced to his own negligence or foolishness or high-risk behavior is not normally seen as making it legitimate to deny him the care he needs. Still less do people automatically forfeit any claim to assistance if it turns out that their urgent needs are the result of prudent or well-considered choices that simply turned out badly.[33] We are neither so systematically alienated from the unchosen aspects of our own identities nor so uniformly confident of and identified with our role as choosers as to regard the presence or absence of choice as having this kind of make-or-break significance. This helps explain why the appeal of luck egalitarianism may seem tacitly to depend on a form of metaphysical libertarianism, for libertarianism may appear to promise a basis in metaphysics for a dichotomy that would otherwise seem so stark as to be morally untenable.[34]

Some luck-egalitarian writers have sought to address these difficulties by qualifying the luck-egalitarian principle or limiting its application in various ways. And some writers have suggested that certain of the difficulties can be avoided by drawing the line between choices and

---

33. See Anderson, "What is the Point of Equality," pp. 296–300.
34. In "Responsibility, Reactive Attitudes, and Liberalism in Philosophy and Politics" (*Philosophy & Public Affairs* 21 [1992]: 299–323, reprinted in *Boundaries and Allegiances*, pp. 12–31), I argued that contemporary liberalism has been exposed to conservative attack because of a perceived tendency among many liberals, both in politics and in philosophy, to rely on a reduced conception of individual agency and responsibility. The points made in the last two paragraphs might be taken to suggest that what luck egalitarianism has done, in effect, is to overcompensate for that perceived tendency.

circumstances differently. Dworkin, for example, in explaining the differences between his view and Cohen's, argues that the line should be rooted in "ordinary people's ethical experience."[35] If the distinction is drawn in this way, he says, then various aspects of one's personality that are not in any straightforward sense chosen—including one's ambitions, tastes, preferences, convictions, and traits of character—will nevertheless fall on the choice side of the line. The reasons are twofold. First, all of these features of personality are relevant to the choices that one makes, either because they supply motives for one's actions or because they "affect [one's] pursuit of" one's ends.[36] Second, people normally identify with these aspects of their personalities and see themselves as having to take "consequential responsibility" for them, in the sense that they expect to have to bear the costs of possessing them.[37] One conclusion Dworkin draws from this is that people cannot normally demand compensation for expensive values or tastes. Even though such tastes are not actually chosen, they nevertheless fall on the choice side of the line by his standards, at least when people identify with them. Eric Rakowski, who takes a similar position, says that people's values and beliefs are "constitutive elements of themselves for which they must assume responsibility,"[38] and that even though one does not choose one's preferences, one can nevertheless choose to strengthen or weaken them, so that they too are appropriately situated on the choice side of the line.[39]

35. Dworkin's reply to Cohen takes up sections II through IV of chap. 7 of *Sovereign Virtue*. The quoted phrase occurs on pp. 289–290. There is additional discussion of the ethical interpretation of the distinction between choices and circumstances on pp. 322–325. It is worth noting that in his original formulations of his equality of resources scheme, Dworkin did not characterize the relevant distinction as a distinction between choices and circumstances at all. He tended to speak instead of a distinction between the person and his circumstances. See, for example, *Sovereign Virtue*, pp. 81 and 140. He was criticized for this by Cohen (in Section IV of "On the Currency of Egalitarian Justice"), who argued that the relevant notion is choice rather than personality. In more recent discussions, such as those cited at the beginning of this note, Dworkin does indeed characterize the distinction as a distinction between choices and circumstances (or choice and chance), but he preserves a link with his earlier characterization by asserting that people's "choices reflect their personalities" (*Sovereign Virtue*, p. 322). My argument in the text is that this does not yield a distinction between choices and circumstances that is helpful to Dworkin's position.
36. Dworkin, *Sovereign Virtue*, p. 322.
37. Ibid., p. 290.
38. Rakowski, *Equal Justice*, p. 63.
39. Ibid., pp. 57–72.

However, this way of drawing the line between choices and circumstances leads to further difficulties. By the criteria that Dworkin and Rakowski suggest, people's talents and abilities, no less than their ambitions and preferences, may also deserve to be situated on the choice side of the line. After all, people's talents and abilities are often relevant to their choices, either because they shape people's motives or because they affect people's pursuit of their ends. In addition, people frequently view their talents, no less than their values and preferences, as importantly constitutive of their identities. And even if talents are themselves unchosen, people can nevertheless choose whether to develop them. Furthermore, many people also expect to take "consequential responsibility" for their talents, in the sense that they believe they are entitled to the differential rewards that such talents may enable them to secure. If this is correct, then the effect of broadening the category of choice to include not only the actions one actually chooses but also the various constitutive features of oneself that underlie one's choices, is to cast doubt on the capacity of the distinction between choices and circumstances to support the substantive positions that luck egalitarians favor.[40]

There is a further point that a number of critics have made. Luck egalitarianism, as it is often presented, appears to treat equality as being an essentially distributive ideal whose fundamental aim is to eliminate the effects on distribution of "brute luck." Because of this concern to neutralize brute luck, the luck egalitarian arrives at allocative decisions on the basis of judgments that are strongly "inward looking." That is, an individual's claim to be compensated in the name of equality for some disadvantage always depends on a judgment about the source of the disadvantage in different aspects of the self. We cannot know whether an individual's disadvantage entitles her to egalitarian compensation without disentangling the respective contributions made by her will, on the one hand, and by unchosen features of her talents and personal circumstances, on the other hand, to the processes that put her at that disadvantage. For this reason, luck egalitarianism encourages her to look inward

---

40. At one point (*Sovereign Virtue*, pp. 260–263), Dworkin himself insists on the importance, for ethical purposes, of identification with aspects of one's unchosen circumstances. These "parameters," which help define what counts as a good life for an individual, are distinguished from those circumstances that count instead as "limitations" on one's ability to lead a good life. However, as Anthony Appiah suggests in his review of *Sovereign Virtue*, it is very unclear how a recognition of the ethical role of parameters is to be reconciled with the assignment of fundamental significance to the distinction between choices and circumstances. (See K. Anthony Appiah, "Equality of What?" *The New York Review of Books* April 26 [2001]: 63–68.)

in deciding whether she has a legitimate claim on fellow citizens, and, as Anderson and Wolff have emphasized,[41] it encourages those fellow citizens both to scrutinize the deepest aspects of her self and to arrive at heavily moralized judgments about the degree of responsibility she bears for her own misfortune.

In all of the respects I have mentioned, the luck-egalitarian conception of equality diverges from a more familiar way of understanding that value. Equality, as it is more commonly understood, is not, in the first instance, a distributive ideal, and its aim is not to compensate for misfortune. It is, instead, a moral ideal governing the relations in which people stand to one another. Instead of focusing attention on the differing contingencies of each person's traits, abilities, and other circumstances, this ideal abstracts from the undeniable differences among people. It claims that human relations must be conducted on the basis of an assumption that everyone's life is equally important, and that all members of a society have equal standing. As Anderson insists, in defending a version of this ideal, equality so understood is opposed not to luck but to oppression, to heritable hierarchies of social status, to ideas of caste, to class privilege and the rigid stratification of classes, and to the undemocratic distribution of power. In contrast to the inward-looking focus of luck egalitarianism, it emphasizes the irrelevance of individual differences for fundamental social and political purposes. As a moral ideal, it asserts that all people are of equal worth and that there are some claims that people are entitled to make on one another simply by virtue of their status as persons. As a social ideal, it holds that a human society must be conceived of as a cooperative arrangement among equals, each of whom enjoys the same social standing. As a political ideal, it highlights the claims that citizens are entitled to make on one another by virtue of their status *as* citizens, without any need for a moralized accounting of the details of their particular circumstances. Indeed, it insists on the very great importance of the right to be viewed simply as a citizen, and to have one's fundamental rights and privileges determined on that basis, without reference to one's talents, intelligence, wisdom, decision-making skill, temperament, social class, religious or ethnic affiliation, or ascribed identity.

Of course, things are not quite so simple. The *social and political ideal* of equality, as I will call it, itself has distributive implications. Furthermore, even if that ideal emphasizes the importance, for certain purposes, of abstracting from the differing contingencies of individuals' situations,

---

41. Anderson, "What is the Point of Equality?" (at, for example, p. 310); Wolff, "Fairness, Respect, and the Egalitarian Ethos" (especially pp. 113–118).

it must also concede the necessity of attending to such differences for other purposes. People may claim equal rights as citizens, but the interpretation and application of those rights will often depend on features of their individual circumstances. And special circumstances may at times give rise to special rights. Still, one will think about the distributional implications of equality very differently than luck egalitarianism tempts us to do if one insists that, in the end, the relevant question is about the bearing on distribution of a morally-based ideal of human social and political relations—and not about the optimal way of reflecting in our economy a metaphysical distinction between individuals' choices and their unchosen circumstances. Granted, the social and political ideal of equality may itself be understood in different ways.[42] But unless distributive egalitarianism is anchored in some version of that ideal, or in some other comparably general understanding of equality as a moral value or normative ideal, it will be arbitrary, pointless, fetishistic—no more compelling than a preference for any other distributive pattern.

If one keeps firmly in mind the fact that questions about egalitarian distributive norms must be controlled by some broader understanding of equality, then the appeal of luck egalitarianism seems to me limited. As I have already suggested, many people accept what I have called the social and political ideal of equality. That ideal does not support the ambition of purging the influence of brute luck from human relations, which is just as well since one has only to describe that ambition for its folly to be evident. As Anderson argues, questions of distribution are important, for people who are committed to the social and political value of equality, not because a properly designed set of distributive institutions can help to minimize the influence of luck, but rather because certain kinds of distributive arrangements are incongruous with that social and political value. Clearly, for example, people whose basic needs have not been met—people who lack adequate food, clothing, shelter, education, or medical care—cannot participate in political life or civil society on a footing of equality with others, or can do so only with great difficulty. Even if basic needs have been met, a society cannot be considered a society of equals if the resources that individuals have available to pursue their most cherished ends is left entirely at the mercy of market forces. Moreover, significant distributive inequalities can all too easily

---

42. One important interpretative issue, about which there is no general consensus, is what the ideal implies about the relations among people who are not citizens of the same country or members of the same political society. Debra Satz discusses this issue in her unpublished paper, "Inequality of What and Between Whom? When and Where Does Inequality Matter? The Case of Inequality Between Nations."

generate inequalities of power and status that are incompatible with relations among equals. Thus, those who accept the social and political ideal of equality will have compelling reasons to avoid excessive variations in people's shares of income and wealth, and this will mean, among other things, that they have reason to oppose institutions that allow too much scope for differences in people's natural and social circumstances to translate into economic inequalities. But, on the one hand, this is very different from having the general ambition of eradicating the distributive effects of brute luck, and, on the other hand, it does not assume that inequalities arising from people's choices are always acceptable.

From this perspective, the most important questions concern not the neutralization of luck but rather, for example, the nature of people's "basic needs," the proper criteria for political institutions to use in distinguishing between genuine needs and what are merely very strong preferences, the appropriate measure for the social and political institutions of a complex modern society to employ when assessing the well-being of individual citizens, and, especially, the degree of material inequality that is compatible with a conception of society as a fair system of cooperation among equals. Depending on how these questions are answered, people who are committed to the social and political ideal of equality may end up supporting a system that tolerates either more or less inequality of income and wealth than luck egalitarianism does. In either case, however, the motivation for their position will be different from the motivation for a luck-egalitarian outlook. Since the position that adherents of the ideal favor will have been developed in response to questions that differ, at least in part, from the ones that luck egalitarians ask, the basis for their position will lie in considerations that differ from the ones that luck egalitarians cite.[43]

III

All of this helps to explain why it is misleading to treat Rawls's theory of justice as representing a kind of incipient luck egalitarianism. Notwithstanding his remarks about the moral arbitrariness of people's natural attributes and of the social positions into which they are born, his failure to

43. In "Equality and Justice," in *Ideals of Equality,* Andrew Mason (ed.) (Oxford: Blackwell, 1998), pp. 21–36, David Miller draws a distinction between distributive equality and social equality that is similar to the distinction I have drawn in this section, although Miller takes a different view of the relations between the two notions than I would. In the same volume, Richard Norman ("The Social Basis of Equality," pp. 37–51) invokes Miller's chapter in defending what he calls "socially-located egalitarianism."

claim that justice requires people to be compensated for all disadvantages resulting from unchosen features of their circumstances is no mere oversight. Despite occasional remarks to the effect that his conception of justice "nullifies the accidents of natural endowment and the contingencies of social circumstance as counters in [a] quest for political and economic advantage,"[44] it is quite clear from his discussion as a whole that the underlying motivation for Rawls's theory of justice is not the general elimination of the influence of brute luck on distribution. Indeed, Rawls explicitly emphasizes the differences between his own theory and what he calls "the principle of redress." This is "the principle that undeserved inequalities call for redress; and since inequalities of birth and natural endowment are undeserved, these inequalities are somehow to be compensated for."[45] Rawls says that the principle of redress is plausible "only as a prima facie principle, one that is to be weighed in the balance with others."[46] His own theory, accordingly, "gives some weight to the considerations singled out by the principle of redress,"[47] but it is clearly "not the same as"[48] that principle.

Rather than trying to devise a conception of justice that will minimize the effects of brute luck, Rawls aims to identify the most reasonable conception of justice to regulate the basic structure of a modern democratic society. For the purposes of this enterprise, a society is conceived of as a fair system of cooperation among free and equal people, each of whom is taken to have the capacity for a sense of justice and the capacity to develop and pursue a rational plan of life that is constitutive of his or her good. Different plans are rational for different people, and the human good is irreducibly heterogeneous. Rawls cites the "moral arbitrariness" of natural attributes and social contingencies, not because his ultimate aim is to extinguish the influence of all arbitrary factors but rather because he thinks the arbitrariness of the factors he cites serves to undermine both an important objection and an influential alternative to his view. The objection is that those people who are more talented or intelligent or hard-working than others deserve greater economic rewards than his theory would permit them to secure. And the alternative that many of those who press this objection favor is "the system of natural liberty," which, as we have seen, allows people to compete in a largely unregulated free market, constrained only by

44. Rawls, *A Theory of Justice*, p. 15.
45. Ibid., p. 100.
46. Ibid., p. 101.
47. Ibid., p. 100.
48. Ibid., p. 101. Rakowski believes (mistakenly, in my view) that Rawls relies on the principle of redress as a premise of his argument. See *Equal Justice*, pp. 112–114.

the need to respect one another's basic liberties and by a requirement of formal equality of opportunity.

Rawls believes that the appeal of the system of natural liberty is morally spurious. The extent to which the system allows people's material prospects to be influenced by their natural assets and the social circumstances into which they are born is indefensible. It is indefensible because it is incongruous with people's status as equals and because the distribution of those contingencies does not itself have any moral basis. If we take seriously the idea that all citizens have equal standing in society, and the idea that each has an equally important interest in developing and pursuing a rational plan of life within a fair cooperative framework, then it is inappropriate to set up an institutional scheme that makes people's chances of carrying out their plans depend so heavily on natural and social contingencies that in themselves have no moral authority. Rawls's emphasis on the moral arbitrariness of people's natural attributes and social starting points is meant to undercut our tendency to treat those factors as morally authoritative, especially when doing so would compromise something morally fundamental.

What is relevant for Rawls, in other words, is the conjunction of two points. The first point is that the distribution of natural and social contingencies lacks any moral basis. The second point is that a system that allows the economic distribution to track the distribution of those contingencies too closely will compromise the status of some citizens as equals, for it will undermine their ability to satisfy the equally legitimate interest that each citizen has in developing and pursuing a rational plan of life that is constitutive of his or her good. If Rawls is right, the conjunction of these two points gives us reason to reject the system of natural liberty, once we conceive of society as a fair system of cooperation among free and equal people. But the importance of these points neither derives from nor commits Rawls to the general ambition of neutralizing all of the distributive effects of bad brute luck. For Rawls, what is fundamental is the status of citizens as equals, and the moral arbitrariness of people's natural and social starting points is important because it helps to clarify the distributive implications of taking equal citizenship seriously.

Rawls's defense of his reliance on primary goods as the basis for interpersonal comparisons of well-being also looks very different when it is not seen through the lens of luck-egalitarian concerns. In saying that citizens in a well-ordered society are expected to take responsibility for their ends, in the sense that they are expected to "regulate and revise their ends and preferences in the light of their expectations of primary goods,"[49]

49. Rawls, *Collected Papers*, p. 370.

Rawls is certainly not making a claim about the moral significance of a putative metaphysical distinction between voluntary choices and unchosen circumstances. Instead, he is making an observation about how his principles of justice serve, in effect, to allocate responsibility between society and the individual. He writes:

> This conception [of justice] includes what we may call a social division of responsibility: society, the citizens as a collective body, accepts the responsibility for maintaining the equal basic liberties and fair equality of opportunity, and for providing a fair share of the other primary goods for everyone within this framework, while citizens (as individuals) and associations accept the responsibility for revising and adjusting their ends and aspirations in view of the all-purpose means they can expect, given their present and foreseeable situation.[50]

As Rawls notes, this allocation of responsibility would make no sense if, in general, people were unable "to moderate the claims they make on social institutions"[51] because they lacked the capacity to adjust their plans in light of the resources they could expect to have at their disposal under the terms of a fair distribution. By the same token, the allocation of responsibility would make no sense if society as a whole lacked the capacity to establish institutions capable of guaranteeing the basic liberties and fair equality of opportunity. In fact, as Rawls suggests, it does not seem unreasonable to suppose that people normally do have the capacity to adjust their plans in light of their fair expectations. What is more important for the purposes of our discussion, however, is that the suggestion that they have such a capacity is not a metaphysical thesis about the relation of causation and the will, nor, in any case, does it provide the *motivation* for the allocation of responsibility. People are asked to accept responsibility for their ends, in Rawls's sense, not because the metaphysics of the will makes it fitting that people should bear the costs of their choices, but rather because it is reasonable to expect people to make do with their fair shares. And what makes shares fair, according to Rawls, is not that they compensate people for all unchosen disadvantages while leaving them to bear the costs (or reap the rewards) of their voluntary choices. Shares are fair when they are part of a distributive scheme that makes it possible for free and equal citizens to pursue their diverse

50. Ibid., p. 371.
51. Ibid.

conceptions of the good within a framework that embodies an ideal of reciprocity and mutual respect.[52]

In addition, Rawls emphasizes that his reliance on primary goods as the basis for interpersonal comparisons is limited to the special case of social justice. As he says, "Primary goods are not...to be used in making comparisons in all situations but only in questions which arise in regard to the basic structure. It is another matter entirely whether primary goods are an appropriate basis in other kinds of cases."[53] What is distinctive about the case of social justice is that interpersonal comparisons must be capable of providing grounds for adjudicating among conflicting claims in a way that all citizens can recognize as fair. It follows, Rawls believes, that we need a practical basis for making these comparisons and that this basis must lie in features of people's situations that are publicly accessible and can be appraised without violating people's liberties or subjecting them to unduly intrusive examination. As he says, "the idea is to find a practicable basis of interpersonal comparisons in terms of objective features of citizens' social circumstances open to view."[54] This is in striking contrast to the inward-looking focus of luck egalitarianism. Whereas the aim of neutralizing the distributive effects of brute luck requires intrusive and conceptually problematic judgments about the inner sources of people's disadvantages, the aim of adjudicating fairly among the claims of free and equal citizens requires judgments that rest on a practicable and public basis.

None of this is to suggest that Rawls's views are beyond criticism. It is perfectly possible to argue, for example, that the difference principle inappropriately rewards those who are among the worst-off, as measured in terms of primary goods, only because they prefer greater leisure to greater income and so choose to work at less demanding jobs or not to work at all. It is also perfectly possible to argue that Rawls's reliance on primary social goods as the measure of well-being renders him incapable of taking adequate account, as an acceptable theory of justice surely must, of those who have special medical conditions that are unusually costly to treat.

52. For a related discussion of the passage from Rawls discussed in this paragraph, see T. M. Scanlon, "The Significance of Choice," in *The Tanner Lectures on Human Values*, vol. 8, Sterling McMurrin (ed.) (Salt Lake City: University of Utah Press, 1988), pp. 151–216, at 197–201. I have also discussed Rawls's doctrine of "responsibility for ends" in Section IV of "Responsibility, Reactive Attitudes, and Liberalism in Philosophy and Politics" (see *Boundaries and Allegiances*, pp. 29–30).
53. Rawls, *Collected Papers*, p. 364.
54. Rawls, "The Priority of Right and Ideas of the Good," in *Collected Papers*, pp. 449–472 at pp. 454–455.

Indeed, Rawls himself concedes the force of both of these criticisms. In response to the first, he indicates that despite some reservations, he is prepared to contemplate an expansion of the list of primary goods to include leisure time.[55] In response to the second, he acknowledges the importance of making provision for those with special medical needs but treats this as a "problem of extension"[56] that is to be deferred until after "the first problem of justice"[57] has been addressed. This problem concerns the relations among "citizens who are normally active and fully cooperating members of society over a complete life."[58] Accordingly, for the purpose of addressing this problem, Rawls makes the frankly idealized assumption that all citizens have, "at least to the essential minimum degree, the moral, intellectual, and physical capacities that enable them to be fully cooperating members of society over a complete life."[59] Elsewhere he describes himself as assuming "that all citizens have physical and psychological capacities within a certain normal range."[60] He speculates that the problem of special medical needs can be dealt with "at the legislative stage when the prevalence and kinds of these misfortunes are known and the costs of treating them can be ascertained and balanced along with total government expenditure."[61]

These tentative lines of response may or may not prove adequate. Perhaps they are too ad hoc or require intuitionistic balancing of a kind that Rawls had hoped to avoid. But it is a mistake to regard the criticisms to which he is responding as the thin end of a wedge: that is, as leading inexorably to luck egalitarianism. The aim that informs Rawls's response to the problem of special medical needs, and that would also have to inform any better response, is the aim of "restor[ing] people by health care so that once again they are fully cooperating members of society."[62] This, once again, is entirely independent from and does not commit Rawls to the aim of compensating people for all disadvantages resulting from unchosen circumstances. Instead, the aim of enabling people to be fully cooperating members of society provides an independent standard for judging which disadvantages should be compensated. By this standard,

---

55. See Rawls, *Collected Papers*, pp. 252–253 and 455.
56. See Rawls, *Political Liberalism* (New York: Columbia University Press, 1993), pp. 21–22, and *Collected Papers*, p. 531.
57. See Rawls, *Collected Papers*, pp. 259 and 368.
58. Ibid., p. 368.
59. Rawls, *Political Liberalism*, p. 183.
60. Rawls, *Collected Papers*, p. 368.
61. Rawls, *Political Liberalism*, p. 184.
62. Ibid.

some disadvantages should be compensated even if they result from bad "option luck," whereas others should not be compensated even if they result from bad "brute luck." For example, the standard may require that people be provided with medical care even if their need for care results from choices that they made voluntarily but that turned out badly. On the other hand, it does not require that people be compensated for expensive tastes simply because those tastes result from unchosen features of their upbringing, for such compensation is not normally necessary to enable people to be cooperating members of society. As Rawls says, "We don't say that because the preferences arose from upbringing and not choice that society owes us compensation. Rather, it is a normal part of being human to cope with the preferences our upbringing leaves us with."[63]

In discussing the relation between Rawls's view and the luck-egalitarian position, my primary concern has not been interpretative. By emphasizing the differences between the two positions I have hoped instead to accomplish two things. The first is to make clear that the philosophical underpinnings of luck egalitarianism are not to be found in Rawls's work. Thus, if luck egalitarianism is to be supplied with a compelling motivation, that motivation will need to come from somewhere else; it cannot simply ride piggy-back on Rawls's remarks about the arbitrariness of the natural lottery or about the need for citizens to take responsibility for their ends.

My second aim has been to illustrate how a plausible form of distributive egalitarianism can be anchored in a more general conception of equality as a social and political ideal. Rawls's theory shows how this can be done. For Rawls, people are conceived of as free and equal citizens, and the aim is to determine which principles of distributive justice are most appropriate for a modern democratic society whose members are so understood. In other words, the question is which principles of justice are most consistent, in modern conditions, with the freedom and equality of persons. Equality is understood as a social and political ideal that

---

63. Rawls, *Political Liberalism,* p. 185n. Of course, luck egalitarians disagree among themselves as to whether people should receive compensation for expensive unchosen tastes, for they disagree about whether such tastes are properly subsumed under the heading of "choice" or of "circumstance." Dworkin, as we have seen, assimilates most preferences to the "choice" side of the luck-egalitarian divide, despite the fact that they are not themselves chosen, and he concludes that in general no compensation is called for. For Rawls, however, the question is not whether preferences are properly subsumed within the category of "choices." The question, instead, is whether compensation for expensive tastes is necessary to enable people to participate in the scheme of social cooperation.

governs the relations in which people stand to one another. The core of
the value of equality does not, according to this understanding, consist
in the idea that there is something that must be distributed or allocated
equally, and so the interpretation of the value does not consist primarily
in seeking to ascertain what that *something* is. Instead, the core of the
value is a normative conception of human relations, and the relevant
question, when interpreting the value, is what social, political, and economic arrangements are compatible with that conception.

IV

As I have suggested, proponents of luck egalitarianism often give the
impression that they conceive of equality as an essentially distributive
ideal. They begin from the premise that there is some currency that
should be distributed equally and then proceed to investigate what that
currency might be. I have argued that this is misguided. Any form of
distributive egalitarianism, if it is to be at all plausible, must be anchored
in some more general conception of equality as a moral value or normative ideal. This does not by itself disqualify luck egalitarianism as the best
form of distributive egalitarianism since it is open to luck egalitarians
to argue that it can be so anchored. Yet I have also argued that once we
remember that egalitarian distributive norms must flow from a broader
conception of equality, the appeal of luck egalitarianism is limited.

It may be protested that, in developing these arguments, I have not
done justice to the luck-egalitarian position. Luck egalitarians often present their view as expressing the intuitive idea that it is unfair if some
people are worse-off than others owing to factors beyond their control.[64]
And, in response to my arguments, they may assert that this idea in turn is
rooted in a conception of people as having equal moral worth, so that luck
egalitarianism does flow from a broader conception of equality as a moral
value. It does not treat equality as being an essentially distributive ideal.

However, the idea that it is unfair if some people are worse-off than
others owing to factors beyond their control captures only part of the
luck-egalitarian position. Luck egalitarians also believe that it is *not* unfair
if some people are worse-off (or better-off) than others as a result of
their voluntary choices. Thus, the luck-egalitarian claim must be that the

---

64. For versions of this formulation, see Arneson, "Equality and Equal Opportunity for
    Welfare," p. 85, and Larry Temkin, *Inequality* (New York: Oxford University Press,
    1993), p. 200.

position that results from combining these two formulations is rooted in a conception of people as having equal worth. This claim requires argument. Most theories of justice purport to treat people as having equal moral worth or importance. If luck egalitarians believe that their position is the best expression of the equal worth of persons, then that claim requires some defense; it cannot simply be assumed. This is particularly true because it is by no means clear that most people actually have the intuitions to which luck egalitarians appeal. To be sure, there are some contexts in which it does seem unfair that people should suffer disadvantages as a result of circumstances beyond their control, and there are some contexts in which it does not seem unfair that people should suffer disadvantages as a result of their voluntary choices. But these observations alone do not suffice to establish the intuitive credentials of luck egalitarianism, for luck egalitarianism asserts something more sweeping. It claims that, in general, it is unfair if people are better or worse off as a result of factors beyond their control and that, in general, it is not unfair if people are better or worse off as a result of their voluntary choices. It is far from clear that, in its generalized form, this claim enjoys widespread intuitive support.[65] The more common or intuitive view, I believe, is that the fairness or unfairness of differences in advantage resulting from, on the one hand, factors beyond people's control and, on the other hand, people's voluntary choices, is highly dependent on the prevailing social context and institutional setting.

For example, if I have a less successful career as a philosopher than you do because your superior philosophical gifts enable you to refute all my arguments, then, contrary to what the generalized claim might lead

---

65. The generalized luck-egalitarian claim bears a superficial similarity to the equally generalized claim that it is inappropriate to blame people, or to judge them morally responsible, for things that are beyond their control. The latter claim, which is of course central to discussions of free will and responsibility, is indeed widely accepted. Despite the superficial similarity between the two claims, however, there are also important differences. The claim about blame and responsibility articulates a precondition for responsible agency that strikes most people, upon reflection, as compelling. The luck-egalitarian claim, by contrast, is a first-order normative judgment that treats equality as the default distributive baseline and claims that departures from that baseline are justified if and only if a suitable condition of control is satisfied. As I argue above, the intuitive plausibility of that normative judgment cannot be taken for granted. Moreover, such plausibility as it does have may depend on seeing it, wrongly in my view, as a natural extension of the claim about the pre-conditions of responsible agency. This is related to my earlier observation (at pp. 187–188) that luck egalitarianism may tacitly depend for its appeal on a perception that it can be validated metaphysically.

us to expect, most people would not regard that as unfair. Nor would most think it unfair if a naturally gifted professional athlete were offered a more lucrative contract than his less talented teammate. On the other hand, most people would consider it outrageous if an emergency room doctor left an injured patient untreated simply because the patient's injury resulted from a foolish but voluntary decision. And few would think it acceptable to deny legal counsel to an indigent defendant on the ground that her inability to pay for an attorney was the result of poor financial decision making on her part. If this is correct, then the intuitive credentials of luck egalitarianism cannot be taken for granted, and it is all the more important for luck egalitarians to explain how exactly their position is supposed to follow from a conception of persons as having equal moral worth.

Moreover, I have argued that equality is most compelling when it is understood as a social and political ideal that includes but goes beyond the proposition that all people have equal moral worth. It is this ideal that we invoke when we say that our society should be organized as a society of equals. The case is analogous to other human relationships that we take to be governed by an ideal of equality. When we say, for example, that a friendship or a marriage should be a relationship of equals, we do not mean merely that the participants are of equal moral worth but also that their relationship should have a certain structure and character. Similarly, I believe, our notion of a society of equals expresses a normative ideal of human relations. Luck egalitarians must either reject this ideal or argue that it too supports their distributive principles. It is not clear what grounds they have for rejecting it, but, as I have already indicated, I see no reason to think that it supports the generalized luck-egalitarian position. Since, as I have argued, neither complete choice-sensitivity nor complete endowment-insensitivity seems morally plausible in its own right, and since neither reflects our intuitive understanding of the implications of equality, we have no reason to think that either would be a feature of a society of equals.

Ronald Dworkin is one writer who can be interpreted as attempting to anchor luck-egalitarian principles in an ideal of equality that goes beyond the proposition that all people are of equal worth, but his ideal of equality is not the same as the social and political ideal I have described. Dworkin states that a "full theory of equality" seeks to answer the question of what it is to treat people as equals. A theory of distributive equality addresses one aspect of this question, namely, which scheme of distribution may be said to treat people as equals. Thus Dworkin presents his equality of resources scheme neither as a set of first principles nor as rooted merely in the idea that people are of equal worth but rather as part of a spelling out of the idea of equal treatment. In effect, then, he can be interpreted as attempting to anchor luck-egalitarian principles in a more general ideal of equality—namely, the ideal of treating people as equals.

Dworkin says that treating people as equals means treating them with equal concern. Indeed, he says that "[e]qual concern is the sovereign virtue of political community" and that "[n]o government is legitimate that does not show equal concern for the fate of all those citizens over whom it claims dominion and from whom it claims allegiance."[66] Some writers have denied that the ideal of equal concern really does support luck-egalitarian principles. G. A. Cohen, for example, says that, contrary to what Dworkin supposes, "it seems quite unclear that a state which forthrightly refuses to pursue a norm of strict distributive equality *ipso facto* shows failure to treat its subjects with equal respect and concern."[67] Anderson goes further, arguing that luck egalitarianism fails "the most fundamental test any egalitarian theory must meet: that its principles express equal respect and concern for all citizens."[68]

Whether or not Dworkin's ideal of equality supports his distributive principles, however, there is a prior question about the adequacy of that ideal itself. It is noteworthy, I think, that when, in his famous two-part article "What is Equality?,"[69] Dworkin first broaches the question of how the ideal of treating people as equals might best be applied to issues of distribution, he does so with reference to the example of a wealthy man who is deciding how, in drawing up his will, to divide his wealth among his children, each of whom has different needs, ambitions, and tastes. He then moves on to consider a putatively analogous question that arises in "an ordinary political context," namely, the question of how "officials" should make decisions about the distribution of resources among citizens.[70] Now the first thing to notice is that the model of testator and

66. Dworkin, *Sovereign Virtue*, p. 1.
67. G. A. Cohen, *If You're an Egalitarian, How Come You're So Rich?* (Cambridge: Harvard University Press, 2000), p. 165.
68. Anderson, "What is the Point of Equality?" p. 289.
69. Reprinted as chaps. 1 and 2 of *Sovereign Virtue*.
70. Dworkin, *Sovereign Virtue*, p. 13. Dworkin is not the only luck-egalitarian writer who uses the model of testator and heirs to illustrate what I refer to in the text below as an "administrative conception" of equality. In his article "Equality and Responsibility" (*Boston Review* 10 [April/May 1995]: 3–7 at p. 3), John Roemer uses the same model to illustrate his own version of an egalitarian distributive theory. And Roemer says elsewhere that the aim of his theory is to provide "an algorithm" ("A Pragmatic Theory of Responsibility for the Egalitarian Planner," p. 182) that could be used by "an egalitarian planner" (p. 180) to "implement" (p. 182) the "correct egalitarian ethic" (p. 180).

heirs is an asymmetrical model, with one party distributing benefits and
the others receiving them. Thus, when this model is applied to questions of economic distribution within society, citizens are represented,
again asymmetrically, as objects of treatment by some kind of centralized subject. In this case, there are important questions that arise about
the identity of the subject. Is it, as Dworkin's language seems at times
to suggest, a group of "officials"? Is it, as he suggests at other times, "the
distributive scheme" itself? Or is it, as some of his formulations appear
to imply, the society or community as a whole? And how is any of these
to be understood as a locus of agency? Whatever the answers to these
questions may be, what is really striking is that the model of testator and
heir does not describe a *relationship among equals* at all. An autocratic
parent might write his will in such a way as to treat all of his children
as equals in Dworkin's sense, but that would not transform his family
into an egalitarian social unit. Similarly, an autocratic government might
impose an economic system that treated individuals as equals in Dworkin's sense,[71] but that would not transform the society into an egalitarian
political community. In short, Dworkin's ideal of equality, as applied
to questions of distribution, is not itself a model of social or political
equality at all; it is perfectly compatible with social hierarchy, inasmuch
as it involves one relatively powerful party choosing how to distribute
resources among those with relatively less power.[72] Of course, it might be

71. Indeed, Dworkin himself says that a "benevolent tyranny" might bring about
    "a more egalitarian distribution than a democracy could" (*Sovereign Virtue*, p. 187).
72. In a discussion of this point, Stephen Perry objected that the device of the auc-
    tion, which plays a much more developed role in Dworkin's argument than does the
    model of testator and heirs, is not comparably hierarchical. In the auction, a number
    of shipwreck survivors on a desert island are given an equal number of clamshells,
    which they use to bid for available resources. Since no role is envisioned for a govern-
    ment, and since all the participants in the auction have the same status (leaving aside
    the role of the auctioneer), the auction might be thought to provide a model of genu-
    ine social equality. But the primary role of the auction, as Dworkin describes it, is to
    tell us what kind of distribution of resources should properly be counted as an equal
    distribution. It is intended to undercut the idea that distributive egalitarians want
    each person at all times to have the same amount of wealth. The auction is not meant
    to illustrate a more general ideal of social equality, nor do the participants in the
    auction ask themselves what distributional practices are appropriate to a society of
    equals. Indeed, Dworkin gives no general characterization at all of the social relations
    among the participants. Instead, they are simply stipulated to accept the assumption
    that resources shall be "divided equally among them" (*Sovereign Virtue*, pp. 66–67),
    and the auction presupposes that aim. Dworkin's underlying idea of equality, which
    is not itself illustrated by the auction, is the (asymmetrical) idea that a government
    must show equal concern for all of its citizens; as he insists, equal concern is "the
    special and indispensable virtue of sovereigns" (*Sovereign Virtue*, p. 6).

protested that there is no reason why the same model could not also be applied to the distribution of power itself. But then who would be doing the distributing?

In fact, however, Dworkin does not advocate the equal distribution of power. After distinguishing what he calls "the two modes of power,"[73] impact and influence, he goes on to argue, "If a community is genuinely egalitarian in the abstract sense—if it accepts the imperative that a community collectively must treat its members individually with equal concern—then it cannot treat political impact or influence as themselves resources, to be divided according to some metric of equality the way land or raw materials or investments might be divided."[74] Accordingly, Dworkin would allow a "limited place for equality of impact but none for equality of influence."[75] The upshot is that Dworkin's ideal of equality does not require or even permit an equal distribution of power; and the kind of equal distribution of resources that it does require is not incompatible with social hierarchy or even, as he himself says, with "benevolent tyranny."[76]

Dworkin has developed his ideal of equality in great detail over a period of many years, and he has applied it with great force to an impressive range of issues. The observations I have made do not detract from the many virtues of his view. But those observations do, I think, suggest that Dworkin's ideal represents what might be called an *administrative conception* of equality. A "genuinely egalitarian" community, he believes, is one that accepts the abstract principle that people should be treated as equals (or treated with equal concern) and whose "officials" then administer social and political institutions in accordance with the best conception of what treatment as equals requires. But an egalitarianism that begins from the question of how best to administer or operationalize an abstract principle of equal concern contrasts sharply with an egalitarianism that begins from the question of what relationships among equals are like and goes on from there to consider what kinds of social and political institutions are appropriate to a society of equals.[77]

73. Dworkin, *Sovereign Virtue*, p. 199.
74. Ibid., pp. 209–210.
75. Ibid., p. 200.
76. Ibid., p. 187. Dworkin would of course reject a "benevolent tyranny" for other reasons. His point (and mine) is merely that considerations of distributional equality do not in themselves furnish grounds for doing so.
77. My characterization of Dworkin's conception of equality as administrative is closely related to G.A. Cohen's description of it as "statocentric" (see *If You're an Egalitarian, How Come You're So Rich?* p. 165). Cohen writes:

> Within Dworkin's theory of equality, the locus of the norm of equality proper...is in the relationship between the state and those whom it claims the right to govern. Because it

If the administrative conception of equality supports luck-egalitarian distributive principles—and this is the claim that Anderson denies and about which Cohen expresses doubts—then Dworkin's version of luck egalitarianism is indeed anchored in a more general ideal of equality. But people who think of themselves as egalitarians need to consider how well the administrative conception captures the value of equality as they understand it.

It will already be clear that, in my view, the *social and political ideal* of equality has greater resonance for most people. This does not mean that there is no room for distributive egalitarianism or even for Dworkin's administrative conception of equality. But it does mean that these distributive and administrative ideas will be most compelling if they can be shown to have strong roots in the ideal of a society of equals.[78] The recent history of political discourse in liberal societies seems to me to confirm this. I have already noted that the rise of luck egalitarianism among philosophers took place during a period of giddy triumphalism about markets that largely displaced a concern with economic equality in many liberal societies. Yet it is a striking fact that during this very same period, the power of equality as a social and political ideal continued to make itself felt. One of the great preoccupations of liberal societies in recent decades has been with the normative implications of diversity:

---

claims that right, the state must treat its citizens with equal respect and concern, on pain of being a tyranny, and it must *therefore* distribute resources equally to its members. But if the state fails to do so, then no analogous duty falls on individuals. It is not the individual's duty to treat everyone (relatives, friends, and strangers alike) with equal respect and concern. (p. 164)

This is perhaps an appropriate place to record my sense that there is a tension within Cohen's own writings between his apparent endorsement, in "On the Currency of Egalitarian Justice," of choice as an inequality-legitimating factor and his criticism, in his Tanner Lectures ("Incentives, Inequality, and Community," in *The Tanner Lectures on Human Values*, vol. 13, ed. Grethe Peterson [Salt Lake City: University of Utah Press, 1992], pp. 263–329) and in *If You're an Egalitarian, How Come You're So Rich?* of incentive-based inequalities as unjust precisely because of their choice-dependence. I am inclined to view this as symptomatic of a broader tension between the luck-egalitarian attitude toward choice and the attitudes associated with what Cohen calls an egalitarian "ethos." The emphasis on the importance of a choice-constraining egalitarian ethos is quite congenial to the social and political ideal of equality, but the luck-egalitarian motivation for such an emphasis is less clear.

78. Dworkin comes close to recognizing the importance of that ideal in his discussion of campaign finance reform in chap. 10 of *Sovereign Virtue*, in which he places great emphasis on the notion of "citizen equality." But that is not the notion of equality to which he appeals in defending his version of luck egalitarianism.

with questions about how best to accommodate differences of race, gender, religion, culture, and ethnicity. And these questions have almost always been addressed through an (implicitly if not explicitly) egalitarian lens. The central issue, in effect, has been this: What must a modern liberal society do to constitute itself as a genuine society of equals given that its membership will inevitably be highly diverse in many socially and normatively salient respects? It is this profoundly egalitarian question that has animated the intense debates in liberal societies about pluralism and multiculturalism; about race, gender, and ethnicity; and about the politics of identity. One lesson we should learn from the very intensity of these debates, and from the remarkable social changes that have accompanied them, is the continuing vitality of the idea of a society of equals. And this in turn tells us something—or so it seems to me—about the appeal of distributive egalitarianism. What it tells us is that the most compelling versions of that idea, both politically and philosophically, will be those whose source in an ideal of genuine social equality can be vividly and convincingly demonstrated.[79]

---

79. Thus, I believe that Will Kymlicka gets things more or less backward when, in chap. 9 of *Liberalism, Community, and Culture* (Oxford: Clarendon Press, 1989), he seeks to ground a conception of equality for minority cultures in Dworkin's luck-egalitarian distributive principles.

8

Choice, Circumstance, and the Value of Equality

1. Introduction

One of the most familiar conservative criticisms of the welfare state is that its policies rely on and enforce a diminished conception of individual responsibility and choice. Over the past quarter-century, this criticism has been pressed, to great advantage, by conservative politicians in the United States and elsewhere. Within political philosophy, similar criticisms have been directed against various forms of economic egalitarianism, including the kind of egalitarian liberalism developed most

Originally published in *Politics, Philosophy & Economics*, Volume 4 Number 1 (February 2005): 5–28. © SAGE Publications Ltd. All rights reserved. Earlier versions of this article were presented at a Yale Philosophy Department colloquium, at a conference on The Theory and Practice of Equality at the Kennedy School of Government, Harvard University, and (in my absence) at a conference at Tulane University sponsored by this journal. I am grateful to all of these audiences for valuable discussion and I am particularly indebted to Richard Arneson, Amélie Rorty, Peter Vallentyne, and Andrew Williams for insightful written comments.

prominently by John Rawls. In response to such criticisms, many political philosophers have attempted, since the 1980s, to demonstrate that choice and responsibility can be incorporated into the framework of an egalitarian theory of distributive justice. Indeed, the attempt to develop a responsibility-based conception of egalitarian justice has become one of the central preoccupations of contemporary political philosophy.

The first proposal along these lines was the "equality of resources" scheme initially presented by Ronald Dworkin in 1981.[1] Dworkin's scheme is complex, but it holds that economic inequalities deriving from differences in people's tastes and ambitions are justifiable in a way that inequalities deriving from differences of talent or external circumstance are not. Dworkin views one's tastes and ambitions as aspects of one's personality for which one may reasonably be held responsible. By contrast, he thinks that one cannot reasonably be held responsible for one's natural abilities or the circumstances of one's birth or for other matters of "brute luck." Dworkin, therefore, draws a basic "distinction between a person and his circumstances, and assigns his tastes and ambitions to his person, and his physical and mental powers to his circumstances."[2] Although Dworkin did not, in his early articles, highlight the notion of choice in particular, G. A. Cohen subsequently argued that Dworkin's differential treatment of ambitions and talents seems plausible only insofar as the former, but not the latter, are taken to be objects of choice. Accordingly, Cohen argued that choice was "in the background [of Dworkin's argument], doing a good deal of unacknowledged work."[3] Indeed, Cohen went further, asserting in a famous passage that "Dworkin has, in effect, performed for egalitarianism the considerable service of incorporating within it the most powerful idea in the arsenal of the anti-egalitarian right: the idea of choice and responsibility."[4]

In the same spirit, however, Cohen insisted that the crucial distinction for egalitarians is the distinction between *choice* and circumstance, rather than between the *person* and his circumstances. Once this is appreciated, he maintained, Dworkin's own position needs to

---

1. See Ronald Dworkin, "What is Equality? Part I: Equality of Welfare," *Philosophy & Public Affairs* 10 (1981): 185–246 and "What is Equality? Part II: Equality of Resources," *Philosophy & Public Affairs* 10 (1981): 283–345. Both of these essays are reprinted in Ronald Dworkin, *Sovereign Virtue* (Cambridge, MA: Harvard University Press, 2000), pp. 11–64, 65–119, respectively. When citing these articles hereafter, I will give the page references in *Sovereign Virtue* only.
2. Dworkin, *Sovereign Virtue*, p. 81.
3. G.A. Cohen, "On the Currency of Egalitarian Justice" *Ethics* 99 (1989): 928.
4. Ibid., p. 933.

be modified in important respects. In particular, egalitarians must acknowledge, as Dworkin does not, that people are entitled to compensation for expensive, but unchosen, tastes or preferences. It is *not* reasonable, Cohen argued, to hold people responsible for such tastes. In the ensuing debate, Dworkin has accepted the vocabulary of *choice* and *chance* as an appropriate way of characterizing the crucial distinction, but he has continued to deny that compensation for expensive preferences is justified.[5] Many others have developed alternative versions of responsibility-based egalitarianism.[6] Some of these versions have been closer to Dworkin's position and some have been closer to Cohen's. What these various proposals share is the core "luck-egalitarian" idea that there is something unjust about inequalities deriving from unchosen aspects of people's circumstances, but nothing comparably unjust about inequalities deriving from people's voluntary choices.[7] Like Dworkin and Cohen themselves, however, the authors of these proposals often disagree with one another about which factors should be counted among people's circumstances and which should be subsumed within the category of choice.

5. See, for example, Dworkin, *Sovereign Virtue*, Chaps 7, 9.
6. There are also views that are closely related to responsibility-based egalitarianism, but that depart from it either by substituting priority for equality or by giving responsibility a more limited role. An example of the first is Richard Arneson's "responsibility-catering prioritarianism," as described in his "Luck Egalitarianism and Prioritarianism," *Ethics* 110 (2000): 339–349. An example of the second is the version of egalitarianism defended by Peter Vallentyne in his "Brute Luck, Option Luck, and Equality of Initial Opportunities," *Ethics* 112 (2002): 529–557.
7. The term *luck egalitarianism* is taken from Elizabeth Anderson, "What is the Point of Equality?" *Ethics* 109 (1999): 287–337. My discussion has been influenced in many ways by Anderson's criticisms of luck egalitarianism. Other important critical discussions include: Jonathan Wolff, "Fairness, Respect, and the Egalitarian Ethos," *Philosophy & Public Affairs* 27 (1998): 97–122; Seana Valentine Shiffrin, "Paternalism, Unconscionability Doctrine, and Accommodation," *Philosophy & Public Affairs* 29 (2000): 205–50; Seana Valentine Shiffrin, "Egalitarianism, Choice-Sensitivity, and Accommodation," in *Reason and Value: Themes from the Moral Philosophy of Joseph Raz*, edited by R.J. Wallace, P. Pettit, S. Scheffler and M. Smith (Oxford: Oxford University Press, 2004); Timothy Hinton, "Must Egalitarians Choose Between Fairness and Respect?" *Philosophy & Public Affairs* 30 (2001): 72–87; Timothy Hinton, "Choice and Luck in Recent Egalitarian Thought," *Philosophical Papers* 31 (2002). See also the important series of articles by Marc Fleurbaey: "Equal Opportunity or Equal Social Outcome?" *Economics and Philosophy* 11 (1995): 25–55: "Equality Among Responsible Individuals," in *Freedom in Economics*, edited by J.F. Laslier et al. (London: Routledge, 1998), pp. 206–234; "Egalitarian Opportunities," *Law and Philosophy* 20 (2001): 499–530; "Equality of Resources Revisited," *Ethics* 113 (2002): 82–105; "Freedom with Forgiveness," *Politics, Philosophy, and Economics* (2004).

The reason why these debates are of more than scholastic interest is that they purport to anchor economic egalitarianism in a fundamental moral idea that is taken to have widespread appeal among people of otherwise diverse political orientations. The debates are animated by a conviction that there is broad support for what Brian Barry calls "the principle of responsibility," which he defines as "the principle that unequal outcomes are just if they arise from factors for which individuals can properly be held responsible, and are otherwise unjust."[8] Barry says that rich and poor alike accept the principle of responsibility, and he adds: "this principle is widely shared not only in the USA but also in other affluent western societies. Its appeal is probably a great deal more broad than that."[9] If this is correct, then a persuasive demonstration that the principle supports economic egalitarianism would appear to be a remarkable achievement.

In this article, I will distinguish between two different roles that the principle of responsibility may be asked to play in egalitarian arguments. The first role is more limited and defensive. The second is more ambitious and affirmative. I will argue that, although the principle can legitimately play the first role, it cannot play the second. Yet it is the second role that is central to the project of developing a responsibility-based conception of egalitarian justice. If my arguments are correct, that project is misconceived. The attempt to develop a responsibility-based conception of justice should not be the focus of egalitarian political philosophy.

2. Defensive Arguments and Affirmative Arguments

Let me begin, then, by distinguishing between the two different ways in which the principle of responsibility figures in egalitarian arguments. As I have said, the principle's role in arguments of the first sort is limited and defensive. Arguments of this kind are intended solely to rebut those criticisms of economic egalitarianism that themselves appeal to the principle of responsibility. They are meant to establish that the principle of responsibility does not support conservative conclusions, so that even if the principle is granted, at least for the sake of argument, it fails to undermine the egalitarian position.

---

8. Brian Barry, "Does Responsibility Undermine Equality?" paper presented to the Workshop in Law, Philosophy, and Political Theory, University of California, Berkeley, 20 March 2003.
9. Ibid.

For example, conservatives often claim that egalitarian policies violate the principle of responsibility by rewarding those who are lazy or unwilling to work and by penalizing those who are industrious and hardworking. In response, egalitarians argue that characterological differences (differences in levels of personal industry or energy) cannot plausibly be seen as the primary cause of existing inequalities. Far more important are differences in social class, family background, inherited wealth, and natural ability, none of which individuals choose for themselves and for none of which can they plausibly be held responsible. Moreover, some egalitarians add, even if characterological features are among the factors that contribute to economic inequality, it is no more proper to hold individuals responsible for their own characters than it is to hold them responsible for their native talents or intelligence. Rawls takes a position like this when he says that we do not deserve "the superior character that enables us to make the effort to cultivate our abilities," because "such character depends in good part upon fortunate family and social circumstances in early life for which we can claim no credit."[10] In a similar spirit, he adds that "Even the willingness to make an effort, to try, and so to be deserving in the ordinary sense is itself dependent on happy family and social circumstances."[11]

In advancing these "defensive" arguments, egalitarians do not commit themselves to the principle of responsibility. They simply dispute the conservative's assessment of the implications of that principle. They do this by challenging the conservative's claims both about the causes of inequality and about the factors for which individuals may plausibly be held accountable. Neither of these challenges presupposes that the egalitarian actually endorses the principle of responsibility.

By contrast, those who advocate responsibility-based conceptions of egalitarian justice not only endorse the principle but argue that it provides the basis for an egalitarian position. Like many conservatives, in other words, the "luck-egalitarian" philosophers who offer these "affirmative" arguments treat the principle of responsibility as a fundamental norm that should guide the design of society's social, political, and economic institutions. Of course, these luck egalitarians differ sharply from conservatives in their interpretation of the principle and its implications. Rather than limiting themselves to purely defensive arguments, however, they join conservatives in asserting the principle of responsibility as a

10. John Rawls, *A Theory of Justice*, revised edn. (Cambridge, MA: Harvard University Press, 1999), p. 89.
11. Ibid., p. 64.

CHOICE, CIRCUMSTANCE, AND THE VALUE OF EQUALITY 213

fundamental principle of political morality. On the assumption that the principle is as widely shared as Barry and others believe, this enables them to claim that the egalitarian position has its roots in a basic tenet of ordinary moral thought.

I will have little to say in this article about the egalitarian arguments that I have characterized as defensive. Although I am sympathetic to such arguments, my primary focus will be on the affirmative arguments, which I believe to be ill-conceived. I believe that it is a mistake to try to ground an egalitarian position in the principle of responsibility, and the bulk of my discussion will be devoted to explaining why this is so. My explanation will encompass a number of different considerations, which I will group together under four headings: justification, metaphysics, moralism, and equality as a social value.

3. Justification

As I have said, the justificatory ambition of those who advance affirmative arguments is to demonstrate that egalitarianism can be anchored in a fundamental moral principle that has broad appeal among people of different economic classes and diverse political orientations. But I believe that the principle of responsibility has this kind of appeal only if it is interpreted so abstractly as to be nearly devoid of content, a virtual tautology. Once it is given more content (the kind of content that it has to have if it is to support an egalitarian conception of distributive justice) then it no longer has the broad appeal that recommended it to egalitarians in the first place.

The principle of responsibility asserts that unequal outcomes are just if, and only if, they arise from factors for which individuals can properly be held responsible. What is it to hold an individual responsible for a factor? It is at least to say that nobody is required to mitigate the effects of that factor on the individual's situation. It is, in that sense, to treat the fact that some aspect of the individual's situation was caused by the designated factor as a justification for that aspect of the situation. On one interpretation, then, the principle of responsibility amounts to little more than the claim that unequal outcomes are just if, and only if, they arise from factors that serve to justify them or, more briefly, that inequalities are just if, and only if, there is some justification for them. Construed in this way, the principle surely does have widespread appeal, for it is very nearly a tautology. Just for that reason, however, it is incapable of providing support for any particular conception of justice. Since it leaves open the question of which inequalities are in fact justified, and since that is the issue about which different conceptions of justice disagree, the principle so understood provides no basis for choosing among those conceptions.

The principle can be given a more substantive interpretation, of course, by supplementing the abstract interpretation just considered with a specific account of the factors for which individuals are properly held responsible. In this spirit, as we have seen, luck egalitarians interpret the principle to mean that inequalities deriving from people's voluntary choices are acceptable, whereas inequalities deriving from unchosen features of their circumstances are unjust. Once the principle of responsibility is given this interpretation, it may indeed support a conception of justice that is redistributive enough to deserve the label "egalitarian," provided that the extent to which economic outcomes are affected by unchosen circumstances is sufficiently great. Of course, as this suggests, the substantive principle itself needs to be supplemented with an account of how the line between choices and circumstances is to be drawn and, as I have said, this is one of the central points at issue among different versions of luck egalitarianism. For present purposes, however, the question is whether any version of the substantive principle that is strong enough to support an egalitarian position can claim the kind of widespread support on which the force of the affirmative arguments depends.

The answer to this question, I believe, is no. Any version of the substantive principle that is strong enough to support an egalitarian conception of justice will, at a minimum, need to count individuals' native talents and abilities as being among their unchosen circumstances. Other putatively egalitarian versions go further and subsume additional features of the person (such as unchosen preferences and character traits) within the category of circumstance rather than choice. But even the weakest egalitarian versions will be controversial, as we can see if we think about the claim that inequalities deriving from voluntary choices are acceptable, whereas inequalities deriving from differences of natural talent are not. As I have argued elsewhere,[12] and as is in any case obvious, both parts of this claim are contested. To be sure, most people agree that there are some contexts in which inequalities deriving from people's voluntary choices are acceptable and some contexts in which inequalities deriving from differences of natural ability are unacceptable. Yet few people hold the general view that inequalities resulting from choice are always legitimate but that it is always unfair if people are better or worse off as

12. Samuel Scheffler, "What is Egalitarianism?"; Chapter 7 in this volume. See also Samuel Scheffler, "Equality as the Virtue of Sovereigns: A Reply to Ronald Dworkin," *Philosophy & Public Affairs* 31 (2003): 199–206.

a result of their differing talents and abilities. On the contrary, many people believe that individuals should be compensated for certain kinds of disadvantages, even if their own choices are among the causes of those disadvantages. In addition, many people regard material inequalities deriving from differences of talent and ability as acceptable within limits. This means that any version of the principle of responsibility that is strong enough to support a luck-egalitarian conception of distributive justice is bound to be controversial. In attempting to justify such a conception by reference to one of these versions, one cannot claim to be anchoring egalitarianism in a simple moral idea that represents common ground among people of otherwise diverse political orientations. This claim rests on an equivocation between two different versions of the principle of responsibility: the abstract version, which has broad appeal but does not support an egalitarian conception of justice, and certain specific substantive versions, which may support an egalitarian conception of justice but do not have comparably broad appeal. In addition to undermining the justificatory ambitions of those who advance affirmative arguments, this equivocation reveals a parallel between the luck-egalitarian and conservative positions, for many conservative arguments equivocate in just the same way between abstract and substantive versions of the principle of responsibility.

There is one additional point that is worth noting. *Any* conception of distributive justice can be viewed as *producing* an interpretation of the principle of responsibility, for any such conception will specify which inequalities are acceptable and which are unacceptable, and from the fact that a given inequality is deemed acceptable it follows that the factors from which it arises are ones for which individuals may properly be "held responsible," in the sense that nobody is required to mitigate the effects of those factors on individuals' situations. Clearly, however, no interpretation of the principle of responsibility that is derived in this way from an independently specified conception of justice can serve as the basis for that very conception.

4. Metaphysics

I have said that, at a minimum, to hold an individual responsible for a factor, in the sense that is relevant to the interpretation of the principle of responsibility, is to treat that factor as serving to justify those aspects of the individual's situation that were caused by the factor. As we have seen, the abstract version of the principle of responsibility makes no claim about the specific factors for which people are properly held responsible in this sense. By contrast, the luck-egalitarian versions assert that individuals are properly held responsible for their voluntary choices, but not for unchosen features of their circumstances. If, as I have argued, this is a substantive claim with which many people will disagree, it requires some defense. What might lie behind it? Why might it be tempting to suppose that people are properly held responsible for their choices, but not for their circumstances?

There is one possible answer that I will mention only to set it aside. It might be suggested that people identify with their choices but not with their circumstances, and that this is why they are appropriately held responsible for the former but not the latter. Claims to the effect that there is a connection between identification and responsibility have some appeal, although they obviously need additional elaboration. Such claims play an important role in Dworkin's arguments, where they are used to help explain why people's values and preferences, even if unchosen, should not be treated as features of their circumstances that entitle them to egalitarian compensation.[13] Whatever the merits of those arguments, however, and whatever general appeal there may be to the idea that there is a connection between identification and responsibility, it is clear that that idea cannot explain why people should be held responsible for their choices, but not for their circumstances. That is because, however the line between choices and circumstances is drawn, some of the factors with which people identify will fall on the circumstance side of the line. After all, people often identify not only with their choices, and not only with their values and preferences, but also with their unchosen talents, abilities, and physical characteristics, which all luck egalitarians (including Dworkin) would include among their circumstances. People identify with these things in the sense that they regard them as constitutive elements of who they are. So if the factors for which people are properly held responsible are the personal factors with which they identify, then they cannot be held responsible solely for their choices.[14]

What other reason might there be for treating the distinction between choices and circumstances as constituting the dividing line separating those factors for which people are properly held responsible from those for which they are not? It is important to remember that, according to the luck-egalitarian view, this dividing line has profound economic and

13. See, for example, Dworkin, *Sovereign Virtue*, pp. 287–291; Ronald Dworkin, "Equality, Luck and Hierarchy," *Philosophy & Public Affairs* 31 (2003): 194.
14. See Scheffler, "What is Egalitarianism?" pp. 188–190; Scheffler, "Equality as the Virtue of Sovereigns," p. 201.

political significance. The factors for which people are properly held responsible are those that justify inequality, and the factors for which they are not properly held responsible are those that do not justify inequality. So the question is why the distinction between choices and circumstances should be thought to have this kind of significance. Why should it be thought to mark the boundary between legitimate and illegitimate inequality?

Perhaps the most obvious answer that suggests itself is this. Voluntary choices are seen as inequality-justifying because they are thought to be under individuals' control in a way that makes individuals morally responsible for them. Unchosen circumstances, by contrast, are seen as not being inequality justifying because they are not under individuals' control and so individuals are not morally responsible for them. On this interpretation, luck egalitarianism postulates a substantive, normative connection between two different notions of responsibility. People are properly held responsible for their voluntary choices, in the sense that they must bear the distributive consequences of those choices, because they are morally responsible for having made them. By contrast, people cannot properly be expected to bear the distributive consequences of their unchosen circumstances because they are not morally responsible for finding themselves in those circumstances.

It is worth repeating that this is a substantive thesis. The claim that people should be expected to bear the distributive consequences of their choices, but not their circumstances, neither entails nor is entailed by the claim that they are morally responsible for the former but not the latter.[15] The plausibility of the thesis will depend on how the relevant notions of choice, control, and moral responsibility are understood. The thesis will seem most plausible if those notions are given a "libertarian" or "incompatibilist" interpretation, according to which genuinely voluntary choices belong to a different metaphysical category than do other causal factors. If the distinction between choices and unchosen circumstances is viewed as a fundamental metaphysical distinction, then it may seem capable of bearing the enormous political and economic weight that luck egalitarianism places on it. Of course, any plausible moral or political view will treat choice as a significant notion. However, it is far from obvious that, in general, the justice of assisting those in need or of compensating those who have suffered special disadvantages depends primarily on the causal role of their choices in contributing to their plight. Nor

15. For a related discussion, see Kasper Lippert-Rasmussen, "Egalitarianism, Option Luck, and Responsibility," *Ethics* 111 (2001): 571–572.

is it obvious that any scheme of differential reward that is sensitive to unchosen differences in talent or natural ability is to that extent unjust. These views are likely to press themselves upon us, to the extent that they do, insofar as we are in the grip of a simple but seductive metaphysical picture, according to which the ontological distinctiveness of genuine choice gives it a privileged capacity to express our identity and worth as persons, and hence, perhaps, to ground any entitlement we may have to differential reward.

In saying this, I am not making a claim about what luck egalitarians actually believe. Few, if any, proponents of a luck-egalitarian position endorse the picture I have just described. Instead, some accept one version or another of a compatibilist understanding of choice.[16] Others say that they are agnostic about the nature of genuine choice, and even about whether human beings are capable of genuine choice. They limit themselves to the claim that only genuine choice (whether or not we turn out to be capable of it and whatever it may turn out to consist in) can legitimate inequality. G. A. Cohen takes this view, and he is happy to accept the implication that if genuine choice is not possible for us, then no inequalities are justified.[17] My claim, however, is that, whatever luck-egalitarian philosophers may themselves believe, the plausibility of a luck-egalitarian position tacitly depends on a libertarian conception of what genuine choice would look like. In the absence of such a conception, it is simply not clear why choice should matter so much—why such fateful political and economic consequences should turn on the presence or absence of genuine choice.

Suppose, for example, that one accepts some version of a "compatibilist" conception of voluntary choice, according to which genuine choices enjoy no exemption from the normal causal order. They are neither metaphysically anomalous nor categorically unique. Instead, the hallmark of such choices is, roughly, that they exhibit certain characteristic

---

16. See, for example, Eric Rakowski, *Equal Justice* (Oxford: Oxford University Press, 1991), pp. 76–77, 113–115.
17. Cohen writes: "Equality of access to advantage is motivated by the idea that differential advantage is unjust save where it reflects differences in genuine choice … but it is not genuine choice as such…which the view proposes to equalize. The idea motivating equality of access to advantage does not even imply that there is such a thing as genuine choice. Instead, it implies that if there is no such thing, because, for example, 'hard determinism' is true, then all differential advantage is unjust… my view tolerates the possibility that genuine choice is a chimera." See G.A. Cohen, "Equality of What? On Welfare, Goods and Capabilities," *Recherches Economiques de Louvain* 56 (1990): 381.

relations to the agent's deliberations, or that they are sensitive in specifiable ways to the agent's values and preferences, or that they are free of certain specific forms of causal interference, or that they possess some combination of these features. If one accepts a view of this kind, then the relation of choice to the agent's values, deliberations, and preferences will make the presence or absence of choice an important factor in many contexts. Still, it will be only one factor among others, and its relative importance will vary depending on the context. In some contexts, other factors may loom larger. Moreover, it will seem pertinent, on such a view, to observe that a talent for choosing wisely is just one human skill among others. What we call practical wisdom is affected in complex ways by other traits of character and temperament, and is not itself distributed equally among people. In addition, any given person's skill as a chooser may vary depending on the nature of the choice and on features of the social or institutional context. The person who is good at choosing friends may not be good at choosing investments, and the person who is good at choosing fruitful research topics may not be good at choosing vacation destinations. Nor can luck egalitarians say that the choices made by those who are less skillful choosers are for that reason alone less genuine choices, for luck egalitarians hold that, if there are genuine choices, then people may reap the rewards of the good ones and must bear the costs of the foolish ones. The capacity for genuine choice must therefore be understood by luck egalitarians as a capacity that can be exercised with varying degrees of judgment and skill. But then unless genuine choices (both the wise and the unwise) are conceived of as metaphysically distinctive in a way that makes them privileged indicators of our true identities or ultimate worth, it is obscure why they should have the kind of across-the-board, make-or-break significance that luck egalitarianism assigns them.[18]

18. This question suggests itself with special force in relation to the work of Arneson, for he has long insisted that "among an individual's talents and traits are talents at value forming, choice making, and choice executing," and that some people have "very poor choicemaking abilities." See, respectively, Richard Arneson, "Review of *Sovereign Virtue*," *Ethics* 112 (2002): 371; Richard Arneson, "Equality of Opportunity for Welfare Defended and Recanted," *Journal of Political Philosophy* 7 (1999): 496. Nor does his work display any evident sympathy for a libertarian conception of choice. (Although see his criticism of J.J.C. Smart's "premature dismissal of libertarianism" in Richard Arneson, "The Smart Theory of Moral Responsibility and Desert," in *Desert and Justice*, edited by S. Olsaretti (Oxford: Oxford University Press, 2003), pp. 233–258. The quoted phrase appears on p. 258.) It is therefore unclear why he gives the presence or absence of choice as much importance as he does, both in his original luck-egalitarian scheme and, it seems, in his subsequent prioritarian view. For Arneson's

In short, my second reason for thinking that it is a mistake to ground egalitarianism in the principle of responsibility is this. Those substantive versions of the principle that might plausibly be thought to support a form of egalitarianism tacitly depend for their appeal on a metaphysical account of choice and moral responsibility that seems to me implausible, and which egalitarians who rely on the principle certainly make no attempt to defend.[19] In this respect, as in the matter of justification previously discussed, the luck-egalitarian position inherits the deficiencies of the conservative position whose advantages it explicitly seeks to incorporate. The appeal of the conservative position also tacitly depends on a metaphysically inflated conception of the significance of choice.

5. Moralism

To describe a person as moralistic is to say that the person is too prone to make moral judgments: that the person relies on moral categories to an excessive degree, invoking them prematurely or in contexts where

original luck-egalitarian scheme, see Richard Arneson, "Equality and Equal Opportunity for Welfare," *Philosophical Studies* 56 (1989): 77–93; Richard Arneson, "Liberalism, Distributive Subjectivism, and Equal Opportunity for Welfare," *Philosophy & Public Affairs* 19 (1990): 158–194. For his prioritarian view, see Arneson, "Luck Egalitarianism and Prioritarianism"; Arneson, "Equality of Opportunity for Welfare Defended and Recanted." In fact, however, it is possible to read some of Arneson's later writings as expressing second thoughts about the degree of weight that should be attached to considerations of choice and responsibility. See, in addition to Arneson, "The Smart Theory of Moral Responsibility and Desert" and Arneson, "Review of *Sovereign Virtue*," Richard Arneson, "Welfare Should be the Currency of Justice," *Canadian Journal of Philosophy* 30 (2000): 497–524.

19. Andrew Williams has suggested in correspondence that the appeal of luck egalitarianism may depend, not on a set of tacit metaphysical assumptions, but rather on an opposition to restricting choice and spreading responsibility. In other words, if we reject the luck-egalitarian requirement that people should internalize the costs of their own choices, then our only options are either to prevent individuals from making certain choices or else to force others to share the costs of those choices. The first may seem like unwarranted interference and the second may seem unfair. But the impression that this is an alternative explanation of the appeal of luck egalitarianism is illusory. After all, the luck-egalitarian view itself restricts people's ability to profit from their unchosen natural abilities or from other favorable circumstances of their birth, and it insists on spreading the costs of unfavorable personal circumstances. So luck egalitarians need to explain why restrictions and cost spreading are acceptable as responses to differences in unchosen circumstances, but not as responses to differences in people's voluntary choices. The metaphysical diagnosis continues to suggest itself.

they are out of place, or using them in a rigid and simplistic way that ignores the nuances and complexities of human predicaments. Doctrines and policies can also be described as moralistic if they either support or are supported by misplaced moral judgments. Moralism is the enemy of insight and illumination, and one of its most common functions is to place obstacles in the way of genuine understanding. There are critics of morality who think, in effect, that all moral judgment is moralistic, but moralism is in fact a moral flaw: a deformation or disfiguration of the moral. It is a moral failing to neglect the often complex reality of people's circumstances or to subject them to unjustified criticism.

Political moralism involves the use of moralistic judgments to justify political positions or policies. It is a particularly pernicious form of moralism. Like all forms of the phenomenon, it combines a claim to authoritativeness with a fatal insistence on the oversimplification of complex situations. In political contexts, the characteristic function of this combination is to provide a pretext for neglecting legitimate claims or interests, or for silencing dissident voices.

One familiar form of right-wing moralism appeals to ideas of desert and individual responsibility in order to delegitimate the claims of the poor to assistance. Of course, *desert* and *responsibility* are important normative concepts that play a significant role in moral thought, and policies for the alleviation of poverty are quite properly the subject of extensive debate and disagreement. Yet there is also a long-established tradition within conservative politics of using a simplifying and highly moralized discourse of individual responsibility as a way of placing the onus for the alleviation of poverty squarely on the poor themselves. Indeed, the concepts of *desert* and *responsibility* seem especially vulnerable to moralistic misappropriation, and what might be termed *the moralism of responsibility* is one of the most popular forms of political moralism. In part, this is because the defensive exaggeration of a sense of individual authorship and control provides a bulwark against the fear of contingency, luck, and powerlessness. In addition, the conservative version of the phenomenon enables those who are well-off to feel that they can take credit for their own success and that they need not be troubled unduly by the plight of those who are less fortunate.

One of the aims of luck egalitarianism is to undermine conservative moralism by turning the principle of responsibility against conservatives. In this spirit, luck egalitarians employ what I have called defensive arguments in order to show that those who are well-off owe much of their success to their natural talents and favorable social circumstances, which they did not choose and for which they cannot plausibly be thought to be responsible. Similarly, the plight of the poor is said to derive largely from unchosen natural factors and from the social circumstances into which they were born. The aim of these arguments is to undermine conservative moralism by demonstrating its dependence on an unwarranted complacency about the actual sources of inequality in our society.

Yet, as we have seen, another aim of luck egalitarianism is to incorporate "the most powerful idea in the arsenal of the anti-egalitarian right," namely, the idea of choice and responsibility. It is in order to achieve this aim that luck egalitarians go beyond defensive arguments and make the affirmative claim that inequalities deriving from people's voluntary choices are justifiable whereas inequalities deriving from unchosen circumstances are not. In making this claim, however, luck egalitarians court their own form of moralism. As I have already suggested, the idea that, because individuals are responsible for their voluntary choices, they must bear the full costs of those choices, flies in the face of the more nuanced and context-dependent judgments about the significance of choice that are characteristic of ordinary moral thought. Most people do not insist, as a general matter, that someone who makes a bad decision thereby forfeits all claims to assistance. They do not take such a sweeping view either in matters of personal morality or in political contexts.[20] In their personal lives, for example, they do not refuse to comfort a friend whose foolish, but voluntarily undertaken, romance has come to a painful end; or to give directions to a driver who has predictably become lost after failing to consult a map; or to help a family member who finds

---

20. Hence, I agree with Thomas Scanlon's criticism of what he calls the "Forfeiture View" of the significance of choice. See Thomas Scanlon, *What We Owe to Each Other* (Cambridge, MA: Harvard University Press, 1998), pp. 251–267. Indeed, one way of putting the points I have been making would be to say that luck egalitarianism depends on a particularly strong and implausible version of the Forfeiture View, inasmuch as it relies to an extraordinary degree on what Scanlon calls "the special legitimating force of voluntary action." See Scanlon, *What We Owe to Each Other*, p. 260. Andrew Williams has suggested in response that luck egalitarians can make do instead with what Scanlon refers to as a "Value of Choice" account, thereby avoiding the threat of moralism. However, my argument has been, in effect, that if one rejects the Forfeiture View in favor of a Value of Choice account, then the idea of constructing a master principle of distributive justice on the basis of the choice–circumstance distinction loses its appeal. Of course, someone who accepts a Value of Choice account may say, plausibly enough, that there are contexts in which what justice demands is that people should be provided with equally valuable sets of choices or opportunities rather than with equal outcomes. On such an account, however, it will be appropriate in each of the relevant contexts to ask for a further explanation of why this is so. The distinction between choices and circumstances does not have the kind of general justificatory significance on a Value of Choice account that the Forfeiture View assigns it.

himself unemployed as a result of a poor career choice. In short, most people do not have a blanket policy of refusing assistance to anyone who has made a mistake or a poor decision. Such a policy would strike us as harsh, unforgiving, insensitive to context, and unduly moralistic.

A similar point applies to the judgments people make in wider social and political contexts. Most people do not believe that an indigent defendant should be denied legal representation, even if her inability to afford an attorney was the result of bad financial planning or imprudent credit-card use and, indeed, even if she freely and voluntarily committed the crime of which she is accused. Nor do they believe that people whose poverty has resulted from poor financial decision-making should be denied emergency medical care or assistance in obtaining food or shelter. Once again, a blanket policy of this kind would strike us as harsh, unforgiving, insensitive to context, and moralistic.

It is also worth noting that few people endorse a blanket policy of refusing to reward unchosen talents or traits of character. In their personal lives, for example, few people have a general policy of refusing to praise their friends and acquaintances for anything other than effort or hard work. Such a policy would also be liable to strike us as strange and moralistic. Nor do most people believe that grades, literary or scientific prizes, friendships, or surgical residencies should be allocated solely on those bases. The case of income is more controversial, even in a society that is as market-oriented as ours, but clearly there are relatively few people who believe that effort and choice (as opposed to talent) are the sole legitimate bases for income differentials.

The libertarian conception of choice may seem to promise a defense against the charge of moralism. If choices and circumstances belong to different metaphysical categories, then the attitudes that strike us as moralistic may be said to have an independent philosophical justification. Perhaps that is why the conservative discourse of responsibility is so often accompanied, if only tacitly, by a maximalist conception of the metaphysical significance of choice. In any case, the upshot of the considerations I have been rehearsing is that the successful incorporation of "the most powerful idea in the arsenal of the anti-egalitarian right" may come at a price. Luck egalitarians may find that, along with that powerful idea, they have also incorporated one of the least attractive features of the anti-egalitarian position: its tendency to a rigid and unsympathetic moralism.

Granted, the charge of moralism may not apply equally to all attempts to ground egalitarianism in the principle of responsibility. That is partly because different versions of luck egalitarianism draw the line between choices and circumstances in different ways. It is partly because few luck egalitarians present the luck-egalitarian principle as an absolute requirement or as constituting the whole of political morality; most acknowledge that the principle needs to be supplemented or qualified in various respects. It is also because some luck egalitarians, such as Dworkin, interpret the notion of choice sensitivity in such a way as to give certain kinds of hypothetical choice schemes a role in determining which disadvantages should be compensated. For all of these reasons, there may be versions of luck egalitarianism that can deflect some of the moralistic implications of the unadorned luck-egalitarian principle that I have been considering.[21] Even so, the fact that the unadorned principle has such implications, and that they can be avoided only by qualifying or moving away from it, should make us uneasy about the idea of grounding egalitarianism in a version of that principle.

6. Luck Egalitarianism and Conservatism

The three considerations I have thus far cited as reasons for rejecting an egalitarianism that is based on the principle of responsibility all point to features that such an egalitarianism shares with the conservative, anti-egalitarian position it officially opposes. These two positions, I have argued, share an unsustainably ambitious justificatory aim, an unacknowledged reliance on a maximalist metaphysics of choice, and an unappealing tendency toward excessive moralism. But perhaps this is not really surprising. Perhaps it was never reasonable to hope that one could incorporate the most powerful features of the anti-egalitarian position while at the same time excluding all of its unattractive features. My own view is that the project of developing a responsibility-based conception of egalitarian justice represents an overreaction to conservative criticism of the welfare state and of egalitarian liberalism more generally. To be sure, that conservative criticism requires a response, and part of its value lies in the way it challenges defenders of liberal egalitarianism to clarify their own conceptions of individual responsibility. Nevertheless, I believe it is a mistake to respond to the conservative criticism by trying to develop a responsibility-based conception of egalitarian justice. The project of developing such a conception is misguided both because, in attempting

21. Not surprisingly, some of these implications could also be avoided by forms of egalitarianism that endorse part, but not all, of the luck-egalitarian position as I have characterized it. This is true, for example, of views that condemn inequalities deriving from unchosen circumstances as unjust, but do not commit themselves to the acceptability of inequalities deriving from voluntary choices.

to duplicate some of the central virtues of the conservative position, it is likely to duplicate some of its central vices as well and because it misrepresents the nature of our concern with equality as a value.

Admittedly, the criticisms of that project that I have developed to this point have not been conclusive. There are many different versions of luck egalitarianism and they differ from one another in many significant respects. I have not discussed any of these versions in detail, but have instead focused on their shared aspiration to construct a fundamental principle of distributive justice using a distinction between choices and circumstances. I have conceded that, despite my arguments, there may be forms of luck egalitarianism that can deflect the charge of moralism, and perhaps some version of the position can be freed from the untenable justificatory ambitions and undefended metaphysical associations to which I have called attention. Since, however, I believe that the luck-egalitarian project rests, in any case, on a misunderstanding of the nature of our concern with equality, I shall not pursue these possibilities any further. Instead, my aim in the remainder of this article will be to suggest what I take to be a more satisfactory characterization of the way in which equality matters to us. Ultimately, the most serious reason for declining to ground egalitarianism in the principle of responsibility is that to do so is to lose touch with the value of equality itself.

7. Equality as a Social Value

Why is equality a value? Why does it matter to us? Concerns about equality arise in many different contexts and there may be no single answer that is appropriate to all of these contexts. Insofar as equality is understood as a substantive social value, which is distinct, for example, from the formal principle that one should treat like cases alike and from the axiological judgment that all people are of equal worth, the basic reason it matters to us is because we believe that there is something valuable about human relationships that are, in certain crucial respects at least, unstructured by differences of rank, power, or status. So understood, equality is in some ways a puzzling value and a difficult one to interpret. After all, differences of rank, power, and status are endemic to human social life. Almost all human organizations and institutions recognize hierarchies of authority, for example, and most social roles confer distinctions of status which in turn structure human relationships, such as the relationships of doctors to patients, teachers to students, parents to children, attorneys to clients, employers to employees, and so on. If there is any value at all in such relationships, then at least one of the following two things must be true. Either some relationships can be valuable despite having a fundamentally inegalitarian character or else it is not necessary, in order for a relationship to qualify as having an egalitarian character, that it should be altogether unmarked by distinctions of rank or status. The egalitarian need not deny the first point, but, given the ubiquity of the distinctions mentioned, the second point is crucial if equality is to be understood as a value of reasonably broad scope. In fact, both points are almost certainly true. This means that, in order to understand the value of equality, one needs to investigate the specific respects in which egalitarian relationships must be free from regimentation by considerations of rank or status. One needs to characterize in greater detail the special value that egalitarian relationships are thought to have and to consider which differences of authority or status have the capacity to compromise that value.

There are limits to how much progress one can make in addressing these issues if one treats them purely as subjects for abstract investigation. To some extent, the participants in putatively egalitarian relationships must work out the terms of those relationships for themselves. This is especially true of the participants in close interpersonal relationships. They must establish for themselves the divisions of authority and labor and the patterns of mutual dependence that will characterize their dealings with each other, and they must determine what kinds of role differentiation their relationship can sustain while remaining a relationship of equals. Even in such cases, however, the judgments of the participants are not infallible, and some generalizations are surely possible, both with respect to the value of conducting relationships on a footing of equality and with respect to the circumstances that make that impossible.

Here I will limit myself to some remarks about one special but crucial type of relationship. This is the relationship that the members of a political society bear to one another. I will begin by asking why exactly it is important to us (assuming that it is) to live in a society in which citizens relate to one another as equals. Let me mention two different answers to this question. The first answer purports to be thinner and philosophically less committal, while the second answer is morally and philosophically more ambitious. Rather than appealing to any particular "comprehensive moral doctrine" to explain the importance of equality, the less committal answer starts by pointing out that the idea of equal citizenship is part of the broader notion of society as a fair system of cooperation among free and equal people. This broader notion, in turn, is implicit in the public political culture of a modern democratic society. As such, it represents a point of normative convergence among people whose values and outlooks may differ sharply in other respects and who may, indeed, disagree about the philosophical underpinnings of this notion itself. In other words, the value of equal citizenship is more widely acknowledged than is any particular account of the source of this value. Precisely because it represents a settled conviction shared by people whose other evaluative commitments may differ profoundly, the idea of society as a fair system of cooperation among free and equal people has a special importance in modern constitutional democracies. The pluralistic character of these democracies calls into question their ability to identify any shared basis for a public conception of justice. Yet the idea of society as a fair system of cooperation is so firmly embedded in their political traditions and cultures that it may help to provide such a basis. A modern democracy may be able to achieve a just and stable social order despite the prevalence of pluralism, provided that its major institutions establish a fair cooperative framework within which people who relate to one another as equals can pursue their divergent conceptions of the good.[22]

Whereas the first answer avoids endorsing any particular philosophical account of the value of equal citizenship, and instead suggests that the diversity of outlooks affirming this value gives it a special importance within the public political culture of a modern democracy, the second, philosophically more venturesome answer does not hesitate to assert that living in a society of equals is good both intrinsically and instrumentally. When the relationships among a society's members are structured by rigid hierarchical distinctions, it claims, the resulting patterns of deference and privilege exert a stifling effect on human freedom and inhibit the possibilities of human exchange. Because of the profound and formative influence of basic political institutions, moreover, patterns of deference and privilege that are politically entrenched spill over into personal relationships of all kinds. They distort people's attitudes toward themselves, undermining the self-respect of some and encouraging an insidious sense of superiority in others. Furthermore, social hierarchies require stabilizing and sustaining myths, and the necessity of perpetuating and enforcing these myths discourages truthful relations among people and makes genuine self-understanding more difficult to achieve. In all these ways, inegalitarian societies compromise human flourishing; they limit personal freedom, corrupt human relationships, undermine self-respect, and inhibit truthful living. By contrast, a society of equals supports the mutual respect and the self-respect of its members, encourages freedom of interpersonal exchange, and places no special obstacles in the way of self-understanding or truthful relations among people. It also makes it possible for people to develop a sense of solidarity and of participation

---

22. See John Rawls, *Political Liberalism* (New York: Columbia University Press, 1993).

in a shared fate without relying on unsustainable myths or forms of false consciousness. For all of these reasons, an egalitarian society helps to promote the flourishing of its citizens. Nor is the value of living in such a society purely instrumental. On the contrary, to live in society as an equal among equals is a good thing in its own right.

Obviously, these two different ways of characterizing the importance of equal citizenship differ from one another in significant ways. For our purposes, however, the pertinent point is that proponents of both characterizations need to address a common set of questions. They need to consider what forms of political authority are compatible with a society of equals, what regime of rights and freedoms such a society requires, and how, compatibly with a commitment to egalitarian membership, individuals' differing aims, values, identifications, and group affiliations can best be accommodated. They also need to decide what system for the allocation of economic resources is appropriate to a society of equals and what bases for the assignment of benefits and burdens such a society would recognize. In my view, an egalitarian scheme of distributive justice is best understood as one that tries to provide answers to these questions.

Yet this is not the approach that has generally been taken by those who have tried to develop responsibility-based conceptions of egalitarian justice. Rather than exploring the implications for distribution of the ideal of a society of equals, these philosophers have generally addressed themselves directly to questions of distribution. They have assumed that an egalitarian conception of justice is one that seeks to distribute *something* equally, and they have asked what the proper *equalisandum* might be. Thus, they have debated the "currency" of egalitarian distribution and, as we have seen, they have tried to fix the scope of egalitarian compensation by establishing an authoritative distinction between choices and circumstances,[23] but they have made little attempt to situate the distributive principles they favor within a broader conception of the nature of egalitarian social relationships.

Sometimes writers in this tradition simply present us with an array of possible distributions and invite us to make judgments about which of these distributions is best "from the point of view of equality," as if the word *equality*, considered in the abstract and cut loose from any serious

---

23. As John Roemer says, "If the first issue of contention in modern egalitarian theory is what the equalisandum should be, the second is the distinction between a person's actions that are caused by circumstances beyond his control and those for which he is personally responsible." See John Roemer, "A Pragmatic Theory of Responsibility for the Egalitarian Planner," *Philosophy & Public Affairs* 22 (1993): 147.

reflection about the nature of human societies or relationships, sufficed to define a perspective from which optimal principles of egalitarian justice could be discerned. Insofar as they draw connections between egalitarian distributive principles and more general ideas of equality, these writers tend to argue that distributive egalitarianism follows, not from an ideal of egalitarian social relationships, but rather from an abstract conception of the equal worth of persons or from the principle that a government should treat its citizens as equals. Sometimes they assert that there simply is no egalitarian idea more basic than the intuition, which is presented as a brute moral datum, that it is bad if some people are worse off than others through no fault of their own.[24] Richard Arneson captures the spirit of this tradition when he describes egalitarianism as the view that "people should get the same, or be treated the same, or be treated as equals, in some respect."[25] The idea that egalitarianism is concerned with the nature of the relationships among the members of society fades into the background or disappears altogether.[26]

24. In Larry Temkin's representative formulation, "the ultimate intuition underlying egalitarianism is that it is bad (unfair or unjust) for some to be worse off than others through no fault of their own." See Larry Temkin, *Inequality* (Oxford: Oxford University Press, 1993), p. 200.

25. Richard Arneson, "Egalitarianism," in *The Stanford Encyclopedia of Philosophy (Fall 2002 Edition)*, http://plato.stanford.edu/archives/fall2002/entries/egalitarianism/.

26. The tendency among philosophers discussing or defending egalitarianism to focus solely on questions of distribution, in isolation from any consideration of equality as an ideal of human relationships, is not limited to proponents of responsibility-based conceptions. In the article cited in note 6 above, for example, Peter Vallentyne exhibits the same tendency. So too do many others, including Dennis McKerlie, "Egalitarianism," *Dialogue* 23 (1984): 223–38; Derek Parfit, "Equality or Priority?" *The Lindley Lecture* (University of Kansas, 1995). Of course, equality is an intrinsically relational notion; the fact that two people have equal amounts of some good constitutes a kind of relation between them. This is what McKerlie means when he writes: "Equality is a relationship between different people. There is equality when they are equally supplied with resources, or equally happy. Whether there is equality or inequality, and how much there is, will depend on the overall distribution of whatever is valued. A moral view based on the value of equality will give us the goal of creating this relationship in outcomes. It will tell us to aim at outcomes with the overall pattern of distribution that maximizes equality or minimizes inequality." See Dennis McKerlie, "Equality," *Ethics* 106 (1996): 274. It should be clear, however, that when I speak of equality as an ideal of human relationships, I am expressing a view that is very different from McKerlie's. Equality, as I understand it, is an ideal that governs the terms on which independently existing human relationships should be conducted; it is not the "relationship" that consists in two people's having the same amount of something. As McKerlie's comments reveal, his understanding of the relationship of equality makes equality an inherently distributive notion.

One possible explanation for this neglect is suggested by Thomas Nagel, who writes:

> There are two types of argument for the intrinsic value of equality, communitarian and individualistic. According to the communitarian argument, equality is good for a society taken as a whole. It is a condition of the right kind of relations among its members, and of the formation in them of healthy fraternal attitudes, desires, and sympathies. This view analyzes the value of equality in terms of a social and individual ideal. The individualistic view, on the other hand, defends equality as a correct *distributive* principle—the correct way to meet the conflicting needs and interests of distinct people, whatever those interests may be, more or less. It does not assume the desirability of any particular kinds of desires, or any particular kinds of interpersonal relations. Rather it favors equality in the distribution of human goods, whatever these may be—whether or not they necessarily include goods of community and fraternity.[27]

Nagel says in this passage that those who defend equality as a distributive principle give it an individualistic interpretation, and that the only alternative is a communitarian defense according to which equality is good for society as a whole because it is a condition of the right kind of relations among its members. Although he blurs the contrast a bit by saying that the communitarian interpretation analyzes the value of equality in terms of a social *and individual* ideal, Nagel's basic claim is that distributive egalitarianism is the only thoroughly individualistic form of egalitarianism.

I agree with Nagel that, insofar as defenders of distributive egalitarianism abstract from any consideration of equality as an ideal of human relationships, there is a clear sense in which their view may be described as individualistic. However, I think it is a mistake to suppose that the only alternative to this kind of individualism is a communitarian understanding of equality, if such an understanding is taken to require a departure from basic liberal principles. To say that it is important to us to live in a society of equals is not to deny, for example, that a just society must provide a fair framework of cooperation within which people can pursue their diverse schemes of value and conceptions of the good. On the contrary, we have already seen that, at least on one view, a shared commitment to living in a society of free and equal citizens is precisely what

27. Thomas Nagel, "Equality," in *Mortal Questions* (Cambridge: Cambridge University Press, 1979), p. 108.

underwrites that conception of justice. Indeed, I doubt whether it is possible adequately to characterize the liberal vision of a just society without at some point invoking the idea of a society of equals.

Whether or not I am right about that, I am quite confident that there is no prospect of successfully defending a responsibility-based conception of egalitarian distribution without attempting to anchor it in the ideal of a society of equals. As I have already argued, the luck-egalitarian version of the principle of responsibility cannot plausibly be grounded in the metaphysics of choice. Nor, as I have argued elsewhere, can it be grounded in a bare appeal either to the equal worth of persons or to the idea of equal treatment.[28] Responsibility-based conceptions address questions about the extent to which people should be required to bear the costs and allowed to reap the rewards of their own choices, about the extent to which people should be compensated for, and prevented from profiting from, unchosen personal characteristics, and about whether people's values, preferences, talents, and character traits should, for distributive purposes, be treated as aspects of their choices or numbered among their unchosen circumstances. But all of these questions concern the terms on which we want to live with one another. They are questions about the kinds of burdens that we want to be able to share with others and are willing to have them share with us; and they are questions about the kinds of advantages we want to be able to retain for ourselves and are willing to have others retain for themselves. To answer such questions, we must determine the kinds of relations in which we want to stand to our fellow citizens. We must decide when and on what terms we want to share one another's fate and when and on what terms we want to face the future alone. If there are distinctively egalitarian answers to these questions, they do not lie in metaphysics or in axiology or in the idea of equal treatment. They must rest instead on some conception of the importance of living together as equals.

Once we recognize this, we are led away from the idea that economic distribution should be regulated by a luck-egalitarian version of the principle of responsibility. There is no reason to believe that the members of a society of equals would wish to be regulated by such a principle, especially if I have been correct in arguing that the luck-egalitarian position tends toward moralism, exaggerates the significance of choice, and diverges in many ways from people's judgments in particular cases. To be sure, the idea of internalizing the costs of one's choices represents an

28. See Scheffler, "What is Egalitarianism?"; Scheffler, "Equality as the Virtue of Sovereigns."

important value, which people who were deliberating about the appropriate distributive regime for a society of equals would surely take into account. So, too, the idea that individuals should be protected from the ravages of bad fortune or bad brute luck. But there are a number of other values that would also figure in the deliberations of people who were concerned to establish a society of equals, and which would undercut any temptation they might have to assign the choice-circumstance distinction a dominant role in fixing the scope of permissible economic inequality. For example, reflection on the significance for human relations of practices of forbearance and accommodation might temper their insistence that individuals must fully internalize the costs of all of their choices.[29] Similarly, reflection on the centrality for individual identity of unchosen personal characteristics might temper their refusal to allow any reward that is based on such characteristics. On the other hand, reflection on the factors that make some people better choosers than others might limit their willingness to privilege choice as an inequality-justifying consideration. In addition, a recognition of the effects on their relations to one another of significant inequalities of income and wealth would almost certainly lead them to limit the extent of such inequalities from any source. In short, the regulative concern governing their deliberations would be, not the enforcement of the line between choice and circumstance, but rather the effects on their relationships to one another of different regimes for the allocation of advantage.

Let me briefly summarize my argument in this section. Equality as a social and political value expresses an ideal of how human relationships should be conducted. That ideal has distributive implications, and the task for an egalitarian conception of distributive justice is to draw out those implications. In general, however, philosophers who have sought to develop responsibility-based conceptions of egalitarian justice have not conceived of their task in this way. They have not sought to ground their proposals about justice in the ideal of equality. To that extent, I believe, they have lost touch with the reasons why equality matters to us. In principle, it remains open to them to argue that a responsibility-based conception follows from a proper understanding of the ideal of equality. Indeed, I have maintained that they must attempt to show this if such a conception is to have any chance of being compelling. However, I have also expressed skepticism about the prospects that such an attempt can succeed, for, in thinking about what a society of equals would be like, there is no evident

---

29. See, in this connection, Shiffrin, "Paternalism, Unconscionability Doctrine, and Accommodation"; Shiffrin, "Egalitarianism, Choice-Sensitivity, and Accommodation."

reason to suppose that its fundamental principle of distribution would track a version of the distinction between choices and circumstances.

8. Conclusion

I hope I may be forgiven for concluding on a somewhat self-referential note. In 1992, I published an article in which I observed that some of the most prominent contemporary liberal theories (including, most notably, the egalitarian liberalism of John Rawls) avoid using the notion of *desert* at the level of fundamental principle.[30] In consequence, I said, such theories seem to rely on an attenuated conception of individual responsibility, and this exposes them to a kind of criticism that is similar to the criticisms directed by conservative politicians against familiar liberal programs and policies. I went on to argue that judgments of desert and responsibility serve to express reactive attitudes and emotions that play a vital role in our social practices and interpersonal relations. I concluded that the political prospects of egalitarian liberalism may depend on whether its proponents can successfully demonstrate that their position does not, in the end, require an unacceptably revisionist conception of individual responsibility.

At first glance, the project of developing a responsibility-based conception of egalitarian justice seems directly responsive to this line of thought. In assigning choice and responsibility a central place within their distributive scheme, many luck egalitarians explicitly aim to improve on the perceived deficiencies of the kind of egalitarian liberalism associated with Rawls. In treating a version of the principle of responsibility as a fundamental distributive norm, their goal is to demonstrate that, far from being an unacceptably revisionist position, egalitarianism has its source in a widely shared and deeply entrenched conception of individual responsibility.

Nevertheless, I have argued in this article that the project of developing a responsibility-based conception of egalitarian justice is ill-conceived. The participants in that project seek to defuse conservative criticism by demonstrating that the notions of choice and responsibility can be installed at the core of an egalitarian doctrine. In so doing,

---

30. Samuel Scheffler, "Responsibility, Reactive Attitudes, and Liberalism in Philosophy and Politics," *Philosophy & Public Affairs* 21 (1992): 299–323. This article is reprinted in Samuel Scheffler, *Boundaries and Allegiances* (Oxford: Oxford University Press, 2001), pp. 12–31.

however, they overcompensate for the perceived deficiencies of Rawlsian egalitarian liberalism and incorporate the vices of the conservative position along with its virtues. By mimicking the conservative's emphasis on choice and responsibility, they unwittingly inherit the conservative's unattractive moralism and questionable metaphysical commitments, and they lose touch with some of the most important reasons why equality as a value matters to us in the first place.

If an egalitarian conception of justice is to be defended against conservative criticism, I believe that it will have to take a different form. The fundamental aim should be to identify the distributive regime that is best suited to a society of equals. In thinking through this issue, the role of individual choice and responsibility will, of course, be important, as will the desirability of protecting people against misfortune, but these will not be the only factors. Other kinds of considerations, such as those I mentioned earlier, will also need to be taken into account. The conception of justice that results may, to one degree or another, be revisionist of people's ordinary beliefs about desert and responsibility. The lesson of the conservative criticism is not that such beliefs are immune to revision. It is, rather, that proposed revisions must be compatible with a realistic account of the role played in human psychology and social relationships by ideas of desert and responsibility. This is really just one aspect of a more general truth. Once we recognize that equality is a normative ideal of human relations, it should be clear that an adequate egalitarian conception of justice must be complemented by a serious psychology of egalitarianism. Such a psychology would include, for example, an account of the motivational structures and resources that egalitarian institutions could be expected to engage, a demonstration of how egalitarian norms would support the reactive attitudes and emotions that are an important part of human relationships, and a description of the psychological processes by which egalitarian social forms would sustain individuals' self-respect and their sense of themselves as free and effective agents.[31]

The basic point is this. A conception of distributive justice, whether egalitarian or nonegalitarian, cannot be just a self-standing distributive formula. It must be part of a larger normative vision of society. It must enter into individuals' motives and attitudes, regulate their practices and

31. Here I draw on and extend some remarks I made (on May 24, 1991) as part of my unpublished comments on G.A. Cohen's Tanner Lectures at Stanford University. For Cohen's response to those remarks, see G.A. Cohen, "Incentives, Inequality, and the Difference Principle," in *The Tanner Lectures on Human Values*, Vol. 13, edited by G. Peterson (Salt Lake City: University of Utah Press, 1992), pp. 291–293.

institutions, and help to structure their relationships with one another. If there is merit in the conservative claim that some versions of the liberal egalitarian vision are defective because they assign too small a role to individual choice and responsibility, then egalitarians will want to find ways of responding to that criticism. But they will want to respond in a way that avoids the punitive moralism of the conservative position itself, and preserves their own fundamental vision of a society in which citizens relate to one another as equals.

9

Is Terrorism Morally Distinctive?

The term *terrorism* may by now have become too ideologically freighted to have any analytic value. If the
term is to be an aid to understanding, two opposed but complementary
ways of employing it will have to be resisted. On the one hand, there
is the tendency, among the representatives and defenders of governments facing violent threats from nonstate groups and organizations,
to use the term to refer to all forms of political violence perpetrated by
nonstate actors. On the other hand, there is the tendency, among the
representatives and defenders of nonstate actors engaged in political
violence, to insist that "the real terrorists" are the officials or the military forces of those states with which they are locked in conflict. Under
the combined influence of these two tendencies, the word *terrorism* is
in danger of becoming little more than a pejorative term used to refer
to the tactics of one's enemies.

Originally published in the *Journal of Political Philosophy* 14 (2006): 1–17.

In this paper, I will proceed on the assumption that the concept of terrorism retains more content than that, and that we recognize a use of the term in which it refers to a special kind of phenomenon or class of phenomena. My primary aim will not be to produce a definition of the term but rather to consider whether there is anything morally distinctive about the type of phenomenon to which it refers. Clearly, it will be impossible to do this without making some attempt to characterize the phenomenon. Still, my aim is not to produce a definition of the term *terrorism* or to identify necessary and sufficient conditions for its application.[1] What I will do instead is to describe a certain familiar pattern to which terrorist actions often conform, and to argue that instances of terrorism that fit this pattern do indeed have a morally distinctive character. There is no doubt that the term *terrorism* is frequently applied to conduct that does not fit this pattern. I will not insist that this is always inappropriate. I believe that the term is misapplied in some of these cases, but I do not mean to deny that there are cases in which its use is appropriate despite the absence of the morally distinctive features to which I will call attention.

Two other caveats are in order. First, I will assume that terrorism is a prima facie evil, and that the use of terrorist tactics is presumptively unjustified, but I will remain agnostic on the question of whether there can ever be circumstances in which such tactics may nevertheless be justified, all things considered. Second, I take it to be obvious that, although terrorism is a prima facie evil and its use is presumptively unjustified, it may sometimes be a response to policies that are also unjustified and that may be as objectionable as the terrorist response itself. Furthermore, the fact that terrorism is unjustified does not mean that all of the measures used to oppose it are themselves justified. In short, I assume that terrorism is a prima facie evil and my concern is with the kind of evil it is. Terrorism may sometimes be a response to great wrongs, and great wrongs may be committed in opposing it. But I will not be concerned here with the nature of those other kinds of wrongs nor will I address the question of whether the presumption against engaging in terrorism can ever be defeated.

Some other recent writers have taken a different approach to this subject. Their primary focus, understandably enough, has been on questions about the justification of terrorism, and they have sought to arrive at a definition of the term that would cohere with their justificatory conclusions.

---

1. Many different definitions have been proposed. For discussion, see C. A. J. Coady, "Terrorism and Innocence," *Journal of Ethics* 8 (2004), 37–58, and Jenny Teichman, "How to Define Terrorism," *Philosophy* 64 (1989), 505–517.

This has led many of them to endorse a broad definition according to which terrorism is simply politically or ideologically motivated violence that is directed against civilians or noncombatants. In fact, this broad definition has become sufficiently widespread that Jeff McMahan refers to it as the "orthodox definition."[2] Its popularity may reflect a concern about some of the apparent implications of relying on a more narrowly circumscribed definition. Since any narrower definition will presumably fail to classify certain types of political violence against civilians as forms of terrorism, any such definition may seem to imply that the types of violence it excludes deserve less severe condemnation. This implication is bound to seem troubling, especially if it is assumed that a narrow definition would single out forms of violence characteristically engaged in by nonstate actors and exclude forms of violence characteristically engaged in by states. Given this assumption, it may seem that reliance on a narrow definition would unwittingly import an uncritical pro-state bias.

Although I understand this concern, I think it is a mistake to begin an inquiry into the morality of terrorism by endorsing a broad definition. Such a starting point may lead us to overlook relevant distinctions and to give an oversimplified description of the moral terrain. I prefer to begin, not by trying to settle on a definition, but rather by thinking about certain familiar forms of violence that most people would not hesitate, prior to analysis, to classify as instances of terrorism. I want to ask whether there is anything morally distinctive about these specific patterns of activity. As I hope will emerge from my discussion, this relatively narrow focus will serve to highlight some morally salient features and distinctions that might otherwise be easier to overlook. And, as I will try to make clear, such a focus need not import an uncritical pro-state bias, both because state activity can fall within the narrower sphere of activity on which I will concentrate and because many forms of violence that do not fall within that sphere nevertheless deserve severe condemnation, whether or not they are classified, in the end, as instances of terrorism.

Although terrorism is a political phenomenon, the resources of contemporary political philosophy are of limited assistance in trying to understand it. In recent years, a valuable new philosophical literature on terrorism has begun to emerge, and philosophical interest in the subject

---

2. See Jeff McMahan, "The Ethics of Killing in War," *Ethics* 114 (2004), 693–733, at p. 729. Variants of the broad definition have been defended, for example, by C. A. J. Coady and David Rodin. See Coady, "The Morality of Terrorism," *Philosophy* 60 (1984), 47–69; Coady, "Terrorism and Innocence;" Coady, "Terrorism, Morality, and Supreme Emergency," *Ethics* 114 (2004), 772–789; Rodin, "Terrorism without Intention," *Ethics* 114 (2004), 752–771.

has, of course, intensified since the September 2001 attacks on the World Trade Center and the Pentagon.[3] But, with one or two exceptions, the major political philosophies of the past several decades have been little concerned with the political uses of terror or with political violence more generally. On the whole, they have been philosophies of prosperity, preoccupied with the development of norms for regulating stable and affluent societies. To a great extent, for example, they have concerned themselves with issues of distributive justice, and they have implicitly addressed this topic from the perspective of a secure and well-established society with significant wealth to distribute among its citizens. Even when philosophers have looked beyond the boundaries of their own societies and have addressed issues of global justice, as they have increasingly begun to do, they have generally done so from the perspective of affluent, western societies whose responsibilities to the rest of the world are in question precisely because their own power and prosperity are so great. Contemporary political philosophers have not in general needed to concern themselves with threats to the survival or stability of their societies or with the conditions necessary for sustaining a viable social order at all. None of this is intended as criticism. It is entirely appropriate that political philosophers should address themselves to the questions that actually vex the societies in which they live. But it does suggest that the recent political philosophy of the affluent, liberal west may not afford the most useful point of entry for an investigation into problems of terror and terrorism.

A number of contemporary writers on terrorism have found it natural to situate their discussions in relation to the traditional theory of the just war.[4] For my purposes, it will be helpful to begin instead with the pre-eminent philosopher of fear in our tradition, Thomas Hobbes. It is

3. Two valuable early anthologies are R. G. Frey and C. W. Morris (eds.), *Violence, Terrorism, and Justice* (New York: Cambridge University Press, 1991), and M. Warner and R. Crisp (eds.), *Terrorism, Protest, and Power* (Aldershot: Edward Elgar, 1990). Two significant post-9/11 anthologies are V. Gehring (ed.), *War after September 11* (Lanham, MD: Rowman and Littlefield, 2003), and I. Primoratz ed., *Terrorism: The Philosophical Issues* (London: Palgrave Macmillan, 2004). See also the symposia on terrorism published in special issues of *Ethics* (Volume 114, Number 4) and *The Journal of Ethics* (Volume 8, Number 1) in 2004.

4. See, for example, the writings by Coady and Rodin cited above. See also F. M. Kamm, "Failures of Just War Theory: Terror, Harm, and Justice," *Ethics* 114 (2004), 650–692, and Noam Zohar, "Innocence and Complex Threats: Upholding the War Ethic and the Condemnation of Terrorism," *Ethics* 114 (2004), 734–751. The pioneering contemporary revival of just war theory is, of course, Michael Walzer's *Just and Unjust Wars* (New York: Basic Books, 1977). Walzer devotes one chapter of that book to terrorism, and he also discusses terrorism in several of the essays included in *Arguing*

striking that, in his famous catalogue of the "incommodities" of the state
of nature, Hobbes describes fear as the worst incommodity of all. The
state of nature, he says, is characterized by a war of "every man against
every man," and such a war comprises not merely actual battles but an
extended "tract of time" in which "the will to contend by battle is sufficiently known."[5] This means that, in the war of every man against every
man, a condition of general insecurity prevails for an extended period. "In
such condition," he says, "there is no place for industry, because the fruit
thereof is uncertain; and consequently no culture of the earth; no naviga-
tion, nor use of the commodities that may be imported by sea; no commodious building; no instruments of moving and removing such things
as require much force; no knowledge of the face of the earth; no account
of time; no arts; no letters; no society; *and which is worst of all, continual
fear, and danger of violent death.* And the life of man, solitary, poor, nasty,
brutish, and short" (Ch. 13, para. 9, pp. 95–96, emphasis added).

Hobbes makes at least three points in this passage and the surrounding text that are relevant to our topic. First, there is his insistence on
how bad a thing fear is. Continual fear—not momentary anxiety but
the grinding, unrelenting fear of imminent violent death—is unspeak-
ably awful. It is, he suggests, worse than ignorance. It is worse than the
absence of arts, letters, and social life. It is worse than being materi-
ally or culturally or intellectually impoverished. Fear dominates and
reduces a person. A life of continual fear is scarcely a life at all. Someone
who is in the grip of chronic terror is in a state of constant distress; he
"hath his heart all the day long gnawed on by fear of death, poverty, or
other calamity and has no repose, nor pause of his anxiety, but in sleep"
(Ch. 12, para. 5, p. 82).

The second point is that fear is incompatible with social life. On the
one hand, sustained fear undermines social relations, so that in addition
to being worse than various forms of poverty and deprivation it also
contributes to them, by destroying the conditions that make wealth and
"commodious living" possible. Fearful people lead "solitary" lives. Alone
with their fears, trusting no one, they cannot sustain rewarding forms of

---

about War (New Haven, CT: Yale University Press, 2004). The application of just war
   theory to terrorism is vigorously criticized by Robert Goodin in *What's Wrong with
   Terrorism?* (Cambridge: Polity Press, 2006).
5. Thomas Hobbes, *Leviathan,* chapter 13, paragraph 8. Quotation taken from the edition edited by A. P. Martinich (Peterborough, Ont.: Broadview Press, 2002), p. 95.
   Subsequent references, including chapter, paragraph, and page number in the Martinich edition, will be given parenthetically in the text.

interpersonal exchange. On the other hand, the establishment of society offers relief from fear and, in Hobbes' view, it is to escape from fear that people form societies. The fear of death, he says, is the first of "the passions that incline men to peace" (Ch. 13, para. 14, p. 97). Indeed, and this is the third point, it is *only* within a stable political society that the miserable condition of unremitting fear can be kept at bay. In addition to being incompatible with social life, sustained fear is the inevitable fate of presocial human beings.

Terrorists take these Hobbesian insights to heart. In a familiar range of cases, at least, they engage in violence against some people in order to induce fear or terror in others, with the aim of destabilizing or degrading (or threatening to destabilize or degrade) an existing social order. Without meaning to beg the very questions of definition that I said I would not be addressing, I will call these "the standard cases." I do so in part on the boringly etymological ground that these cases preserve the link between the idea of terrorism and the root concept of terror. But I will also go on to argue—indeed, it is my primary thesis—that the etymology points us to something morally interesting, which might otherwise be easier to overlook.

In "the standard cases," terrorists undertake to kill or injure a more or less random group of civilians or noncombatants;[6] in so doing, they aim to produce fear within some much larger group of people, and they hope that this fear will in turn erode or threaten to erode the quality or stability of an existing social order. I do not mean that they aim to reduce the social order to a Hobbesian state of nature, but only that they seek to degrade or destabilize it, or to provide a credible threat of its degradation or destabilization, by using fear to compromise the institutional structures and disrupt the patterns of social activity that help to constitute and sustain that order. The fear that terrorism produces may, for example, erode confidence in the government, depress the economy, distort the political process, reduce associational activity and provoke destructive changes in

---

6. The relevance of civilian or noncombatant status to the definition of terrorism is contested, but since I am setting aside questions of definition I will not address the issue. For pertinent discussion, see Coady, "The Morality of Terrorism" and "Terrorism and Innocence;" Robert Fullinwider, "Terrorism, Innocence, and War," in Gehring (ed.), *War After September 11*; Virginia Held, "Terrorism, Rights, and Political Goals," in Frey and Morris (eds.), *Violence, Terrorism, and Justice*, pp. 59–85; Virginia Held, "Terrorism and War," *Journal of Ethics* 8 (2004), 59–75; Igor Primoratz, "The Morality of Terrorism," *Journal of Applied Philosophy* 14 (1997), 221–233; Noam Zohar, "Innocence and Complex Threats." There is, of course, a large literature on the principle of noncombatant immunity in wartime.

the legal system. Its ability to achieve these effects derives in part from the fact that, in addition to being intrinsically unpleasant to experience, the fear that terrorism produces may inhibit individuals' participation in a wide range of mundane activities on which a polity's social and economic health depends. In some cases people may become mistrustful of the other participants in the activity (one of the other passengers may be a hijacker or suicide bomber), while in other cases they may fear that the activity will be targeted by terrorists who are not participants (someone may toss a hand grenade into the night club or movie theater). In the various ways I have mentioned and others that I will describe, the fear that is generated by terrorism can lead to significant changes in the character of society and the quality of daily life, and at the extremes these changes can destabilize a government or even the social order as a whole. In the standard cases, then, terrorists use violence against some people to create fear in others, with the aim of degrading the social order and reducing its capacity to support a flourishing social life—or at least with the aim of credibly threatening to produce these effects.[7]

Terrorist violence may, of course, have many other aims as well, even in the standard cases.[8] The terrorists may hope that their violent acts will attract publicity for their cause, or promote their personal ambitions, or provoke a response that will widen the conflict, or enhance their prestige among those they claim to represent, or undermine their political rivals, or help them to achieve a kind of psychological or metaphysical liberation. Nor need they conceive of their actions exclusively in instrumental terms. They may also be seeking to express their rage. Or they may believe that their victims are not in the relevant sense innocent, despite being civilians or noncombatants, and they may think of themselves as administering forms of deserved punishment or retribution.

There are many other respects in which what I am calling standard cases of terrorism can differ from one another. But they all have the following minimum features: (1) the use of violence against civilians or noncombatants, (2) the intention that this use of violence should create fear in others, including other civilians and noncombatants, and (3) the further intention that this fear should destabilize or degrade an existing social order, or at any rate that it should raise the specter of such destabilization or degradation. The destabilization or degradation of the social

---

7. For a related discussion, see Jeremy Waldron, "Terrorism and the Uses of Terror," *Journal of Ethics* 8 (2004), 5–35, at pp. 22–23.

8. Waldron has a good discussion of many of these aims in "Terrorism and the Uses of Terror," Section 6.

order may itself have many different aims. Among other things, it may be intended (a) as a prelude to the imposition of a different social order or the reconstitution of the existing order on different terms, (b) as a way of effecting some change in the policy of an existing state or society, (c) as a form of deserved punishment, and hence as an end in itself, or (d) as some combination of these.

What makes terrorism of the standard kind possible is the corrosive power of fear. As Hobbes suggests, sustained or continual fear is a regressive force both individually and socially. It can induce the unraveling of an individual's personality and, as we have already seen, its cumulative effects on large numbers of people can degrade the social order and diminish the quality of social life. Its capacity to achieve these effects is enhanced by the infectiousness of fear, the fact that it can so easily be transmitted from one person to another, even when the second person is unaware of the reasons for the first person's fear. The latter case is the one that Hobbes called "panic terror," and which he described as "fear without the apprehension of why or what." In such cases, he added, "there is always in him that so feareth, first, some apprehension of the cause, though the rest run away by example, every one supposing his fellow to know why. And therefore this passion happens to none but in a throng, or multitude of people" (Ch. 6, para. 37, p. 45). The fear induced by terrorism does not ordinarily fit the description of panic terror, since those who are subject to it normally know the reasons for their fear. But terrorism still benefits from the infectiousness of fear, because the fact that something has frightened one person may itself frighten another person, and the fearful attitudes of different people can exert mutually reinforcing and intensifying effects. In this age of instant communication, moreover, the capacity of terrorist acts to cause fear, and to exploit the phenomena of mutual reinforcement and intensification, is greatly increased. The news media can be counted on to provide graphic coverage of each terrorist outrage, so that a bomb blast anywhere can generate fear and insecurity everywhere. These attitudes in turn become newsworthy and are dutifully reported by the media, thus contributing to the syndrome of mutual reinforcement.

I said earlier that, in the standard cases, terrorist violence is usually directed against a "more or less random" group of civilians or noncombatants. It is difficult to be more precise. Sometimes virtually any civilians will do. At other times, terrorists will select a particular population group, defined by occupation or ethnicity or religion or social class, and will target people indiscriminately within that group. Or they will select a symbolic target (the World Trade Center), and those who are killed or injured will be those who happen to be in the chosen location at the

wrong time. Even when the target class is maximally wide, the victim-
ization is random in the sense that it is indiscriminate within that class
but not in the sense that it is pointless or irrational. And even when the
target class is relatively narrow, there is an advantage in preserving some
degree of indiscriminateness within that class. In both cases, the randomness or indiscriminateness has the same point. It is to maximize (within
the relevant parameters) the numbers of people who identify with the
victims, thus subverting the defensive ingenuity with which people seize
on any feature that distinguishes them from the victims of misfortune to
preserve their own sense of invulnerability. In this way, the appearance of
randomness is used to exploit the psychic economy of identification in
such a way as to maximize the spread of fear.

   This is not to say that it is always easy to achieve one's aims using
terrorist tactics. In fact, it is usually difficult for terrorist acts to destabilize an otherwise stable social order. This is not merely because such
acts can backfire, and reduce support for the terrorists' goals. Nor is it
merely because of the large armies, police forces, and intelligence services
that stable societies normally have available to fight those who employ
terrorism. Just as important is the fact that stable societies, and individuals raised in such societies, have substantial social and psychological
resources with which to resist the destructive effects of fear. People can
be remarkably tenacious in their determination to preserve the lives they
have made for themselves in society, and if fear can be infectious so too
can courage and the determination to persevere in the face of great danger. These too have mutually reinforcing and intensifying effects.

   But terrorism does not need to destabilize a social order altogether in
order to transform and degrade it and, as we have seen, often such transformation and degradation will suffice to enable those who employ terrorist tactics to achieve some or all of their aims. The problem is that living
with fear can have corrosive effects even for those who are courageous
and determined to persevere. One might put the point provocatively and
say that courage itself—or the need to sustain it over long periods of
time—can be corrosive. Living each day with the vivid awareness that
one's children may be killed whenever they leave home, or that a decision
to meet one's friends at a restaurant or café may result in violent death,
or that an ordinary bus ride on a sunny day may end with lumps of flesh
raining down on a previously peaceful neighborhood, exacts a cost. Nor
is this true only if one yields to one's fears and keeps one's children at
home, gives up socializing and avoids public transportation. It is also true
if one grits one's teeth and resolves to carry on as normal. People often
say, in explaining their determination to maintain a normal routine in
the face of terrorist activities or threats, that to do otherwise would be to

"give the terrorists what they want." This is not wrong, but it understates the problem. Maintaining one's normal routine does not suffice to preserve normalcy. Terrorism undermines normalcy almost by definition. One cannot, simply through an act of will, immunize oneself against the effects of continual fear and danger on one's state of mind or on the quality of one's life. These effects are distressingly easy for groups that use terrorist tactics to achieve and distressingly difficult for the members of targeted populations to avoid.

This is one reason why terrorism is so popular, even if it is not always ultimately successful. Apologists for terror often claim that it is the weapon of the weak, who have no other tools available for fighting back against their oppressors. This may be true in some circumstances. As far as I can see, however, those who engage in terrorism rarely invest much time in exploring the availability of other tools. All too often terrorism is the tool of choice simply because the perceived advantages it offers are so great. It costs relatively little in money and manpower. It has immediate effects and generates extensive and highly sensationalized publicity for one's cause. It affords an emotionally satisfying outlet for feelings of rage and the desire for vengeance. It induces an acute sense of vulnerability in all those who identify with its immediate victims. And insofar as those victims are chosen randomly from among some very large group, the class of people who identify with them is maximized, so that an extraordinary number of people are given a vivid sense of the potential costs of resisting one's demands. Figuratively and often literally, terrorism offers the biggest bang for one's buck.

If what I have said to this point is on the right track, then it does seem that terrorism is morally distinctive, at least insofar as it conforms to the pattern of what I have been calling "the standard cases." In these cases, at least, it differs from other kinds of violence directed against civilians and noncombatants. By this I do not mean that it is worse, but rather that it has a different moral anatomy. By analogy: humiliation is morally distinctive, and so too are torture, slavery, political oppression and genocide. One can investigate the moral anatomy of any of these evils without taking a position on where it stands in an overall ranking of evils. Many people are pluralists about the good. We can be pluralists about the bad as well.

In the "standard cases," some people are killed or injured (the primary victims), in order to create fear in a larger number of people (the secondary victims), with the aim of destabilizing or degrading the existing social order for everyone. The initial act of violence sets off a kind of moral cascade: death or injury to some, anxiety and fear for many more, the degradation or destabilization of the social order for all. Nor is this simply a cascade of harms. It is, instead, a chain of intentional abuse, for those who employ terrorist tactics do not merely produce these harms, they intentionally aim to produce them. The primary victims are used—their deaths and injuries are used—to terrify others, and those others are used—their fear and terror are used—to degrade and destabilize the social order.

The fact that the secondary victims' fear and terror are used in this way is one thing that distinguishes the standard cases from other cases in which civilians are deliberately harmed in order to achieve some military or political objective. In other cases of deliberate, politically motivated violence against civilians, the perpetrators display a callous disregard not only for the lives of their victims but also for the misery and suffering of the people who care about or identify with them. Since those who commit such acts are willing to kill or injure their victims, it is hardly surprising that they should be indifferent to the intensely painful human reactions—fear, horror, and grief—that their acts are liable to produce in others. In the "standard cases," however, the primary victims are killed or injured *precisely in order* to elicit such reactions—precisely in order to elicit fear, horror, and grief—so that those reactions can in turn be exploited to promote the perpetrators' ultimate, destabilizing objectives. Using Kantian terminology, we might say that the primary victims are treated not just as means to an end but as means to a means; that is, they are treated as means to the end of treating the secondary victims as means to an end. Those who engage in this kind of terrorism do not merely display callous indifference to the grief, fear, and misery of the secondary victims; instead, they deliberately use violence to cultivate and prey on these reactions. This helps to explain why there is something distinctively repellent about terrorism, both morally and humanly.[9]

As I have said, not all instances of terrorism fit the description of the "standard cases." Sometimes, for example, terrorist tactics may be employed not to destabilize or degrade an entire social order but rather to make the place of a particular social group or class within that order

9. There are three misunderstandings to be avoided. First, in saying that there is "something distinctively repellent" about terrorism, I am not saying that it is *more* repellent than any other type of atrocity. I am saying only that some of the reasons why it is repellent are distinctive. Second, I am not saying that *all* of the reasons why terrorism is repellent are distinctive; obviously, it is also repellent for some of the same reasons that other types of unjustified violence are. Finally, I am not claiming that what is distinctively repellent about terrorism is also what is *morally worst* about it. What is distinctively repellent about terrorism is, roughly, that it treats the primary victims as means to a means, but what is morally worst about it may simply be that it involves (for example) the unjustified killing of the innocent.

insecure, as in cases where the ambition is to drive the members of the targeted group into another country or territory ("ethnic cleansing"). In cases like this, the description of the "moral cascade" will differ some-what, but the moral anatomy of these cases will still bear a clear and recognizable relation to that of the standard cases. Other instances in which the term *terrorism* is likely to be employed may differ more substantially from the standard cases. An example might be a situation in which violence is directed against civilians solely for the purpose of provoking a response and thereby producing an escalation in the level of a conflict; the fact that the violence also generates fear, although predictable and not unwelcome, is no part of the perpetrators' aim. In a similar vein, insurgents might take civilian hostages simply as a way of pressuring a government to release some of their imprisoned comrades, and not for the purpose of spreading fear, although fear may be one predictable effect of their actions. Still other examples, meanwhile, may seem sufficiently different from the standard cases that the propriety of the term *terrorism* becomes doubtful, even if it is often applied to them. This may be true, for example, of targeted political assassinations or acts of sabotage.

In general, we should be sensitive to the wide variety of actual cases we are likely to encounter, and we should avoid theory-driven oversimplifications of the phenomena. My own aim, as I have already said, is not to produce a definition of the term *terrorism* or to provide a set of necessary and sufficient conditions for its application. Accordingly, I will take no position on the question of how far an act can depart from the standard cases while remaining an instance of terrorism. In any event, the fact that some form of conduct is not best thought of as amounting to terrorism does not mean that there is no objection to it. As the doctrine of the pluralism of the bad reminds us, there are many different kinds of atrocities and many different forms of horrific behavior, and we learn more by attending to the differences among them than by assimilating them all to a single category. One of the many unsettling features of the Bush administration's post-9/11 moral discourse, with its frequent references to "evildoers" and "bad guys," is that it uses moral categories to inhibit rather than to promote moral understanding. It relies on simplifying dichotomies that appeal to psychologically primitive sources of moral motivation and, in so doing, it encourages a dangerously reductive conception of the moral domain.

As I noted at the outset, the term *terrorism* is sometimes used, by representatives and defenders of governments facing violent threats from nonstate groups and organizations, to refer to all forms of political violence perpetrated by nonstate actors. This makes it impossible by definition for states to engage in terrorism. Although I have not endorsed this—or any other—definition, my narrow focus on the standard cases and my emphasis on terrorism's destabilizing aims may seem to imply that it can only be the tactic of insurgents or other nonstate actors. But this is not in fact a consequence of my view. States can certainly employ terrorist tactics in the manner I have described as a way of destabilizing other societies. They can do this in wartime, through the use of such tactics as "terror bombing," or in peacetime, through covert operations targeting another country's civilian population. And domestically, a government might use such tactics in order to create a limited degree of instability, with the aim of discrediting its opponents or generating increased support for repressive policies. Of course, it is crucial in such cases that the government should not appear to be the perpetrator of the terrorist acts, since its aim is precisely to ascribe those acts to others. Still, the fact remains that governments can engage in terrorism both against other societies and, with the qualification just mentioned, domestically as well.

Governments may also use terror as an instrument of policy without this amounting to terrorism of the "standard" type. Indeed, here I am prepared to engage in at least partial, stipulative definition, and to say that governments may use terror as an instrument of policy without this amounting to terrorism at all. This will be true, in my view, when a government uses terror internally—and is willing to be seen as doing so—in order to stifle dissent and opposition, to maintain its grip on power and to preserve the established order. I will use the term *state terror* to describe this phenomenon, and in the usage I have stipulated there is an important contrast between state terror and terrorism, even terrorism that is perpetrated by states. The point of the stipulation is not to suggest that one of these phenomena is better or worse than the other, but rather to highlight what I take to be a significant distinction between two different political uses to which terror may be put. Terrorism, as I understand it, standardly involves the use of violence to generate fear with the aim of destabilizing or degrading an existing social order. State terror, as I understand it, standardly involves the use or threat of violence to generate fear with the aim of stabilizing or preserving an existing social order. Of course, other people may use the terms *terrorism* and *state terror* in different ways, but the point is not merely terminological, and anyone whose use of the relevant terminology differs from mine needs to find some other way of expressing the contrast I have described.

It is an interesting fact that fear and terror can be used either to undermine an existing social order or to preserve one. They can be made to serve not only revolutionary but also conservative purposes. How is this possible? How, in particular, is it possible that fear and terror can be used to preserve a social order if, as I said earlier, they undermine social life? Hobbes, who certainly understood the second of these points, also emphasized the first. He wrote: "Of all passions, that which inclineth men least to break the laws is fear. Nay, excepting some generous natures, it is the only thing (when there is appearance of profit or plea- sure by breaking the laws) that makes men keep them" (Ch. 27, para. 19, p. 222). For Hobbes, fear can be used to preserve order because it is a passion "that relate[s] to power" (Ch. 31, para. 9, p. 269). In the state of nature—in the war of all against all—each person has sufficient power to pose a threat to every other person. Hence each person has reason to fear every other person, and this undermines the conditions of social life. But the concentration of power in a sovereign produces a redistribution of the capacity to inspire fear, and this makes social life possible. On the one hand, people's attitudes toward one another need no longer be dominated by fear and mistrust, and so the development of social relations is no longer inhib- ited. On the other hand, everyone has reason to fear the sovereign's power, and hence to obey the sovereign's laws, and so the social order is stabilized.

But this suggests that fear does not, after all, undermine social life, at least not in all cases. It undermines social life only when, in the absence of a common authority, fear is radically decentralized, and each person has reason to fear every other person. There is something to this, but as stated it overlooks the differences between ordinary political author- ity and a regime of state terror. In a decent society that is governed by the rule of law, crimes are punished and the fear of punishment can be said to provide individuals with a reason for obeying the laws. Here the phrase *fear of punishment* functions as a way of characterizing a certain kind of reason for action; people's presumed desire to avoid punishment is a consideration that counts in favor of obedience. But this does not mean that people are actually afraid or that they lead lives full of fear.[10] On the contrary, one of the primary advantages of the rule of law, and of a predictable, publicly promulgated and impartially administered system of punishments and sanctions, is that it enables people to avoid fear. By structuring their lives in accordance with what the law allows, they can predictably avoid the punishments and sanctions attached to violations. Of course, people who break the law, or are accused or suspected of doing so, may find themselves genuinely fearing punishment. But, leaving aside false accusations and unwarranted suspicions, law-abiding citizens need not actually experience any fear of the state, even if we can truly say that

---

10. This is related to Jeremy Waldron's distinction between "Jack Benny-style coercion" and "Arendtian terrorization." See Waldron, "Terrorism and the Uses of Terror," pp. 15–16.

the fear of punishment gives them a reason to obey. In a well-functioning state, the "fear of punishment" is not normally a condition of fear at all. For this reason, it provides no obstacle to the development of rich social relations, and indeed helps to facilitate them. For the very same reason, however, it also provides no counterexample to the thesis that a state of continual fear undermines social life.

Things are very different under a regime of state terror. Here the state deliberately keeps people afraid as a way of maintaining its grip on power and preserving the established system. In order to do this, it deliberately eliminates the features of impartiality and predictability associated with the rule of law. Power is exercised and laws are administered arbitrarily. Although there may be forms of conduct that can reliably be expected to result in arrest and punishment, there are few if any reliable ways of avoiding such outcomes. Networks of secret agents and informers may denounce people for any reason or none, and there is no independent judiciary or regime of rights to protect those who are accused. People may be imprisoned, or lose their jobs, or have their property confiscated, or be tortured or killed, without ever knowing why. Since citizens have no basis for confidence in their ability to avoid such calamities, they are kept perpetually fearful, uncertain, anxious. And since they have no way of knowing who may be an informer or an agent of the state, they are kept perpetually wary and mistrustful of one another. The point of inducing this Hobbesian condition of ongoing mutual mistrust is precisely to restrict the development of social relations and to inhibit the cooperative and solidaristic attitudes that accompany them. A regime that rules by terror recognizes these relations and attitudes as potential threats. By using fear to constrict and impoverish social life, it confirms both that fear undermines social relations and that a free social life is the antidote to fear. Thus, the fact that genuine terror can be used to preserve an established order does not falsify the observation that fear undermines social life, for social relations are indeed inhibited under a regime of terror. Notwithstanding the existence of centralized rule and a set of rigidly constrained social and economic institutions, such a regime has as much in common with the Hobbesian state of nature as it does with a political society that is subject to the rule of law.[11]

I have drawn the contrast between a regime of terror and the rule of law starkly, but I do not mean to deny that there can be intermediate cases. On the one hand, even the most brutal totalitarian states may need

11. My discussion in this paragraph is indebted to Waldron, "Terrorism and the Uses of Terror," pp. 18–20.

to provide selective relief from terror for certain groups of people in order to achieve their aims.[12] On the other hand, even relatively decent governments may find it irresistible at times to use fear as a way of deflecting criticism or deflating political opposition. A judiciously administered dose of alarm can do wonders in inducing a compliant frame of mind and encouraging people to rally round their leaders. Ironically, the fear of terrorism—which is in part to say the fear of fear—seems to be a particularly effective tool for this purpose. This is one reason why governments are so eager to label their enemies as terrorists; in addition to discrediting them, the very use of the label may help to induce a state of timid docility in an otherwise restive population. But none of this undermines the argument I have been developing.

The upshot of that argument is that there are two different ways in which fear might be said to be capable of contributing to the preservation of order. Although Hobbes, to the detriment of his political theory, did not distinguish between them, neither of them falsifies the claim that fear undermines social life. It is true that, when the rule of law prevails, the fear of punishment gives people a reason to obey, yet social life is not inhibited. But since the "fear of punishment" is not, in these circumstances, a condition of actual fear, the idea that fear undermines social life remains intact. Under a regime of terror, by contrast, genuine fear is indeed used to preserve order, but since social relations are severely restricted under such a regime, the tendency of fear to compromise social life is confirmed rather than disconfirmed.

This argument may seem to prove too much for my purposes, however. If, as I have insisted, a regime of state terror does indeed undermine social life, then it may seem that such a regime cannot, after all, be said to aim at stabilizing or preserving the existing social order. Surely undermining social life is incompatible with preserving the social order. What my analysis really shows, it may be suggested, is that both terrorism and state terror use fear to destabilize or degrade the social order. The difference between them is just that terrorism hopes thereby to destabilize the existing *political* configuration, whereas state terror hopes to reinforce or consolidate that configuration. I resist this interpretation because I believe that state terror typically aims to stabilize more than just the existing political configuration. It also seeks to preserve a set of tightly

---

12. Indeed, just as terrorist tactics are sometimes used, not to destabilize the entire social order but rather to make the place of a particular group within that order insecure, so too the apparatus of state terror is sometimes used against a subset of the population rather than against the population as a whole. Of course, such limitations tend to be unstable. Once terror is put to political use, it is hard to keep it within bounds.

controlled social and economic institutions, and in this sense it aims to stabilize an entire social order—albeit a severely constrained one—and not merely a government. Despite the fact that it uses fear to inhibit certain kinds of social relations and thus to restrict social life, in other words, it does nevertheless seek to preserve a rigidly constrained social order, in the sense just specified. To be sure, the fact that social life is so severely compromised under such a regime means that the social order that is preserved is bound to be a grim and dystopian one. Still, I think it would be a mistake to deny that it is a social order at all or to ignore the fact that the regime aims to stabilize and preserve it.[13]

If this is correct, then it is possible to reaffirm and to expand upon my earlier observations about the relationship between terrorism and state terror. In the standard cases, I have said, terrorism involves the use or threat of violence to generate fear, with the aim of degrading or destabilizing an existing social order. State terror, on the other hand, standardly involves the use or threat of violence to generate fear, with the aim of stabilizing or preserving an existing social order—albeit a grim and tightly controlled one. There is, accordingly, a significant difference between terrorism—even terrorism perpetrated by a state—and state terror. They represent different ways of using terror for political purposes. But they exploit a common mechanism: the capacity of fear to undermine social life. As I have argued, terrorism of the standard kind uses this mechanism to degrade the institutional structures and patterns of activity that help to constitute and sustain an existing social order. State terror, by contrast, uses the same mechanism to subvert or prevent the emergence of cooperative social relationships that might pose a threat to the power of the state or to the character of the prevailing social and economic arrangements. People are kept chronically fearful and mistrustful of one another so that, even if they have the resources and opportunities to do so, they will be unwilling or unable to form the kinds of groups, associations and social networks that might become independent centers of influence, facilitate the emergence of critical voices and perspectives, or in other ways challenge the status quo. Under a regime of state terror, fear is used by the state to keep social relations impoverished so that a rigidly constrained social and economic order can be preserved and protected from challenge.

I think that this contrast helps to explain why terrorist violence is so often calculated to attract maximum publicity, whereas so much of the

13. I am grateful to Jay Wallace and to an anonymous referee for prompting me to clarify these points.

violence associated with state terror is carried out in secret. Terrorists aim to promote chaos and disarray as a way of subverting the social fabric. They want people running for cover. The perpetrators of state terror want to promote order and regimentation. They want people marching in step. Spectacular acts of public violence are designed to produce disruption and panic. The shadowy operations of secret police and paramilitary groups are designed to produce silence, conformity and the desire to make oneself inconspicuous, to attract no notice.[14]

One additional complication should be noted. I have been distinguishing between terrorism and state terror: between the use of fear to degrade or destabilize an existing order and the use of fear to stabilize or preserve an existing order. But I have emphasized that states can engage in both forms of activity. It is natural to wonder whether the reverse is also true. Can nonstate groups use fear to stabilize an existing order? Although the label "state terror" is obviously not appropriate to such cases, I believe that the answer is yes. For example, nonstate groups may use violence to terrorize an oppressed or subordinated population, with the aim of reinforcing an established system of caste or hierarchy or defeating attempts to dismantle such a system. (Think, for example, of the Ku Klux Klan.) We can think of these as cases of "substate terror," in which fear is used to police the boundaries of a social hierarchy, to block the development of new social movements, or to inhibit social change. The use of fear to stabilize an existing order is no more the exclusive province of the state than the use of fear to destabilize such an order is the exclusive province of nonstate actors. The reason for distinguishing between terrorism, on the one hand, and state or substate terror, on the other, is to highlight the distinction between these two different uses of fear, and not to suggest a distinction between two different categories of agents.

Conclusion

The title of this paper poses a question. The answer that has emerged from my discussion is as follows. Terrorism is morally distinctive insofar as it seeks to exploit the nexus of violence and fear in such a way as

14. Of course, show trials and public executions can also help to produce these effects, and they too are familiar devices of state terror. But silence and conformity are not normally achieved by setting off bombs in public places or by using other standard terrorist tactics.

to degrade or destabilize an existing social order. Terrorist acts may have many functions other than the degradation of the social order, and the degradation of the social order may itself be intended to serve different purposes. But insofar as it conforms to the "standard" pattern I have described, terrorism has a morally distinctive character, whatever other functions and purposes individual instances of it may also serve. If, as is often the case, the term is applied more widely, then one consequence may be that terrorism so understood is not always morally distinctive. For example, we saw earlier that many philosophers now believe the term should be taken to refer to any politically motivated violence that is directed against civilians or noncombatants. If we accept this usage, then some acts of terrorism may turn out not to differ much in their moral character from murders and assaults that do not qualify for the "terrorist" label. David Rodin, who advocates a definition of this sort, concludes that terrorism is just "the political or ideological species of common violent crime."[15] This usage makes the distinctive character of the "standard cases" easier to overlook. And the distinctiveness of those cases will certainly be easier to overlook if terrorism is defined instead as political violence that is perpetrated by nonstate actors. If we rely on this kind of definition, then some of what I have been calling "the standard cases" will turn out to be instances of terrorism whereas others will not.

I do not take these considerations as reasons for insisting on a definition of terrorism that limits it to the standard cases. But I do think that the word *terrorism* is morally suggestive precisely because *terror* is its linguistic root, and that if we define the term in a way that effaces or even breaks the connection between terrorism and terror, as the definitions just mentioned do, then we are liable to miss some of the moral saliences toward which the word *terrorism* gestures.[16] The currency of that particular word, which adds to the already rich vocabulary we have for describing violence of various kinds, testifies to the power of fear and to the peculiar moral reactions evoked by its deliberate use for political ends. It is perfectly possible that, under the pressure of ideology or confusion or convenience, our usage of the term may evolve in such a way that it applies in some cases where fear plays no role and does not apply in some

---

15. See David Rodin, "Terrorism without Intention," p. 757.
16. Many other writers have insisted on the importance of fear for an understanding of the morality of terrorism. See, for example, Robert Goodin, *What's Wrong with Terrorism?*; Jeremy Waldron, "Terrorism and the Uses of Terror"; and Carl Wellman, "On Terrorism Itself," *Journal of Value Inquiry* 13 (1979), 250–258.

of what I have been calling the standard cases. Indeed, this may already have happened. But then we will need to find other ways of reminding ourselves of how bad a thing fear is, of the diabolical ways in which it can be provoked and exploited for political purposes, and of the specific character of our moral reactions when that happens.[17]

17. This paper was originally written for a conference on terrorism organized by Joseph Raz at the Columbia Law School in December 2004. A later version was presented as a lecture at the Mershon Center at Ohio State University in May 2005. I am indebted to both audiences for valuable discussion. I also received helpful written comments from Julie Tannenbaum, Jay Wallace, Robert Goodin, and three anonymous referees for this journal.

IO

Immigration and the Significance of Culture

"We didn't want to publish anything that can be perceived
as inflammatory to our readers' culture..."
—Robert Christie, spokesman for The Wall Street
Journal, *explaining why the* WSJ *declined to reprint the*
caricatures of the Prophet Muhammad whose
publication in the Danish newspaper Jyllands-Posten
sparked a worldwide furor[1]

It is often said that immigration poses a threat to national identity. A country that experiences a large influx of immigrants will find it more difficult to sustain its national traditions and the practices in which they are enshrined. A country's unity is

Originally published in *Philosophy & Public Affairs*, 35, no. 2. Copyright © 2007 by Blackwell Publishing, Inc. Used by permission of John Wiley & Sons, Inc. This article was originally written for a conference on "Multiculturalism and Nationalism in a World of Immigration" at the University of Copenhagen in May 2006. Versions of it were also presented under the auspices of the Humanities Center at the California State University, Chico; the Montreal Political Theory Workshop; the Ethics Center at the University of Zurich; the Department of Political Science and the Ethics Programme at the University of Oslo; the Columbia Law School; and the Colloquium in Legal, Political and Social Philosophy at NYU Law School. I am indebted to the members of all of these audiences and to many other people for helpful discussion and comments. I want particularly to thank Arash Abizadeh, Sarah Aikin, Norbert Anwander, Barbara Bleisch, Lene Bomann-Larsen, Joseph Carens, Ronald Dworkin, Jakob Elster, Samuel Freeman, Pablo Gilabert, Kent Greenawalt, Moshe Halbertal, Dale Jamieson, Troy Jollimore, Sandy Kadish, Ethan Leib, Jacob Levy, Kasper Lippert-Rasmussen, Catherine Lu, Liam Murphy, Thomas both expressed in and sustained by its citizens' shared sense of history; by their mutual recognition of national holidays, symbols, myths, and ceremonies; by their allegiance to a common set of values; and by their participation in a range of informal customs and tendencies covering virtually every aspect of life, including modes of dress, habits of thought, styles of music, humor, and entertainment, patterns of work and leisure, attitudes toward sex and sexuality, and tastes in food and drink. Immigration transforms these sources of cultural unity into grounds of contention and conflict. Immigrants arrive with their own histories and traditions, customs and values, habits and ceremonies. The features and practices that define the host nation's distinctive identity—the very features that give its nonimmigrant citizens the sense of belonging to a single people—are experienced by immigrants as unfamiliar at best, and alienating or oppressive at worst. All too often, the symbols of inclusion and commonality are thus transformed into emblems of exclusion and discord. Once this happens, a country has in theory only two choices. It can resort to a kind of cultural apartheid, refusing to grant equal recognition or status to the traditions and practices of the newcomers, and enforcing as best it can the symbols of the old identity. Or it can abandon the old identity and reconceive itself as a multicultural society with a new, pluralistic identity. In practice, of course, there is also a third option, which may be the most popular one of all. This is to avoid honestly confronting the choice between the first two options, and to muddle along trying to have it both ways: paying lip service to the ideas of pluralism and multiculturalism without abandoning the privileged position of the dominant culture, and resorting to serious national soul-searching only when, periodically, the conflict simmering just below the surface of the social fabric erupts into a full-fledged crisis.

Some people conclude from reflections like these that immigration must be severely limited. A country need not apologize, they believe, for its desire to sustain its distinctive national culture and identity, so long as that culture is not intrinsically unjust or oppressive. And since large-scale immigration threatens a country's ability to sustain its national

Nagel, Anne Phillips, Joseph Raz, Cristina Rodríguez, Peter Schaber, Kathryn Scheffler, Rosalind Scheffler, Sharon Street, Sarah Stroud, Dag Einar Thorsen, Jeremy Waldron, Daniel Weinstock, Jay Wallace, Wai-hung Wong, and the Editors of *Philosophy & Public Affairs*.

1. Quoted in *The New York Times*, February 4, 2006, p. A3.

identity, a society may legitimately impose strict limits on the number of immigrants it will accept. Other people argue, by contrast, that limiting immigration is neither feasible nor desirable, and that nations must abandon their old identities, which are often largely fictional constructions in any case, in favor of newer, genuinely multicultural forms of self-understanding.

For myself, I agree that immigration poses many challenges, both practical and theoretical, which host societies can ill afford to ignore. Yet I am uneasy about the tendency, which is by now nearly universal, to frame those challenges, as I have so far been doing, using the discourse of "national identity," "national culture," and "multiculturalism." I have come to think that this discourse encourages a way of thinking about the challenges of immigration that is in some respects oversimplified and in other respects distorted. In this article I want to explain the sources of my uneasiness. I do not think that simply framing the challenges in other terms will make them disappear. But I do believe that, in this case as in others, the unsatisfactory description of a problem may place obstacles in the way of understanding, and make the shape of possible solutions harder to discern.

Let me begin with a story drawn from my own family history. In about 1911, my great-grandfather, Josef Zuckerbrod, fearing for the future of his fourteen-year-old son Yidel (my grandfather), took him to the local train station in the southern Polish territory of Galicia, then under Austrian control, and put him on a train to begin the long journey to Glasgow, where Yidel's married sister lived. Yidel never again saw his father, who died a few years later, and the pain of their separation stayed with him for the rest of his life. He made his way across Europe alone, and joined his sister and brother-in-law in Glasgow. He remained there until early in 1914, when, traveling alone again, he boarded a ship bound for New York, where an older brother had settled.

The ship's manifest, filed upon arrival in New York, includes a statement from the Master that asserts that, to the best of his belief, none of the "aliens" on board "is an idiot, or imbecile, or a feeble-minded person, or insane person, or a pauper, or is likely to become a public charge, or is afflicted with tuberculosis or with a loathsome or dangerous contagious disease, or is a person who has been convicted of, or who admits having committed a felony or other crime or misdemeanor involving moral turpitude, or is a polygamist or one admitting belief in the practice of polygamy, or an anarchist, or under promise or agreement, express or implied, to perform labor in the United States, or a prostitute, or a woman or girl coming to the United States for the purpose of prostitution, or for any other immoral purpose."[2] The manifest also includes a notation of the race and nationality of each "alien," and the accompanying instructions specify that, in completing the manifest, "special attention should be paid to the distinction between race and nationality." The instructions go on to explain this distinction with exemplary clarity. Nationality, they specify, should "be construed to mean the country of which [the] immigrant is a citizen or subject." Race, by contrast, should "be determined by the stock from which the aliens sprang and the language they speak," although it is further explained that "stock" is of primary importance, and that language is relevant only insofar as it may help to determine stock. "The original stock or blood shall be the basis of the classification independent of language. The mother tongue is to be used only to assist in determining the original stock."[3] A putatively exhaustive list of forty-six races is provided.[4]

Having been assigned a race (Hebrew) and a nationality (Austrian), and the ship's Master and Surgeon having certified that he did not appear to be suffering from a contagious disease or to be an idiot, imbecile, criminal, pauper, or anarchist, my grandfather was cleared to enter the United States. Years later, a stray checkmark on the ship's manifest led the anonymous person entering the passengers' names into an immigration database to misread the elaborately scripted "Y" of my grandfather's first name as an "F," and so he is listed in immigration records as having entered the country with the improbably multicultural-sounding name of "Fidel Zuckerbrod." "Yidel," in any case, soon gave way to "Julius," and, with the name "Julius Zuckerbrod," my grandfather settled in New York and lived there for the rest of his long life.

Although my grandfather never received a formal education, he read the newspapers avidly and took a strong interest in world affairs. Yet if someone had asked him whether it was important to him to have his culture recognized by his new country, or whether he thought the

2. "Affidavit of the Master or Commanding Officer, or First or Second Officer," included in the ship manifest of the SS *Nieuw Amsterdam*, dated January 12, 1914. Available electronically at http://www.ellisisland.org.
3. "Instructions for Filling Alien Manifests," ibid.
4. Here are the forty-six "races": "African (black), Armenian, Bohemian, Bosnian, Bulgarian, Chinese, Croatian, Cuban, Dalmatian, Dutch, East Indian, English, Finnish, Flemish, French, German, Greek, Hebrew, Herzogovinian, Irish, Italian (North), Italian (South), Japanese, Korean, Lithuanian, Magyar, Mexican, Montenegrin, Moravian, Pacific Islander, Polish, Portuguese, Roumanian, Russian, Ruthenian (Russniak), Scandinavian (Norwegians, Danes, and Swedes), Scotch, Servian, Slovak, Slovenian, Spanish, Spanish-American, Syrian, Turkish, Welsh, West Indian" (ibid., commas added).

national identity of the United States should be replaced by a new, multicultural identity in order to accommodate him and other immigrants, I doubt that he would have known what to say. And I doubt this not merely because the terminology would have been unfamiliar to him, and not merely because he was a quiet man who was not in the habit of talking about himself. Even if the terminology had been familiar and he had been prepared to engage in the kind of reflection required to answer the question, I think he would have found the formulation of the question puzzling.

What, to begin with, might he have seen as "his culture"? Not Polish culture, surely. My grandfather was not a Polish citizen—Poland was not a state at the time—nor was he of Polish "stock"; as the ship's manifest says, Poles and "Hebrews" were taken to belong to different "races." Was there such a thing as "Galician culture"? If so, then I am sure that my grandfather would not have been tempted to claim it as his own. Might he have thought that "his culture" was the culture of the Habsburg Empire? The suggestion is comical. Perhaps, then, the most plausible suggestion is that his culture was "Hebrew culture." But what is Hebrew culture? Judaism is a religion, which my grandfather took seriously, and which, like most religions, admits of many versions and variants. In addition, Jews, both religious and nonreligious, have sustained a sense of themselves as a distinct people over many centuries, and of course their enemies have always been happy to reinforce that sense if it was ever in danger of waning. Yet if there is a monolithic Jewish "culture," I have no idea what it is. Jews live in many different countries and participate in many different ways of life. The Jewish world, if it makes sense to talk in those terms, is notoriously variegated and even fractious. Jews are divided along lines of class, region, politics, language, ideology, skin color, sexual orientation, and religious practice and interpretation. They display wildly divergent attitudes toward Judaism as a religion, toward each other, and toward their own Jewishness. Whatever it is that Jews may be said to have in common, I am sure that it does not add up to a complete "culture."

So what, to repeat, might my grandfather have seen as "his culture"? It may be suggested that, even if there is no common culture that all Jews share, perhaps the Jews of his time and place—Eastern Europe in the late nineteenth and early twentieth centuries, say—did share a culture. However, although it may seem natural today to speak of "Eastern European Jewish culture," this way of speaking seems to me to owe a great deal to a combination of simple ignorance and gauzy post-Holocaust sentimentality. Even a glancing familiarity with the history of the Jews of Eastern Europe makes it evident that there were profound differences, of many different kinds, among and within the Jewish communities in that part of the world. This is true even of the Jews of Galicia. Yet it is also true that Galician Jews ("Galitzianers") were often regarded by other Eastern European Jews as forming a recognizable group or type. So perhaps, despite my reservations, this is as close to an answer as we can come; perhaps my grandfather's culture was the culture of Galician Jews.

If that was his culture, however, then two facts seem striking. The first is that he, like so many other Galician Jews, took great risks and endured painful separations in order to uproot himself from Galicia and to begin a new life elsewhere. Furthermore, and this is the second point, there is no indication that something called "Galician Jewish culture" was a salient category for him, still less that it was something that he wanted recognized and preserved in the United States. To be sure, my grandfather wanted to live freely and without fear of persecution, and he wanted to be able to practice his religion as he saw fit. And he certainly wanted to maintain family relations, and to reestablish family networks that were disrupted by mass migration. Furthermore, many of his personal tastes, habits, and customs carried over from Galicia to New York; the formative influence of his upbringing in the old country did not simply disappear upon arrival in the new world. Immigration is not amnesia; and it does not wipe the slate clean. Yet immigration does involve change—*that's the point*—and my grandfather, who as a teenager traveled halfway around the world by himself to begin a new life, knew that as well as anyone. The life he made for himself was a life in New York, not in Galicia, and that, I assume, was how he wanted it. And if some of the customs and practices of his Galician past persisted, many others gave way to the new customs and practices that he inevitably acquired in his new surroundings. If, upon meeting him later in his life, you had been asked to say what his culture was, you would have been unlikely to say that it was "Galician Jewish culture." You might have been tempted to say that it was "New York Jewish culture," although that phrase conjures up a stereotype that in many ways he did not fit, and, once again, there is no evidence that it picks out a category that he operated with or cared about. More to the point, this culture could hardly have been one that he brought with him *to* New York from Glasgow and Galicia, or whose preservation might have been of concern to him upon his arrival in the United States. If it was his culture at all, it was a culture he acquired as the result of immigration. Indeed, if there is such a thing as "New York Jewish culture," then it is a culture that was created by immigration; if the Jewish immigrants who settled in New York had simply brought a fixed and determinate culture with them, and if the United States had somehow contrived to preserve that culture unaltered, then "New York Jewish culture" would never have existed.

In expressing doubts about what my grandfather might have taken "his culture" to be, I do not mean to suggest that he was a "cosmopolitan" or that he lacked particular loyalties and allegiances. Nothing could be farther from the truth. After the upheavals of his youth, he seldom traveled outside of New York. A man of great warmth and humor, he led a stable life that was firmly embedded in a web of family and communal relations and in which Jewish religious practice and observance continued to play an important role. There is no doubt that his identification of himself as a Jew and his sense of solidarity with the Jewish people were fundamental to his self-understanding. My point is not that he was so sophisticated and worldly that he transcended his culture; it is rather that, despite his strong family, religious, and communal allegiances, it is not clear that he ever had, still less that he brought with him from Galicia, a single fixed and determinate "culture."

My grandfather's story is not extraordinary, except in the sense in which every immigrant's story is extraordinary. But neither does it instantiate a pattern to which all immigrant narratives conform, for there is no such pattern. My grandfather's story contains some elements that are unique to him and his experience, other elements that are typical of the particular cohort of immigrants to which he belonged, and still others, such as the elements of separation and dislocation, that are, if not universal, then much more nearly so. Despite these more nearly universal elements, however, it would be rash to make generalizations about immigration based solely on my grandfather's experiences. Yet I do find that his story suggests certain broad lessons, primarily of a cautionary character, and that it helps to reveal some of the limitations of some recently popular ways of thinking about immigration.

The first lesson has to do with the difficulty, and the danger, of trying to identify for each immigrant a single culture to which that individual belongs. Many others have warned eloquently against the twin tendencies to reify cultures and to assign each individual to a single culture.[5] Sometimes these warnings emphasize the emergence of new, distinctively cosmopolitan ways of living and hybrid forms of identity, which are contrasted with more traditional ways of life, and which are said to imply

5. See, for example, Kwame Anthony Appiah, *The Ethics of Identity* (Princeton, N.J.: Princeton University Press, 2005) and *Cosmopolitanism* (New York: W. W. Norton & Company, 2006); David Hollinger, *Postethnic America* (New York: Basic Books, 1995) and *Cosmopolitanism and Solidarity* (Madison, Wisc.: The University of Wisconsin Press, 2006); Jeremy Waldron, "Minority Cultures and the Cosmopolitan Alternative," *University of Michigan Journal of Law Reform* 25 (1992): 751–793.

that some individuals cannot be assigned to any single, relatively homo-geneous culture. I take my grandfather's story to suggest a different and more far-reaching point, though also one for which I claim no original-ity, which is that even for people whose lives may seem, superficially, to be assimilable within some fixed cultural framework, the appearance of cultural fixity and determinacy is often illusory or at least misleading.

This point does not apply only to immigrants, and it does not depend on a person's having undergone the changes that immigration by defi-nition involves, although the fact that immigrants must undergo such changes suggests that the point holds even more strongly for them. The basic point has wider application, however. Most individuals in mod-ern societies belong to groups of many different kinds; they participate in practices, customs, and traditions of very different provenance; and they have tastes, interests, and affinities in common with different sets of people.[6] Which of these multiple affiliations is salient, even for the indi-vidual himself, can vary depending on the context. Consider a simple example. From a European standpoint, it may seem natural to speak of "American culture," and for an American who is traveling in Europe, his status *as* an American may seem especially salient. Yet in other contexts the same person may feel—or be told—that he is part of "Western cul-ture," where the West is taken to comprehend *both* Europe *and* North America. And, on the other hand, when this same American is in the United States, famously in the throes of its "culture wars," his status as a resident of one of the "blue states"—as a Californian, for example—may at times (on election night, say, or when he is visiting Texas or Alabama) seem more salient than his identity either as an American or as someone who belongs to Western culture. But it does not stop there. A Northern Californian and a Southern Californian may feel that they share a strong cultural bond if they meet in Appalachia or Addis Ababa, but Northern Californians who visit Southern California often profess to find it cultur-ally alienating, and vice versa. Moreover, neither of these regions is itself culturally monolithic; indeed, there are significant cultural differences even between the neighboring Northern California university towns of Berkeley and Palo Alto, as residents of either will attest. And I have so far said nothing of those many identifications and allegiances that cut across and transcend regional and political boundaries: identifications and allegiances based, for example, on class, religion, occupation, race, gender, or sexual orientation. Yet it is obvious that there are contexts in which one's identity as a Catholic, a physicist, a trade unionist, a black

6. This is a prominent theme in the seminal essay by Waldron cited in note 5.

man, a soldier, or a lesbian may loom larger than any identification based on region or citizenship. And then there are identifications or cultural affinities based on shared interests in music, painting, literature, or other forms of artistic activity or appreciation; or on a shared commitment to a cause like environmentalism, vegetarianism, or pacifism; or on a shared passion for railroads or slow food or a particular football team; or for mountain climbing, surfing, collecting antiques, or playing bridge.

All of these identifications and passions and affiliations, and countless others, are aspects of human culture, and to live a human life is to trace a particular path through the space of possibilities they define. Admittedly, some people explore that space more intrepidly than others, and few people regard all of their identifications and affiliations as equally significant. For some people, there is a single affiliation that is central to their sense of themselves, while for others there may be a small number of such affiliations. Yet to insist that, for each individual, there must be some one identification that corresponds to his or her *real* culture is to misunderstand both identity and culture. Identity is a protean notion. Most people have multiple identifications and, even though some of those identifications are likely to be more central to their sense of themselves than others, people's perceptions of the relative importance or salience of their various identifications are almost always context-dependent to one degree or another. People's identifications are also subject to change over time, and even strong identifications sometimes change or fade away. Moreover, the idea that each person's most fundamental identification or identifications must have their source in some fixed and determinate culture is simply untrue. So although there may be room for legitimate variation in the extent to which different societies attempt to police the space of cultural possibilities, the idea of having the state assign each individual to a single culture chosen from a fixed menu of options based on geography, religion, skin color, or language, should—like the list of forty-six races—strike us as comically (if not tragically) misguided. It is misguided not least because of its self-fulfilling character; there is no surer way to make a particular form of group affiliation a dominant feature of individual identity than for the state to make it the ascriptive basis for the assignment of legal status.[7]

In saying this, I do not mean to imply that states should always be insensitive to racial or religious or ethnic differences. On the contrary,

---

7. This and related points are emphasized by Chandran Kukathas, "Are There Any Cultural Rights?" *Political Theory* 20 (1992): 105–139. See also Donald Horowitz, *Ethnic Groups in Conflict* (Berkeley: University of California Press, 1985); the writings by David Hollinger cited in note 5; and Appiah, *The Ethics of Identity*, pp. 134–135.

there are contexts in which it is essential that they be sensitive to such differences. However, this sensitivity should be rooted in, and should encourage, an appreciation of the enormous variety of human experience. It should not be based on the false and pernicious idea that for each individual there is ultimately only one identification that really counts. Nor should it be allowed to degenerate into something that is the antithesis of a respect for human diversity, namely, the oppressive attempt to confine each individual, politically and legally, within some rigidly defined region of social space. In short, the presumption that each individual ultimately "has" a single, well-defined culture is false, and if we decide fundamental political questions based on that presumption, we are bound to go seriously astray.

The second lesson has to do not with the relation between individuals and cultures but with the nature of immigration. The reasons why people leave one country for another vary, as do the reasons why host countries accept new immigrants. As I have already said, however, immigration always involves change: *that's the point of it*. It changes the immigrants and it changes the host country. To the extent that there are costs and benefits associated with these changes, there are important questions about how they should be distributed. One thing is clear, however. It cannot be the aim of a reasonable immigration policy to insulate either the host country or the new immigrants against cultural change. To think that we must choose between preserving the national culture of the host country and preserving the imported culture of the immigrants is to accept a false dilemma. The truth is that we cannot preserve either of them. Or, at any rate, we cannot preserve either of them in unaltered form. This is so even if we waive, for the moment, the doubts I have been expressing about whether it is appropriate to think of each individual as having a single, determinate culture. Even if, for the sake of argument, we suspend our challenge to that assumption, the fact remains that neither the immigrants' culture nor the national culture can be preserved unaltered. *Of course* the immigrants' culture— their practices, customs, ways of living—will change. It will change because their new society presents them with a new predicament. They must come to terms with new rules, new options, new neighbors, new institutions, new history, new ideas, new customs, new values, new modes of dress, new climate, new cuisine, new tastes, new expectations, new language. How could their ways of living possibly be unaffected by these changes in their social and geographical surroundings? Even if they adopt as radically isolationist or separatist a stance as they can muster and as the new society will allow, their way of life will now be shaped by the need to insulate themselves against *these* options, neighbors, ideas, customs, modes of dress, expectations, values..., and that means that "their" culture will change. It will change because changing is what cultures do when they confront new situations, and immigration, by definition, presents immigrants with a new situation.

Equally, however, the "national culture" will change. It will change because the introduction into society of a new set of people presents the old residents—the putative bearers of the national culture—with a new predicament. They must come to terms with the presence in their midst of new neighbors, new customs, new ideas, new values, new modes of dress, new expectations, new languages, new cuisine, new tastes. Even if they adopt as radically exclusionary a stance as they can muster, their way of life will now be shaped by the need to exclude *these* neighbors, ideas, customs, modes of dress, expectations, values..., and this means that the national culture will change. It will change because changing is what cultures do when they confront new situations, and immigration, by definition, presents the host society with a new situation.

For cultural preservationists—for those concerned to preserve either the preexisting culture of the immigrants or the national culture of the host country—these reflections may seem to support a rejectionist attitude toward immigration. If, as I have been arguing, immigration inevitably brings cultural change, then, it may seem, the lesson for the first kind of preservationist is that prospective immigrants should stay put, and the lesson for the second kind is that prospective host countries should refuse to accept those who do not. Wholesale rejectionism is not a tenable attitude, however. It is not tenable because it fails to engage with the compelling reasons that immigrants usually have for migrating, or with the compelling reasons that host countries usually have for accepting them. More fundamentally, it is not tenable because it rests on a misunderstanding of the nature and prospects of cultural preservation. Suppose that our country were today to seal its borders and reduce to zero the number of immigrants that it accepted. The fact remains that, within a relatively short period of time—let us be very optimistic and say 150 years—every single one of the country's current residents will be dead. If the country survives, it will be populated entirely by people who are as yet unborn—immigrants from the future, if you like. Do we really suppose, or could we really wish, that, despite undergoing a complete population replacement, our country's national culture might remain *exactly the same* in 150 years as it is today? To think that this is either possible or desirable is to imagine nothing at all happening in or to the country in the intervening period: no new ideas, no new challenges, no new discoveries or inventions, no advances in science or medicine or technology, no new works of literature or art or music, no new heroes or villains, no changes in fashion or style or entertainment, no new achievements, no new successes, no new failures. It is, in short, to imagine that our successors might not actually lead human lives, that history might simply be frozen, that our country might go on functioning with a past but no future. If cultural preservation is to be a reasonable or even a coherent goal, it cannot possibly mean this.[8] Cultures survive only by changing: by accumulating and interpreting and producing new ideas and experiences. There is no other way. So to the extent that the impulse behind blanket rejectionism is to preserve a culture by preventing it from changing, it is fundamentally misguided.[9]

To this point I have warned against an oversimplified understanding of the relation between individuals and culture, and I have argued that immigration inevitably changes both the culture of the immigrants and the culture of the host country. This suggests, on the one hand, that there

8. Compare the following passage from Alice McDermott's novel *After This* (New York: Farrar, Straus, and Giroux, 2006): "The piano player was just coming up the steps as Monsignor McShane opened the front doors. He was a young guy, small and dark-haired. A young man's beard under the fair skin. He wore a suit and carried a briefcase and introduced himself with a Scots Irish name that Monsignor didn't bother to retain. The two walked up the aisle together. 'This is some church,' the kid said, craning his neck to take in the Danish modern stained glass, the circus-tent ceiling. He then mentioned that he occasionally played at another Catholic church, an old-fashioned one, St. Paul's, near his school. 'I went to St. Paul's,' Monsignor said, 'as a boy.' And knew immediately, as if he had never understood it before, what his parishioners were lonesome for, in this monstrosity of his. It was not the future they'd been objecting to, but the loss of the past. As if it was his fault that you could not have one without the other" (p. 277).

9. These remarks leave open the question of whether and for what reasons immigration may ever legitimately be restricted. There is, of course, a large literature on these questions. Two valuable anthologies are W. Schwartz (ed.), *Justice in Immigration* (Cambridge University Press, 1995) and B. Barry and R. Goodin (eds.), *Free Movement* (University Park: The Pennsylvania State University Press, 1992). One of the most influential arguments for the legitimacy of immigration restrictions is developed by Michael Walzer in *Spheres of Justice* (New York: Basic Books, 1983), chap. 2. Joseph Carens presents an influential argument for open borders in "Aliens and Citizens: The Case for Open Borders," *Review of Politics* 49 (1987): 251–273. Many writers defend intermediate positions. See, for example, Veit Bader, "Fairly Open Borders," in *Citizenship and Exclusion*, Veit Bader (ed.) (New York: St. Martin's Press, 1997), pp. 28–60. Carens maintains that Rawls's theory of justice provides support for open borders, but Rawls himself cites Walzer's position with approval and expresses support for "a qualified right to limit immigration" (in *The Law of Peoples* [Cambridge, Mass.: Harvard University Press, 1999], p. 39 note.). On the other hand, Rawls suggests that immigration would cease to be a problem in the "Society of liberal and decent Peoples" (ibid. pp. 8–9), whereas Walzer insists that "immigration will remain an issue even after the claims of distributive justice have been met on a global scale" (*Spheres of Justice*, p. 48).

is no general right of immigrants to resist changes demanded by the host society whenever those changes would conflict with norms or practices of the immigrants' culture. But it also suggests, on the other hand, that there is no general right of the host society to impose constraints on new immigrants whenever this is thought necessary to protect the national culture from change. These points serve to undermine strong preservationist claims, whether on behalf of immigrant culture or on behalf of national culture. They are worth making, obvious though they may seem, because strong preservationism is influential, and because debates about immigration are often distorted by unrealistic ideas about the extent to which it is either possible or desirable to resist cultural change. However, these points take us only so far. They do not tell us, for example, whether there are any demands for cultural change that new immigrants *are* entitled to resist, or any that the host society *is* entitled to press.

The general tenor of my remarks may seem to support negative answers to these questions. The spirit of those remarks suggests a general position that might be described as *Heraclitean pluralism*. Heraclitean pluralism asserts that culture and cultures are always in flux, and that individuals normally relate to culture through the acknowledgment of multiple affiliations and allegiances, and through participation in diverse practices, customs, and activities, rather than through association with some one fixed and determinate culture. It further asserts that, in light of these facts, states should be maximally accommodating of the cultural variety that free individuals will inevitably exhibit, without seeking to constrain that freedom in the vain and misguided attempt to preserve some particular culture or cultures in the form that they happen to take at a given historical moment.

Yet it is important to see that there is room within Heraclitean pluralism for a certain kind of conservative or traditionalist project. Most human beings have strong conservative impulses, in the sense that they have strong desires to preserve what they value, including what they value about past and present practices, forms of social organization, and ways of life. As we have already seen in the case of strong preservationism, these impulses sometimes issue in support for foolish or even dangerous policies based on false or incoherent ideas about the possibility of inhibiting cultural change. However, the problem with these policies lies not in the conservative impulse itself, but rather in the assessment of how best to act on it.[10] In fact, it is difficult to understand how human beings could

10. I am indebted here to G. A. Cohen's unpublished paper "Rescuing Conservatism: a Defence of Existing Value," in R. Jay Wallace, Rahul Kumar, and Samuel Freeman (eds.), *Reasons and Recognition: Essays on the Philosophy of T. M. Scanlon* (Oxford University Press).

have values at all if they did not have conservative impulses. What would it mean to value things but, in general, to see no reason of any kind to sustain them or retain them or preserve them or extend them into the future? Joseph Raz has argued that "there is a general reason to preserve what is of value."[11] By this he means that each person has reason to preserve anything at all that is of value, whether or not the person himself values that thing (or, in Raz's terms, is "engaged with" it). When it comes to the things that the person himself does value, however, a conclusion even stronger than Raz's seems warranted, for the idea that I might see no reason at all to preserve or sustain any of the things that I myself value seems not merely mistaken but incoherent. What then would it mean to say that I valued them? Even people who claim that they live only for the moment—that they value only momentary experiences—presumably value, and wish to sustain, a life that is rich in the right kind of momentary experiences. And even radicals who wish to overturn the established order seek to entrench the values that animate their revolutionary ambitions. If there is a conceptual gap between valuing and the impulse to conserve, it is not a very large one.[12]

For this reason, it would be fatal to Heraclitean pluralism if it could not in any way accommodate the conservative impulse, particularly the impulse to conserve valued traditions, customs, practices, and modes of living. However, the failure of strong preservationism helps point the way toward an alternative strategy of accommodation that is compatible with Heraclitean pluralism. Strong preservationism fails as a strategy for accommodating the conservative impulse because it fails to recognize that change is essential to culture and to cultural survival, so that to prevent a culture from changing, if such a thing were possible, would not be to preserve the culture but rather to destroy it. In other words,

---

11. Joseph Raz, *Value, Respect, and Attachment* (Cambridge: Cambridge University Press, 2001), p. 162.

12. In "Relationships and Responsibilities" (*Philosophy & Public Affairs* 26 [1997]: 189–209, reprinted in *Boundaries and Allegiances* [Oxford: Oxford University Press, 2001], pp. 97–110), I argued that if one values one's relationship with another person noninstrumentally, then one will see oneself as having reason to devote special attention to that person's needs and interests. In "Projects, Relationships, and Reasons" (in *Reason and Value: Themes from the Moral Philosophy of Joseph Raz*, R. J. Wallace, P. Pettit, S. Scheffler, and M. Smith (eds.) [Oxford: Clarendon Press, 2004], pp. 247–269), I argued that, similarly, if one values a personal project noninstrumentally, then one will see oneself as having reason to devote special attention to the flourishing of that project. These claims might be seen as instances of a more general thesis about the relation between valuing something and seeing reasons to sustain or preserve it.

strong preservationism is self-defeating.[13] But this suggests that, para-doxical though it may sound, the right way to preserve a culture is to allow it to change. Of course, not every change in a culture will preserve it, and merely allowing a culture to change does not guarantee that the culture will survive: nothing can guarantee that. Still, what it takes for a culture to survive is for an ever-changing but sufficiently large and continuous group of people to use enough of the culture's central ideas, practices, values, ideals, beliefs, customs, texts, artifacts, rites, and cer-emonies to structure sufficiently large portions of their lives and experi-ences. Obviously, this is not a precise formula; the multiple judgments of sufficiency that it calls for are all subject to interpretation, and in border-line cases there may be disagreement about whether a particular culture has survived or not. What is important for our purposes, however, is to understand what is meant in speaking of the use of cultural materials to "structure" people's lives. What this structuring involves is not the algo-rithmic application of the culture's values and ideals to new situations, nor the uncritical and unrevisable adherence to its ideas and beliefs, nor the exact reproduction of its ceremonies and practices and customs in precisely their original form. What it involves is the use of judgment and intelligence in determining which elements of a cultural heritage require modification and which should be carried forward unchanged; in inter-preting the relevance of older values and ideals for novel problems and predicaments; in deciding how the culture's traditional ways of thinking can best be extended so as to assimilate the never-ending accumulation of new historical experience; and in deciding which influences from other cultures are to be welcomed and which are to be resisted.[14]

In short, the survival of a culture is an ongoing collective achievement that requires the exercise of judgment, creativity, intelligence, and interpre-tive skill. It also requires a healthy dose of good luck, for whether a culture will survive depends on whether its resources, effectively developed, are well suited to dealing with the contingent and ever-changing historical circum-stances that the culture actually confronts. But one thing is certain. Any

---

13. Compare Jeremy Waldron: "Cultures live and grow, change and sometimes wither away; they amalgamate with other cultures, or they adapt themselves to geographical or demographic necessity.... To preserve or protect [a culture], or some favored ver-sion of it, artificially, in the face of...change, is precisely to cripple the mechanisms of adaptation and compromise (from warfare to commerce to amalgamation) with which all societies confront the outside world" ("Minority Cultures and the Cosmo-politan Alternative," pp. 787–788).

14. Here I draw on my discussion in "Conceptions of Cosmopolitanism," reprinted in *Boundaries and Allegiances*, pp. 111–130.

culture that survives will have changed over time; it will have assimilated new experiences, absorbed new influences, reaffirmed some prior practices and ideas, modified others, and dispensed altogether with still others. Survival is successful change. A reasonable cultural preservationism strives to achieve such change rather than seeking to preserve the past unaltered.

This explains why I said that there is room within Heraclitean pluralism for a certain kind of conservative or traditionalist project. Although it is opposed to any strong preservationist attempt to preserve a particular culture in the form that it happens to take at a given historical moment, Heraclitean pluralism has no quarrel with the desire to preserve a culture per se. On the contrary, inasmuch as it seeks to accommodate cultural variety and change, it is hospitable in principle to the kind of change in which cultural preservation, properly understood, consists. Moreover, if the points about value made earlier are correct, then almost everyone is a conservative with respect to some values, and the difference between reasonable cultural preservationism and other cultural orientations is more a matter of degree than one of kind. Heraclitean pluralism asserts that the best way of accommodating the conservative impulse in general is also the best way of accommodating reasonable preservationist projects: namely, by giving individuals the freedom to structure their lives with reference to a diverse array of values, practices, and ideas.

This is, it must be said, a deeply counterintuitive position. How can it possibly be true that the conservative impulse is best accommodated by allowing people to change? And how can it possibly be true that the aim of cultural preservation is best accommodated within a pluralistic framework? To these questions Heraclitean pluralism responds as follows. The world is constantly changing, and so the successful conservation of valued practices, ideals, and ways of life necessarily involves their extension, modification, and reinterpretation in changing circumstances. It is a creative and dynamic process. To prevent people from changing in response to changing conditions would inhibit rather than facilitate cultural conservation, because it would prevent the creative reinterpretation and reinvention of inherited cultural materials that is essential to a culture's long-term survival. Cultural preservation is possible only if people have the freedom to engage in this interpretive process and to act on its conclusions. And since free people will inevitably be drawn to diverse ways of living and schemes of value, a genuinely free society must have a pluralistic framework. That is why, the Heraclitean maintains, the aim of cultural preservation is best accommodated within such a framework.[15]

---

15. In claiming not merely that the aim of cultural preservation can be accommodated within a pluralistic framework, but that this is the best way of accommodating it, the

What is the bearing of Heraclitean pluralism on questions of immigration? As I have said, immigration on any significant scale inevitably alters the cultural landscape both for the immigrants themselves and for the host society. There is no possibility of preserving unaltered either the imported culture of the immigrants or the national culture of the host society, and neither the immigrants nor the host society has any general right to such preservation. As I noted earlier, however, these observations take us only so far. They leave open the question of whether there is *anything* that immigrants may demand of the host society, or that it may demand of them, in the name of cultural preservation.

Heraclitean pluralism, as I am understanding it, delivers a negative answer to this question. What immigrants may demand of the host society, it asserts, is justice, where justice is understood not to include any special cultural rights, entitlements, or privileges. Justice does include the basic rights and liberties—including freedom of thought, expression, association, and conscience—that are familiar from egalitarian liberal theories like that of John Rawls. It also includes, let us suppose, fair equality of opportunity and some conception of the just distribution of economic resources. More abstractly, the principles of justice set out fair terms of cooperation among free and equal citizens.[16] So in addition to demanding all the rights, liberties, opportunities, and economic resources that are made available to other citizens, immigrants may legitimately demand to be treated as free and equal persons who are full-fledged participants in the scheme of social cooperation, and are entitled to be respected as such.

Heraclitean is not maintaining that cultural preservation is possible *only* within such a framework. That would be implausible, for a society might allow people enough interpretive freedom to enable them to sustain their culture without establishing a thoroughly pluralistic social framework. Nor is the Heraclitean claiming that the odds of any given culture's survival are always maximized within a pluralistic framework. It is possible that providing additional freedom beyond what is strictly necessary for cultural preservation may in some cases make such preservation more difficult. Instead, in saying that the aim of cultural preservation is best accommodated within a pluralistic framework, and not merely that it can be so accommodated, the Heraclitean is making an independent normative judgment about the importance of a wider freedom. I am grateful to Samuel Freeman and Kasper Lippert-Rasmussen for raising the question to which this note is a response.

16. Throughout this article I simply assume—I will not try to defend the assumption here—that all immigrants who enter a country lawfully and who continue to abide by its laws must be given the opportunity to become citizens after a reasonable period of time. I set to one side the question of whether the same applies to those who enter a country unlawfully. Nor shall I consider the legitimacy of "guest worker" programs.

The fulfillment of these demands, Heraclitean pluralism asserts, gives ample scope for immigrants (and others) to pursue reasonable preservationist projects. Within the framework of laws that themselves conform to the principles of justice, immigrants and others may take full advantage of their rights, liberties, opportunities, and economic resources to develop and extend inherited practices, customs, ideals, and traditions. What they cannot do is demand additional rights or resources, beyond those they are owed as a matter of justice, in the name of cultural preservation specifically. There is no guarantee, of course, that their preservationist efforts will be successful, but, as I have indicated, there is nothing in any case that the host society could do to guarantee that.

By the same token, however, there is nothing that the host society may legitimately demand of immigrants in the name of preserving the national culture. What it may legitimately demand of them is that they live peacefully in society and uphold the duties and obligations of citizens. These include the familiar duties to obey just laws, pay taxes, and the like. More abstractly, they include the obligations of citizens to do their fair share to uphold the scheme of social cooperation, but they do not include any obligation to preserve or uphold or participate in the historical culture of the nation per se. Individual citizens may, of course, pursue reasonable preservationist projects with respect to the national culture, just as they may with respect to any other culture, but they cannot use the coercive power of the state to require others to support those efforts, and laws that have this aim or effect are, therefore, unjust.

Understood in this way, Heraclitean pluralism is evenhanded in its refusal to endorse special state protections aimed at preserving a particular culture or cultures. Neither the national culture nor any immigrant culture should receive such protection. Within a liberal framework, individuals are free to structure their lives in accordance with inherited traditions of practice and conviction as they see fit, provided that they fulfill their duties as citizens and do not violate the rights of others. So, on the one hand, immigration inevitably changes both the culture of the immigrants and the culture of the host country, and neither of them can or should be immunized against change. Yet, on the other hand, change is compatible with cultural survival and renewal, and in a just society immigrants and nonimmigrants alike will have the freedom and the opportunity to engage in the dynamic and interpretative process of extending their inherited cultures in the altered circumstances to which immigration gives rise.

As will be apparent, I have a great deal of sympathy for Heraclitean pluralism, and I think that there is much to be said for the stance that I have just described, especially with respect to claims made on behalf of immigrant cultures. In general, the considerations I have been rehearsing about the relations between individuals and cultures and about the relations between conservatism and change serve to undermine strong preservationism and are congenial to the spirit of the Heraclitean position. In addition, I think that the demand for justice, which is central to that position, has great force when deployed on behalf of immigrants, and that it provides more support for reasonable preservationist efforts by the members of immigrant communities than is often recognized. Some people interpret the legitimate grievances of immigrant communities in existing liberal democracies as evidence that the familiar liberal conceptions of justice are inadequate and should be modified to incorporate a regime of cultural rights. The alternative conclusion that seems to me more plausible in many of these cases is that the societies in question have failed to meet the requirements of liberal justice, and that the remedy for the grievances of immigrants is not to modify those requirements but rather to ensure that they are satisfied.

Nevertheless, I do not think that Heraclitean pluralism as it stands provides a fully satisfactory way of thinking about issues of immigration and culture. Its limitations are most apparent in its attitude toward national culture. As we have seen, the Heraclitean position is that the power of the state may not be used to coerce citizens into supporting reasonable efforts to preserve the national culture. The problem with this is that the state cannot avoid coercing citizens into preserving a national culture of some kind. To begin with, the institutions of state and their laws and policies themselves define a political and civic culture, or what Rawls called a "public political culture,"[17] and that culture in turn shapes and constrains the conduct of daily life in countless ways. In effect, then, the political and civic culture serves partly to constitute and partly to shape a broader national culture, and in demanding obedience to its laws and support for its institutions the state is, in effect, requiring citizens to contribute to the preservation of that culture. For this reason, the national culture has a different status than other cultural traditions that may be represented within the society. It cannot be treated by the state as just one culture among others, nor can the state be expected to refrain from deploying its coercive power in support of a national culture. To suppose otherwise is to fall prey to a conceptual confusion, and to the extent that Heraclitean pluralism neglects this point it is unsatisfactory.

Nor is it reasonable to insist that the content of the public political culture should be determined solely by universal moral or constitutional

17. John Rawls, *Political Liberalism* (New York: Columbia University Press, 1993).

principles that treat all citizens as equals, and that it should not contain any distinguishing ethnic or linguistic or particularistic elements. A country is a contingent historical formation. The history of any country is also the history of particular people—of its original population and their successors over time—with their contingent array of practices, affiliations, customs, values, ideals, and allegiances. Inevitably, elements of that array will help to shape the character of those basic social, political, and legal institutions that serve to enforce the political and civic culture. They are likely to influence everything from the choice of official languages, national holidays, and public monuments and ceremonies to the regulation of work, education, and family arrangements. In enforcing the political culture, then, and so in shaping the broader national culture, the state will inevitably be enforcing a set of practices and values that have their origins in the contingent history and traditions of a particular set of people.[18] This is not in itself inappropriate, and there is in any case no alternative. The state can neither avoid promoting a national culture nor invent that culture *ab initio*. It is worth noting that there is an important difference in this regard between religion and culture. A state need not recognize an official religion, but it cannot avoid promoting a national culture. Where culture is concerned, neutrality is not an option.[19]

This suggests the need to modify the Heraclitean position to recognize the special place of the "public political culture," to acknowledge the contingent historical circumstances that will inevitably have influenced both its form and its content, and to allow for its role in shaping a broader national culture. Although immigrants may find the public political culture alien and although its historical roots may be remote from their

---

18. Thus, although my ultimate conclusions differ significantly from his, I am generally in agreement with Will Kymlicka when he writes: "Some people suggest that a truly liberal conception of national membership should be based solely on accepting political principles of democracy and rights, rather than integration into a particular culture. This non-cultural conception of national membership is often said to be what distinguishes the 'civic' or 'constitutional' nationalism of the United States from illiberal 'ethnic' nationalism. But... this is mistaken. Immigrants to the United States must not only pledge allegiance to democratic principles, they must also learn the language and history of their new society. What distinguishes 'civic' nations from 'ethnic' nations is not the absence of any cultural component to national identity, but rather the fact that anyone can integrate into the common culture, regardless of race or colour" (*Multicultural Citizenship* [Oxford: Clarendon Press, 1995], pp. 23–24).

19. Compare Kymlicka: "It is quite possible for a state not to have an established church. But the state cannot help but give at least partial establishment to a culture when it decides which language is to be used in public schooling, or in the provision of state services" (*Multicultural Citizenship*, p. 111).

own, the coercive pressure that the culture exerts is not by itself unjust. It is not by itself unjust that immigrants should be expected to obey the laws and support the institutions of their new society, even when the character and the content of those laws and institutions has been shaped in part by historical circumstances and traditions with which the immigrants have no antecedent identification.

But if this suggests a modification of the Heraclitean position that works, so to speak, in favor of the host society, there are also considerations that pull the other way. First, and most obviously, although it is not *by itself* unjust that immigrants should be expected to obey the laws and institutions of their new society, it *is* unjust to expect them to obey gravely unjust laws or support severely unjust institutions, especially if the burdens imposed by those unjust laws and institutions fall primarily on the immigrants themselves.[20] Nor is it enough that the laws should be just; they must also be applied fairly and impartially to immigrants and nonimmigrants alike. Like any other citizens, immigrants are entitled to the equal protection of the laws, and they cannot be expected to acquiesce in the denial of equal protection or in unjust treatment more generally.

Second, the principles of justice may themselves require, by virtue of their guarantees of liberty of conscience and association, that certain limited exemptions from otherwise just laws should be provided to people for whom compliance would conflict with deeply held conscientious convictions, whether religious or nonreligious in character. Justice may also require other forms of legal accommodation for conscientious convictions in some circumstances. To the extent that this is so, the conscientious convictions of immigrants must be considered on the same footing as those of nonimmigrants and must be judged by the same criteria; they too must be eligible for whatever exemptions or other forms of legal accommodation justice requires.[21]

---

20. This point is not specific to immigrants, of course. If severely unjust laws or institutions impose special burdens on any group of people, the duty of those people to comply is called into question.

21. In the United States, the discussion of legal accommodation is controlled by the religion clauses—the establishment and free-exercise clauses—of the First Amendment of the U.S. Constitution. However, I am assuming that, as a matter of justice, the legal accommodation of conscientious conviction should not be restricted to religious convictions. In *Religious Freedom and the Constitution* (Cambridge, Mass.: Harvard University Press, 2007), Christopher Eisgruber and Lawrence Sager argue that the religion clauses should be interpreted as equality or antidiscrimination norms, which single out religion for special mention, and which may support exemptions from otherwise valid laws or regulations in a limited range of cases, not because religion is uniquely privileged but rather because it is specially vulnerable to hostility and

Third, it is not quite true that what the society owes its immigrants is justice and nothing more. In expecting them to accept a civic and political culture that includes many contingent elements that are not requirements of justice, the society is in effect demanding that immigrants accommodate themselves to the commitments, traditions, and values of the preexisting population. If a society is conceived of as a fair system of cooperation among free and equal people with diverse aims and values, then the willingness of people to accommodate one another will be indispensable to its successful functioning. But accommodation is not a one-way street. If, as I have been arguing, it is not in general unreasonable to expect immigrants to accommodate themselves to aspects of the national culture that are not themselves required by justice, neither is it unreasonable to expect the wider society to make some effort to accommodate the traditions, practices, and values of immigrants, even when a failure to do so would not violate any principle of justice. Here I am thinking not of formal legal exemptions like those that may sometimes be required to accommodate religious or conscientious conviction, but rather of informal, ad hoc adjustments made by individual citizens and social institutions as a way of helping new immigrants to feel at home. In general, it is essential to the successful functioning of any society that its members be prepared to accommodate one another on an informal basis in a wide range of contexts, and this willingness to engage in informal accommodation is an especially important element of a society's treatment of new members, whose place in the society might otherwise seem marginal or precarious.[22] The territory of informal accommodation is

---

neglect. See also the earlier article by Eisgruber and Sager, "The Vulnerability of Conscience: The Constitutional Basis for Protecting Religious Conduct," *University of Chicago Law Review* 61 (1994): 1245–1315. In "Religion and the Exemption Strategy" (Chapter 16 of *Religion and the Constitution, Volume 2, Establishment and Fairness*, Princeton University Press, 2008), Kent Greenawalt interprets the religion clauses as supporting exemptions in a wider range of cases than Eisgruber and Sager recognize, and he argues that at least some of those exemptions rest on valid claims of privilege rather than on considerations of equality or nondiscrimination, but he also argues that conscientious convictions of a nonreligious character should sometimes be treated the same way. The whole idea of providing exemptions from otherwise justified laws is sharply criticized by Brian Barry in *Culture and Equality* (Cambridge, Mass.: Harvard University Press, 2001), especially Chapter 2. For a critical assessment of Barry's position, see Samuel Freeman, "Liberalism and the Accommodation of Group Claims," in *Multiculturalism Reconsidered*, Paul Kelly (ed.) (Cambridge, UK: Polity Press, 2003), pp. 18–30.

22. Compare Timothy Garton Ash: "It's the personal attitudes and behavior of hundreds of millions of non-Muslim Europeans, in countless small, everyday interactions, that

bounded, on the one side, by what the state owes immigrants as a matter of justice and, on the other side, by the duties and obligations that the principles of justice and political morality assign to immigrants and other citizens. It is within this territory that many of the conditions of daily life are fixed. Unless the wider society makes a significant effort within this territory to accommodate the tastes, values, and traditions of newcomers, they are likely to feel that they have been denied equal respect and equal citizenship even if no principle of justice has been violated, and the consequences of persistent feelings of this kind can be explosive. In this arena, as in the content of the principles of justice themselves, there is an ideal of reciprocity that a decent and well-functioning society must strive in good faith to honor, and which it ignores at its peril.[23]

Finally, the points that I have made about the special role of the national culture should not be understood to reinstate strong preservationism. The contingent historical character of the national culture is not in itself objectionable, and a society is not obligated to purge all of the contingent elements of the culture in order to accommodate new immigrants who may find those elements alien or unfamiliar. On the other hand, once a society accepts immigrants as new members, then they have as much of a part to play as anyone else in shaping the future character and culture of the society. They now belong to the society and are contributors to its ongoing history. Although the society remains subject to the standing requirements of justice, the character of its national culture cannot be insulated against change, any more than the character of any other culture can. Its new members are now part of the mix of people who will help to determine how the culture evolves, and it is only to be expected that large-scale immigration will lead to more or less gradual and more or less radical changes over time.

The various considerations I have been rehearsing suggest a number of modifications or qualifications of the Heraclitean position on immigration, but they do not undercut its central claims. It is true, as the Heraclitean says, that there is no possibility of preserving unaltered either

will determine whether their Muslim fellow citizens begin to feel at home in Europe or not" ("Islam in Europe," *The New York Review of Books* LIII [2006]: 32–35, at p. 35).

23. Seana Shiffrin has discussed the importance of mutual accommodation as a general phenomenon with great insight and sensitivity. See her "Paternalism, Unconscionability Doctrine, and Accommodation," *Philosophy & Public Affairs* 29 (2000): 205–250, and "Egalitarianism, Choice-Sensitivity, and Accommodation," in *Reason and Value: Themes from the Moral Philosophy of Joseph Raz*, R. J. Wallace, P. Pettit, S. Scheffler, and M. Smith (eds.), pp. 270–302.

the imported cultures of immigrant communities or the national culture of host societies, and that neither side has any general right to such preservation. It is also true that, in a just society, immigrants and nonimmigrants alike should have the freedom and the opportunity to engage in the dynamic and interpretative process of extending their inherited cultures in the altered circumstances to which immigration gives rise. Finally, I believe that the Heraclitean position is correct to forswear any appeal to cultural rights or to the language of multiculturalism in thinking about these questions. The constituents of political morality that are most relevant in thinking about the mutual responsibilities of immigrants and host societies are the principles of justice, which define a fair framework of social cooperation among equals (and which are understood to exclude special cultural rights); the basic liberties, including especially the liberties of speech, association, and conscience; and the important idea of informal mutual accommodation within the bounds of justice. Talk of cultural rights and of multiculturalism adds little that is useful to this, and it provides an invitation to mischief both by encouraging us to think in unsustainable, strong-preservationist terms and by promoting a distorted and potentially oppressive conception of the relations between individuals and cultures.[24]

My resistance to employing the discourse of cultural rights and multiculturalism runs counter to strong currents in contemporary liberal thought, so it may be worth pausing for a moment to expand a bit on the reasons for that resistance. After all, the idea of treating diversity with respect to culture as calling for explicit protection under a regime of liberal rights and toleration may seem like a natural extension of basic liberal ideas and values. Historically, liberalism had its origins in the practice of religious toleration. Subsequent liberal theorists secularized and generalized the notion of a religious affiliation so as to include commitments of a nonreligious character as well. It is in this spirit that contemporary liberals emphasize diversity with respect to people's "conceptions of the

24. Anne Phillips has suggested to me that these remarks may have an unfortunate resonance in the contemporary European context, where public discourse about the "failure of multiculturalism" has functioned as a kind of code in which to express hostility to immigration and support for anti-immigrant policies. I hope it is evident that, in arguing that the concepts of "culture" and "multiculturalism" are of limited analytic value in thinking about the rights and duties of immigrants and host societies, I am very far from endorsing such attitudes or policies. Nor, as Joe Carens has persuaded me, would I wish to reject all of the policies that have been implemented in Canada under the heading of "multiculturalism" or "cultural rights," even though I am skeptical about the way those policies have been conceptualized and justified.

good" or "comprehensive moral doctrines," which are understood to include but not be limited to distinctively religious commitments.[25] It is in this spirit, too, that many modern liberals speak, as I have done in this article, about "freedom of conscience" rather than "freedom of religion," since the assumption is that a person's conscientious convictions need not have a religious character. And just as the modern liberal focus on competing conceptions of the good represents a generalization from the case of diverse religious commitments, so too the idea that liberalism should protect diverse cultures may seem like a natural next step.[26] If it is important to protect diversity with respect to religion, conceptions of the good, and comprehensive moral and philosophical outlooks, then surely it is reasonable to protect diversity with respect to culture as well. A person's cultural affiliations may be just as central to her identity as her religious commitments or her moral and evaluative convictions, and so a liberal polity that is concerned to promote and protect fundamental human interests should be just as concerned to safeguard cultural diversity as it is to protect moral, religious, and philosophical diversity.

However, I believe that it is a mistake to extrapolate from the case of moral, religious, and philosophical convictions to the case of cultural affiliations. Moral, religious, and philosophical outlooks, as conceptualized within liberal theory, are explicitly justificatory structures; they are systems of norms and values that provide guidance about how to live. To the extent that there is a principled liberal case for accommodating diverse outlooks of this kind, it rests on the importance to people of being free to order their lives in accordance with values, norms, and ideals that they perceive as authoritative, that is, as defining the conditions of a good or worthy life. The special status of moral, religious, and philosophical doctrines derives from their role as perceived sources of normative authority. We may think of this role as follows. Many people have—and think of themselves as having—moral, religious, or philosophical convictions about how best to live. To describe these convictions as *convictions* is to say that those who hold them believe them to be true. And to describe

25. For discussion of this point, see Jeremy Waldron, "Theoretical Foundations of Liberalism," *Philosophical Quarterly* 37 (1987): 127–50, especially pp. 144–145.
26. Waldron expresses qualified support for this step in "One Law for All? The Logic of Cultural Accommodation," *Washington & Lee Law Review* 59 (2002): 3–34. He says that it is desirable to think of the issue of "cultural accommodations as a *general* problem, in a way that is uncontaminated by the U.S. Constitution's particular emphasis on religious liberty and the arguably artificial distinction that such emphasis requires us to draw between religious and 'merely cultural' practices and beliefs" (ibid., p. 11 n.).

them as convictions about *how to live* is to say that those who hold them see them as providing reasons for action. Thus, many people recognize moral, religious, or philosophical reasons for action, and take the force or authority of those reasons to derive from their association with presumed moral, religious, or philosophical truths. In that sense, morality, religion, and philosophy are perceived sources of normative authority.

Cultures are not in the same sense sources of normative authority, for they are not explicitly justificatory structures at all. As a first approximation, we may say that a culture is a web of formal and informal practices, customs, institutions, traditions, norms, rituals, values, and beliefs. Although norms and values are important aspects of all cultures, this does not mean that the role of culture is parallel to the role of moral, religious, and philosophical doctrines. To begin with, there is no need for a culture to embrace a uniform normative outlook, and many cultures exhibit a high degree of moral, religious, and philosophical diversity. Moreover, as this formulation already implies, most of the values and principles that are aspects of culture are themselves regarded by their adherents as having a moral, religious, or philosophical character. They are not thought of by those who accept them as constituting an independent normative category. So while many people have what they take to be moral, religious, or philosophical convictions, few have what they think of as "cultural convictions." And while many people accept what they represent to themselves as moral, religious, or philosophical principles, and defer to the authority of considerations associated with those principles, few endorse what they think of as "cultural principles." Even when people realize that the principles they endorse are in fact widely shared within "their" culture, the authority of the principles is normally taken to derive not from their acceptance within the culture but rather from the direct normative force of the principles themselves.

It is true, of course, that we speak of *cultural norms* or *cultural values,* but these expressions are normally used in descriptive or interpretive contexts. To describe something as a cultural norm or a cultural value is not to characterize its perceived authority but rather to indicate its prevalence within a certain social group. Except in special cases, people who actually accept such values and norms, and who feel their force, do not think of them in those terms, still less do they see the authority of the values and norms as deriving from their status within the culture. In fact, for this very reason, to describe something as being (merely) a cultural norm or value can sometimes be a way of debunking it: of denying that it has the kind of authority that its adherents take it to have.

In short, cultures are not perceived sources of normative authority in the same sense that moral, religious, and philosophical doctrines are.

Those who think of them as being on a par commit something like a category mistake, for *culture* is a descriptive, ethnographic category, not a normative one. In other words, to classify something as a moral, religious, or philosophical value or principle is to say something about the kind of authority its adherents take it to have. By contrast, to classify something as a cultural norm or value is not to characterize its perceived authority but merely to indicate that a certain group of people subscribes to it. This explains why, although many people have what they think of as moral, religious, or philosophical convictions, and regard those convictions both as true and as action-guiding, few people think of themselves as having a comparable class of "cultural convictions." And it explains why "cultural reasons" rarely feature as such in individual deliberation; from a deliberative perspective, these supposed reasons do not constitute a special class of norm- or value-based considerations over and above the various norm- and value-based considerations that agents already recognize.[27,28]

27. Brian Barry makes very similar observations about the concept of "culture" in *Culture and Equality*, especially at p. 253. However, although he comes close to noticing (on p. 33) that these observations point to important disanalogies between culture and religion, he seems not to consider the possibility that, in so doing, they may provide reasons for treating culture and religion differently.

28. One important question, which I cannot address adequately here, concerns the implications of these arguments for debates about the so-called cultural defense in criminal law. One preliminary observation is that the idea of a cultural defense appears to hover uneasily between "interpretive" and "normative" readings. That is, it appears to hover between (a) the claim that information about a defendant's cultural background is sometimes necessary for the interpretation of his or her beliefs, intentions, and other mental states, which the law already deems relevant in establishing culpability or deciding on an appropriate sentence; and (b) the claim that an otherwise criminal act should sometimes be treated less harshly if, in performing the act, the defendant was acting in accordance with the norms of his or her culture. Consider, for example, the case of Jacob Zuma, who, before he became President of South Africa, was tried on rape charges and acquitted in 2006. According to Michael Wines of *The New York Times* ("A Highly Charged Rape Trial Tests South Africa's Ideals," April 10, 2006, p. A3), Mr. Zuma claimed in his trial that he was "being persecuted for his cultural beliefs," and "cast himself as the embodiment of a traditional Zulu male, with all the privileges that patriarchal Zulu traditions bestow on men." More specifically, he argued that his accuser "had signaled a desire to have sex with him by wearing a knee-length skirt to his house and sitting with legs crossed, revealing her thigh." Furthermore, "he said, he was actually obligated to have sex. His accuser was aroused, he said, and 'in the Zulu culture, you cannot just leave a woman if she is ready.' To deny her sex, he said, would have been tantamount to rape." Here, it seems, we have (a) an interpretive claim about what, in light of his relation to Zulu culture, it was reasonable for Zuma to believe about his accuser's behavior (that she was signaling a desire to have sex with him), and (b) a normative claim to the effect that Zuma should be exonerated because his purportedly criminal

Perhaps this will change as the discourse of multiculturalism becomes increasingly pervasive and begins, in self-fulfilling fashion, to alter the way that we think and deliberate, and the kinds of consideration that we deem authoritative in practical reasoning. To some extent, this may already be happening. In the course of a discussion about the remarkable global spread of the concept of culture, Kwame Anthony Appiah relates the following story about an experience he had in his hometown of Kumasi, Ghana: "I was setting out with a friend who works at the palace of the Asante Queen Mother for some celebration about which he was greatly excited, and I asked him why it mattered so. He looked at me in puzzlement for a moment and replied: '*Ēyē yē kōkya.*' It is our culture."[29] So perhaps people are already starting to think of themselves as having "cultural reasons." On the other hand, Appiah's story would hardly be worth telling if his friend's comment did not strike us as in some way surprising or anomalous, and I have tried to suggest one reason why that might be so.

I do not mean to deny that the fact that one is associated with a particular culture may be an important aspect of one's identity. By the same token, however, a commitment to a particular moral, religious, or philosophical doctrine may also be an important aspect of one's identity, and yet these identity-based considerations are not what ground the special status of such doctrines within liberal thought. Thus, the relation between culture and identity does not support an extrapolation from the case of moral, religious, and philosophical convictions to the case of cultural affiliations. Of course, one might propose that the need to protect individual identity should be treated as an independent basis for a regime of cultural rights. However, as I argued earlier, "identity" is too protean and variable a notion to warrant this sort of protection. Individuals' identities are fluid, context dependent, and mutable. In providing the familiar liberties of thought, speech, association, and conscience, a liberal polity already affords individual identity the only kind of legal protection that it can or should receive. Furthermore, as I also argued earlier, the relations between individuals and cultures are complex, and

<hr />

conduct was in fact obligatory according to the norms of Zulu culture. I believe that the arguments of the first part of my article have implications for interpretive versions of the cultural defense, while the arguments of the last several pages have implications for normative versions. I am grateful to Sarah Aikin for pressing me on this question, which I hope to address more fully at some point.

29. Appiah, *The Ethics of Identity*, p. 119. Chapter 4 of Appiah's book, "The Trouble with Culture," where this passage appears, provides a trenchant critique of the language of culture and cultural diversity.

it is a mistake to suppose that each individual "has" a single fixed and determinate culture. So if one reifies cultures as privileged sources of individual identity and seeks to protect them on that basis, the effect is to rigidify the notions of culture and identity in a way that is false to the facts and is liable to encourage illiberal social arrangements.[30]

To avoid misunderstanding, there are two points that I particularly want to emphasize. First, my arguments against relying on the language of culture and identity in thinking about problems of immigration should not be mistaken for a general skepticism about the moral significance of particularistic attachments and group affiliations. People's lives are enriched beyond measure by such attachments and affiliations and, as I have argued elsewhere,[31] the responsibilities that we acquire by participating in personal relationships and belonging to groups and associations are among the most important and deeply rooted responsibilities that we have. In these respects, personal relationships and group affiliations are of the greatest moral significance. The doubts that I have registered in this article have to do with the normative significance of the concept of culture in particular, and with the idea that cultural preservation as such is a goal that the state should take special measures to advance or achieve.

Second, although I have argued that cultures are not explicitly justificatory structures in the same sense that moral, religious, and philosophical outlooks are, I do not mean to deny—indeed I wish to insist—that

30. In *Multicultural Citizenship* and in his earlier book *Liberalism, Community, and Culture* (Oxford: Clarendon Press, 1989), Will Kymlicka has argued forcefully that liberal societies must provide special protections for threatened "societal cultures." For Kymlicka, a societal culture is "an intergenerational community, more or less institutionally complete, occupying a given territory or homeland, sharing a distinct language and history" (*Multicultural Citizenship*, p. 18). Kymlicka argues that it is through one's membership in a societal culture that one comes to have the options that are preconditions for the kind of autonomous choice that liberals value. National minorities with distinct societal cultures, such as indigenous or aboriginal peoples, may require, and should receive, special protections so that they can continue to provide their members with the preconditions of freedom and autonomy. Kymlicka also cites the importance of individuals' identifications with their societal cultures to explain why the members of threatened minority cultures cannot simply be absorbed into the surrounding societal culture. I am skeptical of Kymlicka's option-based defense of cultural rights. However, since he distinguishes between national minorities and immigrants, and explicitly denies that the latter have the right to preserve their societal cultures, I shall not address his arguments here. Brian Barry subjects Kymlicka's position to severe criticism in *Culture and Equality*, as does Kwame Anthony Appiah in *The Ethics of Identity*.
31. For example, in the essays cited in n. 12 and 14. See also Chapter 2 in this volume.

cultures include normative materials of many different kinds. As I have emphasized, for example, the moral, religious, and philosophical values that people accept also belong *eo ipso* to those people's cultures. In arguing that culture is nevertheless not a normative category in the same sense that morality and religion are, my point is simply that the fact that something is part of a culture does not itself confer any normative authority on it, even for those who belong to the culture. After all, many things can be part of a culture, including, for example, not only social norms but also patterns of deviation from those norms. So the mere fact that something is a feature of a culture to which one belongs does not confer any normative authority on it, nor is it ordinarily seen as so doing. Instead, people respond to perceived values, ideals, and principles, when they do, *as* values, ideals, and principles, and not as features of culture. In the same spirit, my contention is not that we should ignore the values, ideals, and principles that the members of a culture espouse, but rather that we should assess the significance of those values and ideals as such, instead of supposing that what gives them their normative character is the fact that they are part of a culture.

The implication of my argument, then, is not that all of the political claims advanced under the heading of cultural rights or cultural preservation should automatically be dismissed, but rather that those claims should be redescribed in such a way as to make clear the values, ideals, and principles that are at stake. Very often, I believe, these will turn out to be moral, religious, or philosophical values or ideals, so that the appeal to culture will turn out to have been redundant. Occasionally, the values or ideals in question may be ones that cannot naturally be subsumed under the heading of "moral, religious, or philosophical values," in which case it is the weight and significance of these new values, rather than their status as features of the culture, that need to be assessed. Finally, it may in some cases turn out that there was really no value at all at stake, and that the appeal to culture was sheer bluff—that it was simply an appeal to the brute fact that some people behave in a certain way, which by itself has no normative force.[32] In cases of all three kinds, I believe, the elimination of the language of culture will have proven salutary.

32. The obvious exceptions to this claim are cases of purely conventional solutions to coordination problems. The brute fact that everyone else is driving on the right does give me a compelling reason to drive on the right. But precisely because driving on the right is a matter of pure convention, and expresses no distinctive value, it would be mad to think that we should find ways to preserve the practice of right-hand driving in a world in which driving on the left was becoming the dominant convention.

My discussion has been very abstract and has provided little specific guidance about how societies should organize themselves to accommodate new immigrants. My primary proposal, some may complain, has been the purely verbal or terminological recommendation that we avoid using *culture* and *cultural preservation* as central analytic categories in thinking about the challenges posed by immigration. Yet this, it may be protested, provides no assistance in coping with those challenges. It tells us nothing about the specific policies and practices that societies should implement to deal with problems of immigration. It tells us nothing about how to resolve hard cases or about how to defuse the most serious conflicts.

To this I can only reply by reiterating some points that I made at the beginning of my discussion. I believe that, in thinking about the challenges of immigration, an excessive reliance on the discourse of culture and identity has produced distortions and oversimplifications both in the theoretical literature and in popular debates. Framing the challenges in other terms will not by itself make them disappear. However, understanding a problem is the first step toward solving it. And since the unsatisfactory description of a problem can cloud the understanding and make the shape of possible solutions harder to discern, there is much to be said for trying to frame the issues in ways that enable us to keep the real challenges clearly in view. It is true that I have not provided solutions to those challenges here. The challenges are, in any case, only partly philosophical, and real solutions will require political judgment and institutional resolve at least as much as they will require philosophical analysis. I have tried to indicate some of the categories and principles that may guide us in attempting to devise such solutions, however, and to warn against some ways of conceptualizing the problems that seem to me unhelpful or worse.

The Normativity of Tradition

I

Tradition plays an important role in many people's lives. Many people, and perhaps most people, participate in traditions of one kind or another. By this I mean that they take the fact that an act is called for by some tradition as giving them reason to perform that act. For convenience, I will say that they see themselves as having "reasons of tradition" or simply "traditional reasons" for acting in certain ways.

The force of traditional reasons is not immediately apparent. These reasons may appear to be subject to a reductive dilemma. On the one hand, it may seem that to act in a certain way for traditional reasons is simply to act in that way because people have acted that way in the past. But the mere fact that people have acted some way in the past is not by itself a reason to act that way in the future. If it were, then every act that has ever been performed would give us reason to perform a relevantly similar act. This seems absurd. On the other hand, most traditions endorse or embody or exemplify certain values, principles, or ideals. So perhaps to act for traditional reasons is just to act for reasons that derive from those values, principles, or ideals. But if traditional reasons are just reasons deriving from certain values, principles, or ideals, then the reference to tradition seems otiose. The force of the reasons, on this assumption, does not derive from the fact that they are part of a tradition. It is not the existence of the tradition, but rather the normative significance of the values or principles, that gives rise to the reasons. So, someone who has never participated in the tradition may have just the same reasons for responding in just the same way to the relevant values or principles as someone who is a participant of long standing.

In the past I have argued that something like this reductive dilemma actually holds in the case of culture.[1] On the one hand, to act on "cultural reasons" might be to act in a certain way simply because other people have acted that way. So understood, cultural reasons have no normative force; they are not reasons at all. On the other hand, to act on cultural reasons might be to act in response to certain values or principles, values or principles that are, as a matter of fact, widely accepted within a cultural group. But then the reference to culture seems otiose. The normative force of the reasons derives from the relevant values or principles, and not from the fact of their acceptance by the cultural group. The upshot is that cultural reasons do not represent an independent class of reasons over and above the reasons deriving from the values and principles that people recognize.

From a deliberative perspective, this conclusion can be accepted without significant loss, for *culture* is primarily a descriptive or ethnographic category, not a normative or deliberative one. In other words, to describe something as a cultural norm or cultural value is simply to indicate that it is a norm or value that is widely shared within a certain social group. Except in special cases, people who actually accept the values and norms in question, and who feel their force, do not think of them as cultural norms, nor do they see the authority of the norms as deriving from their status within the culture. Similarly, "cultural reasons" rarely feature as such in individual deliberation.

The case of tradition seems different. People do, I believe, act on reasons whose force they themselves ascribe to the authority of some tradition. In this sense, *tradition* appears to be a normative notion. So the reductive dilemma with respect to tradition has significant skeptical

---

1. See "Immigration and the Significance of Culture," Chapter 10 in this volume. The next two paragraphs summarize arguments developed at greater length in that paper.

implications. This is reason enough to pursue the investigation further. But questions about the normative force of tradition are of interest for at least two additional reasons.

First, these questions are relevant to issues of political morality. The diversity of traditions is characteristic of a modern, pluralistic society, and the question of how a political society should organize itself so as to accommodate this form of diversity is a pressing one. Liberal societies have a long history of attaching special significance to *normative diversity*, particularly diversity with respect to people's differing moral and religious outlooks and conceptions of the good life. This suggests that questions about how best to respond to the diversity of traditions may depend on the normative force of traditional reasons. There is of course, a parallel issue about the proper response to the diversity of cultures, and in that instance I have argued that the reductive dilemma undercuts the case for special "cultural rights" or for "multiculturalism," at least on some interpretations of those contested and highly charged terms. The case that is undercut depends, in effect, on an equivocation between the ideas embodied in the two horns of the dilemma. On the one hand, the fact that cultures comprise actual group practices is used to establish that cultural diversity is something over and above the diversity of individual moral, religious, and philosophical convictions. This paves the way for the claim that a special regime of rights may be required to accommodate this form of diversity. Yet, on the other hand, the examples of cultural considerations that are cited are almost always considerations that are perceived, within the relevant cultural groups themselves, as deriving their normative authority from moral, religious, or philosophical values or principles, and not from the group's acceptance of those values or principles. The upshot is that cultural diversity is not, in the end, a species of *normative* diversity that is independent of moral, religious, and philosophical diversity. The question whether the same is true of diversity with respect to tradition is of obvious political relevance.

The second reason is this: Questions about the normative force of tradition bear on the more general topic of the role in human life, and the importance for human flourishing, of our attitudes toward the past and the future. Many people care intensely, though in ways that are rarely made explicit or articulate, about certain things that happened in the past and certain things that may happen in the future. Of course, they care about their own pasts and their own futures. But their time-related concerns are not limited to concerns about other temporal periods of their own lives. They also care about things that happened before they were born, and things that will or might happen after their deaths.

It is a commonplace, of course, that many people wish to feel a part of something larger than themselves, and contemporary philosophers have relied on this commonplace in their investigations of the moral and political significance of membership in a community or a nation. But I am interested in the specifically temporal dimension of people's attitudes, which seems to me to have received insufficient attention. Our attitudes toward the past and the future are complex, puzzling, and poorly understood. It may or may not be the case that they involve something that is best described as a desire to be part of something larger than ourselves. Part of the interest of an investigation of the normative force of tradition lies in the light it may shed on these attitudes.

Two points of clarification are in order. First, in one broad and standard sense of the term, a tradition is a set of beliefs, customs, teachings, values, practices, and procedures that is transmitted from generation to generation. However, a tradition need not incorporate items of all the kinds just mentioned. For example, we speak of intellectual traditions, and these are traditions that comprise ideas and beliefs but may not include practices or norms of action and may not have any direct implications for how people should behave. In this essay, though, I am interested in those traditions that are seen by people as providing them with reasons for action, and so I will limit myself to traditions that include norms of practice and behavior. This still includes traditions of many different kinds, including, for example, national traditions, religious traditions, literary or artistic traditions, and the traditions associated with particular institutions, organizations, communities, and professions.

Second, there is a looser sense of the term in which a tradition need not extend over multiple generations. A family or a group of friends may establish a "tradition," for example, of celebrating special occasions by going to a certain restaurant, without any thought that subsequent generations will do the same thing. Even a single individual may be described as having established certain traditions, in this extended sense of the term. For example, a person may have a "tradition" of taking a walk by the river on Saturday afternoons. These uses of the term are suggestive, and I have no desire to police ordinary usage, but my primary interest is in the more standard cases in which traditions are understood to involve multiple people and to extend over generations. Except where I explicitly indicate otherwise, those are the kinds of traditions I will have in mind in this discussion. I will refer to personal "traditions" like those just mentioned as *personal routines*.

II

Why might the fact that some act is called for by a tradition to which one subscribes seem like a consideration in favor of performing that act? A short but unhelpful answer would be to say: because one subscribes to the tradition. As I have already said, to subscribe to or participate in a tradition just is to see the fact that it calls for certain actions as reasons for performing those actions. But this invites the question: why subscribe to a tradition? What is it about traditions that leads people to treat them as reason-giving? There is, I believe, no single answer to this question. Instead, one of my aims in this essay is to show that there are many different factors that may contribute to the perceived normative authority of a tradition.

To begin with, one important feature of traditions is that they serve to establish and entrench certain social conventions. Indeed, virtually any well-established convention may be said to constitute a tradition in an extended sense of the term. The fact that red traffic lights are normally used to indicate that vehicles should stop might be expressed by saying that red lights are traditionally used as stop signs. But some conventions belong to wider traditions of thought and practice that include many other elements. Like all conventions, the conventions that belong to wider traditions serve to co-ordinate behavior and, in so doing, to facilitate social interaction and make it easier to achieve various individual and collective goods. So, for example, a religious tradition may establish a sabbatarian practice, which designates one day each week as a day of rest. If it is desirable for each person to observe a weekly day of rest, and if there are advantages to having an entire community observe the same day of rest, then a convention that establishes a particular day as the day of rest has obvious advantages. In treating the fact that that day is the traditional day of rest as a reason not to work that day oneself, one acknowledges these advantages and defers to the normative force of the convention.

Second, if it is an essential feature of conventions that they play a useful co-coordinating role, then there may be room for a distinction between conventions and what might be termed *collective habits*. Suppose that the people in a given community always go to the beach on a certain holiday. On balance, most of them find this a pleasant thing to do. Yet the fact that they all do it on the same holiday is not itself a useful piece of social co-ordination, for it results in heavy traffic and overcrowded beaches, and does not make beach-going more pleasant than it would be if different people went on different days. So we might describe the practice of going to the beach on this holiday not as a convention but rather as a collective habit. Although collective habits can have their dis-advantages, such as heavy traffic and overcrowded beaches, they also have advantages. Like all habits, they enable us to settle without excessive and repetitive deliberation on courses of action that have, on balance, proved successful in the past. We gain deliberative efficiency by relying relatively unreflectively on successful past practice as a defeasible guide to future conduct. If we distinguish collective habits from social conventions in this way, then it seems clear that traditions will often embody collective habits as well as social conventions. If one goes to the beach because it is the traditional thing to do on this holiday, one reaps the benefits of the deliberative efficiencies of these habits.

A third, closely related factor that may speak on behalf of adherence to a tradition is the fact that a tradition of reasonably long standing may be regarded as a repository of experience and of the kind of wisdom that comes from experience. Traditional practices take shape in light of an accumulation of historical experience, judgment, and perspective that outstrips what any single individual can reasonably aspire to achieve in the course of a lifetime, and someone who adheres to the tradition may gain the advantages of that accumulated experience and judgment.

Fourth, there may be reasons for adhering to a tradition that derive from the fact that the tradition embodies certain values, ideals, and principles. The reductive dilemma suggests otherwise. It maintains that any reasons of this kind will derive from the values, ideals, and principles themselves, and that the tradition is not a source of reasons over and above these value-, ideal-, or principle-based reasons. But this may be too hasty. For one thing, values, ideals, and principles are not self-interpreting. In addition to endorsing or embodying a set of values, a tradition will typically incorporate a well-developed body of advice and instruction about how to interpret those values and how best to apply them to the concrete circumstances of daily life. Actually, there are two closely related phenomena that need to be distinguished here. First, there is the fact that abstract values and principles require inter-pretation if they are to provide any concrete guidance about how to live. Most traditions do not limit themselves to endorsing some set of val-ues and principles, but also provide useful guidance about their imple-mentation and application. Second, many values, principles, and norms are "imperfect" in the Kantian sense; that is, they articulate norms of living with which we are supposed to comply, but these norms leave the timing and manner of our compliance up to us. The discretionary character of these norms, which might seem to make them less bur-densome for individuals, actually makes them more so, at least in one respect. The very indeterminacy of the norms places special burdens on the will and the deliberative capacities of the individual, for there is no particular occasion on which one is required to fulfill the obligations they establish. This turns the decision about when to fulfill them into a significant deliberative task.[2] Phenomenologically, moreover, it also creates the impression that their fulfillment is always supererogatory, for on each occasion, discharging such an obligation goes beyond what one is, then and there, required to do. This in turn makes it easier to convince oneself, on each particular occasion, that one need not discharge the obligation *then*. One function of traditions is to establish customs and conventions regarding the time and manner in which we fulfill these imperfect duties and ideals, thus reducing the indeterminacy of the norms and the burdensomely discretionary character of the demands that they make of individuals. For example, many traditions establish conventions concerning the timing and proper amount of charitable giving, and thus make the demands on individuals more determinate and clear-cut. This point illustrates, incidentally, the way in which the various advantages of subscribing to a tradition may operate in tandem. In this case, the tradition establishes a convention whose function is to make it easier for people to implement some principle or live up to some ideal. And such conventions themselves normally reflect a long history of experience in trying to develop effective ways of encouraging compliance with the relevant principles and ideals.

Fifth, in addition to embodying or endorsing certain values and principles, traditions may themselves be seen as valuable, in something like the way that libraries or cathedrals or museums are seen as valuable. They may be regarded as valuable repositories of human knowledge, experience, creativity, and achievement. As I have argued elsewhere,[3] we can distinguish between recognizing something as valuable and valuing it oneself; we recognize the value of many things that we ourselves do not value. For example, I may regard bird watching as a valuable activity without valuing it myself. Valuing includes but goes beyond the recognition of value. Like me, those who value bird watching will see it as a valuable activity, but unlike me they will also see themselves as having reason to engage in the activity. In the case under consideration, similarly, one

---

2. This is related to a point that Thomas Nagel makes in criticizing Robert Nozick's libertarianism: it "is acceptable to compel people to contribute to the support of the indigent by automatic taxation, but unreasonable to insist that in the absence of such a system they ought to contribute voluntarily. The latter is an excessively demanding position because it requires voluntary decisions that are quite difficult to make" ("Libertarianism Without Foundations," *Yale Law Journal* 85[1975]: 136–149, at p. 145).
3. "Valuing," Chapter 1 in this volume.

may recognize the value of a tradition without valuing it oneself, and people who are in this position will not normally see the fact that some act is called for by the tradition as a reason for performing that act. But the situation is different for people who do value the tradition. For them, the fact that the tradition calls for some act to be performed may well be seen as a reason for performing it. Indeed, this may be part of what valuing the tradition consists in.

Sixth, even if the mere fact that people have acted in a certain way in the past does not by itself provide one with a reason to act that way now, the fact that particular people to whom one feels closely tied acted in a certain way in the past—and attached special value to that way of acting—may give one reasons of loyalty to act that way now. Subscribing to a tradition and acting in accordance with that tradition may be ways of expressing one's loyalty to others who adhered to the tradition and to whom such adherence was important. Loyalty is itself a value that many traditions endorse, of course, and in so doing these traditions are, in effect, self-reinforcing: that is, they confirm for their adherents the importance of acting in accordance with the kinds of reasons that lead many people to adhere to them in the first place. If a tradition itself endorses loyalty as a virtue or value, then one effect of this is that people may have reasons of loyalty for acting in accordance with reasons of loyalty.

Seventh, the fact that traditions normally embody certain values, principles, and ideals means that traditions normally *stand for* something. They are not simply intergenerational chains of replicated behavior. Accordingly, when a tradition has played a formative role in a person's development, the person may come to feel that what the tradition stands for is also what he or she stands for. The values of the tradition have been internalized in such a way that they have come to occupy a central place in the person's self-conception. The person may or may not regard these values as binding or mandatory for everyone, but she feels that she would be unrecognizable to herself without them. For someone who is in this position, acting as called for by the tradition is not only a matter of responding to the intrinsic normative force of the values. It is also a matter of being true to oneself. In this sense, acting on traditional reasons may be experienced as a requirement of personal integrity.

To this point, I have identified seven different kinds of consideration that may speak in favor of adherence to a tradition: we may label them *convention, habit, wisdom, guidance, value, loyalty,* and *integrity*. In acting on reasons of tradition, people may be seen as tacitly acknowledging the force of some or all of these kinds of consideration. This by itself is sufficient to show that the reductive dilemma fails as a diagnosis of traditional reasons. It is not true that, in acting on traditional reasons, one must either be acting in a certain way simply because other people have acted that way in the past or else responding to a principle-based reason that applies with just as much force to people who do not adhere to the tradition. Traditional reasons are neither normatively empty nor otiose.

III

The seven types of consideration I have mentioned so far do not exhaust the normative force of traditional reasons. To make further progress, we need to consider the general question I mentioned earlier, namely, the role of tradition in relation to broader human attitudes toward the past and the future. One place to begin is with what I call personal routines. As I have noted, these may sometimes be spoken of as traditions in an extended sense of that term, but for the sake of clarity I will generally avoid using this terminology. Whatever we choose to call them, these routines help to illuminate the normative significance of traditions in the standard sense, because they provide clues about the attitudes toward time that help to account for that significance.

So consider, to begin with, the pleasures of repetition and familiarity. Someone who goes to the same café and orders the same coffee and pastry every morning may take pleasure in the regularity of this routine over and above the pleasure derived from the coffee and pastry themselves. There may also be an extra pleasure involved if the café proprietor or waiter knows without asking, when the person walks in each day, what the person wants: that he will have "the usual." Many people have routines of one kind or another that have this character. In saying this, of course, I do not mean to deny that many routines are not pleasurable at all, but are instead boring, tedious, or even soul-deadening. The point is not that our familiar personal routines are always pleasurable, only that they sometimes are. To the extent that these routines *are* pleasurable, it is worth asking why this is the case. What is the source and character of these distinctive pleasures—the pleasures of routine and familiarity? These are questions that do not seem to me to be often enough discussed, perhaps because we are accustomed to thinking of novelty, adventure, and excitement, rather than familiarity and repetitiveness, as sources of pleasure and fulfillment, and we are too quick to associate routine with boredom and tedium. The pleasures of "the usual" are easily overlooked.

Let me venture three tentative suggestions about what accounts for these pleasures. The first two have to do with what might be called the problem of temporal mobility. It is a striking fact about human life that we have almost no control over our movement through time. The one

exception is that we can influence the time of our deaths, either by killing ourselves or, less dramatically, by taking steps that will predictably
raise or lower the odds of our survival. But as long as we are alive, we
move through time at a uniform rate in a single direction, and we have
no alternative. This contrasts sharply with the degree of control we exercise over our mobility in space. Unless we are severely incapacitated, the
ability to move our own bodies from one place to another, at a rate and
in a direction of our choosing, is a fundamental feature of our lives, and
we rely on it so ubiquitously that we tend to take it for granted. Yet its
importance to us can hardly be overstated.

Although we also take our inability to control our mobility in time for
granted, it is nevertheless experienced as a constraint. The twin urges to
revisit the past and to see into the future can be almost unbearably powerful. Since they cannot be satisfied, we must make do for the most part
with memory in the one case and anticipatory imagination in the other.
But these mental capacities are highly imperfect surrogates for genuine
temporal mobility. In a modest way, personal routines help to compensate for the lack of such mobility. If I visit the same café and order the
same coffee and pastry every morning, then during any given visit my
experience is, in relevant respects, the same as it has been in the past
and as it will be in the future—or so it seems to me. This means that
I experience what might be thought of as a kind of quasi-mobility in
time, for the invariant character of the daily routine effaces the temporal
specificity of any particular café visit. I am having coffee here today, but
it is as if I were having it yesterday—or tomorrow. Of course, when it
comes to living in the past or in the future, "as if" is not good enough,
but then again it is better than nothing, although the phenomenon can
also be taken too far. If our life is altogether dominated by routine, then
the years may seem to blend into or become indistinguishable from one
another. In these circumstances, all our experiences may seem to lack
temporal specificity, and we may find it difficult to say whether any given
experience took place three years ago or five years ago or ten years ago.
When this is not just a symptom of failing memory, it may instead be a
symptom of our life's impoverishment. An excess of routine may give us
quasi-mobility at the expense of a narrow and unrewarding existence. Yet
without any personal routines at all, a life may come to seem fractured
and disjointed. One reason why such routines can be rewarding is precisely that they efface the temporal specificity of particular experiences
and, in so doing, enable us to feel, as we engage in the routine activity,
that we are making contact with other stages of our lives.

A second function of personal routines is as follows. One consequence of our lack of temporal control is that we cannot establish for

ourselves a "home" in time, in the way that we can establish a home in space. A home (in space) is not merely a place that we happen to occupy. It is also a place to which we normally have both a claim to return and the capacity to return. It is a place where we feel that we belong, and where others treat us as belonging. By establishing a home, we ward off feelings of being lost or adrift in the world. The very idea of a home is, in effect, a response to the vastness and impersonality of the universe and the precariousness and insignificance of our own place in it. A home is a tiny piece of the world to which we lay claim, and which we experience as our own. It is, in a sense, our world. This is one reason why homelessness is such a terrible condition, even if one does not lack for shelter from the elements. Those who have no home have no place in the world.

But we are all homeless in time. That is, we cannot carve out a piece of time that becomes our own and to which we can return at will. The constraints on our temporal mobility make this impossible. Yet the vastness and impersonality of time are every bit as chilling and awe-inspiring as the vastness and impersonality of space, and the need for a refuge—for something that serves the function of a place in time—is, for many people, almost as strong as the need for a place in space. Since we cannot establish homes in time the way we can establish homes in space, we must address this need in other ways. This is a second function of personal routines. By ordering the same coffee and pastry at the same café each morning, I domesticate a slice of time. In other words, I dedicate that slice of time each day to a specific purpose of my choosing, and in so doing I lay claim to it. It becomes "my time," as people sometimes say. And since a routine is by its nature temporally extended, "my time" extends beyond a single day. The routine establishes a kind of temporal corridor, which passes through the succession of days, and which "belongs" to me. So, although we cannot establish a home in time by strict analogy to a home in space, we can establish something that serves some of the same function. Obviously, we cannot return to any particular point in time the way we can return to a particular location in space. But when we dedicate the same hour each day to a particular activity of our choosing, the recurrence of the designated hour substitutes for the ability to return to a particular temporal location. And the comfort and familiarity of the routine is not unlike the comfort and familiarity of a home. In this sense, the routine domesticates a piece of time in the way that a home domesticates a piece of space. In both cases, the effect is to make ourselves feel *at* home in the world. We ward off the vastness and chilliness of time, in the one case, just as we ward off the vastness and chilliness of space, in the other. So the second function of personal routines is to domesticate time: to help us establish something that fulfills the function of a temporal "home."

Now the example of a personal routine that I have been using is in one way misleading. If I go to the same café every morning, then my routine involves repetition both with regard to time and with regard to space. It is not an example of an exclusively temporal regularity. Many personal routines have this kind of mixed character. They involve a repetitive activity that is always undertaken at the same time *and* in the same place. Indeed, one of the most familiar and ordinary sorts of personal routines, though not always one of the most rewarding, involves leaving and returning to one's (spatial) home at a certain time each day. Yet a personal routine need not have this mixed character. One's routine may be to take a walk at a certain time each day, following a different route each time. Or perhaps one devotes an hour each evening to reading fiction or listening to music, wherever one happens to find oneself. But even when a routine does involve regularity with regard to both time and space, my point has been that the temporal regularity serves some distinctive purposes.

I have so far mentioned two of these purposes. There is also a third purpose, which has to do with the reality of the self. The philosophical problem of personal identity concerns the conditions under which a person who exists at one time is the same person as a person who exists at another time. There is a related question that arises from the perspective of the individual agent. What gives me confidence at any given moment that I am a temporally persisting being, that I have a reality that extends beyond the present moment? As I am interpreting it, this is not exactly a philosophical question. That is, it is not a request for a statement of the conditions for the persistence of the self over time. It is rather a psychological question, a question about the sources of my confidence (whether justified or unjustified) that I am a persisting creature. After all, the past is gone and the future has not arrived yet. I have direct awareness of my existence at the present moment. But what makes me so sure that some person who existed in the past was *me*, or that there is a particular future person whose existence would be *my* existence? In raising this question, I do not mean to suggest that people are normally troubled by it, still less that they are plagued by skepticism about their own persistence. On the contrary, we normally take our persistence for granted, and the question I am raising has to do with the factors that enable us to do this.

Certainly the fact that I have (what present themselves as) memories of the past is of great importance, as is the fact that I have intentions, expectations, and other future-directed attitudes. Also important is the fact that the subjective quality of my consciousness is continuous from moment to moment; there is something that it feels like to be me and this feeling is not normally subject to sharp discontinuities (although more needs to be said about sleep and other forms of unconsciousness). Another factor that contributes to my confidence in my own persistence is my sense of myself as an organism. I am a physical creature with a body that manifestly has a history, and I experience changes in that body as changes in me. All these factors help to establish and to stabilize my sense of myself as a persisting creature.

It would be a mistake, however, to focus exclusively on our own attitudes as sources of our confidence in our persistence. For all its importance, memory is notoriously unreliable, and, in any case, we remember only a small fraction of our lives and experiences. The other factors that I have mentioned are similarly imperfect as devices for instilling confidence in ourselves as temporally extended beings. Rather than focusing exclusively on our own attitudes and faculties, we need also to consider the role of stability in the world around us in giving us a sense of ourselves as persisting creatures. If we were confronted at each moment with an utterly different environment, with no fixed points or continuities from one minute to the next, then it is doubtful that we could achieve a stable sense of ourselves as temporally extended beings. Our confidence in our persistence is inseparable from our confidence in the persistence of the world in which we live. In addition to the generic persistence of the world around us, moreover, it is also important that there should be particular other people who themselves persist and who recognize us as persisting creatures. One of the things that reinforces my sense of myself as a persisting creature, in other words, is the fact that there are other people who treat me as such a creature. In short, my confidence in my persistence is dependent on my confidence in the persistence of the world around me and on the confidence of others in my persistence.

Personal routines contribute in another way to our confidence in our own stability over time. I have so far mentioned two types of stabilizing factor. First, there are "internal" factors, which include various of our own mental and physical states, such as memories, intentions, feelings of being embodied, and so on. Second, there are "external" factors like the persistence of the world around us and of other people who regard us as persistent. Personal routines amount to a third type of factor, which occupies an intermediate position between the other two. By engaging in personal routines, we *enact* our persistence over time. Through the repetitive performance of acts that express our distinctive values and desires, we mark the world with continuities that are expressive of ourselves. In so doing, we confirm our sense of ourselves as persistent creatures, manufacturing, as it were, evidence to support our confidence in our persistence. The result is a kind of self-fulfilling, performative validation of our sense of our own reality as temporally extended beings. And to the extent that others recognize or enter into our routines, as for example when the barista knows what our "usual" is, we receive the added reassurance of knowing that the evidence we have manufactured or performed has been independently confirmed. The barista's response gives pleasure in part because it testifies to our success in making manifest, through willful repetitive doing, our own reality as temporally extended creatures.

IV

I have identified three functions of personal routines in helping to solve problems posed by time. Such routines help to compensate for our lack of control over our mobility in time, they provide a way of domesticating portions of time, and they provide assurance of our own reality as temporally extended creatures. Let me now return to the question of tradition and its normative significance. I said earlier that, in order fully to appreciate the normative force of traditional reasons, we needed to investigate the role of tradition in relation to broader human attitudes toward the past and the future. Our discussion of personal routines was the first step in that investigation, and we are now in a position to notice that traditions fulfill the same functions as do personal routines, although there are some differences in the way they do so.

Consider, first, the problem of mobility in time. I said that a personal routine compensates for our lack of control over our temporal mobility by establishing a regularity that effaces the temporal specificity of any particular instance of that regularity. In so doing, such a routine compensates for our lack of control over our mobility in time by enabling us to feel that each instance is "timeless." Although any given instance does of course have a particular temporal location, the fact that it is, in relevant respects, indistinguishable from all the other instances means that its temporal location is inessential—it takes place in the present, but it might as well be taking place in the past or the future. Now, traditions fulfill this same function, but with an important added dimension. In regularly acting in accordance with a traditional practice, an individual in effect assimilates that practice as a personal routine, and so reaps the advantages just mentioned. But insofar as the tradition extends beyond the lifespan of the individual, the quasi-mobility in time that it affords outstrips anything that the individual could achieve with an ordinary personal routine. In acting in accordance with the traditional practice, the individual acts not only as she has acted in the past and as she will act in the future, but also as others acted before she was born and will act after she is dead. In so acting, then, there is a way in which she is able to project herself backward and forward in time, to transcend not only the specificity of the moment but also the boundaries of her own life. She acts in accordance with the traditional practice today, but her act is in relevant respects indistinguishable from the way others have acted since before she was born and will act after she is gone. In that sense, participating in the practice enables her to travel back to a time before she lived and forward to a time when she will live no more.

Consider next the desire to domesticate time, to create something that plays a role in relation to time that is analogous to the role that a home plays in relation to space. I said earlier that a personal routine affords one way of doing this. By devoting a certain period of time each day (or each week, or . . .) to a specific type of activity of one's choosing, one establishes that recurring time slot as a kind of refuge to which one can "return" more or less at will, and in so doing achieve a sense of comfort and familiarity. It is no accident, I think, that great traditions are often greatly preoccupied with the establishment of temporal rhythms and routines, with the organization and segmentation of time, and with marking time's passage. They establish calendars, holidays and festivals, seasonal practices and ceremonies, daily or weekly or monthly or yearly rites and rituals, and regular commemorations of historical events. As already noted, a person who regularly acts in accordance with traditional practices assimilates these routines as his own, and in so doing such a person comes to inhabit what amounts to a pre-established temporal structure. As a way of domesticating time, this offers certain advantages when compared with the development of purely personal routines. Traditions are public, collective enterprises, so the temporal structures they make available have a social dimension that many people find comforting and enriching, much as many people prefer living with others to living alone. In addition, traditions usually have at their disposal substantial resources of wisdom and experience, and to the extent that they are supported by and embodied in institutions they often have substantial material resources as well. This means that the temporal routines they have established are likely to be both more elaborate and better grounded in the lessons of the past than are the purely personal routines developed *de novo* by individual agents. Moreover, insofar as traditions extend beyond the normal human life span, they offer individuals temporal structures that are themselves more enduring and so temporally more expansive than any routine those individuals could construct for themselves.

Consider, finally, the way that personal routines help to confirm our reality as temporally extended beings, through a kind of repetitive doing that enacts our persistence over time and marks the world with continuities that are expressive of ourselves. I pointed out that, when other people recognize or enter into our routines, they testify to the objectivity of these performative demonstrations of our persistence, and in so doing they confirm the reality we have sought to enact; that is, they confirm our own reality as temporally extended creatures. But traditions are by their nature collective enterprises, which are sustained not only by the allegiance of many adherents over long periods of time, but also by the adherents' mutual recognition of one another as collaborators in a shared enterprise. This recognition is normally expressed in and reinforced by the adherents' joint participation in various public, collective routines: in public rites, rituals, ceremonies, celebrations, and observances. In effect, then, this makes the mutual recognition by each adherent of the others' performative demonstrations of their persistence a structural feature of the tradition itself. So one function of traditions is to provide a stable means by which their adherents can confirm their own reality as temporally extended creatures. The continuing presence of others who participate in the same routines as we do, and who recognize us as fellow participants, provides us with regular confirmation of the reality that our participation seeks to enact.

The upshot of these reflections is that, in addition to the various considerations enumerated earlier, association with a tradition offers some distinctive advantages as a way of addressing the three problems related to time that we have been discussing: our lack of control over our mobility in time, our need to domesticate time, and our desire to assure our own reality as temporally extended creatures. To be sure, some people feel these problems more acutely than others, and some who feel them acutely will nevertheless find other ways to address them than through association with a tradition, perhaps because they regard the traditions that are accessible to them as uncongenial for one reason or another. Association with a tradition is certainly not the only way of addressing these time-related problems. Personal routines continue to have some advantages that are not superseded by the advantages of association with a tradition. In particular, personal routines are by their nature more individualized—more closely tailored to the desires and interests of the individuals whose routines they are—than any ongoing tradition can possibly be. Association with an ongoing tradition requires individuals to accommodate themselves to practices and arrangements that were developed by other people, and these practices and arrangements may have features that are experienced, especially by persons of a more voluntaristic and individualistic temperament, as alien or external constraints. For such individuals, reliance on personal routines may, therefore, be more appealing than association with any tradition. Of course, participation in traditional practices is not incompatible with the development of purely personal routines, and many people incorporate both into their lives.

V

I referred at the beginning of my discussion to the commonplace that many people wish to feel a part of something larger than themselves. This commonplace is often cited in discussions of the moral significance of membership in a community or nation, and it is also cited in explaining the appeal of association with a tradition. But although there is surely something right about the commonplace, its meaning is less clear than it may seem. Taken literally, after all, the desire to be part of something larger than oneself is automatically satisfied by anyone capable of experiencing it. Each of us is a member of the species *homo sapiens*, for example, each of us is an earthling, and each of us is part of the universe. If these truisms do not slake the desire to be part of something larger than ourselves, perhaps it is because we don't want to be part of something quite *that* large. But, it will be said, the size of the group or entity isn't the main thing. The main thing is that we want to *feel identified* with something larger than ourselves, and this feeling involves more than simply recognizing that we belong to some larger group or can be subsumed within some larger category.

I do not doubt that this is true, but it raises at least two sorts of question. First, there is the question of what it is, exactly, to "feel identified with" a group or collective enterprise? If one can recognize that one does in fact belong to a group and yet not feel identified with that group, then what more is involved in the feeling of identification? The second question is why exactly we wish to feel identified with groups or entities or enterprises of some kinds but not of others? We may wish to feel identified with something larger than ourselves but, it seems, not just any larger thing will do. This should lead us to ask about the characteristics that make certain types of groups and enterprises good candidates for identification, and about the human impulses that are addressed by identification with groups and enterprises possessing those characteristics. In seeking to understand the attractions of association with a tradition, for example, we cannot rest content with the commonplace that people wish to identify with something larger than themselves, for that desire underdetermines the specific choice of a tradition as something with which to identify. We should instead ask why traditions in particular are the sorts of things with which people wish to feel identified. What makes it possible and attractive to identify with a tradition, and what do these feelings of identification involve? These, in effect, are the questions I have been discussing.

Still, the commonplace that people wish to be a part of something larger than themselves is suggestive. One of its functions is to call attention to the limits of our egoism. We want to care about, and to value, things other than ourselves and our own flourishing. We think of people who do not care about anything other than themselves as leading impoverished lives. Indeed, it is widely remarked, and sometimes regarded as a paradox, that people who care about things other than themselves are more likely to flourish than people who care solely about their own flourishing. Be that as it may, the logic of valuing implies that, if we do value things other than ourselves, then things other than ourselves come to matter to us, and if they are the kinds of things whose survival can be in question, then their survival normally comes to matter to us as well. As I have argued elsewhere, there is something approaching a conceptual connection between valuing something and seeing reasons to preserve or sustain it.[4] So insofar as we wish to care about, and to value, things other than ourselves, the position in which we wish to put ourselves is one in which there are things other than ourselves whose survival matters to us. It is a further question whether we want to care about things other than ourselves *in order to* care about the survival of things other than ourselves. But the fact remains that most of us do care about, and value, the survival and flourishing of things other than ourselves, and one consequence of this is that we are not indifferent to what happens after our own deaths. What we value, in valuing the survival and flourishing of things other than ourselves, does not depend on our own survival. So if we value the survival and flourishing of things other than ourselves, then it matters to us that those things should survive and flourish even if we are dead. Does this mean that our own death matters less to us? It certainly means that it is not the only thing that matters to us; if we die, but the things we care about and value survive, then, we may feel, all is not lost. The phrase *all is not lost* suggests that we take the survival of what we value to confer on us a kind of immortality, or at any rate, extended longevity. But perhaps this is too strong; perhaps the survival of what we value merely diminishes the significance of our own mortality.

So we want to care about, and to value, things other than ourselves, and in caring about, and valuing, such things, we are led naturally to care about what happens after our deaths: to care about the survival and flourishing of the things that we value. These are time-related

---

4. "Immigration and the Significance of Culture," pp. 268–269.

concerns in addition to the ones discussed previously, and it is clear that they cannot be addressed by purely personal routines, which, by definition, end with our deaths if not sooner. By contrast, it is evident that traditions have a special role to play here. For traditions are repositories of value, and are themselves objects of value, and the whole point of a tradition is to perpetuate the survival of what people value: to hand these values down from generation to generation. Traditions are human practices whose organizing purpose is to preserve what is valued beyond the lifespan of any single individual or generation. They are collaborative, multigenerational enterprises devised by human beings precisely to satisfy the deep human impulse to preserve what is valued. In subscribing to a tradition that embodies values one embraces, or whose own value one embraces, one seeks to ensure the survival over time of what one values. And in seeking to ensure the survival over time of what one values, one diminishes the perceived significance of one's own death.

Of course, participation in a tradition has a backward-looking as well as a forward-looking dimension. If, in the forward-looking dimension, one seeks to ensure the survival of what one values, then, in the backward-looking dimension, one sees oneself as inheriting values that have been preserved by others. One is heir to, and custodian of, values that have been handed down by those who went before. These values themselves enrich one's life, and one's status as heir and custodian gives one's life an additional significance or importance that it would not otherwise have had. One is now part of a custodial chain, a chain of people stretching through time who have undertaken to preserve and extend these values. In addition to imbuing one's own life with a distinctive kind of value, this gives one a value-based relation to the past: a past that might otherwise seem to stand in relation to one's own life as nothing but an eternal void. Just as the forward-looking dimension of participation in a tradition undercuts the sense of the future after one's death as representing nothing more than an eternity of nonexistence, so too the backward-looking dimension undercuts this same sense in relation to the time before one's birth. By giving one a role to play as part of a custodial chain of value, the backward-looking dimension of tradition personalizes one's relation to the past and enhances the perceived significance of one's existence. We might say that, in its forward-looking dimension, participation in a tradition diminishes the perceived significance of one's death, while in the backward-looking dimension it enhances the perceived significance of one's life.

These reflections help give content to the idea that participation in a tradition enables people to feel part of something that is larger than themselves. They help to explain what exactly might be meant by saying this. They also help to explain why the desire to feel part of something larger than oneself, understood in this way, should be a powerful one for many people.

VI

At the beginning of this paper, I said that I wanted to investigate the force of traditional reasons, with an eye toward evaluating the reductive dilemma and the form of skepticism about the normative significance of tradition that it appears to support. I also suggested that such an investigation might help to illuminate questions about people's attitudes toward the past and the future and the role of those attitudes in human life. I have now identified a total of twelve different considerations that may speak in favor of adherence to a tradition. These include the seven considerations that I earlier labeled *convention, habit, wisdom, guidance, value, loyalty,* and *integrity*. They also include five time-related considerations. Participation in a tradition may help to compensate for our lack of control over our mobility in time, it may enable us to domesticate time, it may assure us of our own reality as temporally extended creatures and, by incorporating us into a custodial chain designed to preserve things (other than ourselves) that we value, it may help to enhance the perceived significance of our lives and diminish the perceived significance of our deaths. All of this goes to show, I believe, that the reductive dilemma fails in the case of tradition, and that we should reject the form of skepticism about tradition that is embodied in that dilemma. Acting on traditional reasons is not a matter of doing something simply because people have done the same thing in the past. But neither is it a matter of acting on reasons that derive solely from certain abstract values, principles, or ideals. As we have seen, many of the considerations that speak in favor of adherence to a tradition essentially depend on the existence of the tradition as a collaborative enterprise involving many people over multiple generations. The actual existence of the tradition gives the participants reasons that they would not otherwise have, and which nonparticipants may not share. Tradition is indeed a normative notion.

Several points of clarification are in order. First, my enumeration of this list of twelve distinct considerations should not be taken to suggest that the factors I have listed are entirely independent of one another. To the contrary, I have pointed out in the course of my discussion a number of ways in which these factors may interact with or reinforce one another. I present them as a list of separate considerations for analytic purposes only.

Second, nothing in what I have said is meant to imply that all human beings have the impulses that make participation in a tradition seem compelling, still less that every person either does or should participate in one tradition or another. I believe that participation in a tradition is a very common way of addressing some profound and widespread human concerns, but I make no claims of universality either on behalf of those concerns or on behalf of participation in a tradition.

Third, the list I have presented is not meant to be exhaustive. There may be other considerations, in addition to those I have mentioned, that speak in favor of participation in a tradition as well.

Fourth, I do not mean to suggest that all the considerations I have mentioned apply with equal force to all traditions or to all of the participants in those traditions. Individuals vary in their susceptibility to some of the considerations I have discussed, and traditions vary in their strength, resources, and capacity to fulfill the diverse functions I have enumerated. Nor is the robustness of any individual tradition likely to be invariant over time.

Fifth, although I have emphasized some of the conservative dimensions of traditions, that is, their role in preserving values and establishing rituals and routines that endure over generations, it would be a mistake to think of any tradition as completely fixed and invariant. On the contrary, all traditions change over time and new generations always find ways to modify a traditional legacy in light of changing circumstances and outlooks. Fixity in one area of practice and belief may go hand-in-hand with significant change in other areas. In general, every tradition must strike a balance between continuity and change. If a tradition is too rigid and resistant to change, then it may lose its capacity to speak to the needs, interests, and convictions of new generations, and to help them engage with the novel circumstances and predicaments that they will inevitably face. If, on the other hand, the tradition is too quick to change, or too willing to dispense with older forms of practice, then it risks forfeiting the features that make participation in a tradition seem attractive in the first place. It is a truism that the traditions that are most likely to endure are those that develop successful techniques for balancing continuity and change.

Sixth, although I have spoken at times of the benefits or advantages that traditions make available to their participants, I do not mean to suggest that these advantages should be understood in narrowly self-interested terms. Among the advantages I have mentioned, for example, is the fact that traditions normally embody and perpetuate a range of values and principles, and provide guidance about how to interpret these values and principles and apply them to the concrete circumstances of daily life. To be sure, I have also emphasized that valuing things other than ourselves can help us in various ways to flourish, so the fact that traditions are repositories of value may itself enable them to provide their adherents with eudaimonistic benefits. Still, this does not imply either that the values and principles that a tradition embodies are themselves reducible to values or principles of self-interest, or that the adherents who subscribe to those values and principles are moved by the eudaimonistic advantages they afford.

Seventh, in enumerating the various considerations that may speak in favor of adherence to a tradition, I have not meant to suggest that the participants in a tradition normally have all of these considerations in view when they treat the tradition as a source of reasons for action. As I have said, to subscribe to a tradition just is, in part, to treat the fact that the tradition calls for a certain act as being, other things equal, a reason in favor of performing that act. I have been trying to identify some of the features of traditions that help to explain why people are disposed to treat them as having this kind of practical authority. But in enumerating such features, I do not mean to imply that the individuals who respond to traditional reasons have these features immediately in view or even that they could articulate the features in question if asked. Individual adherents may in fact be able to say little by way of offering reasons for their own actions beyond saying that what they did was what was called for by the tradition. Still, as participants in the tradition they see it as a source of normative authority—that is, of reasons to act in certain ways—and the question I have been discussing is why this should be so.

Eighth, in addressing this question, I have tried to explain why the fact that some act is called for by a tradition to which one subscribes may count as a consideration in favor of doing it. This leaves many other questions unanswered. For example, it does not tell us whether traditional reasons can ever be binding or obligatory. Nor does it tell us what exactly a person's relation to a tradition must be in order for the tradition to be reason-giving for that person. These are important questions, and they deserve careful investigation. But similar questions arise about values in general, and the mere fact that such questions arise does not undermine the normativity either of value or of tradition.

Ninth, although I have discussed some of the advantages that participation in a tradition makes available to individual adherents, we should not overlook the potential social and political advantages of widespread

THE NORMATIVITY OF TRADITION

adherence to a tradition. The successful entrenchment within a society of a tradition that supports humane values may help the society to realize those values, may make it easier for the society to secure various public goods, and may contribute to the political stability of the society.

Finally, I do not mean to idealize or romanticize traditions. Traditions are not all equally admirable, and even the best traditions have their disadvantages. At worst, the (perceived) values that a tradition perpetuates may be misguided or noxious, and the influence it exerts in human affairs may be destructive, oppressive, or in other ways deplorable. A tradition may reinforce social hierarchy, serve the interests of élites at the expense of others, stifle freedom and creativity, place obstacles in the way of social mobility, and make ideals of equality more difficult to achieve. Even a generally benign tradition may at times tend to inhibit desirable forms of change. I have enumerated a large number of considerations that speak in favor of adherence to a tradition, but this should not be taken as a blanket endorsement of all traditions or as a statement of unqualified enthusiasm about all aspects of participation in a tradition. The importance of tradition should not blind us to the deficiencies of particular traditions or to the characteristic disadvantages of participation in any tradition.

On the other hand, the various considerations I have mentioned demonstrate that it would be a mistake to take an unduly dismissive attitude toward tradition as such or to view participation in a tradition as amounting to nothing more than a form of blind conservatism. Most of us do in fact participate in traditions of various kinds, and tradition plays a profound, complex, and wide-ranging role in human life. I have tried to shed light on some aspects of that role, and in so doing to demonstrate the importance of taking tradition seriously.

VII

Before concluding, let me comment briefly on the implications of my argument for the questions of political morality that I mentioned at the beginning of this essay. The failure of the reductive dilemma implies that, unlike "cultural reasons," traditional reasons are normative reasons that are not reducible without loss to other kinds of normative reasons. Although values and principles are important aspects of most cultures, the reasons they generate derive from those values and principles themselves, and not from the fact of their acceptance within a culture. By contrast, I have argued that traditional reasons depend for much of their normative force on the actual existence of the traditions within which they arise.[5] It follows, I believe, that a liberal society that is concerned to accommodate normative diversity needs to pay special attention to diversity with respect to tradition. Contemporary liberal philosophers tend to characterize normative diversity as diversity with respect to people's *conceptions of the good* or *comprehensive moral, religious, and philosophical doctrines.* Insofar as these terms of art are intended as umbrella terms covering all forms of normative diversity, they may be taken by stipulation to include reasons deriving from participation in a tradition. Yet the nontechnical meaning of these phrases makes them less than ideally suited to capture the normative force of traditional reasons, for they suggest forms of normative diversity that consist primarily in differences of individual conviction. By contrast, we have seen that the normative force of traditional reasons essentially depends on the fact that traditions are collaborative enterprises involving many people over multiple generations. And the diversity of traditions is a multifaceted phenomenon, comprising differences of practice, ritual, historical memory, and collective aspiration no less than differences of doctrine or individual conviction. In short, one consequence of acknowledging the multiplicity of traditions as a species of normative diversity is to remind us that normative diversity is neither a purely individualistic nor a purely doxastic phenomenon. This is, I believe, the grain of truth in the appeal to "cultural reasons." It may not have any very immediate or very dramatic consequences for liberal theory. I do not believe, for example, that it supports the establishment of a special regime of rights, on the cultural rights model, to accommodate the diversity of traditions. Still, it is an important point to bear in mind when thinking about the forms of accommodation and mutual understanding that a liberal society will want to encourage.

5. At this point a defender of cultural reasons might propose that they are best understood simply as traditional reasons in my sense, so that my arguments for the normativity of tradition, rather than undermining the normativity of culture, actually reinstate it. If, as this proposal asserts, cultural reasons are stipulated to be nothing over and above traditional reasons, then of course I waive my reservations about the normativity of culture. But culture is normally understood to include all forms of group thought and practice, including both normative materials—such as values, ideals, principles and, indeed, traditions—and nonnormative materials. My argument has been that, when culture is understood in this way, then the mere fact that something is part of a culture is not—and is not normally seen as—a reason for doing it. If our concern is to accommodate normative diversity, then we should focus on the distinctively normative dimensions of human cultures—such as the values, ideals, and traditions that they endorse or embody—and avoid any suggestion that merely being part of a culture in itself confers some kind of normative standing.

Acknowledgments

This paper was presented as a keynote address at the 3rd Annual Conference of the Northwestern Society for Ethical Theory and Political Philosophy in April, 2009. Versions of the paper were also presented to philosophy department colloquia at Brown and the University of Virginia, to my Fall 2008 graduate seminar at NYU, and to a meeting of the Mid-Atlantic Reading Group in Ethics (MARGE). I am grateful to all of these audiences for helpful discussion. I owe special thanks to William FitzPatrick, who served as commentator on the paper at Northwestern. And I am particularly indebted to Jerry Cohen, who provided encouragement as well as valuable written comments, and whose recent death is a source of great sadness.

I 2

The Good of Toleration

Tolerance is often said to be a puzzling or paradoxical value. Within the covers of a single edited volume,[1] for example, David Heyd describes it as an "elusive" virtue, while Thomas Scanlon speaks of the "difficulty" of tolerance and George Fletcher of its "instability." Bernard Williams even goes so far as to suggest that it may be an "impossible" virtue. In this essay, I will explain why tolerance has been seen as an especially problematic value. But the apparently puzzling character of tolerance will not be my primary focus, nor will I attempt directly to dissolve the various puzzles and paradoxes that have preoccupied many writers on the subject.

The appearance of paradox arises in particularly acute form when one tries to provide a general justification of tolerance: that is, a general argument as to why people ought to be tolerant of others. Important as the issue of justification is, however, I will concentrate most of my attention

---

1. David Heyd (ed.), *Toleration: An Elusive Virtue* (Princeton, NJ: Princeton University Press, 1996).

on a slightly different issue. The question that concerns me is the question of what exactly is good about toleration, or, to put it another way, why so many people consider it to be an important value in its own right.[2] What features of the practice of toleration enable it to attract the allegiance of its supporters? Clearly, this question is closely related to the question of justification, since any attempted justification will represent toleration as being good in some respect, and any account of the good of toleration might in principle be taken to provide a reason why people ought to be tolerant. However, questions about the good of toleration are in one way less ambitious than the question of its justification, because the features of toleration that enable it to earn the allegiance of its supporters may not suffice to justify it to others. At the same time, attempts to provide a general justification of tolerance sometimes neglect the less ambitious question with which I am primarily concerned. In attempting to provide reasons, acceptable to all, for endorsing a regime of toleration, they sometimes neglect the question of why some people find toleration an especially good or valuable feature of a society.

So I want to distinguish between the question of *the justification of toleration* and the question of *the good of toleration*. Once this distinction is drawn, however, the answer to the second question may seem obvious. In a pluralistic society, after all, a regime of tolerance is, almost by definition, the only alternative we have to perpetual conflict and strife. If that is right, then the reason why tolerance is good may seem straightforward. It is good because a peaceful and harmonious society is impossible without it.

This is an essentially instrumental argument, and it in no way diminishes the argument's importance to observe that it does not actually address the question I have posed. What interests me is the fact that, while recognizing the evident power and importance of the instrumental case for tolerance, many people also regard tolerance as an intrinsically important value: one whose significance is not limited to its instrumental advantages. My question about the good of toleration is the question of why exactly this should be so? The puzzling or paradoxical features of tolerance serve to sharpen this question, and so I do want to discuss them. But, as I have said, it may be possible to illuminate the good of toleration without fully dissolving the paradoxes that arise when one tries to provide a general justification of tolerance.

2. In keeping with much contemporary philosophical writing on the subject, I will use the terms *tolerance* and *toleration* interchangeably. This represents a slight departure from ordinary usage, but does not, I believe, affect any issue of substance.

Before I address the main issue with which I am concerned, I need to explain what I take to be included under the heading of *tolerance* or *toleration*. There is, of course, an enormous literature on the subject, and in that literature one finds characterizations of toleration that differ along a number of significant dimensions. I will begin by reviewing some of the most important of these differences, with the aim of situating my own discussion in relation to the existing literature.

First, some writers define the attitude of toleration fairly narrowly, so that one does not count as tolerating a belief or practice unless one strongly disapproves of or objects to it. In this spirit, Bernard Williams says that the need for religious toleration arises when one group believes that another is "blasphemously, disastrously, obscenely wrong." Toleration, Williams says, "is required only for the intolerable."[3] Similarly, though less dramatically, Thomas Scanlon interprets tolerance as "an attitude that requires us to hold in check certain feelings of opposition and disapproval."[4] Others, however, take a broader view, insisting that one need not disapprove of a belief or practice in order to count as being tolerant of it. According to this view, it is enough that one does not oneself share the belief or participate in the practice.

Second, most political philosophers think of toleration as a distinctively liberal value that is associated with such familiar individual rights as the right to freedom of religion, conscience, speech, and association. However, some writers take a wider historical perspective, and are prepared to count as an instance of toleration any institutional regime that makes it possible for people with different values and outlooks to live together peacefully. Thus, for example, Michael Walzer takes toleration to consist in any of a wide variety of arrangements that have made possible "the peaceful coexistence of groups of people with different histories, cultures, and identities."[5] Similarly, Benjamin Kaplan, in his fascinating historical account of toleration in early modern Europe, emphasizes that his concern is with toleration understood as a "form of behavior: peaceful coexistence with others who adhered to a different religion."[6] Accordingly, he is prepared to count as an instance of toleration any

3. Bernard Williams, "Toleration: An Impossible Virtue?," in Heyd, *op. cit.*, pp. 18–27, at p. 18.
4. Thomas Scanlon, "The Difficulty of Tolerance," in Heyd, *op. cit.*, pp. 226–239, at p. 226.
5. Michael Walzer, *On Toleration* (New Haven, CT: Yale University Press, 1997), p. 2.
6. Benjamin Kaplan, *Divided by Faith: Religious Conflict and the Practice of Toleration in Early Modern Europe* (Cambridge, MA: Harvard University Press, 2007), p. 8.

arrangement that "enabled people of different faiths to live together in the same towns and villages."[7]

Third, many writers have noted that, on one interpretation at least, the concept of toleration is asymmetrical. In other words, it is the prerogative of the strong to tolerate the weak, but the weak are not in a position to tolerate the strong. This asymmetrical connotation of the term was in fact crucial to the emergence of toleration as a political value during and after the European Wars of Religion. What toleration required was that religious majorities should, within limits—extremely narrow limits by contemporary standards—tolerate religious minorities, but those minorities were not granted equal status, and they certainly could not presume to tolerate the majority. The asymmetrical character of toleration has exposed it to criticism since at least the eighteenth-century: from writers like Goethe, Kant, and Thomas Paine, no less than from contemporary figures like Herbert Marcuse[8] and Wendy Brown.[9] Goethe, for example, famously said that "to tolerate is to insult," and Paine said that "Toleration is not the opposite of intolerance but the counterpart of it. Both are despotisms. The one assumes to itself the right of withholding liberty of conscience and the other of granting it."[10] But although some continue to regard tolerance as being, in view of its asymmetrical character, a limited virtue at best, many others have, in effect, reinterpreted the idea so that it is understood to apply symmetrically to groups and individuals of differing size, strength, and power. Each of us is called upon to tolerate everyone else. It is this notion of toleration, rather than the asymmetrical or hierarchical one, that most contemporary liberal thinkers mean to be endorsing. However, the tension between the two interpretations continues to cast a shadow over discussions of toleration. This is apparent, for example, in Rainer Forst's contrast between the "dark and pessimistic story"[11] of the "permission conception"[12]

---

7. *Ibid.*, p. 162.
8. Herbert Marcuse, "Repressive Tolerance," in R.P. Wolff, B. Moore, and H. Marcuse, *A Critique of Pure Tolerance* (Boston: Beacon Press, 1969), pp. 95–137.
9. Wendy Brown, *Regulating Aversion: Tolerance in the Age of Identity and Empire* (Princeton, NJ: Princeton University Press, 2006).
10. Both quoted in Kaplan, *op. cit.*, pp. 8–9.
11. Rainer Forst, "Toleration and Democracy," unpublished typescript presented to the Colloquium in Legal, Political, and Social Philosophy at the NYU Law School on November 8, 2007, p. 1.
12. *Ibid.*, p. 5.

of toleration and the "bright and optimistic"[13] story of the "respect conception."[14] According to the permission conception, "[t]oleration means that the authority gives qualified permission to the members of the minority to live according to their beliefs on the condition that the minority accepts the dominant position of the authority."[15] According to the respect conception, "democratic citizens respect each other as legal and political equals even though they differ greatly in their ethical-religious views about the good and true way of life."[16] Forst argues that it would be a mistake to suppose that the respect conception has simply superseded the permission conception. He believes instead, and not implausibly, that versions of these contrasting stories continue to be reflected in contemporary thought and practice.

Fourth, most writers recognize that there is a distinction between tolerance as a social practice and tolerance as a personal virtue or attitude. As a practice, tolerance is defined and enforced by a legal or institutional regime. As a personal virtue or attitude, it is instead a feature of individual character. Although some theorists of toleration are more interested in the practice and others are more interested in the attitude, there is a significant question, which is recognized as such by many, about the relation between tolerance as a practice and tolerance as an attitude.

These four distinctions make it easier to appreciate the reasons why toleration has seemed to many people to be an elusive or even paradoxical value. One seeming paradox—we may call it the paradox of suppressed disapproval—arises in particularly acute form for those who concentrate on toleration as a personal attitude and take it to consist, roughly, in a disposition not to interfere with beliefs and practices of which one strongly disapproves. For those who take this position, there appears to be a dilemma. On the one hand, an unwillingness to interfere with the beliefs and practices of others will not count as tolerant at all unless it is accompanied by disapproval of those beliefs and practices. So, for example, a pluralist about value who regards many different ways of life as good, and who for that reason is happy to accommodate a diverse range of beliefs and practices, will not count as tolerant according to this view. Nor will a skeptic who is equally hospitable to diverse values because he or she does not believe that any of them has a distinctive claim to the truth. On the other hand, if we restrict ourselves to

13. *Ibid.*, p. 1.
14. *Ibid.*, p. 9.
15. *Ibid.*, p. 5.
16. *Ibid.*, p. 9.

cases in which the agent deeply disapproves of the practices that are candidates for toleration, then it is unclear why it should be a virtue to tolerate them. After all, it would not be a virtue to tolerate, say, murder or assault, and so it is not obvious why it should be considered desirable to tolerate other forms of behavior that elicit our strong disapproval. The upshot is that many of the cases in which people are willing to accommodate one another are not properly thought of as instances of tolerance, and many genuine instances of tolerance are cases in which accommodation is unjustified. Faced with this dilemma, the scope for justified tolerance can seem to shrink to the vanishing point.

A second seeming paradox, which I will call the paradox of foundational tolerance, arises for those who are concerned to provide a justification of the practice of toleration. As we have seen, there are powerful instrumental arguments to be made on behalf of a regime of toleration. Powerful though they are, however, those arguments, like all instrumental arguments, have their limitations. They are compelling only so long as the practice of toleration remains an effective means of securing the advertised advantages. In circumstances where its capacity to secure those advantages lapses, these arguments lose their force. In particular, if one group in a pluralistic society becomes substantially more numerous and powerful than the others, the members of the ascendant group may feel that they can accomplish more through intolerant policies than they can by adhering to a regime of toleration. The cost to them of suppressing dissent, they may feel, would be minimal and the gains significant. Under these conditions, instrumental considerations may not suffice to tilt the balance of reasons in favor of toleration. So instrumental justifications of toleration, powerful though they are in many circumstances, extend only so far. Yet many people believe that practices of toleration are justified as a matter of principle and not merely on instrumental grounds.

The paradox of foundational tolerance arises in the attempt to provide such a principled justification. The obvious strategy—it may look like the only strategy—is to identify some moral premises from which principles of toleration can be derived. But if one does this, then it seems that one is joining the very argument with respect to which one was advocating a tolerant stance. For one is perforce defending the practice of toleration by appealing to what is, inevitably, just one moral outlook among the many that are represented in the society, and the question is why that one outlook should occupy a privileged justificatory position? Those who advocate other outlooks may reject the proposed regime of toleration, despite the protections it offers them, on the ground that, at a deeper level, it is rooted in, and in that sense favors, the very outlook they oppose. This might not be a problem for anyone attempting to defend a version of the "permission conception."

But for liberals who seek to embed practices of toleration within a broader conception of a society of equals, this result has often seemed embarrassing. It threatens to turn liberalism itself into just "another sectarian doctrine,"[17] to borrow Rawls's memorable phrase. So the "paradox of foundational tolerance" might be expressed as follows: On the one hand, it is hard to see how a regime of toleration can be given a principled justification without appealing to *some* principle. Yet, on the other hand, any particular principle to which one might appeal is likely to be contested in a pluralistic society. If one appeals to such a principle, then partisans of opposing principles are likely to claim that a regime of toleration that is justified in this way is a sham. Although superficially tolerant of diverse outlooks, it is, at a more fundamental level, biased in favor of a particular moral outlook which supports that regime for its own "sectarian" reasons. It is in much this spirit, I take it, that defenders of conservative religious views sometimes argue that a regime of liberal toleration is really just an expression of a kind of "secular humanism" that they reject.

Bernard Williams' solution to this problem is to deny that toleration as a practice does rest on a particular moral value or principle. Toleration as a *virtue*, Williams believes, can only avoid the paradox of suppressed disapproval if it is rooted in a broadly Kantian conception of the value of autonomy, for only a belief that it is good for individuals to be autonomous makes it possible coherently to think that it is valuable to allow the misguided beliefs or practices of others to flourish. But if the *practice* of toleration rests ultimately on the value of individual autonomy, then it is indeed vulnerable to the paradox of foundational tolerance. As Williams puts it, the values of autonomy themselves

> . . . may be rejected, and to the extent that toleration rests on those values, then toleration will also be rejected. The practice of toleration cannot be based on a value such as individual autonomy and hope to escape from substantive disagreements about the good. This really is a contradiction, because it is only a substantive view of goods such as autonomy that could yield the value that is expressed by the practices of toleration.[18]

To avoid the contradiction, liberals could of course simply concede that they are appealing to the contested value of autonomy, but then, Williams

17. John Rawls, "Justice as Fairness: Political not Metaphysical," *Philosophy & Public Affairs* 14(1985), pp. 223–251, at p. 246.
18. Williams, *op. cit.*, p. 25.

says, they will not have given anyone who does not share that value a reason to accept the practice of toleration. What prevents the paradox of foundational tolerance from being fatal to the justification of toleration as a practice, Williams concludes, is the fact that the practice, unlike the virtue, need not rest on the value of autonomy. Instead, he argues,

> …the practice of toleration has to be sustained not so much by a pure principle resting on a value of autonomy as by a wider and more mixed range of resources. Those resources include an active skepticism against fanaticism and the pretensions of its advocates; conviction about the manifest evils of toleration's absence; and, quite certainly, power, to provide Hobbesian reminders to the more extreme groups that they will have to settle for coexistence.[19]

Rawls's idea of an "overlapping consensus"[20] can be thought of as providing a similar solution to the problem of foundational tolerance. Although Rawls applies his idea to the justification of liberal principles of justice in general and not solely to the principle or practice of toleration, he makes clear that toleration has a central place among the liberal values that an overlapping consensus would support. Indeed, he says that the second of the "two fundamental questions" to which his "political liberalism" is addressed, and to which the idea of an overlapping consensus helps supply the answer, concerns "the grounds of toleration understood in a general way."[21] And he illustrates the idea of an overlapping consensus by contrasting it with a hypothetical agreement on the principle of toleration reached on the basis of views like those held by Catholics and Protestants in the sixteenth century. Such an agreement, he says, would be a "mere modus vivendi,"[22] in which toleration was accepted solely on prudential grounds or on the basis of self- or group-interest. An overlapping consensus, by contrast, has a different character. When such a consensus is in place, then toleration and other liberal principles are not justified prudentially but neither are they justified by appeal to a liberal conception of autonomy or to any other "comprehensive moral doctrine." Instead, they are derived from shared ideas that are implicit in the public political culture of a democratic society and which proponents of

19. *Ibid.*, pp. 26–27.
20. See John Rawls, "The Idea of an Overlapping Consensus," *Oxford Journal of Legal Studies*, 7(1987): 1–25, and *Political Liberalism* (New York: Columbia University Press, 1993), Lecture Four.
21. *Political Liberalism*, p. 47.
22. *Political Liberalism*, p. 148; see also "The Idea of an Overlapping Consensus," p. 11.

all reasonable doctrines can accept. The result, Rawls believes, is a principled rather than an instrumental defense of liberal values and institutions, because each of the participants in the consensus has moral reasons
drawn from within his or her comprehensive doctrine for affirming the
shared ideas and the liberal arrangements they support. But sectarianism
is avoided because there is no one comprehensive doctrine that all of the
participants in the consensus affirm or which plays a privileged role in
justifying liberal arrangements.[23]

This suggests a solution to the paradox of foundational tolerance
that differs in one respect from Williams's, inasmuch as all of the diverse
views represented within a Rawlsian overlapping consensus are understood as providing *moral* reasons of one kind or another for accepting
liberal arrangements. But Rawls shares Williams' conviction that it
would be fatal to the case for liberal practices if their defense were to rest
exclusively on an appeal to a Kantian conception of autonomy. He also
shares Williams's view that the preferred alternative is to demonstrate
that those practices can be supported by a "wider and more mixed range
of resources," even if, in Rawls's view, the resources in question are all
supposed to be moral in character.

The two paradoxes I have mentioned—the paradox of suppressed
disapproval and the paradox of foundational tolerance—are responsible
for much of the impression that toleration is an especially perplexing or
elusive value. As I have said, my aim in this paper will not be to dissolve
either of these paradoxes, nor will I attempt to provide a general justification for either the practice or the attitude of toleration. My aim will
instead be to consider what it is about toleration that makes it seem to
many people to be an attractive value or ideal in its own right. To make
this more precise, let me begin by locating my inquiry in relation to the
various distinctions I have mentioned.

My question will be what it is about living under an effective regime
of toleration that seems attractive to people. In speaking of a regime of

---

23. Rawls also says that, by making the justification of liberal institutions independent
    not merely of any particular religious view but also of any particular moral or philo-
    sophical doctrine, an overlapping consensus represents an extension of the principle
    of toleration from religion to philosophy itself. He writes: "Were justice as fair-
    ness to make an overlapping consensus possible it would complete and extend the
    movement of thought that began three centuries ago with the gradual acceptance
    of the principle of toleration and led to the nonconfessional state and equal liberty
    of conscience...To apply the principles of toleration to philosophy itself is to leave
    to citizens themselves to settle the questions of religion, philosophy, and morals in
    accordance with views they freely affirm" (*Political Liberalism*, p. 154).

toleration, I have in mind distinctively liberal practices and institutions. I assume that the general character of a liberal regime is familiar to everyone and requires no special explanation, except to say that I take the ideal of toleration informing these regimes to be symmetrical rather than asymmetrical or hierarchical in character. Although there are variations among different liberal regimes, and although there is room for disagreement at the margins about the proper form for such a regime to take, I will not address these disagreements. Nor will I compare liberal regimes with other arrangements that may make peaceful coexistence possible in some circumstances, and that some would, therefore, consider instances of toleration in a broad sense. I think there is much to be learned from studying the wide range of practices that have made peaceful coexistence among contending groups possible in different times and places. But I assume that liberal toleration comprises a distinctive set of arrangements that extend beyond mere *de facto* coexistence, and I want to consider why such arrangements have seemed to many people to be valuable in their own right. It is possible that the good of liberal toleration, so understood, has also been made available by other practices and arrangements in other times and places, though whether that is so and what it might show are not questions that I will explore.

My inquiry will straddle the distinction between toleration as a social practice and tolerance as a personal virtue or attitude. My primary focus will be on the practice of liberal toleration, but I will be asking what makes that practice appealing to individuals, and in addressing this second question I will be saying something about individual attitudes. In both cases, however, I will construe liberal toleration relatively broadly, and will not take it to require or be defined in relation to feelings of disapproval. So far as the social practice is concerned, a regime of liberal toleration extends a set of privileges and protections to a wide range of beliefs and forms of conduct, and although some of those beliefs and forms of conduct will attract disapproval, the protected class is not restricted by definition to those that do. My discussion of personal attitudes, meanwhile, will focus on the question of what people find valuable about a regime of toleration so understood, and since the practice does not require feelings of disapproval it would be unduly exclusive to insist that the attitudes supporting the practice must involve disapproval.

There are additional reasons for preferring a broader rather than a narrower understanding of liberal toleration. First, to insist on linking toleration to disapproval can lead us to neglect the interesting and important relationships among toleration and other similar practices, such as practices of compromise, accommodation, and the acceptance of reasonable disagreement, for those practices are necessary even where people differ without disapproving of one another.[24] Here the historical concept of toleration, with its contingent history and penumbra of associations, may lead us astray. We may think of toleration as a *sui generis* value with origins in the Wars of Religion, rather than situating it within the wider context of liberal responses to disagreement. Toleration, in other words, is best seen as belonging to a range of values and practices, which, taken together, comprise the complex set of responses toward disagreement that are part of the normative repertoire of a liberal society.

Second, a broader notion of toleration allows for the fact that becoming less judgmental—less disapproving—is a way of becoming more tolerant.[25] By contrast, a narrow notion of toleration requires us to say, unhelpfully in my view, that becoming less judgmental is not a way of becoming more tolerant but rather a way of making tolerance unnecessary. Relatedly, a broader notion of toleration makes it easier to recognize that reflection on the diversity of human value and experience can serve as a resource to combat intolerant tendencies within oneself, by leading one to moderate or suspend one's unreflective attitudes of disapproval. On a broader conception, in other words, pluralistic conviction can be seen as encouraging and supporting tolerant attitudes rather than as offering an alternative to them or rendering them unnecessary.

Finally, if one is interested in the paradox of foundational tolerance, then there is yet another reason for preferring a broader to a narrower notion of liberal toleration. Or, at any rate, there is such a reason if one accepts the Rawls-Williams view about the form that a solution to the paradox must take. According to that view, as we have seen, the solution lies in the idea that a regime of toleration can be supported for different reasons by different people. If one accepts this view, then one will attach significance to any personal attitude that may reliably lead people to support such a regime. Both pluralistic and skeptical beliefs about the nature of the human good are likely to be included among these toleration-supporting attitudes, because either sort of belief may make people more likely to accept practices and ways of life that differ from their own. If this is correct, then a narrow definition that excludes any pluralism-based or skepticism-based acceptance of differing practices from counting as an instance of genuine tolerance is bound to seem misleading at best. Still,

24. On accommodation, see the important papers by Seana Shiffrin: "Paternalism, Unconscionability Doctrine, and Accommodation," *Philosophy & Public Affairs* 29(2000): 205–250, and "Egalitarianism, Choice-Sensitivity, and Accommodation," in R.J. Wallace, P. Pettit, S. Scheffler, and M. Smith, eds., *Reason and Value: Themes from the Moral Philosophy of Joseph Raz*, pp. 270–302.
25. See John Horton, "Toleration as a Virtue," in Heyd, *op. cit.*, pp. 28–43, at 37–38.

my aim is not to engage in a turf battle over the meaning of the word *tolerance*. The interesting questions, in my view, have to do with which social practices a just and liberal society needs in order to accommodate the phenomena of difference and disagreement, and which values and attitudes might help to support or stabilize those practices. My interest in these questions will shape my use of the terms *tolerance* and *toleration* in the ways that I have described, but narrower uses of those terms may be more appropriate for inquiries that have a different focus.

Moreover, despite my general preference for a relatively broad understanding of liberal toleration, my interpretation of the concept does incorporate one significant restriction, which derives from the historical association of the term *toleration* with the phenomena of religious diversity and religious conflict in particular. We now take the practice of liberal toleration to comprehend more than just religion, and for good reason. But in generalizing from the case of religious diversity, we should take care not to overgeneralize. One of the salient features of religious diversity is that it is a species of *normative diversity*, by which I mean diversity with respect to people's values, principles, and ideals. In this respect, it differs from diversity with respect to non-normative features of people, such as their age, physical or biological characteristics, or geographical location. Normative diversity poses special problems and can be the source of particularly intractable conflicts. At the same time, there are distinctive goods associated with the toleration or accommodation of normative diversity, and it is this sort of diversity to which I shall take our practices of toleration to be addressed. The historical emphasis on religious diversity is, from our perspective, too narrow, for religious diversity is not the only significant form of normative diversity. But it has historically been the most explosive—and in that respect the most important—form of normative diversity, and it is, therefore, no accident that practices of toleration emerged historically as a response to the phenomena of religious diversity and religious conflict in particular. In construing our practices of toleration as extending beyond this special but distinctively important case, I will nevertheless continue to interpret them as addressed to normative diversity rather than to diversity of all kinds.

I have distinguished the question I am concerned with, which is "What is it about living under an effective regime of toleration that seems good or attractive to many people?" from the more ambitious question of "What might justify and, in that sense, ground the practice of toleration?" My answer rests on the thought that there is something distinctively valuable about the types of relationship with other people that a regime of toleration encourages. This is a point that Thomas Scanlon has also made. Scanlon says that our reasons to value tolerance lie "in the relation with one's fellow citizens that tolerance makes possible."[26] Although he does not describe in detail the kind of relation he has in mind, the general idea seems to be that people in a tolerant society relate to each other "within a framework of mutual respect."[27] Tolerance expresses "a recognition of others" as being entitled to live as they choose and "to contribute to the definition of our society."[28] The intolerant alternative, Scanlon says, is to regard the standing of others as members of one's society as conditional on their sharing one's values, and this involves "a form of alienation from one's fellow citizens."[29]

I think that Scanlon is right about this, but I don't think that his remarks provide an exhaustive account of the relational goods that are made available within a tolerant, pluralistic society. In the space that remains, I will develop a different (though not incompatible) characterization of the type of relationship among citizens that a tolerant society encourages, with the aim of calling attention to another way in which toleration is a good.

A regime of toleration is a response to normative diversity, and so to the important role played in human life by values, ideals, and principles. For backhanded evidence of the importance of that role we have only to reflect on the extent, ferocity, and persistence of the conflicts that have arisen throughout human history among those who have professed allegiance to differing values or ideals. As Rawls observes, "[t]he most intractable struggles... are confessedly for the sake of the highest things: for religion, for philosophical views of the world, and for different moral conceptions of the good."[30] This may seem surprising. One might expect that the most profound and intense conflicts would arise not from normative disagreement but simply from brute struggles for power or for the control of scarce resources. Yet even when people do engage in battles for power or resources, there is a strong tendency for them to present and to experience those battles as involving clashes of values or principles and, as Rawls observes, such clashes can be the most difficult of all to resolve. Indeed, after making the comment I have quoted, Rawls continues:

> We should find it remarkable that, so deeply opposed in these
> ways, just cooperation among free and equal citizens is possible at
> all. In fact, historical experience suggests that it rarely is.[31]

26. Scanlon, *op. cit.*, p. 230.
27. *Ibid.*, p. 231.
28. *Ibid.*
29. *Ibid.*, p. 232.
30. Rawls, *Political Liberalism*, p. 4.
31. *Ibid.*

As an institutional response to the importance in human life of values, ideals, and principles, a regime of toleration must maintain a delicate balance between two complementary ways of understanding the relevant form of importance. On the one hand, what matters for many institutional purposes is simply the fact that the values, principles, and ideals are important *to* their adherents. Yet, on the other hand, a regime of toleration depends for its effectiveness on an appreciation of the fact that, for the adherents themselves, the authority of the values and principles to which they adhere is precisely *not* perceived as deriving from its importance to them. Quite the reverse: for the adherents, it is the authority of the values that explains why they attach so much importance to them. In seeing the values and principles as important, in other words, they experience themselves as responding to normative ideas with independent authority, and it is this very fact that gives the values and principles their peculiarly important role in the adherents' lives. So a regime of toleration must be sensitive both to the internal role and to the outer-directedness of our normative convictions: both to their internal importance and to their perceived external authority.

The fact that our values and principles have this dual aspect helps to explain why intolerance is both so tempting for its perpetrators and so injurious to its victims. Intolerance is tempting because tolerance, unless justified on purely instrumental grounds, seems to concede authority to values and principles that, by hypothesis, one rejects.[32] Benjamin Kaplan says that, if one surveys the incidents of popular religious violence in early modern Europe, "a striking fact emerges: an extraordinary number of them were triggered by just three types of event: processions, holiday celebrations, and funerals."[33] Kaplan argues that it was the public nature of these events that made them "flashpoints" or triggers for religious violence. Their public character made them potentially explosive partly because, for Europeans of that time, it seemed that

... when a religious group enacted its beliefs in a public space, it was claiming possession not just of that space but of the entire

---

32. As I have said, I construe tolerance broadly enough that it need not always involve disapproval of the values that are tolerated. Yet I am here supposing that one can tolerate only those values that one rejects, and this may seem inconsistent with a broad construal of tolerance. However, even on the broad construal, one tolerates only those values that one does not oneself accept. In that sense, toleration always involves rejection, even if it does not always involve disapproval. Moreover, it is consistent with the broad construal to hold that intolerance generally becomes more tempting in proportion to the degree that one does disapprove of the relevant values and practices.
33. Kaplan, *op. cit.*, p. 78.

community, appropriating the authority to speak and act for everyone, and making those of other faiths accomplices in rituals they rejected or even abhorred.[34]

In other words, intolerance can seem irresistible if one thinks the only alternative is to concede authority to values one rejects or detests. By the same token, of course, intolerance is injurious to its victims in part because they too are, to one degree or another, constrained to defer to values they reject and to neglect values they accept. The temptations of intolerance and the injuries it imposes are two sides of the same coin. Both give evidence of the importance that people attach to the ability to order their lives with reference to values and principles they regard as authoritative. And both give evidence of how unbearable it can seem to concede authority to, let alone to be constrained or compelled to have one's life regulated by, values and principles that one rejects.

But why exactly should this be so unbearable? The explanation, presumably, turns on the importance of the functions that normative and evaluative convictions serve in people's lives. Consider three of the most significant of these functions. First, our values, principles, and ideals determine our deliberative priorities, by defining the ends that we think worth pursuing and the means by which we believe it is acceptable to pursue those ends. In so doing, they determine the kinds of consideration that we count as reasons for action. Second, our normative and evaluative convictions define commitments which, although not immutable, nevertheless endure over time and provide continuity amid the flux and contingency of daily experience. In this sense, they help to stabilize our selves. Finally, these same convictions define what we count as success or failure in our lives, and in so doing they shape our self-assessments and our experience of attitudes such as shame and pride that depend on those self-assessments.

Given that our normative and evaluative convictions serve these functions, it is not surprising that being prevented from acting in accordance with values one regards as authoritative, or being constrained to act in accordance with values that one rejects, should be perceived as a grave injury. By attacking the deliberative and motivational nexus via which our values are translated into actions, these forms of interference and constraint amount to a kind of assault on the self. Depending on their severity and effectiveness, they may compromise the integrity of our deliberations and the exercises of our agency, threaten our capacity to

34. *Ibid.*, p. 97.

lead lives that are successful by our own lights and, in extreme cases, they may even place in jeopardy the stability of our personalities over time.

In his brilliant critique of utilitarianism, Bernard Williams famously asked:

> ...how can a man, as a utilitarian agent, come to regard as one satisfaction among others, and a dispensable one, a project or attitude round which he has built his life, just because someone else's projects have so structured the causal scene that that is how the utilitarian sum comes out?

Answering his own rhetorical question, he continued,

> It is absurd to demand of such a man, when the sums come in from the utility network which the projects of others have in part determined, that he should just step aside from his own project and decision and acknowledge the decision which utilitarian calculation requires. It is to alienate him in a real sense from his actions and the source of his action in his own convictions. It is to make him into a channel between the input of everyone's projects, including his own, and an output of optimific decision; but this is to neglect the extent to which *his* actions and *his* decisions have to be seen as the actions and decisions which flow from the projects and attitudes with which he is most closely identified. It is thus, in the most literal sense, an attack on his integrity.[35]

Moral philosophers continue to disagree about the force of Williams' comments considered as an objection to utilitarianism. But it is striking that the accusation that he levels at utilitarianism in this passage seems to point precisely to what is most injurious about the effects of intolerance on its victims. By making it difficult or impossible for their actions and decisions to be seen as flowing from the projects and attitudes with which they are most closely identified, intolerance is, in the most literal sense, an attack on their integrity. And if, as I have been arguing, the injuries inflicted by intolerance on its victims are closely related to the temptations of intolerance for its perpetrators, then it seems to follow that, just as intolerance threatens the integrity of its victims, so too the perpetrators

---

35. Bernard Williams, "A Critique of Utilitarianism," in Smart and Williams (eds.), *Utilitarianism For and Against* (Cambridge, England: Cambridge University Press, 1973), pp. 77–150, at pp. 116–117.

of intolerance may perceive a willingness to tolerate others as a threat to their own integrity. In other words, the threat that intolerance poses to the integrity of its victims may be mirrored by the threat that tolerance poses to the integrity of the perpetrators. Although this may sound initially implausible, I believe that it is nevertheless true. As I have already suggested, the problem from the point of view of the perpetrators is that tolerating others, unless it is justified on purely instrumental grounds, seems to concede authority to values and principles which, by hypothesis, they reject. And such concessions may seem to them tantamount to the abandonment of their own values and principles, rendering them complicit in practices and ways of life that they do not accept and may well detest. In this way, the prospect of extending tolerance to others may indeed be perceived as a threat to their integrity.

Moreover, it would be wrong to assume that the perceived threat that tolerance poses to the integrity of the perpetrators is less severe than the threat that intolerance poses to the integrity of its victims. The persecutory zeal with which intolerance is frequently pursued suggests otherwise. And it is worth noting that there is one respect in which the threat to the integrity of the perpetrators may actually be more severe than the threat to the integrity of its victims. The victims are, after all, victims, and if intolerance compromises their ability to order their lives in accordance with values and principles that they accept, that is because of the way they have been treated by others, and not because they themselves have been unfaithful to those values. For the perpetrators, by contrast, any extension of tolerance to others would require a decision to defer to the authority of values and principles that they reject. For that reason, it may seem tantamount to a *betrayal* of their own values, rather than a mere failure to act in accordance with them, and as such a much graver compromise of their integrity.

A natural response to this line of thought is to challenge the claim that extending tolerance to others involves conceding or deferring to the authority of values that one rejects. For the extension of tolerance to other people to make sense, all that is required is that one should accept the legitimacy of *those people's* deferring to the perceived authority of the values and principles that they accept. There is no requirement that, in addition, one must oneself defer to the authority of the same values and principles, nor, therefore, is there any implication that one must abandon or betray one's own values and principles.

But this reply, natural though it is, does not do justice to the complaint of the intolerant. And for the very same reason, as I will later argue, it obscures some of the distinctive value of toleration. The problem, in both cases, is that it understates the extent of the transformation in the relations among citizens that a regime of liberal toleration seeks to accomplish. Absent a regime of toleration, the fact that other people take themselves to have value-based reasons for acting in certain ways gives me reason to modify my own behavior only insofar as the fact that they see themselves as having those reasons affects my prospects of achieving my aims. But a regime of liberal toleration requires that we treat the claims of others to act on reasons that they perceive as authoritative as providing us with non-instrumental reasons to modify our own behavior. In this way, it requires us to treat the conflicting claims, values, and principles of other people as an independent source of reasons for action for us. That is why liberal tolerance seems paradoxical. How can values that one rejects provide one with (non-instrumental) reasons for action, especially with reasons for modifying conduct that is rooted in values that one accepts? But it is not the paradoxical character of liberal toleration that interests me at the moment. What interests me is the fact that, in requiring us to treat the value-based claims of others as reasons for modifying our own claims and conduct, there is a sense in which a liberal regime does ask us to concede normative authority to the values and principles of others. The lament of the intolerant is, therefore, correct; they are being asked to defer to the authority of values and principles that they reject.

It may be said in reply that what the intolerant are being asked to treat as reason-giving, and in that sense authoritative, are not the actual values and principles of other people. What they are being asked to treat as authoritative is merely the psychological fact that those people attach importance to their values and principles. But this is not quite right either. It is true, of course, that the intolerant are not required to accept the truth of the values and principles that they reject. So there is a kind of authority that they need not concede. It is also true that they are asked to concede authority to values and principles that they reject only insofar as other people do perceive them as authoritative. To put it another way, they are asked to defer to the perceived authority of the values and principles, not to their actual authority. But the intolerant may reasonably protest that deference to the perceived authority of the values involves a kind of normative bootstrapping that makes it tantamount to a grant of actual authority. One may treat the values of other people as reason-giving only because those people perceive them as authoritative, but in so doing one is nevertheless conceding a measure of actual authority to the values. That is, one is treating them as sources of normative reasons that bear on one's own actions. If, for example, an employee's religion declares that a certain day is a holiday which is to be devoted to prayer and reflection, and if the employee asks her employer for the day off so that she can observe the holiday, then the employer is being asked to guide his conduct in light of reasons deriving from the pronouncements of the employee's religion. In this sense, to defer to the perceived authority of the values is to grant them actual authority. That is because what *deference* amounts to in this context is treating the values of others as sources of reasons to act or refrain from acting in certain ways oneself. Granted, the reasons one acknowledges are not the same as the reasons recognized by the adherents of those values. The adherents see themselves as having reasons to act in ways called for by the values, that is, to participate in the relevant value-based practices. The tolerant, by contrast, see themselves as having reasons to accommodate the value-based practices of the adherents, not to participate in those practices themselves. The employer, for example, sees himself as having reasons to accommodate his employee's wish to devote the holiday to prayer and reflection; he does not see himself as having reasons to engage in prayer and reflection as well. But the intolerant are not wrong to see even this limited and derivative grant of authority as implicating them in the values of others, nor are there a priori grounds for insisting that they must be mistaken if they see this as offending against their own values. So the claim that toleration is a threat to their integrity cannot be dismissed.

If this is right, and it is not unreasonable for the intolerant to perceive toleration as a threat to their integrity, then the prospects for a stable regime of toleration may seem bleak. Echoing Rawls we may say: it seems remarkable that such a thing is possible at all, and historical experience suggests that it rarely is.

This is not the end of the story, however. Rare or not, regimes of liberal toleration have been established and sustained in various societies. Each of these regimes has been imperfect, but all actual political practices and institutions are imperfect. What is surprising is not that they have been imperfect, but that they have been as successful as they have. One aspect of their success, as I have noted, has been their capacity to attract allegiance that is not grounded solely in instrumental considerations. Instead, many people who experience life under a regime of toleration come to regard it as an important value in its own right. In the best cases, a virtuous circle takes hold: practices of toleration come to be perceived by those who are subject to them as intrinsically good or worthy, which helps to stabilize those practices, and this in turn enhances their capacity to attract value-based support from those who are subject to them. How, in light of our discussion, can this possibly happen? If toleration threatens the integrity of those who extend it to others, then why isn't everyone intolerant (at least insofar as they lack instrumental reasons for tolerance)?

For a certain number of people, at least part of the answer is that they have some principled conviction that supports toleration and that outweighs or defuses the threat. Some are committed to an ideal of autonomy, for example, or have a pluralistic understanding of the good, or wish to cooperate with their fellow citizens on a footing of mutual respect. But I don't think that this is the whole story, even for people who have such convictions. Another piece of the explanation is this: the threat to people's integrity does not always materialize. In fact, rather than compromising people's integrity, the very features of toleration that are said to pose the threat are responsible for much of what people find rewarding about the practice. That is because many people experience the fact that they are implicated in the values of the other members of their society—that they are participants in a social practice through which each is implicated in the values of the others—not as undermining their own integrity but rather as establishing a bond with their fellow members.

More specifically, the phenomenon of being linked to others through a practice of mutual deference to one another's values is experienced as a form of fraternity: a way of acknowledging, beneath and despite our differences, that we face a common predicament. This may sound like a strange thing to say, given the emphasis I have been placing on the threat posed to individual integrity by precisely this sort of deference. But consider, by way of comparison, actual fraternal relations—relations among siblings. These relations are usually complex and often have a strongly competitive dimension. Nevertheless, fraternal ties are very powerful and have a distinctive and intimate character. One of the reasons for this, I believe, is that siblings (usually) share the unifying experience of mutual subjection to the authority of their parents. This means that, up to a point at least, they face a common predicament, occupy a common perspective, and have common interests, even if these things coexist with more competitive strands in their relationship. Siblings may simultaneously be rivals, allies, and co-conspirators. Underlying all of these strands is the recognition that they share something that nobody else does—a perspective on their parents' exercise of parental authority from the point of view of those who are subject to it. This common perspective helps to give their relationship its peculiarly intimate character, even when, in other respects, their relations are not especially close.

In general, the shared experience of subjection to a common authority is a powerful basis for relations of solidarity. Many other forms of comradeship and solidarity, in addition to those among siblings, are also forged on this basis. Think, for example, of the relations among students in a classroom, soldiers in a military unit, or workers in a manufacturing plant. In each case, there is room for competition, rivalry, and even dislike—indeed, the full range of human interpersonal attitudes is available to the members of these groups. But, in addition, there is this: a tendency to solidarity deriving from the shared experience of living together under a common authority.

Obviously, we are not all siblings or comrades, and there is (for now) no common human authority to whom we are all subject. So when I say that there is a form of fraternity associated with participation in a regime of toleration, I do not mean to suggest that the model of siblings and comrades carries over straightforwardly to this case. However, although we are not all subject to a common authority, we are all subject to the idea of authority. That is, we must all confront the normative dimension of human experience. We all live in the shadow of norms, principles, reasons, and ideals that, rightly or wrongly, we regard as authoritative. And although our values vary, the experience of responding to normative authority—of trying to be guided by values and norms that we accept—is part of our common experience. And this too makes possible a form of solidarity—a form of solidarity that derives from the shared experience of subjection, not to a common authority figure, but to normativity or authority itself.

It is in this spirit, I believe, that the adherents of different religions sometimes feel a sense of solidarity with one another as participants in the common enterprise of responding to ideas of the sacred or the divine. More generally, the adherents of different values and ideals sometimes recognize one another as participants in the shared human enterprise of trying to live a good or worthy life—that is, of trying to live in accordance with norms and ideals that one perceives as authoritative. I say that they sometimes recognize one another as participants in a common enterprise, not that they must do so or that they always do so. To the contrary, this unifying form of recognition is easily blocked or disabled by any of the numerous factors that give the differences and divisions among people their salience. However, I believe that a regime of toleration, by enforcing the kind of mutual deference to one another's values that I have been describing, encourages such recognition. Indeed, it does more. It gives concrete social expression to a compelling but abstract idea: the idea of an otherwise diverse people who are united by the common experience of confronting the normative or evaluative dimension of human life. In addition, it demands that we relate to one another in a way that acknowledges this bond that unites us. And when we do relate to one another in that way, the experience—for many—is one of fraternity or solidarity with one's fellows.[36] To the extent that that experience is rewarding, toleration comes to be seen as valuable in its own right. In

36. There may seem to be a tension between these ideas and the skepticism about "relational" views of morality expressed in "Morality and Reasonable Partiality," Chapter 2 in this volume. However, the skepticism expressed in that paper concerned the possibility that moral reasons in general might be understood as arising from some valuable ongoing relationship in which all human beings are participants. The common experience of confronting the normative dimension of human life, which I emphasize here, is not itself an ongoing relationship of that kind. Instead, my argument has been that recognition of this shared experience can sometimes encourage the development of relationships of fraternity or solidarity, although it does not do so automatically or universally. I am indebted to Nandi Theunissen for raising this issue.

this way, a regime of toleration that is initially accepted on purely instrumental grounds may begin gradually to attract value-based support and may come over time to be seen as intrinsically worthy. What began as a *modus vivendi* is transformed into a valued way of life.

The rewards characteristically afforded by this way of life might be called the rewards of openness to the other. For some people, the most important of these rewards lies in the sense of enrichment that comes from developing an appreciation for forms of value that are realized in practices other than one's own. Other people simply find it exhilarating to live confidently amidst the whirl of human diversity. For still other people, there are subversive and transgressive pleasures afforded by engagement with unfamiliar customs and practices. What underlies all of these rewards—what makes them available to the participants in a regime of toleration—is the kind of fraternity that is expressed in and realized by the practice of mutual deference to one another's values. And for people who experience and appreciate the rewards associated with that practice, its value ceases to be purely instrumental.

There is, once again, no necessity in any of this. Intolerance persists in liberal societies. Some people who are subject to a regime of toleration continue to find it not rewarding but threatening, all the more so because it asks us to acknowledge what we have in common with those who are different. The most toxic and extreme forms of intolerance almost always involve ideas of purity and separateness that rest precisely on a denial of this commonality. A regime of liberal toleration does not make these ideas disappear. It merely offers an alternative, and displays the charms of that alternative for those who are susceptible to seeing them.

So my claim is that, for some people at least, participation in a practice of mutual deference to one another's values is experienced as a good—as a kind of fraternity—rather than as compromising one's ability to translate one's own values into action. This may give rise to two related worries.

First, if one does experience participation in a practice of mutual deference as a good, then it seems that deference to the values of others is itself among one's own values, in which case it does not really amount to deference to the values of *others* at all. Second, if one experiences toleration as a good, then it is not clear that there is room left to take a critical perspective on the values and practices of others. To the extent that one experiences deference to those values and principles as a good, is it still possible coherently to criticize them? Or does the good of toleration require one to forfeit or disable one's critical faculties?

The answers to both worries turn on the point that, insofar as participation in a practice of mutual deference helps to realize a distinctive value, it is a second-order value: a value associated with deference to the (first-order) values of others. The fact that a person experiences this kind of deference as a good implies that the second-order value is one of that person's values, but not that the first-order values are. So, in reply to the first worry, the deference is still deference to the values of *others*. And, in reply to the second worry, it is *deference* to the values of others that is experienced as a good; the values themselves may leave one cold, and one may have all kinds of critical reservations about them. Of course, as one's reservations about a particular set of values become increasingly strong, one's conviction that deference to those values is a good may weaken, and at the limit one may decide that they should not be tolerated at all. The practice of toleration, or mutual deference, has its limits. Within those limits, however, what is experienced as good is deference to first-order values other than one's own, and the fact that the values are not one's own already implies that one's attitudes toward them fall short of endorsement. I take it that, in addition, one's attitudes may go beyond mere non-endorsement and may be critical to varying degrees as well. The bond of fraternity, like the bonds of love and friendship, can hold among people who are in various respects critical of one another. Were that not so, the world would be even more deficient in love, friendship, and fraternity than it already is.

This last point seems relevant to the paradox of suppressed disapproval. In effect, that paradox questions the justification for allowing people to act in ways that are themselves unjustified. In other words, it represents it as mysterious that we should have compelling reasons to allow others to engage in practices that we believe there to be compelling reasons to avoid. Why don't the reasons against performing the relevant actions translate into reasons against allowing them to be performed? Although the line of thought I have been developing does not directly address this question about reasons and justification, it does suggest a slightly different way of thinking about the supposed paradox. In particular, it invites us to consider the kinds of relationships that people who disagree about reasons for action may nevertheless establish and sustain among themselves, and to assess the value of those relationships. This relational focus contrasts with the emphasis, in the paradox as formulated, on the respective reasons for action of the tolerant and the tolerated, considered in isolation from one another. Similarly, the focus on the good of toleration shifts attention away from questions of reasons and justification toward questions about the human rewards of living under a regime of toleration. There is no paradox in the idea that people may establish ties of solidarity in the face of disagreement, no paradox in experiencing such ties as valuable and rewarding, and no paradox in the observation that a practice of mutual deference to one another's judgments about values may express and facilitate relations of fraternity and solidarity.

I do not want to exaggerate either the force or the significance of the argument I have been developing. As I have tried to make clear, I am not so naïvely optimistic as to suppose that everyone who lives under a regime of toleration will experience it as rewarding in the ways that I have described. It is always a mistake to underestimate the powerful forces that tempt people to intolerance, and nothing in my argument should be taken to encourage this mistake. I have tried only to call attention to the fact that some people do experience toleration as a good in its own right. That fact—surprising enough in its way—marks the limit both of my optimism and of my argument.

Similarly, I do not claim that the value of toleration as I have described it provides the primary justification for toleration as a practice. Instead, I am inclined to believe, with Rawls and Williams, that there are many different strands of conviction that support the practice of toleration, and that that very fact is important both for its stability and for its justification.[37] My point, in describing the "good of toleration," has been merely to highlight one significant strand that seems to me to have been unduly neglected.

Finally, I do not mean to suggest that, if one does experience toleration as a good, then support for the practice follows automatically. To the contrary, for those who appreciate the good of toleration, a new problem arises, namely, the problem of reconciling that good with their other values and commitments. To one degree or another, toleration may put their other values at risk. By the same token, their other values may make their commitment to toleration precarious. So a complete discussion of this subject, which is more than I can undertake here, would have to consider the interactions between the good of toleration, as I have characterized it, and the other values to which a person who experiences that good may be committed.[38]

Nevertheless, the considerations about the good of toleration to which I have tried to call attention in this essay seem to me significant. We are

37. To the extent that Williams believes that autonomy represents the only moral or value-based source of support for the practice, however, my position clearly differs from his.
38. This issue is important for another reason. I have said that toleration poses a threat to the integrity of the tolerant, because it requires them to concede authority to values that they reject. However, I have also said that this threat does not always materialize, and that many people experience participation in a regime of toleration as making possible a valuable form of fraternity rather than as compromising their integrity. In saying this, I mean not merely that they do not think that their integrity has been compromised but that it has not actually been compromised. However, this may seem mysterious. If conceding authority to values that one rejects threatens one's integrity, then how does the fact that it also makes possible valuable relations with other people cause the threat to disappear? After all, even if one experiences those relations as rewarding, it

accustomed to thinking of toleration as being, so to speak, a remedial value or practice: one that is concerned with controlling one's own disapproval or managing disagreement and conflict. Understood in this way, it may seem equivalent to a more or less grudging forbearance. Now a regime of toleration does require us to control our disapproval in many contexts, and it surely *is* a way of managing disagreement and minimizing destructive conflict. Moreover, as we have seen, these dimensions of toleration generate genuine puzzles and paradoxes, and the interest that these puzzles understandably attract tends to reinforce our sense of toleration as a remedial value.

My aim, however, has been to call attention to another dimension of toleration, in which it appears not so much as remedial but rather as facilitating social relations of a distinctive and distinctively attractive kind. It is a rare piece of political good fortune that, in their efforts to defuse violent sectarian conflict, liberal societies have hit upon a way of organizing themselves that makes possible its own intrinsic rewards and satisfactions. This does not make the puzzles and paradoxes disappear, but it may help to explain the intensity with which many people remain committed to toleration despite those puzzles and paradoxes.

Acknowledgments

An earlier version of this paper was presented at a conference on "Themes from the Ethics of Bernard Williams" at the University of Leeds in the summer of 2009. Subsequent versions were presented as the Sikora Lecture at the University of British Columbia and the Parcells Lecture at the University of Connecticut. I am grateful to the members of all those audiences and to the participants in my Fall 2008 graduate seminar at NYU for helpful discussion. I owe special thanks to Gerald Lang, who was the commentator on the paper at the Leeds conference.

---

remains the case that, in tolerating others, one is conceding authority to values that one rejects. So why isn't one's integrity compromised? The answer presumably depends on a point noted earlier, namely, that for someone who experiences toleration as a good, the second-order value of deference to the first-order values of others takes its place within one's own repertoire of values. This in turn makes it easier to reconcile the concession of authority to first-order values that one rejects with loyalty to one's own system of values. Still, the extent to which this succeeds in eliminating the threat to one's integrity will depend on how easy it is to reconcile the second-order value itself with one's other values, and that in turn will depend, *inter alia*, on the content of those other values. I am grateful to Macalester Bell for raising this question.

Index

Note: Page numbers followed by "n" refer to notes.

Bogart, Humphrey, 19
Brown, Wendy, 315
buck-passing account, 32–36, 45–46
Burnett, Murray, 19n

Carens, Joseph, 267n
caring, 17, 23n, 24–26, 36, 304
choice
    vs. circumstance, 176, 178–181, 187–202,
        209–210, 214–217, 220n, 221–223,
        224n, 225, 228, 231–233
    significance of, 187–188, 197n, 206n,
        216–220, 222–225, 231
citizenship
    equal, 191, 195, 203–204, 226–228, 235,
        272, 275, 278
    world, 160 (see also cosmopolitanism)
Coady, C.A.J., 237n, 238n, 239n, 241n
Cohen, G. A., 26n, 234n
    on conservatism, 268n
    critique of Rawls, 6, 116–119, 121, 123,
        126–127, 129–130, 134–158
    on Dworkin, 203, 205n, 206, 209–210
    and luck egalitarianism, 187, 189, 206n,
        209–210, 218
Cohen, Joshua, 127n, 147, 158
collective habits, 291–292, 294, 306
comprehensive moral doctrines, 226, 280, 310,
    319–320
conceptions of the good, 230, 279–280, 289,
    310, 324
consequentialism, 5, 11, 32n, 43, 45, 51
    contrast with egalitarian liberalism,
        112–114, 124–126 (see also Rawls, John,
        on utilitarianism)
    contrast with relational conceptions of
        morality, 44, 56, 69–72
    and distinction between doing and allowing,
        5, 76, 80, 81n, 86n–87n, 100n
    and reactive attitudes, 86n, 96–97
    See also utilitarianism
conservatism, 274, 309
    and criticism of welfare state, 7, 208, 224
    features in common with luck
        egalitarianism, 215, 220, 223–225, 234
    and moralism, 221, 223, 234–235
    and responsibility, 7, 208, 211–212, 215,
        221, 223–224, 233, 235
    and value, 268–269, 271, 307 (see also
        values, preservation of)
contract, law of, 134, 137n, 163
contractualism, 62–63, 66–67 (see also
    Scanlon, Thomas)
convention, 285n, 291–294, 306
cooperation, 198, 199n, 272–273, 324, 330
    advantages derived from, 129
    fair system of, 11, 154, 163, 185, 191,
        193–195, 226–227, 230, 277, 279

cosmopolitanism, 6, 160–164, 170–172, 262
Cottingham, John, 42n
courage, 244
cultural defense, 282n-283n
cultural rights, 8, 10, 272, 274, 279, 284n,
    285, 289, 310
culture
    American, 263
    Asante, 283
    cosmopolitanism and, 160
    immigration and, 8, 257–263, 265–268,
        272–279, 286
    individuals and, 260–265, 267–268,
        270–271, 273–274, 283–284
    Jewish, 260–261
    minority, 207n, 284n
    national, 8, 257–258, 265–268, 272–275,
        278–279
    not a normative notion, 281–282, 285, 288,
        309, 310n
    Polish, 260
    preservation of, 261, 265–274, 278–279,
        284–286
    public political, 226–227, 274–275, 277,
        319
    Western, 263
    Zulu, 282n

deontology, 32n, 56, 58–59
difference principle, 130, 161–162
    lax interpretation of, 127, 138–140,
        142–144, 145n, 146, 148–149, 155, 157
    luck-egalitarian criticism of, 179–181
    moderate interpretation of, 149
    strict interpretation of, 138–140, 142–149,
        155
    ultralax interpretation of, 147n
discrimination, intentional, 176
distributive egalitarianism, 178, 184, 192,
    199–200, 206–207, 229–230 (see also
    egalitarianism, responsibility-based;
    justice, distributive; justice, egalitarian;
    luck egalitarianism)
diversity
    cultural, 9, 206–207, 279–280, 289 (see also
        multiculturalism)
    liberalism and, 9–11, 206–207, 279–280,
        310, 323–324
    moral, 9, 280–281, 289, 310
    normative, 9–10, 289, 310, 323–324
    philosophical, 9, 280–281, 289, 310
    religious, 9, 11, 206–207, 280–281, 289,
        310, 323
    respect for, 265
    of traditions, 9–10, 289, 310
    of values, 3, 6, 11, 116, 123, 125–127, 230,
        277, 323–324
    See also division of moral labor; pluralism

division of moral labor, 6, 11, 113–127,
    134–135, 136n, 141, 158
doing and allowing, 5, 76–103, 109, 113n
doing and failing to prevent. *See* doing and
    allowing
duty to support just institutions, 6, 113,
    117–119, 123, 131, 135
Dworkin, Ronald, 111, 178–179, 186n, 207n,
    224
    on choices and circumstances, 189–190,
        199n, 209–210, 216
    on expensive tastes, 189, 210
    ideal of equality, 202–206

egalitarian ethos. *See* justice, ethos of
egalitarianism
    distributive, 178, 184, 192, 199–200,
        206–207, 229–230
    luck, 7, 175–207, 210, 212, 214–225, 231,
        233
    responsibility-based, 209–213, 224, 228,
        229n, 231–233
    See also equality; justice, egalitarian;
        liberalism, egalitarian
Eisgruber, Christopher, 276n-277n
emotional vulnerability, 4, 22–24, 26–31,
    36–37, 38n, 39, 46
Epstein, Julius, 19n
Epstein, Philip, 19n
equality, 4–6, 111, 113, 124, 145, 161, 193n, 309
    as distributive ideal, 7, 11, 181–182,
        190–191, 200, 228–230
    Dworkin's ideal of, 202–206
    equal protection of law, 276
    equal worth of persons, 48, 111, 191,
        200–202, 225, 229, 231
    gender, 155
    of opportunity, 130, 176, 179, 195–196, 272
    of opportunity for welfare, 182–183
    Rawls's conception of, 7, 193–200
    of resources, 182–183, 185, 187, 202, 204n,
        209
    as social and political ideal, 7, 178,
        191–193, 199–200, 202, 204n, 206–207,
        213, 225–232
    of welfare, 182–183, 185–187
Estlund, David, 150n, 158
ethnic cleansing, 247
ethnicity, 176, 191, 207, 264
expectations
    breaches of, 82–83, 91, 93n, 96
    fair, 196
    normative, 51, 54, 82–83, 91
    of people in different social positions, 115,
        132, 167
    of primary goods, 195
    role in noncoercive institutional structures,
        151–155

expensive tastes, 180, 183, 185, 189, 199

family, institution of the, 140, 151–153, 155
fear, 8, 239–255
Flanagan, Owen, 42n
Fleischacker, Samuel, 166
Fletcher, George, 312
Fleurbaey, Marc, 210n
Foot, Philippa, 79n
Forst, Rainer, 315–316
Frankfurt, Harry, 16–20, 23n, 24
fraternity, 10, 230, 331–334, 335n
free will, 187, 201n (*see also* libertarianism,
    metaphysical)
freedom
    of association, 272, 276, 279, 283, 314
    of conscience, 272, 276, 279–280, 283,
        314–315, 320n
    of expression, 272
    of religion, 280, 314
    of speech, 279, 283, 314
    of thought, 272, 283
Freeman, Samuel, 163, 186n, 277n
Friedman, Marilyn, 42n
friendship, 21n, 23, 31, 33, 37, 39, 57, 63–67,
    68n, 72, 334
Fullinwider, Robert, 241n

Garton Ash, Timothy, 277n
gender, 155, 207, 263
global basic structure, 6–7, 163–164, 170–171
global justice, 6–7, 161–162, 239 (*see also*
    justice, cosmopolitanism and)
globalization, 6, 162, 170–171
Goethe, Johann Wolfgang von, 315
Goodin, Robert, 240n, 254n
Greenawalt, Kent, 277n
guilt, 82, 92

Haase, Kerstin, 67n
Harman, Gilbert, 17
Havel, Vaclav, 16
Heraclitean pluralism, 268–269, 271–276, 279
Herman, Barbara, 42n
Heyd, David, 312
Hinton, Timothy, 177n, 210n
Hobbes, Thomas, 93n, 239–241, 243,
    249–251, 319
Hollinger, David, 262n, 264n
homelessness, 297
Horowitz, Donald, 264n
Horton, John, 322n
Hume, David, 70

identification(s), 189, 216, 228, 244–246,
    263–265, 276, 284n, 303–304
identity, 160, 232, 280
    hybrid, 262

See also consequentialism; deontology; doing
and allowing; Kantian morality; reasons,
moral; utilitarianism)
morally arbitrary factors, 161–162, 179,
193–195, 199 (*see also* choice vs.
circumstance; natural abilities or talents;
social contingencies)
multiculturalism, 207, 257–260, 279, 283,
289 (*see also* diversity, cultural)
Murphy, Liam, 116–120, 123, 136, 137n,
148n, 153, 159

Nagel, Thomas, 42n, 57, 111, 159, 293n
on deontological restrictions, 56, 58–59
on moral division of labor, 114, 118–119,
121–123, 126, 136n
on personal and impersonal standpoints,
102n, 118–119, 121–123
on value of equality, 230
national culture. *See* culture, national
national identity. *See* identity, national
nationalism, 275n
nationality, 259
natural abilities or talents, 161, 163, 176, 179,
190–191, 193–195, 212, 214–216, 218,
221, 223
natural fortune. *See* natural abilities or talents
Norman, Richard, 193n
normative authority, 9, 280–282, 285, 291,
308
experience of being subject to, 10, 332
normativity, 44, 332
reciprocal, 52–57, 64, 67–69, 71–72
Nozick, Robert, 112n, 293n

Oldenquist, Andrew, 61n
original position, 145n, 179

Paine, Thomas, 315
paradox of foundational tolerance, 317–320,
322
paradox of suppressed disapproval, 316–317,
320, 334
Parfit, Derek, 229n
partiality
and morality, 4, 41–74
reasons of, 4–5, 43–44, 49, 51, 57–58, 68,
73–74 (*see also* reasons, membership-
dependent; reasons, project-dependent;
reasons, relationship-dependent)
personal routines, 290, 295–303
pluralism
moral, 115, 121, 124, 130, 134–135
value, 115–116, 121, 124–128, 134–135,
158
See also diversity; division of moral labor
Pogge, Thomas, 145n, 159

power, 154, 161, 191, 193, 204–205, 225,
249–250, 273–274, 319
primary goods, 145n, 180–182, 185, 195–198
Primoratz, Igor, 241n
Pritchard's dilemma, 62–63
publicity condition, 150n
punishment, 243, 249–251

Quinn, Warren, 79n

race, 176, 207, 259, 263–264
Rakowski, Eric, 186n, 189–190, 194n, 218n
Rawls, John, 100, 111, 126–127, 149,
153, 159, 177, 186n, 209, 212, 227n,
233–234, 267n, 272, 274, 318, 322, 324,
330, 335
on background justice, 115–116, 120–121,
132–135, 137n, 138, 141, 150, 158,
168–169, 171
on basic structure, 6–7, 113–117, 119–120,
122, 129–143, 146–148, 150–158,
161–170, 172, 194
and division of moral labor, 6, 11, 114–118,
120–122, 134–135, 136n, 141, 158
and duty to support just institutions, 6,
117–119, 131, 135
on institutional division of labor, 116–117,
120–121, 133–137, 141, 158
and luck egalitarianism, 177–182, 185,
193–199
and moral or value pluralism, 5, 115–116,
121, 130, 134–135, 158
on overlapping consensus, 319–320
on primacy of justice, 11, 161, 166
on sense of justice, 119, 131, 135, 139,
141, 194
on utilitarianism, 70, 130, 136n, 141,
164–166, 169
on virtue of justice, 120, 131–132, 135,
137, 142
See also difference principle
Raz, Joseph, 100n, 269
reactive attitudes, 82–83, 86n, 91–93, 96–98,
122, 233–234
reasons
for action, 4, 27–36, 43–44, 46–74, 86, 90,
99–102, 281, 290, 293–294, 306, 308,
326, 329–330, 334
authority of, 85
to conform with norms, 83–86, 94–98
cultural, 9, 282–283, 288, 309–310
membership-dependent, 4–5, 44, 50–52,
55–57, 60–62, 68n, 72–73
moral, 44, 57–64, 66–69, 71–74, 320, 332n
normative, 22, 85–86, 91, 309, 329
of partiality, 4–5, 43–44, 49, 51, 57–58,
68, 73–74

CPSIA information can be obtained at www.ICGtesting.com
Printed in the USA
BVOW040437081111

275506BV00002B/2/P